REFLECTIONS OF A NEUROPSYCHOLOGIST

Reflections of a Neuropsychologist: Brushes with Brains follows the life of an influential neuropsychologist's fascinating and varied career. Unique in its autobiographical approach, it features coverage of research into human evolution, archaeology and neurology.

Beginning with his earliest memories (and implications for memory processes), John L. Bradshaw reflects on his archaeological expeditions preceding his primary career as a physiological psychologist and a behavioural neuroscientist. His influential research covers such rare neurological disorders as Huntington's disease, Friedreich ataxia, and Williams syndrome, and more common maladies like Parkinson's and Alzheimer's diseases, stroke, Fragile X, Tourette's syndrome, obsessive compulsive and attention deficit hyperactivity disorders, schizophrenia, autism and depression.

His fascinating personal experiences illustrating scientific discoveries will entertain, enthuse, encourage and inspire, and provide established research scientists and practising clinicians with a unique road map.

John L. Bradshaw originally received a scholarship to study Classical Languages at Merton College, Oxford (1958), before transferring to Psychology, Physiology and Philosophy. After two years (1962–1964) as a systems analyst for Imperial Chemical Industries, John completed a PhD in Physiological Psychology at Sheffield University (1967). He then worked at the University of Otago, Dunedin, New Zealand (1967–1968), before moving to the newly-established Monash University in Melbourne, Australia, rising to a Personal Chair and an Emeritus Professorship. His group has worked on movement, neurodevelopmental and neurodegenerative disorders, human evolution and the evolution of language, praxis and tool use, synaesthesia, spatial representation, embodiment, mirror neuron, phantom limb and many other arcane phenomena.

REFLECTIONS OF A NEUROPSYCHOLOGIST

Brushes with Brains

John L. Bradshaw

Routledge
Taylor & Francis Group
LONDON AND NEW YORK

First published 2018
by Routledge
4 Park Square, Milton Park, Abingdon, Oxon OX14 4RN

and by Routledge
605 Third Avenue, New York, NY 10017

Routledge is an imprint of the Taylor & Francis Group, an informa business

British Library Cataloguing-in-Publication Data
A catalogue record for this book is available from the British Library

Library of Congress Cataloging-in-Publication Data
Names: Bradshaw, John L., 1940– author.
Title: Reflections of a neuropsychologist : brushes with brains / John Bradshaw.
Description: Milton Park, Abingdon, Oxon ; New York, NY : Routledge, 2018.
Identifiers: LCCN 2017054793 (print) | LCCN 2017059049 (ebook) |
ISBN 9781351060752 (Master e-book) | ISBN 9781138481190 (hbk) |
ISBN 9781138481237 (pbk) | ISBN 9781351060752 (ebk)
Subjects: LCSH: Bradshaw, John L., 1940–Health. | Neuropsychology. |
Psychologists–Biography.
Classification: LCC QP360 (ebook) | LCC QP360 .B693 2018 (print) |
DDC 612.8/2–dc23
LC record available at https://lccn.loc.gov/2017054793

ISBN: 978-1-138-48119-0 (hbk)
ISBN: 978-1-138-48123-7 (pbk)
ISBN: 978-1-351-06075-2 (ebk)

Typeset in Bembo
by Wearset Ltd, Boldon, Tyne and Wear

CONTENTS

PREFACE

We live in a world of 'fake news' (if we don't like the message, impugn the messenger) and 'alternative facts' (if I don't like what you say, even though you are a 'so-called' expert, my opinion is just as good as yours). I do wonder, however, whether the esteemed President of the (once united and even great) United States of America, if diagnosed with cancer, would trust the recommendations of a shaman or witch-doctor from darkest Africa. That said, and despite a flood, recently, of memoirs (once called autobiographies, but 'memoir' is snappier, even if it did not so long ago simply mean 'a reminder' or memorandum), the reading public seems reassuringly ever curious about the workings of what has rightly been described as 'the most complex structure in the known universe', i.e. the human brain. Maybe not for long, though, given current prognostications that we are soon to be overtaken by IT and AI. I became involved in what was originally known as experimental psychology, later morphing into physiological psychology, neuropsychology and latterly behavioural neuroscience, through a chain of very fortunate accidents and coincidences. Among these, though originally born into poor circumstances in wartime and war-torn Britain, developing interests and fortuitous circumstances led to a superb education in Britain's oldest and most acclaimed university, thence emigration to Australia (truly 'the lucky country'), a life in Melbourne ('the world's most liveable city', according to various such ratings over many years, and one with a health system so configured that it proved possible to study adequate numbers of unfortunate individuals with the most exotic and rare of neurological and neuropsychological disorders), and above all, the opportunity to work with some extraordinary, in every sense of the word, colleagues and graduate students. Also, I soon found a wonderful pleasure in the theatricals and histrionics of lecturing to senior undergraduates, and introducing them to the very latest, and often weirdest, phenomena relating to the human condition. They seemed to love it, I certainly did, and they flocked to join the lab, and frankly, research-wise, 'did us proud', as they say back in the North Country of my old homeland. With such increasing numbers, they practically supervised themselves, or more accurately, each other, as there was always someone around to resolve the most complex or confounding technical questions. My role increasingly became that of overall strategist, generalist, polymath, resources-person and above all midwife, the latter being one that the wise old philosopher Socrates himself adopted 2500 years ago, in Plato's incomparable Dialogues.

This book is an account of what it was like for one person to research in an area, the workings of the human mind/brain, which maybe vies with Theoretical Physics, Cosmology and Molecular Genetics in terms of its complexity, fascination for the general public and the potential significance of its findings; it is also an account, a sample, of just a few of the often bizarre phenomena surrounding the human brain/mind in both health and disease. For when the system fails, it can often reveal something of the arcana, the mysteries, of its normally-functioning complexities; and conversely, a better understanding of normal healthy functioning can help us understand disease processes, leading to better diagnosis, assessment and management.

ACKNOWLEDGEMENTS

I owe an enormous debt of gratitude to my parents, now deceased, who believed passionately in the importance of education, and sacrificed many of life's pleasures on my behalf; to my dear wife Judy, of over 50 years, for the last seven of which she has languished in a nursing home after her devastating stroke; and to my wonderful friend Sara, whose knowledge of IT, librarianship and the many plagues that can beset an author has been of inestimable value. Thank you, Sara! I must also thank Professor Brogyanyi and John Benjamins Publishers for their very kind permission to cite Lehman and Zgusta's version of Schleicher's tale, and John Crossley for his expert photographic skills.

Last but very far from least, let me thank the Australian Broadcasting Corporation who have hosted very many of my numerous radio talks on scientific and other matters, where I developed much of the thinking which went into writing this memoir. In this regard, I owe Robyn Williams an enormous debt of gratitude.

1

THE EVOLUTION OF ALL THINGS

The past is not just another country, or even another continent; it is another island universe, wherein the laws of thought allow one to reverse at will time's speeding arrow.

We were camped, my botanist wife and 9-year-old daughter Catriona and I, just where we always tried to be at nightfall, while travelling in the vast Australian outback – camped in the hard, red-earth centre of a lonely clay-pan, a hollow nestled in the all-surrounding country of dune, sparse scrub, and patches of gibber. These dark stones, polished by aeons of wind, glinted feebly in the rays of a red-setting sun. The best part of the day, with the omnipresent flies at last at rest, and time for a beer and to light a sweet-smelling campfire of resinous wood, rich in volatiles and rare oils, dead and dried by the relentless sun of daytime. A desert, but a friendly desert, alive with little creatures beginning to venture out for night-time activities, calling to each other with faint, pure notes of an exquisite beauty. Above us soon would shine an incomparable night sky, under the sway of the Southern Cross, with a luminosity you could practically read by, beneath the blazing arc of the Milky Way: a jet of milk projected from the full breasts of Hera, consort of the great Greek god Zeus, god of the daytime? Or, mundanely, a cartwheel galaxy, seen almost edge on, from a lonely Earth located near its outer perimeter; a galaxy of billions of stars, many with circling planets like our own, a galaxy among billions of similar astronomical structures scattered seemingly randomly through a measureless, uncaring universe, itself maybe only one of an infinite number of other, similar universes. And we were, are, privileged to gaze upon this emerging glory, from the safe haven of our own little clay-pan in our own little island continent of Australia, on our own little blue planet, our only home, endlessly circling our own little middle-aged sun. Privileged to view this celestial scene, sparked and tracked from time to time by rushing meteorites, burning up in our atmosphere at the end of their journeys from – where? And we are privileged to be able to ask how it all began – the universe (ours?), the solar system, life, humanity, consciousness … the ability to ask, if not always to answer, such questions.

Matter and the universe as we know it may have existed for around 13.6–13.8 billion years or maybe even somewhat longer, depending upon the accuracy of the measurements of the speed of recession of the distant galaxies, their actual distance, and a number of other critical assumptions. It is tempting to try asking what came before this Beginning Big Bang (or First Whimper?) when space, time, energy and matter all supposedly came into being together, almost a theological question, some might say, and nowadays some cosmologists are even returning to this apparently illegal question, although, according to 'traditional' Einsteinian thinking, there can be no time before its beginning, unless perhaps an infinity of universes predated our familiar four-dimensional 'home'. But all such issues belong to the conceptual domain of cosmologists and theoretical physicists. At a more mundane (in every sense) level, our own middle-aged sun, on an outer limb of our parent spiral galaxy, one of maybe 100 billion, and alone composed of 100 billion stars which we know as the familiar Milky Way as seen from many an outback clay-pan, is upwards of 5 billion years old; our ever-orbiting Earth has maybe been around for some 4.6 billion years. Life, in the form of primitive single-celled organisms, first appeared on our little lifeboat maybe a billion years later, almost as soon as the latter had cooled, oceans had appeared, and the rain of comets and giant meteorites, abounding as the solar system settled into an uneasy equilibrium, had diminished to a 'safe' and steady level. Such an early advent of life could almost suggest the presence of precursors then, and now, maybe microbial, on comets in seed form, throughout the solar system and perhaps even beyond. Such providential panspermia, as envisaged by the much-maligned astronomer and sci-fi writer, Fred Hoyle, is currently enjoying a recurrent renaissance, although not perhaps to the extent that it may, as Fred suggested, even be linked to recurrent outbreaks of earthly influenza. It is, however, increasingly evident that simple chemical compounds, capable of combining to form biologically promising precursors, are abundant everywhere in the, our, universe.

Panspermia or not, the currently preferred scenario for life's earthly origin is around hot volcanic 'smokers', plumes of superheated water replete with minerals and metals emerging from the mantle, and located deep in the early ocean. Charles Darwin instead envisioned a warm thermal pool, on land, and it is noteworthy that recent findings of fossils of very early life forms in Australia's Pilbara, dating from 3.5 to 3.8 billion years ago in hot spring deposits, support Darwin's usual, inspired, hypothesis. Modern methanogens, relatives of the oldest microorganisms on Earth, are often found near such hydrothermal vents. In the absence of oxygen, they convert carbon dioxide and hydrogen into methane. They may thus have produced, 3.5 billion years ago, some of the greenhouse gases, needed to stabilise the Earth's early climate, opening the way for other more complex life forms to evolve. Oxygen, of biogenic (photosynthetic) origin from primitive algae, introduced to Earth's atmosphere the element essential for more advanced life, some 2 billion years ago.

Whether life on Earth was of endogenous or exogenous origin, it is composed of chiral molecules. These appear in two forms, mirror images of each other, like a pair of gloves. However, life seems to have preferred molecules of a single chiral, chemical, handedness; all DNA twists clockwise, like threads on a right-handed screw, and consequently nearly all amino acids are left-handed. It is noteworthy that chiral molecules are and have been present in interstellar space, from long before the existence of our solar system. Such observations, and uniformities in the DNA of all living things, support the proposal that life evolved – somewhere – only once, or alternatively that the way it did evolve is perhaps the best solution to the constraints operating.

In my paternal grandmother's house, hundreds of years old, and contiguous with that of my parents', was a very early, and possibly priceless, copy of Darwin's magisterial and iconic *Origin of Species*, one of many books on geology, such as Lyell's *Principles of Geology*, roughly contemporaneous with Darwin's in the mid-nineteenth century. Darwin of course proposed that organisms continually change or mutate, usually with maladaptive consequences leading nowhere. However, the fittest, and only the fittest, will survive and breed, to pass on to their offspring these adaptive changes. Thus, evolution is by 'natural selection', with the inheritance of adaptive characteristics, an essentially gradual change, although from time to time maybe hastened as a result of catastrophic events drastically changing the environmental pressures.

There was even a tattered copy of Alfred Russell Wallace's *The Malay Archipelago*, with its stirring descriptions of travel, danger, butterflies and beetles, in the remains of my deceased grandfather's science library. Wallace, who independently of Darwin developed his own version of evolutionary theory, was a great read notwithstanding. I wish I had known my bibliophile grandfather, but he apparently 'dropped dead' while out cycling with my father, then a teenager.

Lyell's *Principles of Geology* was not a light read, but this book, which almost out of an existing vacuum, set the whole stage of modern palaeontology and maybe even archaeology, came into its own for me when I stumbled upon my very first fossil. Aunty Betty, Grandfather Bradshaw's daughter and my father's sister, in 1950 had a caravan on Britain's south coast, near the tiny Somerset harbour of Watchet; we spent a typical British summer holiday with them when I was 11. The cliffs there expose the famous fossil beds of the Jurassic Blue Lyas (layers, in dialect; the strata are so distinctive), the same as in the iconic exposures at nearby Lyme Regis. Waiting on the beach were wonderful fossil treasures: pearly ammonites, resembling the modern Nautilus, crinoids (stalked relatives of sea urchins and starfish), and, oh delight, the occasional small vertebrae ('wortieberries' in the local dialect) possibly from a dinosaur! All small boys develop obsessive tendencies; until then for me it was stamps, but I soon rearranged my life so as to fill my corner of one of our many decaying greenhouses at home with shelves of fossils gleaned from cliffs, beaches, quarries, stream beds, road cuttings and stone walls all over the country. In Lyell's book I read of what he had believed, well over 100 years earlier, to be the oldest fossil of all, *Eozoon canadense*. What a wonderfully evocative name! The first element, translating (as my expanding education in Classical Greek at the time taught me), means Creature of the Dawn. Lyell we now know was wrong, both on dates and on its status as a fossil, but that is by the way.

Another important local influence was, unexpectedly, the very excellent local fish-and-chips shop, which caused a local commotion when a family portion rose with inflation from 3-pence to 4-pence, and which, curiously, and from some unknown source, for a long time would wrap the precious cargo in old copies of that august medical journal, *The Lancet*, which certainly was excellent at resisting grease. Therein I avidly read intriguing accounts of obscure and euphoniously named creations such as gamma globulin, and determined one day to become a medical doctor, and invent and name some more myself, and was indeed later to tailor my subjects at school so as to include appropriate subjects to qualify for entry into medical school.

It was Richard Dawkins, in the mid-twentieth century, who was the first to radically modify classical Darwinism, with his selfish gene metaphor. (Darwin, of course, writing long before the discovery of genes, could not have known then the exact mechanisms of inheritance.) Dawkins proposed that it is the directing genes, and not the organism as a whole, merely the vehicle for the contained genes, which drives evolution. Very recently a third modification has been proposed (and creationists love modifications, which they claim discredit Darwinian thinking, not realising that modifications are the life-blood of the fundamental principle of self-correction in science). Genes, coding for proteins, the constituents of all things living, are not the whole story. Genes may be turned on or off by epigenetic processes, switches, so that every cell, containing the entire genetic blueprint for the entire organism, throughout its own changes in developmental morphology, and with its many different bodily organs and systems, only ever behaves in a fashion appropriate for its context in place and time – heart cell for heart, liver cell for liver. Think of a butterfly, with its many external and internal parts, radically changing in morphology (larva, pupa, imago) as it passes through life's stages. Moreover, such switches, principally involving methylation, may also be turned on or off as a consequence of adventitious environmental pressures (temperature changes, food shortage or over-abundance, over-crowding). And some switch changes may outlast the organism experiencing them, and be passed on to succeeding generations down the germ line – an additional, fast-acting, adaptive mode of individual inheritance, over and above the much slower classical-Darwinian process of natural selection via variation. I am reminded of memory mechanisms – short-term electrical patterns of storage in neural circuits, followed by a long-term series of structural changes in the neurons and neuronal junctions themselves. A nice recent demonstration of epigenetic changes conserved and transmitted across generations, comes from male mice aversively trained to avoid an otherwise innocuous odour of cherry blossom; their offspring also avoided such odours, and in their sperm exhibited relevant epigenetic changes.

In the geological record, older rocks must have successfully survived the continual recycling of fossil material; consequently there are fewer such survivors, the further one goes back in time. That observation, and the fact that very early life forms almost had to be simple, single cell structures, mean that they are hard to find, hard to see, and are often ambiguous markings in rare silica rocks like chert.

The oldest fossils are often of structures resembling modern stromatolites, layered structures forming through microbiologically modified sediment accretions, such as I have found, and photographed, in the hard red rocks of the Pilbara of Western Australia. Other examples, at 3.5 billion years old, occur in the same general region, surprisingly close to the otherwise fairly uncommon living examples in the hyper-saline waters of adjacent Shark Bay. On the edge of the Greenland icecap, there are slightly older specimens very shortly postdating the period at 3.7 billion years ago when the Earth was battered by asteroids. At the time of writing, there are contested claims of filamentous structures, originating around hydrothermal vents deep in an ancient ocean, said to date from between 3.8 and 4.3 billion years ago. As mentioned above, such vents have long been proposed as possible sources for an anaerobic origin of life.

We must await, it was long said, the so-called Cambrian biological explosion, around 540 million years ago, for evidence of complex life forms, such as the enigmatic *Archaeocyathus* (something seemingly intermediate between a coral and a sponge, and which I once found in a narrow lens of limestone in Big Moro Gorge creek-bed, in the Flinders Ranges of South Australia). Or so it was thought, although the question remained as to why complex life forms seemed to have sprung fully formed out of nowhere, like the ancient Greek goddess Pallas Athene from the forehead of Zeus.

(Parenthetically, mass extinctions, followed by a whole new suite of life forms, have occurred quite regularly during Lifeboat Earth's relatively brief, in the overall scheme of things, history, due variously to adventitious asteroid impacts or violent volcanic eruptions. Nor may we be immune to further such calamities resulting in extra-terrestrial oblivion; there are always bodies passing close to Earth, along with a continual rain of smaller fragments. Indeed, alone with my daughter at mid-day on the dry bed of a small salt lake, again in the lonely yet lovely Australian outback, we both heard a 'whooshing' sound pass us by, but without any sound or trace of impact or of wild (or human) life. Again, micrometeorites containing iron, the commonest type, tiny and very common, may be harvested from one's house gutters with the aid of a small magnet.)

The unlikely rethink, about there being no complex Precambrian life forms, came about as a result of the fabulous finds of a lone geologist, Reginald Sprigg, a specially significant star in my own personal pantheon of luminaries. They were strange, bizarre even, fossils of complex, beautifully preserved organisms often many centimetres long, quite unlike anything seen before or extant later. Like mine, Reg's childhood was spent combing cliffs and scavenging shore lines, roaming road cuttings, quarries and stream beds – for fossils!!. Born in 1919 in South Australia, he was to become a student of Sir Douglas Mawson, a professor of geology and an Olympian figure in polar exploration and survival. Towards the end of the Second World War, he was sent to prospect for uranium, for the nascent nuclear weapons industry, in the vicinity of the Ediacaran Hills in the Flinders Ranges, one of my own favourite destinations for dreaming and discovery. He found masses of uranium, but even more significantly, as it was to turn out, some of the strangest macrofossils ever seen. Moreover, despite vociferous cries of 'Impossible', they appeared to be securely pre-Cambrian. It was all very reminiscent of Alfred Wegener and the theory of Continental Drift. Just as I had done, as a sick child playing with a toy globe of the world, he had noticed how well the continents of Africa and the Americas fit together, jigsaw fashion, just as if they had been pulled apart. Wegener in 1912 proposed that that was effectively what had happened, decades later to be shown as due to sea-floor spreading, due in turn to its modern realisation in plate tectonics. Just so, it was to be at least a decade before Reg Sprigg's extraordinary fossil finds, and similar ones elsewhere on Earth, were to be accepted as pre-Cambrian and dating to an interval between 635 and 541 million years ago. It should, however, perhaps be noted that genetic evidence from modern life forms, extrapolating backwards in time, suggests that basic animal groups may have in fact originated as far back as 750 million years ago. An enormous increase in oceanic algae around 650 million years ago would certainly have both increased oceanic oxygen, and provided an essential food source for animal life.

The fossils that Reg Sprigg found in the Ediacaran Hills are dated to between 560 and 550 million years ago, with finds later made elsewhere commencing around 565 million years ago. However, for the first time in nearly a century, we now have a newly named, authenticated and accepted geological period, the Ediacaran. Again, as a young man in my very early twenties, I read Glaessner's iconic article in the *Scientific American*, and was inspired with a determination one day to visit the area. However, it was to be 30 years before I eventually had my wish, and camped in the arid Ediacaran landscape with my wife Judy, and fossicked among the remains of old mines, within sight of the huge salt lake, Lake Torrens. Another very famous Ediacaran site is in Namibia, at Farm Aar, explored by my friend and colleague, Professor Pat Rich, at Monash University, where we have both laboured in our very different disciplines for decades. When I visited Namibia with mutual friends and colleagues in 2013, I found the countryside surprisingly similar, in features and aridity, to my beloved Flinders, and the fossils at Farm Aar, dating to around 542 million years ago, even more dramatic, although as both regions are designated as of world significance, one cannot and should not remove anything except for scientific purposes, and should take, as I did, only photographs.

The Cambrian period, following the apparently catastrophic extinctions of the prior Ediacaran biota, is noteworthy for an almost unprecedented explosion of complex, multicellular organisms, many of which continued evolving until now. It dates from around 540 million years ago, when, indeed, there appeared the earliest ancestor common to chordates, vertebrates and indeed those species such as the starfish and sea urchins which are, maybe surprisingly, invertebrates related to the chordates. Such ebullient abundance may result from the increasing availability of atmospheric oxygen, from algal or similar photosynthetic processes taking off in earlier millennia. The first chordates promptly appeared, with their stiffening notochord or longitudinal rod in a bilaterally symmetrical body, with mouth and sensors at one end, and propulsive organs down the sides and at the 'trailing' end, wherein there is also located the excretory apparatus. The modern lamprey closely resembles these precursors of the vertebrates (craniates), with backbones/vertebral columns, and crossed (contra-laterally represented) sensory and motor systems. Thus, the left side of the brain or head ganglion manages sensorimotor matters on the right side of the creature's body, and vice versa. Why this crossover? One suggestion is that very early chordates may have evolved from some such creatures as acorn worms, which again for some unknown reason underwent a 180-degree rotation of the body with respect to the head. So many questions yet to be answered.

Fish may first have appeared as early as 480 million years ago, although for a long time they were exclusively cartilaginous, like the sharks, with bony fish (osteichthyes) appearing later. From the latter, a whole series of life forms emerged, apparently intermediate between fish, with fins and relying on gills for respiration, and creatures that could use modified fins as limbs whereby to climb onto the land, like modern mudskippers, and where they could respire like the modern-day lungfish. Such emerging tetrapods were the original amphibians, around 350–375 million years ago, although there seem to have been, contemporaneously and maybe earlier, many 'failed' taxa, resembling each other but not quite making the big jump to a firm and final (except maybe for reproductive purposes) life on the land. Indeed, there are fossil trackways made by apparent tetrapods maybe dating back to 390 million years ago. Descendants of the early amphibians include modern salamanders and the lovely Crested Newt, which occasionally would wander into the ground-level aquaria which as a child I had set up to observe pond life.

Amphibians, obligatory layers of eggs in water, may respire partially or even wholly through the skin, unlike the dry-skinned reptiles with proper lungs, typically laying eggs on land and appearing around 315 million years ago.

While there were earlier, 'failed', mammal-like reptiles, the first true warm-blooded placental mammals on our direct line may stem from around 125 million years ago, although other evidence suggests that marsupial (e.g. kangaroos) and placental (mice and men) stock may have split from that of the monotremes (e.g. platypus) as early as 170 million years ago. Primates perhaps appeared around 75 million years ago, the taxon including monkeys, apes – and ourselves. Some time around 10 million years ago the gorilla's ancestors branched off from our line, with maybe 8 million years ago the chimpanzee/human split occurring.

The march towards mankind is far from an orderly progression towards an inevitable summit, as popularly conceived, but rather a random stumble, driven by adventitious forces, such as climate changes, themselves partly a consequence of underlying tectonic processes, mountain building, etc. Human evolution, it has been noted, is not a linear railroad, but rather a bush with many dead-end branches. Evidence mostly came from fossil remains, although more recently there has been a burgeoning of molecular and genetic studies. The latter depend upon rare and extremely well-preserved material, especially teeth, which, like tiny time capsules, can retain, more or less imperviously, enclosed and encapsulated soft tissue. At any one time, there seem to have been simultaneously present several different species, often with a bewildering array of advanced and archaic features – brain size or configuration, lower limbs adapted for climbing or fast bipedal gait, and upper limbs adapted for grasping, manipulation or tool use. The human brain is of course an expensive luxury; it makes childbirth dangerous and difficult, ties us to an extended and vulnerable childhood requiring long nurture and protection, and consumes up to a quarter of our total energy budget.

A grossly simplified picture is as follows: at around 4.4 million years ago, *Ardipithecus* may have been the earliest precursor to our human family (hominins), followed by bipedal *Australopithecus afarensis* at 3.25 million years ago, with thereafter a gradual evolution tending towards bigger bodies and brains, full bipedalism, smaller jaws and teeth, and more modern upper limbs and hands. Thus, we see adaptations for tool manufacture and use, and eventually language and higher cognitive processes. A diet changing from vegetable material to meat, whether scavenged or hunted, and possibly depending upon fire and cooking, may have had a major influence.

The first true human may have been *Homo habilis* (extant 2–3 million years ago in Africa), which was erect, taller than apes, bipedal, tool-using, as judged from hand shape, although note that birds of various species are now known to make and deploy tools, with a brain now almost half the volume of that of modern humans. There follows *H. erectus* (1.75 million years ago to 100,000 years ago), possibly identical to *H. ergaster*, with a brain more than half the size of ours, and a largely modern skeleton. All the above occurred in Africa. Thence, we see *H. heidelbergensis* (600,000–200,000 years ago, and maybe the same as *H. antecessor*), known to have spread from Africa to Europe around 600,000 years ago, and probably the common ancestor of the Denisovans (which diverged from our line maybe 400,000 years ago, and appeared in Siberia around 50,000 years ago), and of the Neanderthals (which diverged from our ancestral line maybe 500,000 years ago, and appeared in Western Europe around 350,000 years ago, disappearing perhaps around 35,000 years ago). Parenthetically, DNA analysis of the hardened tooth plaque of five Neanderthals from a Spanish cave indicates that members of this so-called primitive subspecies dined on a largely vegetarian diet, rather than meat, as is generally thought. Moreover one unfortunate individual, suffering from a visible tooth abscess and a gut infection caused by an unpleasant bacterium, may have been self-medicating; DNA from poplar trees, parts of which contain salicylic acid (as in the common painkiller aspirin), and *Penicillium* mould (the source of penicillin) were also present. But even chimps are known to self-medicate with appropriate leaves when suffering from gut infections.

Anatomically modern humans appear in East Africa around 200,000 years ago, possibly even 350,000 years ago, as suggested by a reanalysis of material from Jebel Irhoud in Morocco, maybe from African precursors of *H. heidelbergensis*. Such a founder population, on the basis of present-day genetic diversity, may at certain times have been down to just a few hundred individuals, resulting in a tight genetic bottleneck. In Europe, we know from genetic evidence that Neanderthals interbred with anatomically modern people before 40,000 years ago, and in the Far East the Denisovans likewise mated with the anatomically modern people from Africa. Thus Europeans have a small percentage of Neanderthal genes, and Melanesians and Australian aborigines a small percentage of Denisovan genes. However, the absence of Neanderthal genes in native Africans does not necessarily mean that the two groups never mixed; the genetic signature might merely have later been lost. The Neanderthals seem to have made clothing from animal skins, ornaments, tools (possibly less complex than those of the moderns), before becoming extinct around 35,000 years ago, maybe in competition with the invading moderns. Thus, there seem to have been at least two emigrations 'out of Africa' – *H. erectus/ergaster* across Eurasia before 120,000 years ago, and *H. sapiens* (moderns) to South-East Asia (73,000–63,000 years ago), Australia (65,000 years ago), and Western Europe (43,000 years ago). The Tibetan plateau, one of the highest and most inhospitable regions on Earth, may have been populated as far back as 62,000 years ago, in the last Ice Age. Recent controversial finds of 105,000–125,000-year-old archaic *Homo habilis* fossils in China, however, hint at the possibility of a remnant presence there.

In 2003, a skull and partial skeleton of a hominin was uncovered, with other material subsequently, in a cave on the Indonesian island of Flores, with a mixture of primitive and advanced features. It was of extremely small size, both body and brain (one quarter that of moderns, approaching that of *Australopithecus*), with primitive tools, and with evidence of butchering and fire use. As the material dates from 60,000–100,000 years ago, they must nevertheless have deployed early watercraft of some sort to get there. For long, it was claimed that they were modern people suffering from some form of extreme pathology and 'island dwarfism', as has often been found with other animal species marooned on small islands. This mixture of very archaic and advanced skeletal features suggested descent from *H. erectus*, although an even earlier migration of *H. habilis* from Africa cannot be excluded. Indeed, there are now very recent hints of an *H. habilis* presence arriving from Africa in Flores at least 700,000 years ago, and evolving subsequently into *H. floresiensis*, and with an anatomy closer to *habilis* than *erectus*.

As noted, anatomically modern people first appeared in Africa around 200,000 years ago, maybe from an African population of *H. heidelbergensis* which had itself evolved therein, maybe around 600,000 years ago. An exodus from Africa, now thought to have been in one wave only, not two as until recently thought, on the basis of genetic information, underwent some local mixing with pre-existing archaic populations of Denisovans (by Melanesians), and Neanderthals (by Eurasians). Genetic material also provides chronological information about splits from Africans by Australian aborigines, Papua New Guineans and Eurasians about 70,000 years ago, and from Eurasians by Australian aborigines and Papuans between 51,000 and 72,000 years ago. Aborigines and Papuans themselves diversified between 25,000 and 40,000 years ago, with the ancient landmass of Sahul (the Australian continent, Tasmania and New Guinea) being initially settled between 47,000 and 55,000 years ago. Finally, Australian aborigines internally differentiated between 10,000 and 32,000 years ago. Thus, while African populations are nowadays devoid of any Neanderthal or Denisovan genes, East Asians and Europeans possess some Neanderthal ancestry, and Melanesians have also some Denisovan genes. The ancestors of Denisovans and Neanderthals interbred maybe 500,000 years ago.

A complication to the above picture is the Dmanisi evidence, from a cave in the Georgian Caucasus, of material resembling *H. habilis* rather than *H. erectus/ergaster*, dated to 1.8 million years ago, and again suggestive of a separate and early migration from Africa.

Another unresolved question relates to the very recent finds in a cave in South Africa, the Rising Star, near Johannesburg. Cavers stumbled on an enormous and astonishing trove of enigmatic fossils, provisionally labelled *H. naledi*, in a system which was extremely difficult to access, and which required a team of very small and slim female archaeologists. Although the skulls indicated a tiny brain, the size of an orange (500 c.c.), and comparable to *A. afarensis* at 3.2 million years ago, the nature of the trove seemed to indicate ritual burial and would have required some form of illumination for access, both practices not evident until quite late in our own evolution. Provisionally dated to around 300,000 years ago, the skeletons indicate a 1.4 m tall, slender build, weighing about 40 kg, with upper limbs adapted for both climbing and tool use, and lower limbs for a modern upright stance This is a weird mix of primitive and modern traits, reminiscent of the equally puzzling *H. floresiensis*, and like that taxon, clearly not on our direct evolutionary line, even though the tiny brain nevertheless had a surprisingly modern pattern of lobes, gyri and sulci, even compatible with some level of speech and empathy.

Dietary changes, from plant to animal material, may have stemmed from reduced availability of the former consequent upon climate change. High-protein animal meat may have been a first step, scavenged from carcasses, and requiring only the crudest of stone tools for butchering. Cut marks on bone at sites in Ethiopia (2.6 million years ago) indicate that butchering occurred. Competition with other scavengers may have encouraged a move to capture one's own prey, facilitating the evolution of rapid bipedal following of prey until it tired in the hot African day; the pursuers' upright posture would thereby reduce the surface area exposed to the noonday sun. The next stage would be the development of appropriate weapons such as throwing spears. In the absence of actual tools or weapons, due maybe to lack of preservation, cut or other marks on bones may provide circumstantial evidence. Similarly, the absence of actual hearths may not imply absence of roasting or cooking, although charcoal could simply result from bush fires – just as burial of human dead may instead imply hygienic removal, rather than ceremonial activity.

H. sapiens would seem to have experienced a cognitive revolution, around 60,000 years ago, judging from an explosion in so many parts of the world in complexity of tools, personal ornamentation, and of symbolism as evidenced in cave art. Next came an agricultural revolution with large-scale farming at 11,000 years ago, a scientific revolution (the Enlightenment) 500 years ago, the industrial revolution 250 years ago, and we are now witnessing a biotech revolution; what next?

2

TOOLS

Tacit and tactual symbols of civilisation

At the top of our very long, narrow and steep driveway, a nightmare in backing your car down to the road, as attested by the deep gouges ground out of the side of our ancient sandstone house during Mother's many somewhat unsuccessful attempts at reversing, there stood father's old blue shed. Like a relic of America's prairie disasters in the 1930s, it tilted and sagged, bearing evidence of numerous attempts at propping, patching and fixing. In it, apart from an old pre-war sports car up on bricks, 'waiting until I can get round to fixing it', was an antique treadle-operated lathe, with cracked leather drive belts, and an even older seaman's chest. It contained a jumble of rusty, dusty tools, which marked your hands red, and emitted a faintly metallic odour. These had been handed down in the Bradshaw family for generations; indeed, we had a line of ancestors all born, probably, as I was, on the kitchen table, in Number 12, Village Road, Higher Bebington, for many generations, maybe dating back to the days of King Charles I. It was a John Bradshaw, after all, who signed the latter's death warrant.

You could do most things with those old tools if you knew how to use them – they were a lot sturdier than their modern counterparts often sourced to China, having withstood time's challenging tests. They were clumsy, ugly, fascinating, and, as I now realise, more or less priceless. There was also the occasional gem, like the beautifully polished mahogany case, inlaid with moulded velvet inserts shaped to accept a dozen or so of father's Victorian drawing instruments for engineers, finely wrought from beautiful polished brass, and true precision instruments: again priceless, and abandoned or stolen during subsequent moves.

What is a tool? It is generally agreed that it is an object separate and detached from both the substrate and the operator's own person, and intentionally used to facilitate an operation or action of some kind upon another object, which may or may not itself be attached to the substrate. A post against which dairy cow Daisy rubs her bovine bottom is not a tool; a branch held in an elephant's trunk for the same purpose does qualify. As always in the biological sciences, linguistics and philosophy, boundaries are fuzzy. An archer fish may squirt a jet of water at a succulent insect perched above it; it may even compensate for the optical distortion caused by light rays passing through the transition between water and air, by aiming off, and also allow in this way for a moving target. Is that tool use? Is a child's toy a tool, of sorts? Is an octopus, playing with an abandoned jam jar on the sea floor, repeatedly removing and replacing the lid, seemingly for the sake of it, using a tool? It certainly is when, as recently reported, it uses appropriately configured stones to force open mussels for lunch. There are recent claims that bees, having learnt to obtain a food reward by rolling a tiny ball, will continue to do so even when sated, and in the absence of any further need for or availability of food. It clearly is not now just a matter of operant conditioning, but is it a toy or tool?

Apes shape grass stems so as to 'fish' for termites down holes in the earth. Indeed, several species of otherwise naïve crows do much the same with leaf stems, and even suitably bend adventitious bits of wire for similar purposes. And whether or not it is tool use *sensu stricto*, such crows exhibit another indication of cognitive sophistication in problem solving; when presented with a long narrow tube with an inaccessible delicacy at the bottom, if there is accessible water and a means to capture it, they will introduce the water to the tube and float the food item up and out – a capacity beyond most children until aged maybe four or five at least. Parrots may similarly use nut shells to obtain water which is otherwise inaccessible, and apes and macaques may use moss as sponges to transport liquids, whether learning by trial and error, or copying from others. Egyptian vultures have long been known to wield a hammer-stone with their beaks to break open shells, or to drop the shells from a height on to a hard surface, with the same intent. Indeed, bald and shiny-headed Aeschylus, the classical poet of Ancient Greece, is said to have died after being hit on the head by a falling tortoise. Chimp mothers may actively coach their young in cracking nuts open with a hammer stone and stone anvil, suggesting that the mothers know what the offspring do not, and so appropriately tailor their instruction – in other words, they may possess a 'theory of mind'. Some of the putative differences in cognitive capacity between hominins and other primates may be much less than previously thought.

Capuchin monkeys will bash cobbles together, and play with the resultant sharp-edged flakes very reminiscent of the putative tools associated with *Homo habilis*'s very early Oldowan tradition. While the monkeys never seem to actually use the flakes as cutting tools, we have to wonder whether these Oldowan artefacts actually were ever in fact used as tools. Nevertheless, careful analysis of waste chip fragments and flakes from these sites, painstakingly reassembled into the original pebble, indicates a general left-hand-hold and right-hand-operate technique which matches the frequency of right-/left-handedness in modern people.

Just as we have two *visual* systems (parietal, to inform us as to *where* events or actions are occurring), and a temporo-occipital system for their actual *identification*, so too we may have two *motor* systems: the intentional *when* system (basal ganglia, supplementary motor area), and a praxic *how* system involving the frontoparietal axis. Discrete brain damage can dissociate one system (preserved, or lost), from the other – a double dissociation – with corresponding consequences for how various functions are lost or conserved in tool use and deployment.

Anyone who like me has tried to reproduce the beautiful flint arrow heads from the British Neolithic, such as I have found by carefully combing likely sites like newly ploughed fields or recently revealed earlier land surfaces, will testify to the difficulty, and the skill, of these knappers of old. Recently, attempts have been made to image the brain activity of individuals who have spent patient years trying to learn the skill from first principles. In such experts, a region in the parietal lobe, known as the supramarginal gyrus, becomes active. This region is known to be involved in tracking the location of limbs and body parts in space. Another region, the right inferior frontal gyrus, which connects with the parietal lobe, is also active. This prefrontal region is heavily involved in attention, cognitive control, planning and the so-called 'executive functions'. Moreover, with continued practice, brain plasticity may result in enlargement of these active areas. Did apprenticeship to old-time master toolmakers maybe even drive the evolution of language, another skill once held again to separate us from 'brute apes'? Damage to adjacent regions in the inferior dorsolateral frontal cortex, on the left side, affects both praxis (coordinated, purposeful limb control), and the generation of spoken speech, leading to Broca's expressive aphasia, with understanding and comprehension less affected.

Skilled (praxic) manipulation, and the ability to make and deploy tools, even to make other tools, are very much a mark of our own species, no less than the possession of language and a sense of aesthetics. Just as symbolism may underlie both art and language, rapid sequential control of multiple fine muscle systems to discretely defined targets may be common to both speech and praxis, with common underlying neural mechanisms, as shown by deficits with clinical apraxia, where there is loss of skilled manipulative capacity.

An archetypal terrestrial tetrapod typically possessed four limbs, each with five digits, although early species from the Devonian period (390–340 million years ago) did possess more digits. Maybe five is optimal for efficient deployment, and evolution settled on that number. Although we are occasionally born with six digits, we seem to experience no obvious inconvenience. Processing fruits, seeds and nuts may have provided an essential pre-adaptation for tool behaviour and higher cognitive development. The Great Apes are very 'dextrous', and skilled at coordinating the two hands. Such learning likely depends on an evolved prefrontal cortex, with precision, not power, grips essential for habitual, efficient manipulation. Not all of these pre-adaptations may have been available to hands and brains until the time of *Homo habilis*, around 2.6–2.8 million years ago and the Oldowan tradition. That at least is the currently held view, except that at the time of writing I note reports, credible and well supported, of 3.3 million-year-old stone tools in Kenya, long before the oldest known *H. habilis* fossils, the oldest stone tools by far ever found, but so far unfortunately without any associated skeletal remains or cut-marked animal bones, or other indications of butchery. However, by painstakingly refitting the associated flakes found adjacently, back onto the original stone cores from which they had been struck, it became evident that as many as 70 flakes were struck from a single core, a feat demanding an impressive understanding of lithology, and positioning. Around 1.5 million years ago, with *Homo erectus*, we see more advanced, and even to our eyes aesthetically pleasing and symmetrical hand axes of the Acheulian tradition. The next advance in complexity came around 150,000 years ago with the Middle Palaeolithic Mousterian tradition of the Neanderthals, and finally, with anatomically modern humans, we see the beautiful products of the Upper Palaeolithic in Europe emerging around 40,000 years ago.

But what about the Americas, you might ask. Again current thinking has it that prehistoric *H. sapiens* reached that part of the world, presumably crossing the then exposed Bering Straits, around 14,500 years ago, although there have long been hints of settlement some thousands of years earlier. I note that there are currently reports of hammer stones and stone anvils together with fragmentary remains of a mastodon (*Mammut americanum*) dating to 131,000 years ago in California. To which group of hominins might these earlier migrants have belonged? We live in ever more interesting times, but it does seem that hominins might have hit the New World more than 100,000 years earlier than previously thought. And so far we only have their tools to go on.

Tools so far have been discussed in the contexts of pounding or cutting; what about creating holes? Drilled shell fragments, probably as part of personal adornment, go back tens and maybe even hundreds of thousands of years. However, again very recently, at a number of sites in Italy, human teeth have been found, still in skull or jaw, with holes clearly (from striations) drilled, and *filled*, mark you, with bitumen, dating to 14,000 years ago. Did our pre-mesolithic ancestors also view dental visits with as much trepidation as we do?

The initiation and control of movement, whether as praxis (making and using tools), or in language (speaking, or understanding another's speech by covertly anticipating each next syllable, and the oropharyngeal movements required to make it), depend on frontoparietal brain structures (the overall plan), the basal ganglia plus supplementary motor area (sequencing and releasing each next component), and the cerebellum (fine end-point accuracy in terminating each element in a motor sequence). All three massive systems must interplay like a magic orchestra, and later I shall describe our own studies of clinical (developmental, or acquired through injury or disease) disorders of these structures. Interestingly, apraxics are often unaware of their deficits, which tend to be more evident under conscious, volitional control, compared to when an automatic response may be given. Indeed, too much conscious, deliberate and introspective control during your golf stroke may be deleterious, compared to 'just letting it go, and going with the flow', naturally and automatically. Additionally, there tends to be a left side (of the brain) superiority in conscious and language-driven behaviours, and sometimes a weak, right-side superiority in the more automatic, spatial and emotional aspects of behaviour.

I vividly remember finding my first stone arrowhead, a superb Neolithic specimen abandoned on what became a newly eroded land surface on the peat 'hags' of Kinder Scout, high in the English Pennines between Sheffield and Manchester. The point had snapped off in antiquity, rendering this lovely Neolithic artefact useless for the hunt, but still a masterpiece of the maker's art. I have it glued to a card hanging on the wall of my study, along with other specimens I have found with fractures on the shaft, or on the side flanges or harpoon-like barbs, but still lovely to look at.

Using expertise gained from wandering the rock shelters of the remote West Kimberley in Australia, recording rock art sites containing Wandjinas and Bradshaw paintings, so called because they were discovered by Joseph Bradshaw (maybe a distant relation) in the late nineteenth century, back in England I prospected low-lying land adjacent to a stream in places like Budle Bay, Northumberland, close to where my in-laws lived in the historic settlement of Bamburgh, now a mecca for bird enthusiasts. Nor was I disappointed; I found broken axe heads and other fashioned blades. In the English Lakeland District, I came across a fine hand axe, fashioned most likely from the iconic volcanics of Langdale.

An unexpected and rather important find came from one of our student overnight campsites, near Bitlis, while travelling by Land Rover through Eastern Anatolia en route to Persia and Afghanistan in 1966. While collecting water from a nearby creek I noticed an outcrop of obsidian, of a beautiful greenish transparency. I collected a small boxful of adjacent fragments, and when I hosted an archaeological party back in the UK, with specialists familiar with the prehistoric obsidian trade, I showed them the material; we then immediately uncovered among numerous flakes a beautiful little hand axe. Apparently we had stumbled on a previously unknown, but long-sought, source of this lovely volcanic glass. They wanted me the next year to take a jeep, at the expense of the British Institute of Archaeology at Ankara, of which I was an associate, to locate it and find more material, when on our way to New Zealand for a new job in Experimental Psychology at the University of Otago, Dunedin. Unfortunately time did not permit. I still regret a wonderful lost opportunity.

An unexpected coda to that archaeological party, which happened to coincide with when I was writing up my doctoral thesis on pupillary (oculomotor) modulation during information processing, was a wound I suffered to my right, writing, hand. The very eminent, and occasionally bibulous, Professor of Archaeology, listening to our travel adventures and misadventures while we played plaintive Kurdish love-songs on a tape-recorder, pretended to be a love-crossed Kurdish bandit and feinted a lunge at me with our kitchen knife; I automatically raised my hand in defence, and the blade went right through the palm, fortunately not severing any tendons, although stitches were needed in Accident and Emergency. I still have a scar, but did not need to take up his offer of his personal secretary to type my thesis. The perils of archaeology can begin at home.

3

ART, GRAFFITI, JUVENILIA OR KILROY?

Sixty years ago, in Britain, my Father, like many others living in the country, competed in growing the biggest marrow. Naughty children would sometimes surreptitiously carve their initials, or a rude word, on the immature vegetable, and watch it all grow. We would also carve our names on our school desks, on the bark of trees, or on the soft sandstone surface of rocky outcrops. Waiting at the bus stop after school we would bore cupule-shaped holes in the sandstone wall with the large penny coins of the day. (In those days, 'Penny please' secured you a bus ride, and a ticket punched melodiously by a wonderful silver box worn on the conductor's leather belt.) In public toilets we would wonder at the explicit messages and the crude anatomical drawings on the walls, some seemingly reminiscent of the 'vulva' symbols in rock shelters imputed, together with ancient cupule patterns, by archaeologists to fertility rites or other religious rituals. So were these really vulval representations, or are we nowadays seriously missing the point, if they represented in fact something quite different, and we are simply seeing what we might nowadays expect to see on walls in public places? And if they really were crude vulval images, does that merely make them graffiti, maybe juvenilia by immature and hormonally challenged Palaeolithic adolescents? Can graffiti be considered in the context of art, any more than a 'Kilroy was here' message, or modern defacing 'tags' scrawled on buildings and signage?

Graffiti relates to the Italian '*graffio*', or 'scratching'. The Greek '*graphein*' (to write) and English 'grate', 'grind' and even 'scratch' are probably cognate etymologically. Indeed, the urge to mark smooth, unblemished surfaces is as old as humanity. In Pompeii and Herculaneum 2,000 years ago, the Romans decorated city walls with political or salacious remarks or drawings. Indeed, 'art' and the naked female form, along with maybe rather rarer male members, seem to go back more than 250,000 years. A gendered exception is perhaps the very common 'phallus and balls' symbol of (or for) good fortune in classical Rome, and the sculpted stone

'Hermes', plinths with a prominent erect phallus. These were vandalised one scandalous night, systematically snapped off, possibly as a political statement, in the 'Mutilation of the Hermes' incident. They were commonly erected (pardon the pun) outside domestic residences, again to bring good fortune in classical Athens.

Art, like tool use and language, is a quintessentially human activity, but unlike the last two, art seems essentially non-utilitarian, to be undertaken during 'time out' from meeting basic survival needs. The Latin root '*ars*' meant originally 'skill in working', and curiously, equates with '*scientia*' (knowledge), although nowadays art and science tend to be contrasted. Although seemingly great admirers of the naked human form (and in classical times maybe clothing as we know it was rather more revealing), Ancient Romans might or might not have similarly appreciated modern lavatory inscriptions, or recent exploratory assays at deliberately provoking negative emotions with the frankly grotesque or frightening, such as The Scream, by Munch. Indeed, did all forms of what we nowadays call 'ancient art', in all its manifestations, evoke a similar range of emotions, both then, and as now? Did a splendid sunset or view always have such an empirical impact? And why should art, views or sunsets have such an effect on the viewer, when there is no obvious evolutionary benefit or advantage?

Some see art as an attempt, alternative or prior to writing, to render permanent and tangible that which is formally intangible and fleeting. Art seems to involve seeking of order, the expression of a sense of pattern, or constancy amid a chaotic world of confusion. Can we present a natural object, an *objet trouvé* like a beautifully preserved fossil, as a work of art? Or a photographed landscape, or even Duchamp's urinal in all its pleasing technical perfection as an artefact, and thus submitted to the 1917 New York Exhibition? Others note that the purpose of art is not merely to depict or represent reality, which can be done easily enough with a camera, but to enhance, transcend or even distort or caricaturise reality, so as to emphasise or exaggerate what the artist sees as the key, salient, or canonical aspects. Thus artists, consciously or otherwise, may deploy certain rules or principles, almost as if they were neurologists, to activate certain brain regions or mechanisms, via grouping, closure, symmetry, colour contrast or apparent movement, to trigger in the viewer a problem-solving process which is itself intrinsically gratifying. Art may therefore be distinguished from ordinary perception by the intensity of emotional feelings evoked by the artist in the viewer, and it may thereby somehow externalise the artist's consciousness, allowing us access to his or her way of seeing a sample of reality.

Three hundred or more thousand years ago, ochre seems to have been collected, and so perhaps used, for personal or object decoration in the Acheulian culture of *Homo erectus*. The same people crafted stone tools of a satisfying symmetry that seemed to transcend mere utility, and to collect, as *objets trouvés*, rock crystals, fossils and pebbles of pleasing shapes. Indeed, from the Acheulian site of Berekhat Ram in the Golan Heights comes a scoria pebble naturally resembling the female form, which apparently was intentionally modified to produce an enhanced human image. Even earlier, from the Makapansgat site of the South

African Transvaal, comes a jasperite cobble, associated with australopithecine remains, whose entirely natural features startlingly resemble a face; it may have been carried into the cave by beings quite distant and distinct from our own immediate human ancestry.

So what then should we include under the rubric of ancient art? Australia, as so often, provides us with a useful model, in that we find here represented most of the world's major potential categories. Pecked on or ground into smooth hard rock surfaces (petroglyphs), or painted thereon with red, white or yellow ochres, we find in caves or overhang shelters, representations of meandering or intersecting lines, circles, 'sunbursts' and other simple, geometrical, non-representational forms. We see animal and bird tracks similarly marked, animals and birds themselves, often in outline, infilled, or as stick figures. Sometimes animals are in groups or apparently 'doing' something. Occasionally we find human figures, the ancient Guion or 'Bradshaw' figures perhaps being the most noteworthy, and such figures occasionally may be ornamented or apparently engaging in some ceremonial or other activity. We find representations or stencils of hands or artefacts such as boomerangs, throwing sticks or nets. Occasionally, there are sculptures 'in the round'. Finally, there are various forms of personal adornment.

There are perhaps four main regions and types of rock art in continental Australia, and I have been privileged to visit, explore and record in three of these. The one next on my list is the Burrup Peninsula and adjacent Dampier Archipelago in Western Australia's arid Pilbara region some 1,500 km north of Perth, and on Australia's National Heritage list. Almost exclusively petroglyphs, numbering in tens of thousands, the imagery includes marine fauna, lizards, kangaroos, and the long extinct (by at least 5,000 years on the mainland) Thylacine or Tasmanian Tiger. There are also motifs with spiritual significance associated with 'Dreamtime' or Earth-creation myths, and haunting 'archaic' faces maybe 20,000 years old, judging by erosion, patina and content.

In the early 1970s, we were privileged, long before mass tourism, to wander at will in the caves and rock shelters of the Arnhem Land Escarpment adjacent to the East Alligator River, now in Kakadu National Park. Close to Nourlanji Rock (otherwise known as Burruggui), there are yellow, red and white ochre representations in the older Mimi style of ancestral beings from the Dreaming, and of the long-extinct Thylacine. There are also more recent X-ray-style paintings, often of fish or reptiles, showing the internal skeleton or organs roughly *in situ*. We found and filmed cupules (long before pennies!) ground into the rock where ochre had been ground for pigment, and highly polished surfaces where countless bottoms must have sat for equally countless centuries.

On another expedition my wife Judy and I visited Jowalbinna in North Queensland, 'Quinkan Country', near Laura on Cape York. Again, ochre representations are of animals, spirits (often shown inverted if malevolent), and other mythological beings. These 'galleries' are of international significance. They were originally brought to notice by an outback 'bush' character, Percy Trezise, pilot, painter, explorer, writer, and an authority on North Queensland rock art. Pilot of Fokker

Friendship turboprops for the now-long-defunct airline Ansett in the post-war years, he would fly just above ground level with a full load of passengers paying, and hoping, to fly intercity direct, often between canyon walls looking for likely rock art sites – a terrifyingly exhilarating experience for city folk. Later, at week-ends or on leave, he would explore on foot or in his old Land Rover. Hard living, maybe hard drinking, he lived life to the full, and collaborated with aboriginal friends and Mary Haginikitas, artist and illustrator of children's books on mythology. I was privileged to meet both shortly before he died.

In the remote Kimberley, where I have made many visits by four-wheel drive, by boat along the coast, on foot, and by swimming up water-filled gorges, there are countless rock-shelters and caves with Bradshaw (Guion) paintings, eponymous to a Joseph Bradshaw, pastoralist and explorer in the mid to late 1800s. According to my father in England, now no longer with us, Joseph may have been a distant relative. Indeed, he even once had a homestead, still down on maps as the 'Bradshaw Run', on the hillside near Melbourne, less than 1 km from where I have lived for the last 46 years. He was later employed, in the Agricultural Department of what is now the State of Western Australia, in the late nineteenth century to prospect for new grazing lands in the then-unexplored Kimberley, where he first discovered the paintings for which he is known. These are paintings of a unique richness of style and expression, and of great age, as yet indeterminate. With my wife Judy, I was once privileged to be lent by the West Australian Conservation and Lands Management Department (CALM) an early model GPS, to explore the regions north of Bell Gorge for rock shelters and possible art sites. We would swim, naked, up the otherwise inaccessible flooded gorges, equipment and clothing in watertight polythene bags, exploring, finding and recording. Unfortunately, the GPS was of little use those days, when deep in narrow gorges. It was, however, all wonderful, memorable and productive.

The Bradshaws, very often human figures dancing or hunting, are aesthetically beautiful, anatomically correct rather than schematic, and at least 17,000 years old, possibly more than 25,000, and very different from anything else later in the Kimberley or elsewhere. The other, later, major type of Kimberley rock art, the Wandjinas, represent cloud and rain spirits of the monsoonal storm, with eyes, nose, no mouth ('were they to speak, we might all be flooded'), with a radiating halo of rays around the head. If the Kimberley Wandjinas are striking, and the Arnhem Land art can be characterised as varied and interesting, the Guions are just so hauntingly beautiful.

To return to Europe, personal adornment in the form of beads (carved from shells) and pendants (made from shell, bone or teeth) characterised the Neanderthals, our evolutionary cousins as recently extinct as about 30,000 years ago in Western Europe. Thus, there was a brief period of overlap between the two peoples and cultures.

When we think of the European Upper Palaeolithic, we think of those amazing decorated caves, some dated to 30,000 or more years ago, with walls painted with bestiaries of beautifully proportioned and represented animals, many extinct.

However, captive capuchin monkeys, given clay, paint, stones, leaves and sticks, will construct and decorate a range of shapes and forms; they will also mark clay slabs manually, and with stick and stone tools. Chimpanzees will readily draw with pen and paper, introducing variations that seem formally relevant and maybe even aesthetic, and paying attention to the boundaries of the paper. Recently, there was an exhibition in Sydney of artwork produced by elephants, wielding paintbrushes in their trunks and producing aesthetically interesting 'canvases' on paper. What does this tell us about the animals as artists, and us as viewers who experience a sense of the aesthetic? Is art a form of transaction between a producer and a recipient, such that in the absence of an intention to convey something, we have to deny the status of art? The male Australian bowerbird creates intricately decorated bowers adorned with *objets trouvés*, often of human origin, such as blue (a favourite colour, apparently) ballpoint caps, bottle tops, flowers, etc., to woo a potential mate. Surely this implies a transactional arrangement like the proverbial peacock's tail, also an instance – *the* textbook instance – of sexual selection. This of course was Darwin's dilemma until he hit upon the appropriate explanation, a dilemma which he says actually 'made him sick' just thinking about it. The plumage of male birds of paradise, and the antlers of male deer are other such instances whereby the male, although often otherwise disadvantaged, may succeed in convincing a female of his overall genetic superiority despite such impedimenta, and therefore his suitability for breeding. Were the beautiful Acheulian hand axes of *H. erectus*, beautiful certainly to our eyes, and seemingly rather 'over-engineered' for simple chopping tasks, really made to impress the prehistoric ladies of the times? Can the same be said about our own contemporary art, if we see art as an indulgence rather than purely practical? Or is it a by-product of our own overdeveloped brains, a 'spandrel' in Stephen J Gould's terms – a structurally essential architectural prop between buttress and walls which also happens to allow additional decoration in the construction of a medieval cathedral? Is a sense of the aesthetic itself an unselected spin-off or accidental evolution of our uncommonly complex central nervous system? And can the same be said of the evolution of consciousness and the 'illusion of free will'?

The simplest patterns we can produce are straight and curved lines, intersections, star shapes, circles, triangles and squares, and they may correspond to edge, line and intersection detectors which have been identified in the visual system. They are also, in a sense, motor primitives, the simplest non-representational configurations available to the hand. Why, then, do they not systematically precede the earliest representational art of the Upper Palaeolithic, and that found in the magnificent rock shelters here in Australia in the Kimberley, Arnhem Land and Cape York? Such 'primitives' are indeed found, often pecked or pounded into smooth rock surfaces, along with cupules similar to those we made long ago with our pennies. Some see a similarity between such patterns and the visual experiences induced by migraine or hallucinogenic drugs, and invoke shamanic religious ecstasy. Others see them as just a form of doodling! Either way, although 'primitives', there is no evidence for them systematically preceding 'more developed' art forms.

So why then did our ancestors engage in artistic activity, when mere survival may have been demanding? Was it a form of territorial marking, to record or commemorate an event or rite of passage for religious or ritual purposes to do with the tribe, hunt or fertility, or just a form of doodling to occupy a rainy day? The fact that natural features on the rock surface, bulges, cracks and jointing, may be incorporated in an apparently meaningful way into an emerging representation of, say, a horse or bison, suggests that even apparently representational art may have easily built upon natural features, just as we doodle on other materials. The important point is that apart from graffiti, most of our two-dimensional art today relies on paper. Ancient art made do with the three-dimensional rock-face, which seemed to fulfil most of the roles we nowadays assign to a far more perishable substrate. Perhaps to avoid temptations to the ancient urge to graffiti our urban environment, we should avoid providing smooth, flat, unadorned surfaces, as local authorities seem recently to be realising. All of which suggests yet one more possible *raison d'être* for ancient art; maybe, as some latter-day Aborigines and contemporary practitioners of graffiti claim, the ongoing act of doing may be more important than the product itself. And that's how I felt too, when boring cupules with my childhood penny.

An artist, ancient or modern, in painting or drawing a three-dimensional object, must somehow reduce it to two dimensions. More than one perspective may be combined, so as to include as much relevant information as possible. A crocodile painted in an Arnhem Land rock shelter may show the head (as typically seen) side on, and the body (again as typically seen) from above; the creature is immediately recognisable, even though its contorted posture is anatomically impossible. A four-wheeled wagon, pecked into a European rock surface, may be viewed as from above, although with its wheels laid out flat in plan form, as if the whole structure had been squashed from above. Movement or action in human beings may be represented by reducing them to stick or 'pin' figures, anatomically impossible representations but nevertheless surprisingly capable of representing the artist's intention.

When we look at the clouds, we may see a horse, or a face; a bird may appear from what is merely a random configuration of twigs in a tree, a phenomenon known in neurology as pareidolia. The visual system, with inadequate input, may create illusory or spurious images. This is also, of course, the basis of schizophrenic hallucination, or the spontaneous images experienced by those who become blind. The nervous system demands input, manufacturing its own if necessary, and is engaged in a continuous 'effort after meaning', to impose order on seeming chaos. Indeed, the visions apparently experienced by the intensely religious may stem from a combination of such self-organising behaviour, and from the activation of a region within the temporal lobe which researchers, such as Vilayanur Ramachandran, have christened from brain imaging studies, the God Spot. We do not need to appeal to drug-induced or ritual activity to explain experiences that transcend what is given.

Is art, or religion, amenable to scientific study and reductionist explanation? Should it be? Are we all potentially capable of great work? Recent findings involving a number of patients indicate the apparent release of previously unknown and unexpected talent during the progression of dementia. On the other side of the coin, certain otherwise intellectually-compromised autistic 'savants', such as the girl, Nadia, may, from a very early age, exhibit extraordinary untutored artistic talent, which vanishes with special intervention or training in language skills. So is art 'merely' an alternative medium to language? As symbolic behaviours, did they both co-evolve, perhaps mutually, in the past, or were the talented painters of the European Upper Palaeolithic effectively autistic and non-verbal, as has even been proposed? And was the work of lesser quality the play of children? Indeed, was all such rock art performed for the same, or as I believe, for a variety of purposes? Was some, in fact, just good old-fashioned porn for its own sake?

In medicine nowadays, we recognise that a disorder typically involves a number of causative factors. When created, a 'work' may similarly have been inspired by more than one need or drive, or over time, the balance of such impulses may have shifted. The act as an end in itself may have yielded to the symbolic significance of the actual product, which may eventually have come to be appreciated, aesthetically in its own right. We create, and appreciate, for a variety of reasons.

Art, unless done routinely for commercial purposes to earn a living, is nowadays closely associated with the creative drive. As such, it clearly fulfils no direct utilitarian purpose either for the producer or the consumer. While we may never know whether the same situation applied 30,000 years ago in the rocky galleries of Southern France, one wonders whether there was then, as unfortunately there seems to be now, such a high correlation between artistic endeavour and psychopathology. In this context the words of the Roman essayist Seneca sound remarkably apposite: '*Nullum magnum ingenium sine mixtura dementiae fuit*', loosely translated as 'genius is akin to madness', although Seneca was probably thinking of the link between schizophrenic or bipolar mania and creativity, rather than what we nowadays understand by 'dementia'.

I started this chapter by mentioning the cupules we carved as kids; maybe a decade ago a major cupule site, Jinmium, in the Northern Territory, was touted as the world's oldest rock art. We now know the dates were wrong, and maybe also it wasn't even art. While the aesthetically still wonderful Ice Age art of frozen Europe dates back to around 30,000 years ago, we still don't know exactly how far back we can take art in Australia; items of personal decoration, an aspect of aesthetics most likely divorced from any possible religious or shamanistic ritual, have been recorded in Australia, in the form of a kangaroo bone nose ornament dating back to 46,000 years ago. Optically stimulated luminescence, applied to sand grains embedded within a mud-wasp's nest adhering to and overlying a painted motif, measures the elapsed time since the sand was last exposed to sunlight, and so provides a minimum age for dating the art. Such OSL techniques, cutting edge in dating, remind me, within my own professional discipline, of the latest techniques in brain imaging, such as diffusion tensor imaging (DTI), to plot the brain's interconnecting pathways, fibres or neurons. The sand grains of OSL act as proxies for the art; linearly aligned water molecules act as proxies for the axonic pathways. And colour-coded tractography (connectivity mapping) of the human brain, as generated by DTI, can also itself be astonishingly beautiful; art in nature.

I have lived through stirring times, and I want to be around to see where it will all lead to.

4

LANGUAGE

What tales the tongue may tell

Dear departed Aunty Betty, *requiescat in pace*; she was rarely at a loss for *words*, her written and *spoken communications* were largely of trivial gossip, and in the *language* of her times. *Communication*, *speech*, *words* and *language* are not mere redundant synonyms, but themselves capture the hierarchical categorisation of communication generally, and the nested subsets which are included therein. Birds communicate, so do neurons; vocalisation is one mode of communication in the animal world, along with colour changes reflecting mood in the squid, and speech is a form of meaningful vocalisation which we humans uniquely employ. English is one of the world's many language channels to that end, and writing is just another medium which can be employed. Precision in language usage is important in defining concepts, not least when we seek to define language itself. Workers in the field of artificial intelligence sometimes wonder whether a complex IT system can ever model, or 'understand', itself, and philosophers and neuroscientists similarly ask whether a human brain can ever fully comprehend or understand all its operations. Can language adequately and comprehensively define or describe itself? Yes, but it requires precision of terminology and agreement as to correct or intended usage. We must remember that communication is not just language, and language is not just speech (there are also sign and writing). Language is essentially propositional, and composed as it is of sub-units (words, themselves composed of phonemes or graphemes), there may be a near infinity of such possible propositional statements.

It is easy to slip into the teleological position that language evolved, for instance, for the purpose of intraspecific communication, for group hunting or co-operation in defence, or for modelling possible outcomes, or better problem solving, or instructing the young, or for the support of abstract thought ... But evolution is never goal-directed, and the appearance of the precursors of language back in our distant past may have supported the development of any or all of the above, and more, such as, for instance, religion. Indeed, it is difficult to imagine the rituals of religion without some kind of verbal basis, or the slow demise of polytheistic rituals involving multiple deities, before, for instance, modern more or less toxic monotheistic beliefs, all more or less still driven by 'the book', and/or associated political movements, and all too often involving violence to those of differing, and usually equally pointless, persuasions. In a related sense, we cannot dismiss a possible role for group choral song as a bonding mechanism while at the same time supporting the synergistic emergence of true language.

Be that as it may, we are fortunate to have inherited a system so fitted for modelling reality, problem solving, managing abstract concepts (where mere deictic pointing to concrete objects is inadequate), and reducing complexity by labelling and categorisation. However, we do not always need language to think, conceptualise or problem solve. Aphasics, like my wife Judy after a devastating stroke, can still think, plan, problem solve, play simple board games and seemingly reason, without any capacity for speech; and theoreticians may from time to time instead proceed via mental imagery.

The hierarchical recursive inclusivity of language ('John ate the egg laid by the hen in the hedge at the end of the garden at the front of the house up the road') is very reminiscent of that found in computer programming, where there are specific algorithms nested within larger subroutines, which themselves group into entire programs. Language, of course, requires the linking of an arbitrary symbol to represent some object, activity or concept, in a mutually agreed fashion, with other such symbols for understanding and appropriate action or reaction to follow in social exchange. Onomatopoeia and the phenomenon of sound-symbolism, see below, may be exceptions to a purely arbitrary link between word and meaning.

It may be no evolutionary accident that manual dexterity (including right-hand preferences in most individuals), tool-making and deployment, and language all seem to have co-evolved in adjacent brain areas, as evidenced by the tragedies of acquired (i.e. after brain injury or stroke) aphasia (loss of speech), and apraxia (loss of ability to perform skilled, sequential, manual behaviour), as occurred with my own wife Judy.

Such observations have prompted the gestural theory for language origin, as proposed by my long-time friend and colleague Michael Corballis, a view with which I am not entirely in sympathy, preferring to see language in humans as evolving from earlier primate call systems; however, such minor academic disagreements have never come between us, unlike the frequently virulent battles all too often waged between erstwhile friends. Life is too short to spoil it with arcane argumentation. It is of course true that adoption of an upright bipedal gait, itself maybe an ultimate consequence of ancient climate change in the African savannah, freed up the hands for tool use, tool deployment and gesture, upon which we do tend to fall back in default, or when comprehension gets tough, and indeed chimpanzees can be taught rudimentary communication via gesture; gesture, however, is of little use in the dark, at a distance, or when simultaneously deploying tools or weapons. Corballis's gestural-origin hypothesis, in simplest form, might see language developing from an early hominid 'point and grunt' strategy; but at a more sophisticated level it would take heart from the way profoundly deaf communities, where a sufficient number of members who have inherited the disability (an appellation, however, which many such communities vehemently reject, preferring to see it as a 'normal' variant of humanity's rich tapestry of being) each independently evolve in a very short time their own system of signing. These are true sign languages, each with entirely their own syntax, rather than simply alternative coding systems fundamentally derived from and reflecting a parent spoken language. However, there is no evidence of individuals in hearing communities going through a system of signing early in their development of speech – other than maybe just to point and grunt when they want a specific object. I shall return to the question of deaf signing shortly.

Language is certainly unique, seeming to have emerged almost out of nowhere some time in our evolutionary past; via a range of hoots, barks and bird calls many creatures can communicate specific dangers, fear, dominance, anger, desire, and so on, but something as simple as 'she stole my worm' is beyond them. The existence of mirror neurons in primate brains, active both during agency and when observing another's acts, are certainly compatible with the gestural-origin theory, but they do not prove that language evolved *from* mirror neuron activity. It is also true that non-human communication is rather more largely emotional and perhaps under more automatic control, compared to voluntary, propositional human speech, but again that does not prevent the latter having been built upon the former's foundations. Plausible and attractive though the gestural theory is, somehow to me it just does not ring true, even though it is not easily disproved. However, it is never easy to prove what *did* happen in the remote past; far easier, maybe, to show what probably *didn't* happen. We may have faced early evolutionary pressures different from those encountered by other primates, that made our complex communication system adaptive – in the need to coordinate cooperative groups where each individual played a different if complementary role in the group's overall aim, such as hunting where particular strategies might be called for, requiring moment-to-moment variation. Such flexibility may not be called for in a grazing or browsing context or ecology.

Samuel Pepys, in 1669, suggested that we might teach manual gestures and signing to tame chimpanzees, who otherwise seemed to lack communicative capacities with humans. It is now some time since two-way success was reported using manual gestures, or correct selection of hundreds of symbols or tokens. The related bonobos (*Pan paniscus*), the most sociable of the great apes, proved the more adept at communicating with and understanding sign; they were able to request tools or information necessary to perform a task. There were various attempts, more or less successful, at rearing baby bonobos from birth with human infants. However, they were never able voluntarily to generate the full range of human speech sounds (phonemes). This inability is usually ascribed to their possession of a larynx that has not descended like that of humans. Nevertheless, it now seems that baboons *are* capable of generating many human vowels. Absence of the human hyoid bone has also been deemed relevant, and again subsequently refuted. In the wild, chimp call systems do seem to code for a range of relevant environmental events, evoking responses appropriate to a putative aggressor – direction of looking, running, freezing … Vervet monkeys may even use calls to deceive and distract a higher-ranking conspecific, pretending that an aggressor is approaching from a certain direction, thereby enabling theft of a prize 'from under the nose' of the other animal. Not only is this ability indicative of a kind of linguistic communication, but it is also suggestive of a 'theory of mind' – one animal knowing what another believes, a capacity said to be deficient in humans lying on the autistic spectrum.

Working cattle or sheep dogs can recognise up to 1,000 spoken words, and drive the flock accordingly; moreover imaging studies indicate that similar regions, in their brains' left hemisphere, to those active in ourselves, are involved in such communicative behaviour.

In birds, the Japanese tit (*Parus minor*) uses up to ten different notes in its calling repertoire, the order of the notes determining the meaning, an example of compositional syntax analogous to that found in human speech. However, probably the best studied of the birds is Alex, an African Grey parrot now sadly deceased, which could both understand and correctly deploy, in vocal interactions, more than 100 English words, to refer to objects, actions and requests. He could refuse requests, and tell his instructor what she should do, or request information on objects' colour, number (within limits), location, shape or general nature. Separately, we now know that birds' brains, compared to our own, are far more densely packed with neurons and interconnections, so we cannot directly compare intellects between species on the basis of brain volume, without making a substantial (and as yet unknown) correction. Another species of parrot, the wild keas of New Zealand, apparently burst spontaneously into play when exposed to the parrot equivalent of canned laughter. They make a special warbling call, which if played to them invariably triggers behaviour equivalent to our own spontaneous, contagious laughter, soaring in aerobatic loops, kicking and tossing objects to each other, which terminates when the recording is turned off. Separately, lab mice too are said to emit mousey equivalents of human giggles when tickled on the abdomen.

Before electronic communication devices became ubiquitous, rural villagers independently, in very many parts of the world, employed whistled versions of their native languages, the better to communicate over large distances. Indeed, the wonderful old Greek storyteller, teller of tales and of fables, and also of genuine historical events, Herodotus of Halicarnassus, in Book 4 of his *Histories* (440 BC) describes 'Ethiopian troglodytes' communicating thus. Over 70 populations worldwide have independently learnt how to communicate in this way, typically by modulating whistles. Thus, the sounds of speech are not now generated as usual via the vocal cords, but by pitch changes imposed upon a whistle generated in the mouth, and appropriately moving tongue, jaw and lips, analogous to a modified whisper. It is, however, not as accurate or reliable as the naturally spoken parent speech, from which it is directly derived.

Quite different are the independently developing sign languages of the deaf, which in certain congenitally deaf communities independently evolve, with their own gestural syntax, owing nothing to the language of normally hearing speakers of their particular culture. Thus, unlike whistled messages, which are in a sense parasitic on a native language, these deaf-signing languages are indeed true languages, separate in their own right. They also seem to employ similar regions of brain activation to normal spoken languages. Thus, the phonology (speech-related sounds) and basic units of signing both involve widespread left-hemisphere activation; the same is largely true of morphology, the basic units of meaning such as words or word fragments, combined (in spoken speech) by rule from phonemes. The same is again true of syntax, the grammatical rules governing the combination of morphemes into uniquely meaningful strings. With semantics, the formal meaning of a string of morphemes, the left hemisphere may largely contribute denotative meaning ('a file is a tool to rasp away rough edges'), and the right hemisphere may contribute some additional emotional, connotative or contextual meaning ('files can hurt you'). Right hemisphere involvement is also evident with prosodic aspects, changes of pitch, rhythm, stress, intonation, posture or expression, providing extra interpretive, connotative or contextual meaning. Sarcasm, humour, irony, jokes and metaphor also provide additional information via largely right-hemisphere contributions.

It is these apparently right-hemisphere aspects of language, where there is ambiguity often only resolved by context and the speaker's manifest intent, which may remain long beyond the capacity of even the best machine systems of translation or understanding. Consider 'Mary had a little lamb'; did she own one, eat some or give birth to one? Consider also 'I like cooking apples' (do I appreciate the act, or the type of apples?), or a spoken statement such as 'I am now feeling rosie'; is this an impropriety or the consequences of a day spent in too much sunshine?

Correct neurodevelopment is increasingly seen as involving environmental stimulation or input, often before the end of certain critical developmental periods. If for any reason the two eyes are incorrectly aligned at birth, even if corrected by the age of two or three, the child may never subsequently be able to acquire proper binocular vision, and be able to see in 3D depth. A child deprived of exposure to the speech of other members of her family or culture until puberty, may afterwards, if rescued, be unable to learn to speak properly, communicating at best with a series of discrete telegraphic phrases, without grammar, just like an aphasic patient. Such a notorious case was the child Genie, rescued more than a decade after her birth having been kept locked in an attic, and passed the necessities of life by a mute and psychotic parent – almost a real-life instance of the old Egyptian pharaoh's 'Forbidden Experiment', see below.

Even earlier is the critical period for the acquisition of correct pronunciation of certain consonant sounds; an infant who has never heard spoken Japanese or Chinese may never have full phonological mastery when later learning the language. Language exposure in the very first few months of life may be subconsciously retained even when no conscious knowledge of the early experience remains. This subconscious knowledge can then be tapped to speed up learning the language.

Correctly producing a language's speech sounds may even be important in understanding it. According to the old Motor Theory of Speech Perception, when we listen to someone speaking, the redundancy of the message often permits us to guess ahead or predict what the next few words or speech sounds are likely to be; we generate them automatically, subconsciously and sub-vocally. We partly understand the speaker's intent via what we continuously re-create. In a similar fashion, according to the doctrine of affordances in visual perception, we recognise objects, such as a cup, by how we would normally employ them, e.g. picking them up by the handle so as to take a drink. In the last few decades, neurophysiologists have isolated 'mirror neurons' in the brain. These cells, it will be recalled, fire not only when we make a particular gesture, with arm, hand or mouth, but also when we *see* someone else making such movements. These mirror neurons, present in all primates, including ourselves, may facilitate our understanding of someone's intentions, and also our ability to learn to make the same series of movements or gestures.

Clearly we have to learn the language spoken primarily by our family or culture, while at the same time we seem to have an inbuilt hard-wired proclivity to learn a language, any language, even sign if congenitally deaf. Such considerations led Noam Chomsky five or so decades ago to argue that language is an innate and uniquely human trait, programmed into our genes, having been acquired by a sudden mutation at some time in our past. If so, it must have occurred simultaneously in a number of families, as otherwise in the absence of both speakers and listeners able to comprehend, it would have disappeared as non-adaptive from the genome. Children, he said, are born with a language instinct compelling them effortlessly to acquire whatever language within which as toddlers they are immersed. He also invoked the idea of a Universal Grammar shared by all languages, all possessing a common deep structure. However, no evidence has been forthcoming of such a common deep structure or universal grammar, and the idea is nowadays largely discredited. Far more likely, we use a variety of cognitive processes, not necessarily specific to language, such as categorisation, the understanding of relationships, intuiting, learning simple grammatical patterns in a parent language, and, as mentioned above, interpreting the speaker's communicative intent. Indeed, by the third trimester of pregnancy the auditory system is well developed, and after six months within the womb, through to which speech sounds clearly penetrate, infants seem able to discriminate auditory signals, for example, between vowel and consonant sounds, emanating from outside the womb, an ability which is behaviourally demonstrable immediately after birth. Moreover, if exposed even before birth to complex speech sounds from a language other than that which will become their mother tongue a year or so after birth, they can later mimic sounds from that other language, sounds which only native speakers of that language can produce perfectly, far better than infants never exposed to that other tongue. Consequently, right from birth and even before, infants begin to store important aspects of correct phonology, appropriate to their 'mother tongue'.

The acquisition of language seems to use an inherited problem-solving algorithm; what varies, from individual to individual, is the output of that algorithm as determined by additional environmental input.

In the early 1950s, the A5104, the escape route to rural North Wales from the smoke of Merseyside, passed railway-crossings with red Welsh warning notices, 'Perigwl', with the English word 'Danger' beneath. In my early teens and learning Latin and Greek, I wondered whether the Latin 'periculum' (danger) underlay 'Perigwl'; was the similarity due to chance, or to borrowing from the Roman invaders, or the result of cognate origins in a common ancestral tongue? These three possibilities still bedevil philology and the search for the origins of a language. Fossils of a linguistic cocktail still haunted the surrounds of my old home village, Bebington – Anglo-Saxon, the '*Tun*' or 'Settlement' of Bebe's people. Around lay Irby – the Norse '*By*' or 'Village' of the Irish; Wallasey – the '*Eg*' or Isle of the Welsh; and the Norman-French settlement of Egremont, '*AcriMonte*' or the Pointed Hill. Did such factors kindle in me a fascination with language origins? They even led me to become Secretary, and Chairman, of the Oxford University Philological Society, and to personally get to know Robert Graves, poet, historian and novelist.

Whatever traits separate us from our ape cousins, spoken language is a clear candidate, although the creation of the first stone tools three or more million years ago, and increasing brain size and the specialisation of language-related areas half a million years later, were equally clear stepping-stones. Skeletal adaptations, maybe a million years ago or later, hint at the evolution of an anatomically-modern larynx, capable perhaps for the first time of producing our full complex sequences of speech sounds; genes controlling articulatory function, via appropriate brain structures such as the basal ganglia and supplementary motor area – regions with which as a neuroscientist I have long been preoccupied – appeared soon after. While symbolic behaviours are foreshadowed in possible personal ornamentation by our extinct relatives, the Neanderthals, 'proper' art, as we reckon it, may not have emerged much before 50,000 years ago.

Mirror neurons, an imitatory system for matching the observation and production of hand and mouth actions, could underlie the ultimate origins of our own speech. Chewing, sucking, and smacking of tongue and lips may have fostered the development of such mirror neuron mediation, and even directly led to some of the ancient click-languages of Africa. Were the latter in fact perhaps our earliest mode of vocal communication?

The seventh-century BC Egyptian pharaoh Psamtik sought to determine the world's oldest language; he reared newborns in isolation to discover the first word they uttered. 'Bekos' or 'bread' in Phrygian, a now-extinct Anatolian language, apparently emerged. Of course, even were such isolated and abused infants generally to utter such first words, developmental observations of this sort do not tell us anything about the prehistoric origins of language. In 1786, Sir William Jones pioneered another path when he recognised affinities, as indicating common descent, between Sanskrit, the classical language of India, and Persian, Greek, Latin and

Gothic. This was the basis of the reconstruction of the ancient and hypothetical language, Proto-Indo-European, from which we believe are derived most European tongues, and many spoken in Western and Central Asia.

The sounds of all languages slowly change, each set of sounds in each language in their own regular but entirely idiosyncratic fashion, diverging, according to Grimm's Law, ever further from an extinct parent tongue like Proto-Indo-European. Such sound shifts in comparative linguistics parallel, almost uncannily, the slow march of genetic mutations as offspring populations gradually separate from a parent stock. Indeed, many of the same statistical procedures are common both to cladistics in biological evolution, and to studies of the interrelatedness or otherwise of languages. And in neither case, other than as an artificial frozen snapshot in transient time, can we isolate the period of occurrence of, say, *pure* Anglo-Saxon or Early English, on a linguistic or even a genetic basis. As the old Greek once said, you can never step twice into exactly the same river.

Proto-Indo-European (IE) is thought to have been spoken by Neolithic pastoralists somewhere maybe to the north-east of the Black Sea, on the basis of similarities of vocabulary, in its many modern descendants, for the names of certain key plants, animals and activities. Debate continues as to its exact period of origin and homeland, and whether it spread by slow diffusion, or by invasion and conquest. Whatever the truth, the mystery and magic of our Proto-Indo-European heritage have continued to fascinate me and many scholars in the field.

To consider some particular instances: archaeological, demographic and linguistic debate 'centres', appropriately enough, around IE root forms such as '*kwel*' or '*kwol*'. Note, incidentally, that 'e' and 'o' sounds are in a certain fashion interchangeable in many IE languages. Even today this is evident in English, as with 'feed'/'food', 'deed'/'do', 'lend'/'loan', 'get'/'got', 'tell'/'told', etc. Moreover, these two vowel sounds dominated, along with what has become to be known as the zero grade, that is, their absence with instead the somewhat sustained sounding of certain consonants like 'm' and 'n'. The IE '*kwel*'/'*kwol*' seems to have signified 'to move around a centre', or 'dwell'. Its descendants include Greek '*kolos*' ('a herdsman'), Latin '*colo*' ('I cultivate') and '*collum*' ('neck or collar'), and Old Norse '*hals*' (again, 'neck'). With doubling or reduplication of the initial sound, a common phenomenon in many languages, we get '*kwekulo*', a 'cycle' ('*kuklos*', in Greek) or 'circle' ('*circulus*' in Latin). '*Kwekulo*' itself is cognate with Old English '*hweogol*' which indeed gives rise to our modern 'wheel', while Indian Sanskrit '*cakram*' similarly means 'circle'. The unstable 'kwe' sound at an early stage apparently also gave rise, in addition to a 'ke' sound, to such variants as 'te' (for example, Greek '*telos*', a 'cyclical completion') and 'pe'/'po' as in Greek '*polos*' ('pole', around which things revolve).

So did the early IEs till the land and possess wheeled vehicles? The IE root '*wegh*' ('to carry as in a vehicle') gives us Latin '*veho*' ('carry'), '*via*' ('road'), Greek '*wokhos*' ('wagon' – the latter English word itself a direct descendant from the IE root), plus 'weigh' and maybe even, believe it or not, 'wiggle' with its connotation of movement. Thus, many ancient IE roots from thousands of years ago are recognisable even in English, or hint at distant commonalities. And of course we can similarly hypothesise the likely grammar of the ancestral tongue from its various descendants. Readers once able to read Homeric Greek of nearly 3,000 years ago may have, like me, a powerful sense of familiarity if not even a vague understanding, when encountering painstaking attempts at reconstructions, such as a version of Schleicher's short fable in Proto-IE:

> *Owis Ekwoskwe* (The Sheep and the Horse)
> *Owis, kwesyo wlhna ne est* (A sheep, on which wool not was; that is, had no wool), *ekwons espeket* (horses saw, that is, saw horses), *oinom ghe gwrum woghom weghontm* (one a heavy wagon pulling), *oinomkwe megam bhorom* (and one a big load), *oinomkwe ghmenm oku bherontm* (and one a man quickly bearing). *Owis nu ekwobhos ewewekwet* (the sheep to the horses said), *ker aghnutoi moi ekwons nerm agontm widntei* (heart pains me horses man-driving sees, that is, it grieves me seeing a man driving horses).
>
> *(Lehmann & Zgusta, 1979)*

After some further desultory conversation the admittedly rather simplistic story ends:

> *Tod kekluwos, owis agrom ebhuget* (That having heard, the sheep the pasture fled).

Can we go even further back in time? Can we find commonalities between Proto-IE and other similarly-reconstructed superfamilies (from extant or recently extinct languages), such as Altaic (from Central Asia), Dravidian (from southern India), and the North African plus Semitic group? This would take us back ten or more thousand years. Hotly contested are apparent sound similarities, between currently-spoken languages across such diverse groups, for words denoting certain fundamental, key, everyday concepts, such as number, parts of the body, food items, objects in the natural world, etc. One can always come up against spurious similarities, and borrowings like my perigwl/danger pair, although, as mentioned, recent genetic studies are revealing remarkable parallels between world-wide distributions of language and genetic groupings.

Fifty-five years ago, changing my studies from the classical languages to Experimental Psychology, I devised for a course project an experiment to determine whether certain common, key, everyday words, in a range of apparently quite unrelated languages, and unknown to my participants, somehow preserved in their spoken form hints as to their underlying meaning. Students, when asked to pick the correct meaning from four alternatives, slightly but consistently chose the correct one. A year or two ago, someone repeated my unpublished inspiration, with better controls, and with the same results, coining the term 'Sound Symbolism'. This is not simple onomatopoeia, where a word's form reflects the sound of its designate, as with 'sigh', 'whistle', 'crash', and maybe even 'thunder' – or such deliberate constructions as 'the murmur of innumerable bees among the elms'. Try this one yourself: here are two words from a newly-discovered language, 'maluma' and 'takate'. One designates a soft, round ball of wool, and the other a sharp, rough building brick. Which word matches which object? I bet I know how you will choose! We still have a lot more questions to ask about the well-springs of language.

5
THE CHILD IS FATHER TO THE MAN

What is your earliest unequivocal childhood memory and how old were you at the time? And how much might that and similar events around that time have influenced your life subsequently? During the Battle of Britain, in late summer 1940, when I was 6 months old, and for the next 18 or so months, my mother and I were evacuated to a small town in North Yorkshire, Selby. For some reason she always claimed it to be the sootiest place in Britain, and I can clearly remember sitting on the floor in front of a wood fire and saying 'why aren't they dirty?', referring to some newly split logs on the hearth. I also remember lying and screaming in my pram, a tall, blue coach-like vehicle with large wheels and high springs, seeing shops flash past as my mother chased and endeavoured to stop its runaway career. In a corner of our rather large garden, which my father treated as a kind of small holding, to be self-sufficient in fruit and vegetables during the war, he had built an underground bunker, similar to modern Australian fire shelters in our bush-fire-prone southern states. In it there was a crude bench, some blankets and the family's gas masks. I can still smell them now, an odd rubbery odour, and visualise their curious, black goggle-eyed shape. During nights of bombing of the docks and city of Liverpool, some 10 miles away across the River Mersey, we would take refuge in our bomb shelter. My father would take me out when the 'All clear' sounded, and we would gaze at the red sky as Liverpool and Birkenhead burnt. In the morning in our suburbia there would be houses or whole groups missing in adjacent streets, where German bombers had jettisoned unnecessary remaining loads before the hazardous flight back to base. And I had a recurrent nightmare in which I would be chased by a small, black plane which never quite caught up with me. I even learnt to recognise this in my sleep as a bad dream, and somehow taught myself to awaken before the plane got too close. I can still voluntarily terminate the odd, infrequent, bad dream, an ability often reported in what are nowadays recognised as lucid dreaming. Such dreams tend to be particularly vivid and memorable.

The dreamer recognises them as dreams, and can manipulate them at will. Lucid dreams often occur with electrical activity in the brain more typically associated with alert and waking states.

Infantile amnesia, the inability later in life to recall events typically before the age of around two and a half, has analogues in other species. Still not fully understood, it may reflect the absence in infancy of a conceptual or contextual framework within which to place and fully understand events which repeatedly occur with moment-to-moment variations. In our species we call such a framework 'semantic memory', and the multitudinous episodic events which we continue to experience in daily life both help to form and continually modify it. As Wordsworth noted in one of his poems, 'The child is father to the man.' Despite certain claims to the contrary, there is no good empirical evidence that we can recall traumatic events occurring much before two or so years of age; however, early extreme stress can of course have long-term effects, in part via epigenetic mechanisms turning on or off, via methylation tags, certain important gene processes. Thus, environmental influences can determine whether or not a gene is expressed. Indeed, such epigenetic changes can even span several generations, as evidenced by behavioural and health-related anomalies in the grandchildren of people who suffered near starvation in Holland during the wartime German blockade of that country.

Our greenhouses, wherein grew in season tomatoes, grapes and nectarines (the vines and trees were planted outside and trained into the structure), contained a multitude of empty pots and rain water tanks which were home to their own ecology. Diadem spiders, *Araneus diadematus*, an orb weaver of seemingly enormous size, made fascinating webs; I learnt to place them on a stick which I gently shook so that the spider dropped downwards on its thread, which I then rolled up on the stick like a bobbin of cotton or silk. I even organised marine battles between spiders on little boats which I set floating on the tank water. Sometimes they bit me on the hand, but I learnt to ignore the slight nip. In the water were mosquito larvae, and with a magnifying glass I learnt to distinguish between the developmental stages through which the 'wrigglers' passed. Then, under upturned flagstones, there was the occasional devil's coach-horse beetle, *Ocypus olens*. This blue-black, slinky and stinky Rove beetle could give an unpleasant bite and when provoked turned up its abdomen somewhat like a scorpion.

By the age of 10, I was allowed to wander off on my own (shock-horror, I hear parents responding nowadays – and what a lot their children are missing with such freedoms curtailed) into the adjacent Wirral countryside. I went with fishing net and screw-top bottles, to trawl the local ponds with their crystal-clear water and jungles of pondweed species. I returned to my water tanks, themselves now stocked with pondweed, with those small fish known as stickleback, with their bright red bellies from which erectile spines 'clicked out' laterally when provoked. Also in the jars were water spiders and water beetles culled from under pond weeds. Both species could take down to their underwater lairs bubbles of air attached to their rear ends. I soon learnt that the water beetles would attack and eat the small fish. An occasional visitor, uninvited but always welcome, to my ground-level freshwater aquaria, was the stunningly rubescent and mildly toxic great crested newt, *Triturus cristatus*, which is related to the salamanders. These and other water denizens like caddis-fly larvae provided endless fascination and an invaluable basis to lessons in natural history and biology. How tragic that our modern ways of life, mores and fears, have deprived modern youth of such healthy and informative opportunities, and maybe even led to many of the problems nowadays besetting them.

Trips to the seaside were no less fascinating. Again fishing nets were taken at low tide to those small off-shore islands, the Hilbre group, in the Dee estuary, to which you could wade at low tide, fearful of the incoming waters. These could proverbially outrun a galloping horse, and, as in the ballad of 'Mary, call the cattle home, cattle, home, cattle home, Mary, call the cattle home across the sands o' Dee', had taken many lives. We stayed until the next low tide, collecting shrimps and prawns which we cooked over a driftwood fire in old washed-up cans. I learnt to rapidly peel the cooked product, an art I still have. Pollution, whether from nearby industries or the lead from the exposed can seams, was not for us a matter of concern, but local seaside ice-cream was a no-no due to the fear of polio, then exceeding even modern concerns over HIV/AIDS. Return on the top deck of a double-decker bus, with a motion-sick family dog, and an accidentally overturned bucket of seaweed and live shrimps, was frequently a lively and controversial affair.

To return to the greenhouse; my father had a number of probably illegal 22 rifles, and mother for some strange reason liked to carefully line up a series of lit candles planted in earth-filled pots, and try at a single shot to extinguish them all. Whether or not she ever succeeded, I do not remember, but it does bring to mind Homer's returning, disguised, hero Odysseus challenging the invading suitors for the hand of his wife Penelope. In that unforgettable description, two parallel lines of double-headed bronze axes were so placed that an arrow had to be shot through the gaps formed by the paired, adjacent, concave-edged blades. Not only could he alone draw the great bow, but only he succeeded in the overall contest. Father also had a bag of black powder (industrial gunpowder), which as a child himself he had found abandoned in a quarry. On special occasions with it he would fire his 200-year-old blunderbuss, loaded with old nails and ball bearings, once to dispose of a vagrant cat. Years later, when with a school friend looking for fossils in a deserted quarry, we found a series of round drill holes in the sandstone, one with protruding wires. We gently extracted the greasy brown sausage, realising rather late that it was almost certainly extremely unstable gelignite … That narrow escape, however, did not dissuade us from filling screw-top lemonade bottles with calcium carbide covered by blotting paper, and hurriedly topped up with water (acetylene gasses off rapidly when calcium carbide contacts water), and hurled into an adjacent water course. The resultant satisfactory explosion sometimes also yielded the odd briefly-stunned fish for the home aquaria. In later years, travelling as students in an old Land Rover in remote African regions, we would sometimes run an insulated cable connected to the engine's high-tension lead, in rarely successful attempts to stun fish for food in saline lakes.

I was frequently ill as a child, due in part no doubt to the appalling airborne pollution from coal fires and the local gas works. As a result I was sometimes medicated with capsules which could be pulled apart and filled instead with our own homemade gunpowder. My school friend and I could seemingly get whatever we wanted from the local very obliging chemist, from nitric acid to saltpetre, sulphur and anything else to make a bang in what had become a home chemistry lab in one of the greenhouses. Thrown into an open fire, there was a most satisfactory detonation, and we would sell our home-made miniature fireworks to our less innovative school friends. As classrooms in those days often had open fires, this was a good way to enliven tedious lessons. Nitrogen triiodide, safe to manipulate while still wet as a paste from mixing iodine crystals with liquid ammonia, but which when dry on even the slightest contact would dissociate more or less violently, giving off heat and dramatic purple vapour, was another quick-selling stock in trade. It could be pasted on to door handles and inserted into locks with (to little boys) a most satisfactory outcome. I shamefacedly confess to having introduced my daughter and one of her school friends to the pleasures associated with the process.

Weekends spent walking in North Wales led to many interesting chance discoveries. Archaeologists talk about *objets trouvés*, interesting things apparently found by our early ancestors, probably carried around for some time to judge by wear and polish, and subsequently discovered associated with human or near-human remains. I once found in a stream bed, while looking for water creatures, numerous very old dentures, apparently made of pottery, and presumably discarded there by a dentist from a previous age of dentistry. Exactly why that remote stream bed should have been chosen, and why they were in the first place discarded there, remains a mystery. However, it reminds me of my daughter, when she was the same age as I was when I made my discovery, and we were camping in a remote desert region in South Australia. She was poking around in a dried-up torrent bed, and noticed numerous little piles of human teeth. We later concluded that they had eroded out of ancient nearby burials, and being more resistant than the softer jaw bones, had been sorted by erosional processes and collected together like flecks of gold in the creek bed.

Creek beds and cliff faces became stopping points for both of us throughout childhood and later; they were great places to find fossils, which starting as *objets trouvés* themselves, furthered my interest in natural history and led me to collect them and later to become knowledgeable in the area, to the extent that I was appointed curator of my secondary school's geological museum. Hitch-hiking to an interesting geological exposure I met a local archaeologist, who introduced me to the pleasure of weekend digs in the Welsh hill country, with wonderfully eccentric local characters, possessed of such euphonious names as Mervyn Bevan-Evans and Trevor Pennant-Williams. They seemed straight out of the BBC's delightful TV programme, *Time Team*, where similar digs are televised on site all over Britain. This in turn led me eventually to become a member of the British Institute of Archaeology at Ankara, to attend a dig in Eastern Anatolia, and eventually, as a side line to my profession as a research neuropsychologist, to write books on aspects of human evolution.

As mentioned earlier, I and other members of my family had more than our fair share of childhood sickness, which meant compensatory exposure to a range of wonderful children's books, such as Mark Twain's *Tom Sawyer*, R. L. Stevenson's *Treasure Island* and R. M. Ballantyne's *Coral Island*. In consequence, there arose in me a lifelong interest in literature and a desire to see the world, which has remained with me throughout life, and which can be at least partly assuaged in an academic life.

Another life-changing book for me was Cousteau's *The Silent World*. At the age of just 13, I was persuaded to enter a short story I had written for an annual competition sponsored by The Chester Society of Natural Science, Literature and Art. The story dealt in part, I seem to remember, with the demise of a mouse beneath the wheels of a heavy haulage truck. No matter, I won first prize, and at the ceremonial presentation I saw that it was a book entitled *The Blue Fairy Book*. I was wildly disappointed (although it probably dealt in part with the anthropology of folk tales, which might after all have been some interest). Anyway, my mother steamed off the presentation plate from the fly leaf, with household ammonia bleached out a handwritten inscription, and at a bookshop swapped the offending title for one I had recently wanted badly. This was Captain Jacques-Yves Cousteau's immortal *The Silent World*, an account with primitive colour plates of the author's undersea discoveries and adventures, with the first men to dive at record depths without lines to the surface. Cousteau had invented the aqualung. It encouraged me to my own adventures, a little later, with snorkelling and the aqualung. There is, however, a dark coda to this story. For some years after, we would automatically resort to bleach to erase inscriptions from purchases for exchange. We were later to learn that bleached-out inscriptions slowly recover, reappearing, ghost-fashion, as the reduced and faded ink gradually re-oxidises and reappears. Who, I wonder, have themselves wondered at the foreign dedications slowly reappearing on Aunt so-and-so's purported gift?

There are perhaps two morals to this story. The obvious one is that we are not just what we eat, but also what we do and, especially, what we were able to do at certain critical periods in our development. The second, more prescriptive than descriptive, is that we guard and constrain our offspring literally at their peril in later life. They should experience risk, and even possible danger, in order to grow, in personality if not also in stature. The hygiene hypothesis suggests that too much early cleanliness may actually stunt the proper 'education' and development of the immune system so that it can turn against the body instead. Too much care and protection can likewise stunt intellectual and emotional flowering.

6

THE OLD FORGE AND MY FIRST SCHOOL

The tall narrow twin doors stretched from the low black-beamed ceiling down almost to the largely bare flagged floor. It was the only cupboard in the room – lounge, dining room, sitting room – the only downstairs room, apart from the tiny kitchen known as 'the scullery' to my parents. The cupboard doors were painted a dull rough matt black, a utilitarian colour, and a large old-fashioned key hung sloping from the worn fastener – lock would have been far too grand a hyperbole. The cupboard occupied the space between the front window which gave directly on to the main street of the village, and the fireplace. The latter was once the living heart of the Old Forge, as the three-centuries-old sandstone building was eponymously, and rather grandiloquently, known. It was the height of the Second World War, 1943, when I was just three, and the cupboard was – bare, or almost so. On special days a cloth bag was brought down from the top shelf. It normally occupied a space beside another, leather, bag which was never to be touched. The cloth bag contained an assortment of nuts. These – walnuts, peanuts, and hazelnuts harvested in autumn from the local woods – were a rare treat, and a source of plant protein in a period of great stringency and shortage. On rare visits to the seaside, Father would scale the precarious coastal cliffs for eggs from nesting gulls, to be brought down inside his old hat – on his head!

Years later the contents of the other bag – black powder, blasting or gunpowder – were revealed to me, and I, like my father before me, would as a youth frequent the numerous derelict quarries, finding artefacts of bygone times such as the comparatively stable black powder in the leather bag, or the greasy, sweating brown sausage of gelignite, so unstable with time that the very act of discovery could well have proved to be my last.

I have a very vivid memory of the building, directly abutting the village's main street, down which twice a day, noon and evening, after release, the school children's pounding feet would rattle our windows and awaken Father, sleeping after a night-time shift at the local 'works'. I have a bleak black-and-white picture postcard of the Old Forge, as it then was, taken in the time of Dickens; I have a framed colour print which I took just before my parents sold the place, so as to retire to the Welsh countryside, and beside it hangs an oil painting done by the new owners, amateur artists, who may have added a little 'artistic licence' in rendering the exterior floral decorations – but it did 'come up reet loverly' for the sale.

On the floor was a faded Indian carpet, threadbare yet precious enough to be rolled up for safekeeping whenever the house flooded after heavy rains. This would happen once or twice a year, in a house which some decades later would surely have been condemned, or which would have required (as it did) major engineering remedies, but with nightly bombing raids we were lucky to have a roof over our heads, even if it was centuries old, lowering and glowering beneath massive black slates from the enormous quarries of Ffestiniog in North Wales. There was one other precious item of furniture in the room: a magnificent grandfather clock, driven by weights, and pendulum moderated, showing time and phases of the moon, and surmounted by a pair of splendidly carved eagles. So tall was it that a hole had been cut in the ceiling, between two of the rafters, so that the eagles protruded through the floor of my parents' bedroom, right beside the bed, a trap for the nocturnally unwary, and the adjacent source of a wheezy striking of the hours to disturb the sleepers' rest, unless remembered to be disabled. It had its twin next door, in the other half of the old building, inhabited by my grandmother. She, too, had to remember to avoid the eagles if nocturnally exiting her bed.

In the room there was also a table made by my father himself on his ancient pedal lathe in the old tool shed 'up the garden', plus three dining room chairs, and a leather sofa. The leather was soft and rotten, destroyed by the sulphurous gases which lit and powered the house and by the ever-smoking fire. The Old Forge chimney was too broad to 'draw' properly, and had to be swept regularly to preempt destructive ignition; chimney fires were a potential disaster, and ours was no exception, although to me always an exciting event. Once a year father would borrow a fully grown goose to flap its way up the chimney, encouraged if necessary by a small paper fire in the grate below, thereby dislodging the soot. Previously white, it would emerge, angry and black, at the top and have to be caught by a waiting catcher. The other major source of acid pollution was the recurrent acid smog which drifted in from the nearby industries, notably the adjacent gas works. The latter was at the time surmounted by enormous barrage balloons, blimps, floating like grotesque grey-silver elephants, there to protect from air attack the gigantic 'gasometer' which, if hit by a single unlucky (from our point of view) German bomb, would have blown us and our entire neighbourhood and more to eternity.

Did my parents realise the appalling danger we ran, nightly, during the recurrent bomber raids to Merseyside, danger of death by a gigantic fireball? Did it keep them awake at night, or did the grandfather clock do that for them anyway? Or did its wheezy workings, redolent of a distant, stable and peaceful antiquity, quieten their fears? Whatever, when the sirens sounded the almost nightly alarm, I, parents, cat and a few precious possessions and rugs were quickly swept up and carried down to the bomb shelter. This grandiosely named, if pitiful structure, was but a shallow-dug bunker, roofed with corrugated iron and a thin layer of turf, and fitted with plank bench seats. It contained the family's gas masks, goggle-eyed horrors with a rubbery smell which lingered in my memory all my life – that, and the little flappy rubber gasket that covered the attachment retaining the small canister of activated carbon, hopefully to filter the poison gases which the evil Nazis would one day release upon us all.

Nazis, Germans, Hitler – in juvenile innocence I believed they were all derogatory terms related in some way to pejoratives, violence and hatred, such as 'nasty', 'germs', and 'hit'.

The kitchen, hardly even a room, more an alcove accessory to the front room, contained a gas cooker, a primitive and unreliable gas-fired water heater, and a zinc hip-bath kept propped in the corner until at weekends our little family had our weekly all-over ablutions and hair wash, in turn, in the front room before the fire, with the tattered Indian carpet rolled back for the occasion. Outside, on either side of the back door were the washhouse, in the form of a glass-roofed lean-to, and the outside toilet. The former contained a ribbed, barrel-shaped zinc tub to be filled by buckets of warm water on wash day, together with a hand-cranked mangle. This latter I would in a few years' time proudly turn, while my mother guided the wet clothing through in such a way as to save any buttons from pressure damage. Just as proudly I would also hand crank the Singer sewing machine while my mother similarly guided the stitches on cloth which she had cut out from the tissue-paper patterns ordered through the post. As we had no electricity, any ironing was done with ancient flat-irons pre-heated before the smoking coal fire.

On the other side of the back door was to be found the single outside privy, with its wooden bench seat scrupulously scrubbed, overhead cast iron water cistern with dependent chain attached to a protruding lever, and an ornate Victorian toilet bowl. The latter was decorated with embossed bunches of grapes and vine leaves of a pleasing, if deliberate, sepia colour, doubtless to conceal the inevitable stains attracted by the surface irregularities of the artwork. Squares of torn newspaper hung to hand, of a far superior softness and absorbency than offered by the purposed sanitary squares, 'Medicated with Izal Germicide', which in their neat box later superseded the newspaper. Their peculiar chemical smell, harshness and total lack of any absorbency also remain in my memory. Often the next-door's dog had first to be ejected by the intending user of the privy. It was named Dago, apparently 'because it was brown and untrustworthy', perhaps like the prejudice, then, concerning certain foreigners.

In the street outside, massive trucks ('lorries'), driven by steam power (being wartime, any petrol was strictly rationed) ground and smoked their way up and down, with iron-shod wheels, dropping hot coal embers on to the bitumen, thereby pitting the surface. Any fallen and unburnt coal was eagerly scavenged by residents, as were horse droppings 'for the garden'; as my father said, that was the only way, 'when following the horses, to make a quid, not by gambling'. Many drivers in fact preferred horse power to steam. My father would tell how Irish Joe would park his

Stanley Steamer outside the local pub, The Royal Oak, next door, 'with the links thrown over' (the equivalent of parking with reverse gear engaged). After a carefully-timed 10 minutes with a big fob watch, just long enough for the cooling cylinders to cause a partial vacuum and be about to reverse the piston's normal direction of motion, he would exit the pub and whistle for the steamer apparently to obey and move towards him. A nice example of two negatives making a positive. Ever a showman, he is also said to have scandalised local gentry by saddling up his prize, and tame, bull, and joining the hunt.

Uncle Colin was an eminent uncle, on my father's side, who had dared dastardly deeds and visited unspeakable horrors on First World War Germans, thereby winning a coveted medal; he proudly wore a long, polished leather brace on one wounded arm, supposedly resulting from one of his actions, although it was also said that the arm injury in fact resulted from a kick by an angry cow while he was trying to filch milk. Then there was Uncle Ernie, on my mother's side. Later, he was to give me his old car, a 1934 Hillman Minx open-top sports car, which shortly afterwards broke in two in the middle, despite a rusty piece of railway line having been welded on to the chassis to avert, or rather to delay, the inevitable. He had two lovely daughters; one eloped to America with a Polish escapee, who had come out of a conflict zone clinging to axles beneath a train. She told me years later that her stay-at-home sister was now in jail for murdering her husband, an eminent cricketer. 'Grand-dad' on my mother's side was not in fact my mother's father, as Great Nana had remarried after the mysterious disappearance of her first husband. Said by mother to have been a ship's captain, his surviving marriage certificate has him down as a 'ship's rigger'. A harmless exaggeration, maybe, but she would never say what had happened to him. 'Grand-dad' was fond of the Farmer's Arms just up the road, adjacent to a still operating smithy or forge, where I would watch in fascination horseshoes being fashioned, glowing, on the anvil, the bellows fanning the flames, while the smith shod huge, gentle shire horses, with enormous feathery feet. Farmers had reverted to the old ways after years of warfare and privation.

Grandma Bradshaw lived next door to us, and like her maternal counterpart, was a stern, unbending figure, prone to walk naked around the house, with her horribly withered and pendulous breasts – frightful objects of fascination and repulsion to a child. But she did make great pancakes. There was Auntie Annie, a farmer's wife from deep in Wales, who from time to time would visit with wonderful farmhouse salted butter with the farm's insignia pressed into the surface. She had one leg very much shorter than the other, due, I now realise, to childhood TB, doubtless from drinking milk before pasteurisation became mandatory. She had a special, and to me fascinating, built-up boot, 'to stop her falling over', father would say. Uncle Ned, on father's side, was headmaster of a local primary school; he decided to give me an IQ test, which I remember finding ambiguous; he proclaimed me ineducable, to mother's annoyance. He also 'got up her nose' by criticising her for digging up primroses growing wild in the local park, for her own garden; 'They grow even better here', she would say. Nowadays I would agree with him, but not then. In fact, that issue, and the IQ test, led to permanent frosty relations. Finally, Auntie Betty, father's sister and my favourite aunt and tireless reader of stories: father once said that I must NEVER show her a frog, as she would turn green and faint; of course that so intrigued me that as soon as possible I put it to the test; she didn't.

When I was three, my lifelong engagement with asthma started. I used to play with one Lawson Marshal, a slightly older boy, chasing and being chased, and soon found that I could not breathe. We were both regularly taken for 'Sunray Lamp' treatment – ultraviolet, to promote health-giving vitamin D synthesis, an early and laudable form of prophylaxis. Goggles were worn to protect the eyes, but to a child surreptitious peeking was irresistible. When the asthma attacks reached crisis levels, due doubtlessly in part to the unhealthy living conditions of damp, mildew and smog, visits were made to the chemist for powdered ephedrine, presented in screw twists of paper. The bitter taste which persisted long afterwards, despite copious draughts of water, the light-headiness and the racing heart (ephedrine mimics the important pharmacological properties of adrenaline) have stayed in my memory to this day. Years later, playing with my father's motorbike, which employed an old-fashioned magneto ignition, I discovered that if I kicked the engine over with the foot crank, while holding a high tension plug lead, I experienced a tremendous shock which could banish the asthma for a while. Adrenaline release again?

I am reminded of the case report in *The Lancet*, I think, that august medical journal, of an Irishman with chronic cardiac fibrillation; he would end such an episode by jumping off the eaves of his barn. When that manoeuvre eventually failed, he put a tub of cold water below for a double shock. Eventually he apparently added firing his gun while still in mid-air, until his daughter put a timely stop to the progression, fearing ultimate death by misadventure, and sought proper treatment for him.

When I was four, which was then young to commence, I was sent for six years to a Dames' school, a private institution run by six spinsters in a large, and barely modified, old Victorian house. Each pupil came equipped with badge and peaked cap and blazer, of a vivid scarlet, and a slipper bag containing a pair of bedroom slippers. Outdoor shoes were exchanged for slippers on arrival, and the cloth bag, with drawstrings, hung upon a peg. The afternoon ritual of tying shoelaces was a difficult hurdle which took up to a year to master, a bit like telling clock time.

Miss Downey was a bulky motherly old soul, with a large excrescence on the side of her nose, who taught elementary reading, writing and arithmetic. I found her very first lesson a puzzle: she drew on the blackboard schematic front-on representations of seagulls – two convex arcs, one for each wing, with a circular head fitted with a beak which carried a square. The last was described as a box, which could contain a letter. It seemed that there are 26 of these letters, any one of which the seagull could drop into various designated slots. I was familiar with letters as objects delivered to a box by the postman, and for a while I confused them with the intended letters of the alphabet. Was the seagull trained, like pigeons, to deliver the letters? I had heard that pigeons did sometimes carry messages; maybe in wartime seagulls were also to be co-opted? Anyway why did you need seagulls and boxes at all, in order to learn how to read? Metaphors are not always an aid for understanding in little children, and can sometimes be stretched too far.

There was a little girl in the class of 20 or so, whose economical mother, in a time of straitened circumstances, had knitted the child a warm pair of woollen knickers, knickers which evidently caused intolerable itching around the poor kid's bottom, to judge by her classroom contortions, and which in turn led to a length of loose wool hanging below the hem of her dress. One of the boys, probably out of simple curiosity rather than malice aforethought, pulled the end and was rewarded by the continuing emergence of an apparently endless quantity of thread as the knickers progressively unravelled around the pruritic posterior. With my neighbour Derek, who had curiously mouldy front teeth of a distinctly disturbing greenish tinge, we watched in fascination: the little girl either didn't notice, or appreciated the spreading coolness and progressive relief from her intolerable itch.

Despite primitive conditions – the 'playground' was of plain earth, a morass when it rained – it must have offered a good start, as out of an annual intake of around 20, four of us in my year eventually gained entry to Oxford and Cambridge. And I gained a coveted scholarship, again a year early, to one of Merseyside's top Direct Grant schools – single-sex schools, originally private (and therefore in the convoluted logic of Britain's aristocracy, termed 'public'), but with the post-war reforms given government grants, in return for which the school was obliged to take a percentage of local boys, those whose tested intellect was deemed sufficiently superior. One in the eye for Uncle Ned. It was a part-boarding establishment, and in preparation I was expected to learn to play cricket in a local paddock; was not the world conquered by boys on the playing fields of Eton or somewhere? Cricket was fine, as long as one was a fielder, when one's observation of grasshoppers and other interesting denizens of the field could be largely undisturbed. Because of a general lack of ability or drive, I was then made scorer; because I had no idea of or interest in what seemed a strangely complicated and arcane system, and my opposite number on the opposing side generally seemed to know what was happening, I would usually just record whatever he did. Everyone seemed either not to notice or to be happy.

7

SECONDARY SCHOOL EARLY AWAKENINGS, OR WHERE THE WHORE MOANS, THERE MOAN I

'You know when your dick goes all long, thin and stiff', said Sharpy, my new friend in my new school for Big Boys (you never called each other by the first name, and I never even learned his), 'it's called "horn"'. I had indeed experienced the phenomenon, and rather enjoyed the accompanying sensations, but didn't know that there actually was a name for it, which thereby hinted at some remote level of acceptance, if not respectability. I did, however, know, or, rather, guess, that it was extremely impolite to draw attention to it, or even to discuss it openly in the presence of adults. Sharpy looked as if he could confidentially offer me some much-needed background knowledge, although I was not to know at the time that he could also be a fount of unreliable and at times downright misleading information. At 12, he was a year older than me, far more street- and worldly-wise. He went on to say that the phenomenon was associated with procreation – not, of course, in exactly those terms, with which he would have been quite unfamiliar. Thus, when a woman wanted to have a baby, he said, a man had to piss inside her, and you needed horn to achieve this. We both agreed that it seemed an extraordinarily insanitary and rather unappealing thing to want to do, although in a rare moment of insight he hypothesised that that might be why 'horn' felt really rather nice. Indeed, when some time later we encountered, in the school's well-equipped library, very explicit photographs in the latest issue of the *National Geographic* of newly encountered New Guinea warriors, penis sheathed in a tight-fitting tube and held aloft with a cord at the 'present arms' posture, the significance of cultural differences in perceptions of propriety was brought home to us.

This rationalisation of the sexual act, I was also to learn a year later, at least seemed to conform with our new Biology text book. When it came to human reproduction, it coyly invoked the rabbit as a morally acceptable model. Beside an anatomically correct diagram, if sterile and attenuated as to detail, of the male reproductive systems – rabbit, and (very daringly) human – the latter with a politely and tastefully flaccid penis realistically hanging slightly off-centre to its left – how well I remember the details! – the text stated, flatly, that in the rabbit (humans were not mentioned) sperms are shed in the urine. One had to assume that in humans Sharpy was therefore probably right all along. Nor was there any mention of incidental parental frolics; making babies was clearly a grimly serious business, you jointly gritted your teeth, and bravely got on with it for the sake of another generation.

Our classroom, in an old repurposed building, had a frieze, just below the ceiling, and running right round the top of the walls, in the form of a series of plaster 'putti', nude and obese infants of indeterminate although intriguingly nearly-visible sex. They all seemed to subtly differ from each other, and I and my desk-mate (we shared desks in pairs) passed the time during tedious lessons in trying to identify the best-endowed and least ambiguous putto to resolve the issue. The activity also provided a slight frisson of that indefinably pleasing sensation which we were shortly to seek repeatedly, in the pages of the *National Geographic*, consulting the extensive ranges of teenage lovelies with dark skins and almost impossibly pert breasts, that seemed to abound those days in most issues. A marketing ploy before true soft porn became widely available?

Inevitably, the day came round for the biology master, a laconic man with a lazy, superior kind of drawl, to introduce us formally to human reproduction. He commenced by asking one of the form bullies to stand up; 'Tell us, R, what do *you* know about sex?' This was the only time we ever saw R embarrassed and at a loss for words. We then had to draw in our notebooks the male reproductive system, from memory, with the male member at attention. 'Tell me, H', he asked of the smallest, least mature and most timid member of the class, 'does that thing really look like an erect penis?' One felt that H had never seen or experienced such a spectacle. The class ended with the supremely sexist exhortation: 'Boys, just remember the three Ws, whip it in, whip it out, and wipe it.' He had been an army captain 10 years earlier at the end of the Second World War; that is the only excuse I can offer, but if nothing else, it was overall an unusually memorable lesson. Maybe that was the intention all along.

Disliking organised sport, particularly where balls of any size or configuration were involved, but particularly 'rugger', along with a reassuringly sizeable number of like-minded and similarly academically-oriented colleagues, I chose swimming. Just as we were paired as to desks in the classroom, so were we paired as to changing cubicles in the swimming baths. In such relative privacy there was ample opportunity to exchange information, and to compare endowments – length, breadth, erectile rapidity, and so on. Holes conveniently bored through partitions between adjoining cubicles also provided a wider comparative basis, and even inter-cubicle projection. No-one in authority seemed to know (they surely must have known), or even to care. This was in stark contrast to the sad occasion when the police caught a boy with a man in in the toilets of the local market town. Then the whole school was summoned to an address by the headmaster, a formidable figure with impressive paunch, jet black eyebrows and a scarlet gown. He spoke at length on sin, pollution (not the ecological aspects), impure thoughts and worse acts (which were never described or defined), leading to jail in the temporal world, and hell in the one to come. This mostly meant nothing to most of us, who if accused of supposedly homosexual acts at the baths, would have stoutly denied that what we did in any way related to those much darker behaviours between consenting men, about which we had heard improbable rumours. One thing, however, which our intra-cubicular activities did clear up, was that urine played no part in procreation in particular, and sexual pleasure or gratification generally. Further enlightenment came from a specimen of the abundant 'latrinalia' inscribed on the toilet walls:

My grandmother lies over the ocean
My grandfather lies over the sea
My father lay over my mother,
And that's how they got little me.

So *that's* how it was done; it was all beginning to fall into place, even though the picture was as yet incomplete: if not urine, what was it? One day at the baths, my friend H told me he had cracked the puzzle: by adopting a cupped-hand posture, and employing a rapid milking motion, he had experienced a 'wonderful burning sensation', far beyond anything to date, which seemed to spread throughout his body, and was accompanied by repeated pelvic spasms, and copious and repeated spurts of an appropriately milk-like fluid, with a strange smell and a slightly unpleasant taste, and bearing no resemblance whatsoever to the now completely discredited 'piss' theory. We all hurried to confirm the phenomenon, although I, younger than the rest, at first was unsuccessful, and did not like to proceed too long or far, lest I 'broke something', or caused some other kind of internal plumbing disaster. Rumour subsequently had it that one of our colleagues, somewhat older than the rest in our group of five or six juvenile miscreants, roughly a quarter of the class, and ours was not the only such group, produced a product with a slightly greenish tinge, which we were later able to verify.

Although from time to time sharing the effort with mutual 'hot-hand jobs', none of us would in any way have endorsed the potential criticism that we were guilty of homosexual acts. Had there been girls with whom to dally, we would happily have done so instead. That was the problem with single-sex, all-boys schools. In the boarding section, such truly homosexual acts did occur, and certain masters were believed to take certain liberties with certain boys, particularly certain angelic-looking individuals in the choir; and the quarter master of the school's army cadet force stores was fond of ensuring a good crotch fit in the issue of army trousers. All that sort of thing, however, was indeed foreign to our aims or experience.

Not so the tendency for younger boys to develop a (usually very chaste) crush, a form of hero worship, on very good-looking senior boys who generally excelled in sport. Sometimes this rather girlish emotion was reciprocated, and one is reminded of the exactly comparable situation in fifth-century BC Athens, where it was rationalised as a form of apprenticeship. Indeed, in Greek, distinctions are made between 'eros' (sexual love), 'philia' (friendship), and 'agape' (something between the two – maybe what we now call Platonic love). There are just so many faces to male human sexuality.

Another face was the fact that at 14 from time to time I found myself on a morning bus to school, sitting opposite a girl named Jill; she was on her way to her private girls school, our opposite number, as it were, close to my own place of education. Dumpy and unsmiling, in a buttoned-to-the-throat, navy-blue raincoat, which obscured any possible feminine figure within, she would not normally have been any young man's dream; however, she seemed to appreciate my company on the bus, and I began to develop aspirations (Simple companionship? Romance? Rank carnality?), which reached a high point when we sought, and were reciprocally and readily granted, each other's addresses, for an exchange of Christmas cards – it must then have been close to the festive season. However, we both must have got cold feet, or the post doubly failed us (just remotely possible, I now realise, having regularly worked as an emergency schoolboy sorter that time of the year), and by the new year any flickering flames had burnt low in both our breasts.

In part, I now also realise, there had been over that Christmas the distracting and disturbing episode with my cousin A, a month or two my junior. Each year, the family foregathered at my maternal Grandma's place. A fearsome, unbending lady, she lived at the end of a cul-de-sac out in the country, and had, I remember, just discovered Grandpa's First World War souvenirs; a firm believer in the 'out of sight, out of mind principle', she had that week tipped the whole lot into the shallow ditch which separated the property from the adjacent farmer's field. But I digress, merely adding that presumably they still lie there. The house, like many of its type and era, possessed a formal 'drawing room', hardly ever used, and endowed with heavy Victorian furniture and drapes, ideal for a game of hide and seek, a game itself ideal for adaptation and advance to – what else but advances! Flat-chested and gangly, game nevertheless was A, and had not a suspicious Grandma disturbed us behind the most all-enveloping of the velvety drapes, our levels of mutual sex education might have undergone a quantum leap. My friend H, a keen photographer, and to whom I eagerly recounted this episode early in the new year, urged cultivation of the relationship so that as an enterprising threesome we could market a product, but practicalities, logistical problems, and I am glad to say, a modicum of common sense aborted a development ahead of its time, and which nowadays with explicit 'selfies' seems all too depressingly familiar.

There was a gentle, serious, unassuming lad in a lower class, with a twin sister, who had been at my old primary school. It emerged that they were inseparable, and desperately in love with each other, and had been for years. It also emerged, unexpectedly, that they had been having full-on sex together for some of that time. It was not something they would openly discuss, or even acknowledge, except to those they knew well, but for those in the know it was a disturbing revelation, with, of course, the risk of unforeseen and in those days irremediable consequences.

I first experienced the surprisingly common phenomenon, apparently generally known as 'the wandering hand', when obliged, for reasons of space shortage during divinity lessons, to share a desk with its usual resident, someone I did not know well. After an initial surprise, I found the experience a pleasant distraction from the drearily unending reading aloud from Acts, and was relieved to learn afterwards that this activity was widespread in the class, as the entire weekly lesson involved a regularly rotation of reading short biblical passages, and you always knew when it would be your turn. At the end of the lesson, pairs of boys, singly or together, were wont to retire to quiet places for quiet moments.

Some years later, as a school prefect, it would befall me regularly to declaim the daily Lesson from the bible, in the school chapel. Even then an unreconstructed atheist, I had no idea as to how to find the designated readings, but soon solved the problem by opening the bible at random, and reading an appropriately long section also chosen at random. Surprisingly, I soon realised that no-one notices this, as there is such perfectly seamless continuity in the poetry of the King James version, that any excerpt, anywhere, will sound complete and coherent within itself.

An attractive female friend of mine, once one of my PhD students, and now a very senior university administrator, tells me that when at dinner, during an important function, and sitting next to an even more senior delegate from another university, his hand also had tended to wander. And I, too, sitting next to the ageing mother-in-law of a medical professor, have encountered the apparently autonomous and repeated passage of her somewhat inebriated digits. I am reminded of that dirty old ditty:

1st voice: Take your hand off my knee.
2nd voice: It's not my hand.
1st voice: It's not my knee.

There was a boy in the class, a boarder, who boasted unusual success with the opposite sex, for which I was later to discover there was good evidence. A rugby-playing hearty, of flashy good looks, he had little time for aquatic pursuits, and used the back seats of the local cinema for his chosen trysts, which typically commenced with a wandering hand. Target attainment was occasionally barred, which typically, he said, would lead to a bout of testicular aching. Prohibition was usually, it seemed, on the grounds that 'the jam rags had been hoisted aboard'. He was a boarder as his father, a seaman, was frequently away. His son kept a seaman's log book, with girls' names down the side, followed by a grid pattern of columns, headed in order from left to right 'kiss', 'tits', 'grope', and 'bingo'. He would tick as appropriate. I believe he also pioneered ignition of his own farts, which for safety's sake, and to prevent a possibly explosive 'blow back', he performed in the bath. Despite modern claims to the contrary, they really did burn with a blue flame.

Scripture reading was also the time to pass around and peruse decidedly non-scriptural texts which were surreptitiously circulated beneath the desks. 'H' had a maiden aunt who lived with them *en famille*. Unusually, perhaps, she regularly supplied her nephew, an enthusiastic recipient, with a number of 'how to' and similar self-help works, such as Dr Eustace Chesser's *Love Without Fear*. It contained many graphic and improbable accounts, all written in a jocular and avuncular style, to indicate that we are all jolly good chaps together, happily trying to manage what should come naturally. Two anecdotes stick in my mind: one involved a couple, presumably a seaman and a lady of the night, locked long together in a state of vaginismus, such as maybe only dogs can usually experience, in public view behind some objects on the dockside. The other was a detailed account of how to construct a device to give you timely warning, when asleep, that an incipient nocturnal erection was on its way, so that you could take advantage of it for further activity, which he said was always better in the wee small hours. It involved a bridge across the pelvis (unfortunately, you had to sleep on your back), from which an electric buzzer or bell would sound when the member, on rising, caused an electrical contact to be made. He presumably got the idea from devices designed to forestall nocturnal enuresis.

There was a boy in the class, fascinated by and an expert on fungi, who always filled his pen (lever-action fountain jobs, in those days) with home-made ink, such as from the eponymously named Ink Cap. He used also to dabble in invisible ink, and once demonstrated how if using semen on ordinary white paper (I don't know what writing instrument he employed), the writing was invisible, but if the paper was illuminated with light from a source containing a fair proportion of ultraviolet, the writing fluoresced brilliantly. Such 'ink' was also apparently an excellent adhesive for attaching illegally recycled stamps.

I should emphasise that as teenage boys in an all-male environment, we were obliged to assuage our sexual itches with whomsoever was available from among our peers and friends. It involved neither exploitation nor tenderness, at worst, a level of mutual unbridled lust followed by relief, as I understand can be nowadays far from uncommon in jails and naval ships. Schools should be a microcosm of wider society, with roughly equal number of all shades of gender, and the Catholic Church continues to ignore this message about celibacy at its peril. Even though girls were still greatly outnumbered by boys at the Oxford of my day, a situation not to change much for another quarter of a century, it was for us boys 'going up' a time of welcome transition, when most of us were able profitably to redirect our urges.

Sex was not the only issue to address at that age. Then, as now, there was the problem of bullying, although, fortunately, not the horrible modern mode of cyber-attack. I was briefly the victim of a friend of my best friend. The gym master, a ferocious ex-army sergeant-major, while following on a battered old bicycle, used to make us go in midwinter on barefoot cross-country runs; he would prod the laggards with the point of a javelin, which he wielded like a medieval knight on horseback. He also paired every boy with another, roughly matched, and we had to have annual boxing tournaments, sometimes with knock-outs. A dreadful, barbaric activity, which I now abhor, but it did have a salutary consequence for me over the bullying problem. He somehow came aware of the matter, and arranged that we should hold an impromptu match in the main quad, with a surrounding ring of onlookers. Although completely unsporting, and of a generally pacific nature, I realised, rather desperately, that I simply had to take the initiative right at the very beginning, and not let up. It was a wildly and unexpectedly successful ploy; to put it very crudely in modern-day parlance, I literally 'beat the shit' out of him, and had to be physically pulled off him and the match terminated. We actually became guarded friends thereafter, possibly helped by the third-party friendship we both shared. Boxing, and to a lesser extent swimming, were the only sports where I could make a mark, although when being paired with the headmaster's hefty son I won on points, after an unusually bloody match, I realised I might have done better to have been a bit more diplomatic. There were other less fortunate victims of bullying; one poor, shy, nervous and socially incompetent lad, B, I now realise probably lying within the Asperger's spectrum, became incontinent of urine during a long and boring address by some tedious old retired general, and left a permanent stain on a seat, which for years afterwards was always left vacant, and was known eponymously as B's chair, upon which no-one would ever sit: a stark and dreadful reminder. Another very similar boy eventually came out to Australia as a teacher, developed a drink problem, and committed suicide. Somehow his perceptive headmaster discovered our common backgrounds, and asked me if 'he had been picked on at school'. School days can be very cruel.

He of the darkly arching and satanic eyebrows, our headmaster of impressive girth and father of several children, was a self-proclaimed expert on all aspects of parenting. However, his lectures on the topic to parents' groups ended, when, inevitably after puberty, certain problems arising in his own family led to their discontinuation. His wife, noted for her inedible rock-cakes which she freely and embarrassingly dispensed to the boys, achieved the seemingly impossible when she got the family car stuck lengthwise between the Lodge's two stout stone gateposts, requiring dramatic recourse to a crane for extrication; high drama indeed for us boys to observe.

In those early teen years I subscribed to the boys' weekly magazine, *The Eagle*, avidly read by my father. In a time-travel story, the adventurers went back to the Jurassic (which, along with the Carboniferous, would also have been my own destination of choice), vowing only to observe and not to touch anything, to avoid altering time's trajectory forward to their own lifetimes and their return to the present. But one of them could not resist catching a beautiful butterfly; on returning to the present they found that script and the alphabet were now totally illegible to them. Is this story the possible origin of the chaos-theory metaphor of a butterfly flapping its wings in Beijing, and provoking, by runaway amplification and ratcheting up of the consequences of an initial seemingly insubstantial change, the occurrence of example of cyclones in Canada a week later?

'*Triste erat carmen quod cecinit poeta*'; at that point, aged 12, I suddenly appreciated the enchantment of language. It was a perfectly ordinary piece of homework, translation into Latin of a list of English sentences, in this particular instance, 'The poet's song was sad'. An accurate but ordinary translation might have been '*Carmen poetae triste erat*', with the verb at the end, as in German, but a slight tweaking of the syntax, emphasis and word order, which occurred to me out of the blue as it were, seemed to generate something – poetic! I intuitively felt, with a distinct frisson, that I had somehow captured a certain nuance of feeling such as a classical poet might have written 2,000 years ago. And I was indeed congratulated for it.

From then on, 'Latin sentences' homework became less of a chore and more a matter, to me, of exercises in linguistic subtlety, sound, emphasis, expression and balance. I received praise for idiom and good marks, and, I must admit with a certain shame, a bit of money on the side, selling answers to my less facile or motivated fellow colleagues. But I was very careful not to give them exactly my own versions. At the end of the year, we all had to choose between an arts (with Greek) or a science (with German) future – a watershed which then, and now, I firmly believed came far too early, as I also had a passionate interest in scientific research and findings. But my Latin master said that I was an ideal candidate for the Greek option. Who was I to gainsay such praise?

If in Latin there lurked a hidden magic, that magic was amplified manifold in Greek, a 'dead' language of quite extraordinary subtleties of meaning, and endowed yet with a haunting beauty in its phonology when read aloud, slowly. Homer's *Odyssey*, its oldest extant incarnation in extended form, and the magical adventures of its island-wandering hero, Odysseus the Wily, each island inhabited by its own enchanting nymph, call to mind the mystic mythology of the 'Isles of the Southern Seas' which so captured the imagination of eighteenth-century sailors and crafters of hymns. I was hooked, and soon commenced a scrapbook of useful and appealing phrases, culled from classical prose and speech writers and poets, so as to incorporate into English-to-Greek translations. Many of the English passages for translation came from speeches by famous statesmen, such as Disraeli or Churchill, whose oratory reflected quite closely that of, for example, Demosthenes in Greek, or Cicero in Latin. All of this stood me in very good stead some years later when, not yet 18 years of age, I successfully sat for a prestigious scholarship to read Classical Languages at Oxford. I found I could practically 'cut and paste' approximately appropriate and sufficiently high sounding phrases into an amalgam, a 'farrago' (Latin: porridge) of phrases I had memorised. I was in fact complimented upon my grasp of colloquial idiom. Lest this be thought of as taking in some way an unfair advantage, if one wishes to develop an easy colloquial grasp of any language's usage, ancient or modern, it is far better to do it this way, which in a sense approximates the far more naturalistic way whereby we all originally have acquired our mother tongue, literally by listening to her talking, rather than by laboriously learning word lists and grammatical tables in a sterile classroom.

I was committed by then to classical languages, and the only way I could get the necessary School Certificate qualifications in physics, chemistry and biology for a career in medicine was to teach myself. This was in fact aided by my total inability to memorise places, names and dates in geography and history, so with the connivance of a sympathetic geography master, with whom I maintained a friendship until the day he died decades later, I sat in the back of his classes and in successive years mastered theory. The chemistry teacher assured me of failure (the physics master wasn't even interested) without a laboratory component, so I converted my corner of one of the greenhouses into a very satisfactory substitute, where during weekends, with a like-minded friend taking the science subjects, I had a fun-filled and dangerous time which taught me far more than any formal education could have done. Indeed, as a result, I excelled in the eventual examinations, to the chemistry master's chagrin.

The college which awarded me the sought-after scholarship, or 'postmastership' in this case, was Merton, Oxford's oldest (although two others contest this claim in terms of appropriate criteria – buildings, foundation, statutes…). Situated beautifully overlooking the natural expanse of Christ Church Meadows, its lovely and largely intact thirteenth-century buildings are a jewel in Oxford's diadem.

A number of boys in my school had similar ambitions, whether in the Arts or Sciences, and much dedicated study was essential, but every month, I regret to say, a group of us would cycle off into the Cheshire countryside to one or other of the classic country pubs of old England, and even if under age as in my case, get rather disgracefully drunk. Mid-twentieth-century binge drinking by youth who should have known better? A justifiable letting-off of pent-up steam? Take your pick, but it seemed to work, as mine was not the only success.

I still have the exciting letter from 'The Warden and Fellows of Merton College' offering me the longed-for scholarship, dated January 1958, with the date of 10th October, when I was expected to 'go up'. I had eight full months to fill in. Unexpectedly, the school found itself short of a Latin teacher for 15- and 16-year-olds, and I was offered the post. As a gowned prefect with caning rights and privileges (the school still followed barbaric eighteenth- and nineteenth-century models of discipline, although I never needed or wanted to invoke them – the authority itself was more than adequate), I never had a moment's trouble or problems involving discipline. I so enjoyed the experience that I also built up a private tutoring practice for children around my home, being able to teach several languages, maths and even some chemistry, physics and biology. During following university vacations, I continued and extended my 'practice', going everywhere by bicycle.

The school had a debating society, named after and dedicated to an Eminent Old Boy, Lord Birkenhead, F. E. Smith, the Earl of Birkenhead, a noted lawyer and Conservative politician, Britain's Lord High Chancellor from 1919 to 1922. (Fifty years after his death, he was portrayed by the actor Nigel Davenport in the 1981 film, *The Chariots of Fire*.) I became secretary and then chairman of the society, and it stood me in remarkably good stead subsequently, if called upon to make an impromptu address. I will admit, however, that at times the society's debates did become somewhat of an excuse for irrelevant bawdy behaviour. Boys will be boys.

Another feature of the school was its Combined Cadet Force (CCF), to which we had to devote one afternoon a week, and an annual fortnight's stint in a regular army camp, where we engaged in rifle (.22 and old Lee Enfield .303) training, along with Bren and Sten guns, and use of the bayonet (!!!) (boys of 15!!!). Live rounds were used at the firing ranges (we even had one at school), and I have a permanent hearing 'notch' in my right ear (earmuffs were either 'pansy' or not yet invented), although we used blanks for manoeuvres. Someone discovered that a pencil neatly fitted the barrel of a .303, and fired one into the expansive and inviting bottom of the platoon bully while he was bending over, presenting an excellent target. Fortunately, penetration at 100 yards was minimal.

On an exercise in North Wales, I left my rifle leaning against the wall of the White Horse Inn in the tiny village of Cilcain, not discovering that I had done so until we were well on our way back to the Wirral in an army truck. It had to return furiously (in both senses – it occurred at the height of the IRA 'troubles'), with threats of a possible court martial ringing in my ears, if was not still there. It was – but I believe the misdemeanour was held against me when the question of future promotions in the force came up.

In the northern summer, along with three friends, we were lent a Hillman Husky van and drove it down to the West Country, Devon and Cornwall, staying in Youth Hostels, for two or three weeks. It was that holiday that introduced, all of us, naïve as we were, fresh from an all-boys' school in such matters, to the mysteries and allure of the opposite sex. I particularly remember a shop girl, Christine, with whom, together also with her own three friends, we VERY daringly went for a midnight swim. The very name still conjures in me images of Forbidden Delights; nude we all were, but it was a cool, dark, overcast and disappointingly moonless night, so there was not too much to observe, but it was the principle of the thing … Dressing afterwards was obligatory – the temperature soon saw to that, but a first kiss lying in a hollow in the unforgiving, unyielding shingle left its mark, literally and metaphorically. A milestone had been passed, with honours, and honour, intact.

8

DREAMING SPIRES, OXFORD DAYS, *ET IN ARCADIA EGO*

Slow train along the Welsh borders, steam, although soon to be overtaken by the unromantic diesel, fast, efficient, but no longer the living, snorting temperamental 'horse' of a dirtier, sootier past. Arrival at Oxford station, four or five of us all from our old school, but now, like the boys of Harry Potter's Hogwarts school, about to start a new life, away from home, parents, the solidly predictable school routine, with all its inevitable problems now by contrast in deep diminuendo. Some with the family's old cabin trunks rescued from attics and a previous century, some like me, with old suitcases, bursting, roped tight. Shared taxi to colleges we knew not exactly where, hurried promises to meet again when we had found our college feet … My rooms high in an ancient building on Fellows' quad, atop a narrow staircase, and a long, long way down dark stairs and across a quad from where one's nocturnal plumbing needs could be accommodated. Can't descend, can I, to purchase a potty, surely? Milk bottle? But there was a wash basin – which gurgled and kept me awake at night when someone else, below, met his own desperate needs in the same creative fashion, rinsed the basin, and created a vacuum in my own u-bend above. Keep plug in at night? No solution as on the basin there was a patent overflow. So knock small hole in lead pipe below my u bend, and keep chewing gum to hand whenever hole needs resealing. Hurrah! Study shared with fellow first-year student, ex-Winchester and national service, maybe a relative of one of the notorious spies who had defected to Russia; P, a delightful and cultivated fellow, with guitar and repertoire of just one song, with chorus, 'I let a red-headed woman make a fool out of me'. Moral somewhere?

Academic gown to be bought – an impressive, full-length scholar's affair, unlike the short commoners' gown as worn by the majority; attired with pride, and obligatory for dinner at night in the Great Hall, 700 magnificent years old, headed by High Table where dined the Dons, overlooked by a dingy oil painting of our revered founder and eminent philosopher, William of Ockham [*sic*], and to be worn for all Arts (but not Science) lectures, for all exams (when also white bow tie – NOT the pre-tied 'abomination' nowadays), and if hauled before the Proctors, the university's private police force. (There were many returned servicemen then coming up to Oxford, some having achieved very high ranking; one, 'hauled before the 'progs', wore his full military uniform of a Lt. Colonel, complete with swagger stick, and scared the hell out of the awaiting tribunal.)

Bicycles also obligatory; ran to earth for five pounds sterling a dusty, 1914 ladies' model, with skirt guard (my long flowing gown also thereby protected), brakes operated via metal rods, and fitted with a very wide, tractor-type, leather seat to accommodate broad matronly botties – the most comfortable seat imaginable, not at all like modern ball crushers. Gearless and stately, it nevertheless later took me to see the archaeological wonders along the prehistoric downland chalk Ridgeway, with such sites as the West Kennet Long Barrow, enigmatic Silbury Hill, Uffington's Blowing Stone, and the White Horse, to say nothing about the lovely Cotswold country to the North, with such euphonious rivers as the Windrush and the Evenlode. A Greek lexicon was also sine qua non; I obtained an enormous and equally dusty, early-edition mid-nineteenth-century Liddell (Dean Liddell, father of Oxford's very own Wonderland Alice) and Scott, again for a few pounds, probably now nearly priceless – but I will never sell, not even to fund my declining years.

Dinner in Hall was always preceded by the senior Postmaster reciting the college grace: '*Oculi omnium in te respiciunt, domine; tu das escam illis tempore opportuno. Aperis manum tuam et imples omne animal benediction tua. Benedicas nobis, deus, omnibus donis quae de tua beneficentia accepturi simus*...' Why do I remember this so well? Three years later it became my frequent responsibility, a responsibility which one night I maybe exceeded: the noisy college peacocks, for long having disturbed the dons' nocturnal (and diurnal) slumbers, were 'sacrificed' and served up to High Table dinner. I changed '*escam*' to '*pavones*' ('You provide peacocks, oh Lord', instead of the sanctified original 'You provide food...' The chaplain was distinctly unamused, and rebuked me for impiety and possibly heresy.

Food, and opportunities to eat, were overly abundant. Breakfast was in hall – buffet self-service; mid-morning cakes available; lunch (afterwards with free half-loaf, from a fourteenth-century legacy, to be collected as desired); mid-afternoon tea (crumpets, heated on an inverted electric radiator – when they carbonised, they could short the current in an interesting fashion); snacks before dinner in the Junior Common Room (JCR) bar along with beer; high table dinner at 7.30 p.m.; supper, to cap a gastronomic marathon, in a friend's room as desired ... The handwritten and frequently illegible menu was displayed each day in the Porters Lodge; one day it apparently read 'Crap dust', which turned out to be 'Grapefruit', but the quality may have remained the same.

Among Merton's many architectural gems is the medieval library, with the largest collection in England of medieval chained books. Renovated by the famous benefactor and bibliophile, Sir Thomas Bodley (of Bodleian Library fame) a few hundred years ago, its floor was subsequently raised, with the result that his ghost, said to roam his old haunts (what else!), walked upon the old surface. Generations of students are similarly said to have sought to spend the night therein, to ascertain whether or not his feet are to be seen from below, while he progresses from the knees up on the upper floor.

My own experience involving the library was a presumed coincidence, but one also really rather spooky. One winter evening I was entertaining some friends to tea, and suddenly all the lights throughout the college went out, and the library's fire alarm sounded. Within seconds the fire brigade arrived, principally to save the priceless medieval library, should the presumed fire, which turned out to be a false alarm, be threatening it. The next night I also had a (different) cohort of friends to tea, and started to tell them what had happened, commencing with 'Wouldn't it be odd if all the lights went out…', when they did, exactly as I was saying these words. Someone said, 'Good God, go on, turn them on again', thinking I had a hidden means of so doing, just as decades later, in a remote Bolivian settlement in the Amazonas, we found that plugging a faulty light into the generator-driven mains in our lodging house shorted out the settlement's entire system until we unplugged.

There was, in and around Merton, the usual complement of eccentric male characters (there was, I believe, in those otherwise all-male college preserves at that time, a female seamstress to patch your trousers, etc.). A law don, with giant black poodle, apparently was wont in the early hours to enjoy rolling naked in the snow with the dog. Garrod, one-time Professor of Poetry and now in his eighties and nearly blind, would have favoured young men to afternoon tea in his rooms on Sundays, each of the half dozen or so guests provided with a small mechanical toy beside his plate, to – toy with! My fitter-and-turner father had skilled me in minor repairs, and it was my job to fix breakdowns and breakages. I still have, somewhere, his note to me 'Dilly dally has died again, can you come to tea and fix?' A piece of poetry ascribed to him by someone who knew us both (no comment):

> Oh pretty little flower girl,
> How sweet your posies smell.
> I'll buy your pretty roses,
> If you'll sell yourself as well.

When he died, on Christmas Day in an adjacent hotel, as the college was closed that day, he left me a drawing of himself.

Books which made an enormous impression on me were Lawrence Durrell's *Alexandria Quartet*. When I mentioned this to a girl of whom I had become fond, she gave me for Christmas *The Hobbit*, by Tolkien, recommending that I follow it up with his adult triad, *The Lord of the Rings*, not knowing that that eminent scholar of Anglo-Saxon literature and Nordic mythologies had written much of it under the plane trees in Merton's Fellows Garden. Her judgement was unerring. Tolkien was one of a triad of Oxford writers and authors of fantasy at that time, another prominent member being C. S. Lewis of *Chronicles of Narnia – The Lion, the Witch and the Wardrobe*, fame. Old Dyson was the third member of this group, known as

The Inklings; he also was resident at Merton, and when I got to know him, gnome-like, bent, warped and wizened, leaning on a crooked stick, he was for all the world like a character, a friend of Bilbo's, straight out of Tolkien's Shire. The group regularly foregathered in local hostelries to read to each other excerpts of their latest writings.

Oxford, I say, was nothing if not known for its characters. I disturbed one eminent professor underneath an old Land Rover I had just purchased for an expedition into Lapland; it seemed he also had one, in worse condition than mine, and wanted to see how it really should look if healthy 'down there'. A Cambridge colleague of mine years later said that this scholar had subsequently married above his station, into the peerage in fact, with the result he adopted a fancy title, and his wife was disowned. When he died, he expressed the wish for his ashes to be spread in her family's extensive parkland; this required a break-in via a gap in the estate's wall, and she, by now a *persona non grata*, was caught, *in flagrante delicto*, by one of the gamekeepers. Shortly before his untimely end, he, his wife and two colleagues drove a Mini to Italy to a conference, and the fan belt broke, without there being a spare. However, they managed triumphantly to return across the Alps on Lady X's bras. We don't know if they were wired, or how many spares she had. He had also, it seemed, in happier times, having lived for a while in Cambridge on a long-boat (barge), decided to 'sail' the craft to take up his new position at Oxford. This involved taking it down the Cam, where it was moored in Cambridge, out to sea, round the south-eastern tip of England, up the Thames and on into Oxford's local river, the Cherwell (Isis). He had the foresight to be accompanied by another adventurous spirit also possessed of a similar craft. These boats, as the name implies, are of a certain length, such that in choppy waters they may not be strong enough momentarily to be borne simultaneously fore and aft by a pair of sufficiently high waves, with the result that the central section is temporarily unsupported, with foreseeable consequences, if structural reinforcement is adequate amidships only for placid inland waters. Just like the occasional super-tanker known to break in two off the Cape of Good Hope, where there tends to be a characteristic wavelength to the swell, disaster struck. Another eminent figure in his discipline lived near Cambridge, where I later spent many a sabbatical, with wife and son; the latter was painfully shy. When a dinner party was being held, the son retired to the attic above the dining room, and watched proceedings from a trap door in the ceiling; he was refreshed with victuals, as needed and as the courses progressed, by his mother who passed plates up to him. In my later years at Oxford, I became very interested in comparative linguistics and philology, running the Philological Society, along with a serious blue-stocking girl, with whom I attended chaste and frustrating movie sessions. One of our guest speakers (it doubled as a civilised dining club) was the then current Professor of Poetry, Robert Graves. It turned out that he had spent much of his youth exploring the magnificent archaeological wilderness of West Wales' Harlech Dome; we had so much to reminisce. Curiously, an avid hitch-hiker, I was once given a lift by a truck driver, a bibliophile as it turned out, and we had both recently finished Graves' harrowing reminiscences of 'life' in the First

World War trenches; we both remembered that Graves had said that one of the most difficult adjustments he had to remember always to make on return to so-called peacetime civilisation, was never just to unbutton his trousers by the roadside when the urge came to relieve himself. This issue came up also over our philological dinner.

The novelist and cartoonist Max Beerbohm, an alumnus, had a room in college containing samples of his art works. My father had taught me the elements of lock picking, and with my penknife I was adept at gaining entry; with a friend we did a couple of cartoons in his style, framed them, and hung them in a space on the wall beside the Master's own creations. I wonder if they are still there. Would I recognise them now?

Punting the Cherwell was a lovely summer recreation, preferably towing a cooling bottle of wine, and accompanied by a fair maid beneath a parasol. I never got round to parasol purchase, and really only ever had one moderately fairish maid, given the extreme bias then in the sex ratios, although I do remember a friend of mine who lived on the same staircase, and hearing the regular beat of feminine feet, of differing rhythm and timbre, tiptoeing, tottering, up and down the uneven old stairs, pausing at his door, followed by entry. If an enviable 'ladies' man', he nevertheless managed to end up as Professor of Geography. My own 'girl', and similar young ladies resident in a ladies college, if visited by a man for tea (the only period permitted), were required to push their beds outside into the corridor. It was presumably assumed that no young male visitor would be such a cad as to propose consummation, or any other form of 'doing it', on the girl's floor. One of her friends, she told me, returning late from a ball, a well-built young lady, resorted to 'climbing in' over the protected perimeter, a bit like a concentration camp. To preserve her ball gown, at the expense of her modesty, she removed it, rolled it up, and threw it over the wall, planning to scale the latter, but it proved beyond her. In bra and panties, brief for the occasion, she sought the help of a passing policeman, who very willingly gave her a 'leg up', as it were. My own girl Mary, like many of the non-bluestockings, was sweet, gentle, not terribly good-looking, virtuously (and virtually) sex-starved, sadly in love with me (my first real experience of this Janus-like emotion), daughter of a Church of England parson – all of which was tolerable – but, the breaking point, to boot, a Sunday-School teacher with similar worthy and depressing aspirations for me. She did punt with me, ('come punt with me and be my love…'), and as all well-bred young ladies were expected to do, disembarked and walked round and past the two sites, Parsons' Pleasure and Dames' Delight, reserved for (typically elderly and rather degenerate) dons doffing their duds and other apparel for nude sunbathing and, it was rumoured, 'a bit of gentlemanly networking'.

Twice a year, in an attempt to dampen passions in the all-male student body, the Warden held 'a bunfight', a sedate reception to which eligible young ladies at the various local finishing schools and secretarial colleges were decorously bussed in. They seemingly followed a standard stereotype, blonde and otherwise rather colourless, whose 'Daddies' possessed ponied properties often in the New Forest.

One then invited them to tea, but usually after a rather desultory acquaintance, they subsequently seemed to 'fizzle out'. I had to wait for my two years in industry to learn that the world abounded with feisty young females willing to engage enthusiastically in all manner of amorous activities, with carnal urges fully complementary to one's own, girls of whom many a young man's 'Mummy' might well have disapproved, if not despaired.

Darts in country pubs was a pleasant recreation. Practice in the Junior Common Room before dinner had made four of us rather skilled, and we would clamber into my ancient Land Rover, see below, and head for somewhere pleasant and where we were unknown. There we would deliberately play a poor game, which often led to a challenge from the locals. We would let them beat us for one or two games, by which time they would be often ready for a serious challenge, when we would show our true colours and depart with our winnings.

The three Oxford terms were of 12 weeks; the remaining vacation time was supposed to be occupied at least in part, by private study and scholarly contemplation. I had planned to switch, after five terms of Honour Moderations in Classics, to Medicine (pre-clinical, thereafter, one moved on to one of the famous London teaching hospitals for the clinical experience), as I had sufficiently equipped myself while still at school with the necessary qualifications in science and maths, additional to my classics. However, one of the regular reviews of medical numbers revealed that there was currently a surfeit of medicos, and the government would not further extend my scholarship for that purpose. So instead I chose to study the very-new PPP course (Physiology, Psychology and Philosophy), good advice from my tutor, a gaunt chain-smoker with amazingly long thin legs which he could literally coil round each other. However, it turned out, later, that being so new it was not yet accredited as a fit and proper course or precursor to advanced studies, which thereby disqualified me subsequently from being funded for a PhD. Fortunately, as it again turned out, my subsequent two years in industry, with qualifications in the newly developing discipline of business computing, once again made me eligible for funding.

During the long summer vacations I made various trips. With a school friend I hitched around the remote (by British standards) northern islands, the Orkneys and Shetlands, beyond the Scottish mainland, and once in the possession of the King of Norway. This made me wish to visit that country, so with a friend from Magdalen College, I hitch-hiked the next year around the Western Fjords. Sufficiently delighted with that experience, the following year, with four other friends, I bought a dilapidated old long-wheel-base Land Rover, did it up (fitting rubber bushes from dead washing machines as boosters to a failing suspension), and we had a wonderful, adventurous, incident-filled and at times dangerous trip right up to Nord Cap, the ultimate tip of arctic Europe and Lapland, and back down through arctic Finland and Sweden. This set me up in later years to run four-wheel-drive expeditions of an archaeological nature through the Middle East, North Africa and central Asia.

9

STICKING UP LIKE A SORE THUMB

Hitch-hiking

'What must their mothers have been thinking of?' That or similar would have been the sentiments in the last ten or so years, yet in the early to mid-1950s it was deemed perfectly natural for one's young to spread their wings, alone or with a like-minded friend, on voyages of exploration. With Robert, at 15, I became one half of a French tandem bicycle, which we christened Fifi, when we set off on a camping trip hundreds of kilometres in extent, and of several weeks' duration, from England's industrial Merseyside in the north, all the way down to England's south coast. Our destination was Lyme Regis, known for its fossiliferous exposures of the Jurassic Blue Lyas, which the local resident, Mary Anning, had made famous in the early nineteenth century. It was as usual a hermaphrodite tandem, and therefore with a frame rather weaker in the rear half, a weakness later to prove its downfall while simultaneously introducing us to the addictive and economical joys of hitch-hiking. The latter, however, seems nowadays practically a lost art, in part perhaps for reasons, real or imagined, of safety. But more of that later.

My father, a qualified fitter and turner, willingly fashioned us side panniers over the rear wheel, and lent us his 50-year-old, temperamental and decidedly dangerous, kerosene pressure stove. My mother lent us a single, hairy, army blanket apiece and a groundsheet for Robert's two-man tent. We left in September; the nights were bitterly and memorably cold, as we slept directly on the groundsheet, without any intervening mattress or insulation, and there was a gap between the bottom of the tent's walls and the ground. We averaged about 40 miles (65 km) a day, sleeping in fields and where possible foraging for provender, with ripening roadside blackberries for a sweet.

We arrived safely at Lyme Regis, having only once fallen off on a gravelly corner, and collected many fine specimens of fossil ammonites, crinoids, assorted crustaceans, and even (oh, joy!), a fish (shark?) vertebra. These we mailed back home – you could then do that sort of thing!

Things unravelled when we headed home. Fifi was endowed with an early form of derailer gear, of three speeds – nothing like the 20 or so nowadays available; she cracked in the hindquarters, making gear change impossible, and further progress dangerous. So we put her on a train, tying a luggage label to her handle bars, addressed to our homes up north. We decided to try our hands (thumbs?) at hitch-hiking, as beloved by the many servicemen still travelling the roads, to save money. Miraculously, almost the very first passing vehicle stopped just up the road, offering us a lift – all the way up to Merseyside! A blue 'Elizabeth Ann' pantechnicon carrying kitchen furniture, it hurtled along as the driver expounded upon his exploits in outwitting and out-running the police, demonstrating his technique of unexpectedly braking and swerving, to a cacophony of outraged car horns from following drivers; we were hooked!

On my own, with one or occasionally two friends, at every opportunity I hitch-hiked in the English Lake District, and sought fossil sites in North Wales, wandering the lochs, glens, mountains and islands of Scotland. I explored Ireland, the Norwegian fjords, France, Italy, Greece, Turkey … I never had a single bad experience, encountering nothing but kindness and hospitality, ranging from free meals to unexpected nights' accommodation. Apart from alleviating the boredom frequently experienced by long-distance truckies, sometimes hauling heavy rigs at night, I was often of considerable practical assistance as a driver's mate. Thus, on one occasion my role was continuously to roll silver cigarette papers into makeshift fuses, and replace them as they burnt out in the fuse-box beside my seat. On another occasion, encountering a low bridge, I had to reduce tyre pressures all round, just enough to edge the vehicle under, and assist with their subsequent re-inflation. Memorably, a friend and I were picked up in the north of Scotland by the driver of a very old, immaculately maintained, and just purchased veteran car, dating from before 1918. When the engine died, I was able to use the knowledge imparted to me by my father of engine maintenance to strip and clean the carburettor, and get it going again. Shortly afterwards we discovered that the Youth Hostel where we had planned to stay the night was closed. The driver took us on to a five-star hotel without saying a word, and booked us in for dinner, bed and breakfast. Not knowing how far his kindness had extended, we ate the barest minimum to save money, and often afterwards wondered what we had missed out on. But then there was the almost equally ancient truck on a back road in the Greek hinterland. Laden with a badly secured bulldozer, it dropped its shovel with the result that the road behind was blocked, thus preventing me from getting any further lifts.

And then, travelling in the Republic of Ireland, there was the Irish priest who, dropping us off, said: 'Before you go, you must have a wee drap of the hard stuff'; he had a complete still running off his car's motor, tubes, coil and filters all, 'to provide poteen for my poor parishioners'. The 'wee drap' of the urine-coloured, foul-tasting liquid burnt the backs of our throats, and was memorably – horrible!

En route in North Wales to a reputedly good fossil site, I was picked up by a truckie who asked me what I thought of Robert Graves' classic account, *Good-Bye to All That*, of his own time in Wales and the horrors of the First World War.

He then gave me the address of one George Leach who lived not far away, whom I would find interesting; I did, he was an amateur archaeologist, officially in charge of various digs, in which I subsequently participated enthusiastically all over the Welsh hill country for several years.

In those days, there was a particular make of car, a Rover 90, a prestige car beloved of elderly husbands and wives of comfortable appearance and means, with adult children who had fled the nest; we perhaps reminded them of their missing offspring. All such vehicles were always good for a lift. One learnt these little tips, alongside of the best position from which to solicit a lift. There should always be a good straight stretch of road ahead, with room at the side for the driver to pull off. As the drivers approached, one should always look them in the eye, and smile. If one encountered another hitch-hiker already in place, it was an unspoken rule of etiquette that the new arrival moved through and took up the next available slot out of sight up the road. Two people hitching together usually stood less chance of a lift than a single male (and sometimes the second male would sit out of sight until a car stopped, although this was of doubtful form), but if his partner was female, young and attractive, the odds were shortened.

Hitch-hiking, although technically illegal on the German autobahns, followed very strict protocol on the slip roads or on ramps, in terms of positioning and precedence. Cries of 'Polizei' from a sharp-eyed scout led to everyone scattering to the nearest cover.

Hitch-hiking mixed in with a walking holiday with an Oxford friend in the Western Fjords of Norway was my introduction to continental Europe. Although the roads were often unpaved, and at times traffic was infrequent, we never waited long for a lift, and accommodation in the Norwegian equivalent of Youth Hostels was palatial compared to that available in Britain; the worst problem was the superabundance of stunning scenery, and the realisation that we could not keep on asking our drivers to stop for us to take yet another photo. The other worry was the Cuban crisis, then at its peak; we did not know if there would even be an England, sadly degenerate as it was with rust-belt industries and massive pollution, when we returned from the stunning Elysium that is the Norwegian coast. Norway has always been one of my two favourite countries, and one to which my wife Judy and I have returned several times; strange to say, at the same time as I was in Norway's West, Judy, although we had never heard of each other, was leading a women's botanical expedition in Norway's remote Lofoten Islands, up beyond the Arctic Circle.

My other favourite country is Turkey, Norway's polar opposite, to coin a phrase, and again one to which I have often returned. Again, my first visit to Turkey, and the Mediterranean generally, was hitch-hiking. I set out on the modern equivalent of the Grand Tour, to Italy and Greece, so beloved of the English elite two or more centuries ago. Crossing from Belgium to Germany, I had a momentary pang of panic, as atavistic memories of world conflict only two decades previously were still very fresh – indeed, a friend in Norway had made the mistake of wearing Lederhosen and had been spat at. However, a jolly rotund German in an open Porsche picked me up at the border, and all fears vanished. It was summer, and at night I would find a broad-spreading tree under which to lay my 'swag' (a lightweight groundsheet, inflatable airbed and sleeping bag in my case), and be lulled by dappled moonlight filtering through the leaves, and the occasional traces of a meteorite's track.

In Switzerland, I had a wonderful lift with a beautiful blonde girl driving an expensive open-top sports car, hair flowing rapturously in the slipstream. I can still remember the song playing on the radio – the then oh-so-popular '*Girl from Ipanema*'; she will now be an old lady – does she remember me? The same day, I was picked up by an Austrian family who had just won a lottery, and for the very first time in their lives ventured forth, with a new car and impenetrable accents, into the rest of Europe. They had picked up Wim, a gay (in both senses) music student from the Amsterdam Conservatorium, who had proved invaluable as a guide and Mr Fix-it. If one such passenger was good value, two should be even better, so I was installed in the rear seat with a rather amorous companion. We eventually came to a satisfactory (for me anyway) *modus vivendi*, and Wim practised restraint, keeping his word, even when on more than one occasion we had to share a double bed. It was then that I learnt of the pain and anguish associated with a (far from) gay lifestyle and orientation. Later, in Italy, having fled the rather demanding family in Rome, Wim and I were picked up by an Italian pimp who tried to sell us time with his elderly female companion, doubly to Wim's distaste.

And then there was Keith, with whom I travelled for a while, even being briefly arrested with him, when, arriving in a small Italian town at dusk, during a market day, Keith thoughtlessly put his heavy pack down on a tarpaulin-covered table, and broke some hidden religious icons. We were eventually rescued from an angry mob by a rather plain girl in the tourist police, and we paid for the damage. An unforeseen consequence of this was a stream of letters she thereafter sent to my home address, which she had extracted from me in her professional duties, professing undying love and yearning for me, and planning to join me in England; not an easy issue to explain to my mother. We took ship to Corfu, and found a beautiful camp spot under an olive tree on a headland overlooking the sea, where I would venture with my spear gun each morning to catch fish for the mid-day meal. Evenings, we would go down to a tavern for retsina, and sleep the sleep of the blessed under the everlasting stars. Up the hill behind us was a small shrine inhabited by a Belgian priest, with whom I would converse in an amalgam of Latin, French and Classical Greek. The whole area, I now understand, is swamped by a massive holiday resort.

Staying in Athens in a cheap hotel (grandiosely entitled Hotel Megale), I had left Keith cooking our evening meal on my father's dangerous Primus stove, while I went to get some vegetables and meat, to replace our iron, having foolishly sold blood for $5 US each (in those days infection from multi-use needles was still largely below the horizon). Letting me in when I returned, he accidentally kicked over the stove, and set fire to the floor. As management had retained our passports, we had to extinguish the fire with the hurriedly dropped mattress off the bed, afterwards wrapping it up with a sheet to conceal the scorch marks. Thinking that a really rather rapid change of scenery might be advantageous, we settled on Crete, where I wished to view Sir Arthur Evans' momentous excavations of Knossos, the capital of the fabled Bronze Age Minoan civilisation more than three and a half millennia earlier. So we stowed away, briefly 'assisting' in the loading of cement sacks, but staying on the boat.

Knossos, despite far too enthusiastic 'restoration', was a wonder to behold; so too was its equivalent and near contemporary on the Greek mainland, Golden Mycenae of the Cyclopean walls, excavated by the notable German archaeologist, Heinrich Schliemann, who is said to have 'penned' that incredible telegram 'Today I gazed upon the face of Agamemnon'. The latter was the leader of the Greek expedition to Troy three thousand years ago, supposedly to 'rescue' (read, forcibly return) Helen, wife of Menelaus, Agamemnon's brother, who had 'eloped' with Paris of Troy, when the latter was over on a visit. In truth, the gold death mask unearthed by Schliemann almost certainly was not that of Agamemnon, and the real reason for the Trojan War, which was not simply a great myth, was a problem of trade and unduly heavy dues levied by Troy on Bronze Age Greek commerce in the Dardanelles.

An even more mystical experience was sleeping under the stars at Delphi, the ancient centre of religion, culture and oracular pronouncements. It was for me one of life's really great experiences, and the whole place is truly redolent of myth, magic and mystery. Delphi was the seat, literally as well as metaphorically, of the Pytho priestess, whose deliberately ambiguous pronouncements were eagerly sought by all those planning major expeditions; 'You will destroy a great civilisation', would be the message – but as often as not, it might be your own. She is now known to have squatted on a stool, placed over a fissure in the rock, which, as was reported 20 or more years ago in the august science journal *Nature*, releases into the atmosphere volatile and intoxicating gases, and which maybe I too had inhaled, inducing my own mood of exaltation. The word 'Pytho', incidentally derives from a root meaning 'to rot, smell of dead snake'.

Turkey was memorable, mostly for Istanbul/Byzantium/Constantinople (take your pick of these alternative names), a wonderfully cosmopolitan city of Greeks, Armenians and Turks. The very name 'Istanbul' is a corrupt form of '*Eis tan polin*', 'to the city' in late classical Greek. Enough has been written by others about the wonders of that extraordinary city. Returning up through what was then Yugoslavia, a memorable feature was a newly enacted law, presumably to further tourism and encourage the young, that all public buses were required to stop and pick up, free, hitch-hikers if there was a spare seat, as there usually was. Unfortunately, I was unwell, as all too often seems to happen to westerners visiting Turkey for the first time, and war seemed about to break out between Greece and Turkey at any time, over Cyprus. With a similarly unwell Canadian I spent a horribly memorable night, in a massive thunderstorm, under a bridge over the dry bed of the River Euro ('wide'), on the Greek-Turkish border; the bridge was mined with boxes of high explosives, should hostilities commence – and they seemed about to, as we had had to pass through front line army units belonging to both parties, and were questioned at length about the forces ranged against each other. We were both so unwell that we preferred the risk of the bridge being destroyed about us, to lying out in the cold rain. In the event, a beautiful young woman, Mercède, with stunning grey eyes and travelling like us, ministered to us both.

While – and was I merely lucky? – my hitch-hiking career never otherwise encountered any negative events, it was never uneventful, being endowed with a wonderful sense of freedom and curiosity as to how the day would turn out. Wandering through the villages of Crete, for example, equipped at least with a knowledge of Classical Greek of 2,500 years ago, I could still on occasion make myself understood. (A doctor told me it was like an Englishman conversing with Chaucer's grandfather.) Each village was fiercely independent, some royalist, some Communist, and as I travelled I composed little homilies in the archaic tongue on, for example, brotherly love (philadelphia), to smooth the path forward. Once, in the outskirts, I was even mounted on a donkey, pack on my back, and led in triumph, as it were, and like a latter-day messiah, right into the village square.

When I first acquired a car, a 1934 two-seater open-top Hillman Minx, I always tried to repay past acts of kindness to me, picking up hitch-hikers myself. However, in an age when girls, singly or more frequently in pairs, were often on the roads – usually like myself impecunious students – from time to time I was blessed with a delightful companion. And on at least three occasions I was the chief beneficiary, as they totally changed the general direction of my life, for the better, adding dimensions hitherto undreamt of.

Uta, whom I picked up in North Wales' Snowdonia, was a student in southern Germany's incomparably lovely University of Heidelberg, and was later to become my guide and mentor to some of the most romantic scenery, places and buildings imaginable. I soon found myself with her spending idyllic summer holidays exploring her beloved Rhineland, the Neckar, the valleys, rivers, forests, castles and ruins, and learning conversational German from a tutor who was every young man's dream. Memorably, one Easter we did a *Wandertour*, hiking through the snowbound Black Forest from scenic Freudenstadt to Titisee, staying the nights in farmhouses, above the penned cattle wintering immediately below the family home; comforting sounds and smells lulled our romantic slumbers. Most evenings we were close to postcard villages, celebrating Eastertide with a *Knabenchor*, a boys' choir singing the old, traditional Easter pieces in ancient places of worship, into which we would slip in our hiking boots. God! It was just SO romantic and unforgettable. We kept in touch for many years, even though our lives' trajectories diverged.

Then again, I was camping in Scotland's far north-west with a (male) school friend; he was himself in fact about to marry a hitch-hiking girl, as indeed so too was one of *his* earlier travelling companions, to the other of the pair of girl cousins *they* had recently picked up. On the road below our campsite, a girl with a big pack asked me for a lift. When I explained we couldn't oblige as we were setting up a base camp on the adjacent creek for a few days' hiking, Unity asked if she could join us. A recent archaeological graduate from Cambridge, she was shortly to leave for two years research work in East Africa. So, for quite a while she travelled with us, in the back of my old blue panel van, singing the protest songs of the 1960s. Later, from Kenya and Nyasaland (now Malawi), for a couple of years she would send me, every two or three weeks, the most unsettling accounts of her adventures and misadventures, urging me to leave my dreary corporate job and return to university to research for a PhD. Wonderful advice, which I followed and never regretted, and it totally redirected my life, altogether for the better, into its 'proper' paths. Years later, when we had both led separate married lives and each lost our partners, I traced her through a graduate student of mine who was doing her postdoc at Cambridge. Although both now in our late seventies, we have spent time together in each other's countries, camping and exploring, and recaptured tantalising hints of the heady romance of youth.

John Betjeman writes movingly of his dream girl, Joan Hunter-Dunn, in 'A Subaltern's Love Song', in his *Collected Poems*. My friend Liz was just such a girl, studying Medicine at the romantically ancient St Bartholomew's Hospital in London. I got to know her from finding myself sitting opposite her one day while lunching at Bart's with my best friend David from Oxford days, so, strictly speaking, hitch-hiking did not enter directly into the story. When conversation turned to the state of pollution in the Thames, Liz said that 'for a consideration' she would take up my bet that she wouldn't be game to take a dip in it. We set the stake at a new set of underwear, and that I should have the pleasure of accompanying her to approve the purchase. From such chance words … Her parents, real Rover 90 types who most certainly would have offered me a lift had our paths crossed earlier, had a beautiful old house and grounds south-east of London, and Liz became the dream girlfriend of my corporate days. Every fortnight on Friday afternoon I would drive all the way from Teesside down to London, to be with her, her best friend Pat, and David who as a result became Pat's boyfriend; all three were medical students. We became an inseparable foursome, spending memorable weekends together, and a Christmas and New Year in a hut in a remote and beautiful corner, the Duddon valley, of the Lake District, waiting for the adjacent tarn (small lake) to freeze over so that we could go skating. It all suddenly ended when David, born with a defective aorta, unexpectedly died in Pat's arms, while they were revising for an exam. Liz, years later, told me she had never married, and that her professional life had taken precedence.

Then, at this time of writing, a rather extraordinary and unsettling event occurred. I had a vivid dream that we were both young once again and were at a memorable Merton summer ball commemorating the college's 700th anniversary from foundation, and which we had, all four of us, attended in 1964. I hadn't thought of her, or the ball, for a long time. So in the morning I 'googled' her, out of curiosity, knowing from some correspondence we had had some decades earlier, that she had specialised in haematology and practised and lived in the beautiful old town of Salisbury, and sang in the magnificent cathedral's choir. To my shock, horror and emotional turmoil, I learnt that she had died a week or so ago, with a memorial service planned in the cathedral some six weeks later. A spooky and upsetting coincidence? One can never of course know just how many coincidences just fail in reality to eventuate. Is Pat still alive, or am I the only survivor of that golden foursome?

Some other coincidences: Judy, a friend and I were walking one hot summer day in woodland in Snowdonia, and Judy said how nice it would be to find a forest tea garden; she had barely finished speaking when around a corner we encountered a sign 'To Forest Tea Garden'. An enchanted and dangerous 'gingerbread house'? Another coincidence: we were plagued by a youth riding a noisy trail bike on the grass verge outside the house, and I said bad-temperedly to a neighbour that I hoped he would one day run into a tree. Within the week, he did just that – into the tree at the end of our driveway, but while driving his father's car, which compounded the offence.

What does all this reminiscence mean? The recent preoccupation with children's safety, and the ever-increasing cosseting of the young, not only has led to a generation of incompetents, unable to navigate life's thickets and hidden paths, but has also deprived them of the opportunity to experience some of life's most wonderful and memorable experiences. I can only offer my heartfelt thanks to all those who gave me lifts, should any still be around; and to those passengers who have immeasurably enriched my own life. Every young man should some time find himself a Joan Hunter-Dunn. Hitch-hiking can change your life; it is time maybe to restore it to its one-time respectability.

10

AN INDUSTRIOUS INTERLUDE AND INDUSTRIAL INTERVAL

ICI

I had obtained a degree of reasonable quality from arguably Britain's, if not the world's, most prestigious university, terminating in an unaccredited course which would not qualify me for further academic studies. I didn't want to undertake holy orders (I do in fact know a couple of atheist parsons, but it is not normally part of what is nowadays known as the job description), or end up teaching third-rate Classics in a similarly-rated private school. What on earth was I to do? It was then that fate took a hand, two, in fact. I answered an advertisement for a position which is nowadays known as a systems analyst (then, organisation and methods officer), in ICI (Imperial Chemical Industries) head office in Millbank, London. ICI was then Britain's largest manufacturer of chemicals, with branches all over the country and overseas. I was invited to a rather special lunch in a distinctly special restaurant in London's West End, hosted by a very affable interviewer, a bit of a *bon viveur* clearly able to enjoy his job with a bit of self-indulgence. The *flambé* was both novel and particularly appealing. Either the meal or the impression I made was sufficient for me to advance to the next, serious stage in the interviewing procedure; I was summoned with 40 or so other enthusiastic applicants for the two offered positions, to a week at an ICI-hosted house party, 1920s-style, in a large country house recently the domain of a duchess. You could fit an entire restaurant in the grand and grandiosely entitled 'Great Hall of Mirrors', where much of the selection process occurred. We, the applicant hopefuls, were put through various tasks, such as suddenly being asked to give impromptu speeches on abstruse and obscure topics. My experience at running the school debating society, even though it had been largely an excuse for bawdy behaviour, served me in great and unexpected good stead. We were also assessed during drinks and mealtimes, on our ability with the glassware, eating irons and the various courses – our general capacity to accommodate to the wining, dining, entertaining and general social (and to some extent maybe even the work) ethos of a company that openly claimed to be on par with Britain's prestigious Civil Service or Foreign (and Colonial, in those halcyon days) Office. Why, one even 'knocked off' early, at 3.30 p.m., on Friday afternoons 'so that you chaps can get down to your country places for the weekend' was a phrase I was to encounter several times. Yet, and yes, to my surprise, and great relief, I was accepted, with an office in Millbank, a sought-after location overlooking the Queen's stables – although horses failed to make any appearances during my 'watch'. My boss also was in fact an earl, the Earl of Courtown (to be addressed by the staff as 'Lord Courtown' or 'My Lord'). Actually, he was a kindly, rather delightful and definitely vague old gentleman, seeing out his time before returning to his impoverished family seat in Ireland. Moreover, several others in my section also boasted substantial family seats. Courtown (as he was known informally in the office) dressed untidily, frequently with the decaying vestiges of old breakfasts fossilised on his tie, invariably a yellow one, maybe the better to mask the egg stains. At Christmas, in a charismatic and not uncharacteristic burst of charitable bonhomie, he decided that all 15 of us (there was only a single, token female, a blue-stocking type of dubious personal hygiene despite an abundant use of cheap cosmetics) should be taken out, at his personal expense, to a West End show. For convenience, his secretary told me later, as he had asked her advice on the matter, he settled on the nearest theatre in the vicinity of Victoria, and the show was the long-running Black and White Minstrels.

While in London, I had the enormous good fortune to join, in what is nowadays called a 'share house', four young trainee nurses, one of whom I had been introduced to. My role was to ferry all four girls in the mornings to their various hospitals, fortunately all fairly close, in my old blue van which was once the property of a chimney cleaner; I found under the driving seat his calling cards: 'I came today to clean your chimney but you were not in.' I was also in charge of the evening coke stove. (As a fine example of what is known as 'flash-bulb memory', I vividly recall shovelling out the ash just as the assassination was announced on the radio of JFK.) In return for such manly chores, I was fed, my clothes were washed, shirts ironed, and two of the girls enthusiastically performed certain other female services, of which I was still somewhat naïve, and for which I was, and still am, deeply appreciative. They marked a certain rite of passage, and were both enjoyable and educational, as indeed so should be all such experiences. I still remember Pip appearing, wraith-like in a diaphanous white nightie slip one night in my room, and wordlessly climbing into bed with me; dear Pip, what are you doing now? Are you even still in the land of the living? We had, in 44 Collingwood Avenue, near Muswell Hill (I still recall the address, at least in part), a small garden, overgrown with weeds, the target of our neighbours' scandalised opprobrium, to which on one memorable occasion, when challenged as to why 'that young man of yours does not get it in order', one of the girls replied, 'Oh, you see, with all of us to attend to, he is always so very tired.' (An old school friend one Christmas 'accidentally-on-purpose' told my mother about my unconventional domestic arrangements, and she afterwards always coyly referred to them as 'my handmaidens', while my doubtlessly envious father simply made sour comments about me turning out a 'ladies' man'.) It *was* the beginning of the Swinging Sixties, and got me through my two years with ICI, two years somewhat analogous to that reported by soldiers in wartime – '90% tedium, 10% stress'.

A period of stress, but one which unexpectedly contributed immeasurably towards my future prospects for a career in academia; I was seconded for three or four months to IBM, whose massive and lofty headquarters were not too far from ICI Millbank. It involved a crash course in learning how to programme one of the first-ever business computers, the iconic IBM 1401. Occupying a large air-conditioned room, with a processing capacity which a modern mobile phone would doubtless put to shame, it possessed an impressive, to me, daunting even, array of peripherals, tape drives, printers and 80-channel card readers and punches. Although programmed with its own particular IBM autocode, programmers and operators still had to be able to work in machine language to 'patch' faulty routines. I still remember many of the commands, and not only did it subsequently qualify me for research support towards a PhD, otherwise closed to me on the basis of the content of my undergraduate degree's then inadequacy, but it also resulted in my being asked to give a well-paid course of lectures at the university, during a subsequent PhD, on business computing, an emerging area with a great lack of qualified instructors.

London in the Swinging Sixties taught, and matured, me a lot. I came to appreciate good theatre, to which I took 'my girl', using the Luncheon Vouchers, given to 'senior staff' (was that really me?) so that they could attend for nourishment places of an acceptable social standing. I was entirely happy with canteen 'grub', and used the vouchers, as one could, for the theatre. I also did a lot of driving in my old blue panel van, and by choosing my filling stations – surely the aim of the system – I accumulated lots of Green Shield stamps. Although I found nothing useful for redemption, I would give them to the punch girls, so that they would promptly punch up my 80-column programme cards; it worked so well that after a while they wouldn't do anyone else's cards without similar sweeteners, and a memo came round forbidding their further use in the company. One problem with computing in those days was that it was essential always to remember to include an 'end of job' card at a program's termination. One day I didn't, and found on a Monday morning a large tea-chest of cards and printout 'for checking'.

After the excesses of London, I first had a stint at ICI Runcorn, less than an hour's drive from my parents' retirement cottage in North Wales. I particularly remember the introduction of seat belts, which were strongly resisted by the tanker drivers, who said they would prefer to be thrown out in an accident, than to die horribly strapped in. And there were two such hideous accidents, when their tankers of concentrated hydrochloric acid overturned and they were slow in dying. The apprentices at Runcorn amused themselves one lunchtime with the super-abundant seagulls begging for bits of sandwich; one sadistic youth had the bright idea of wrapping in bread a lump of sodium, which resulted in dramatically detonating birds in flight … Another dropped a lump into a bucket of water in the staff car park; the resultant violent reaction sent a highly corrosive fountain over some very expensive vehicles. Decades previously, there had been a tanker spill into the nearby Manchester Ship Canal, and an employee was detailed, twice daily, to take a small boat out to several points on the canal, and test and record the pH. He dutifully did so for some 30 years, and on retirement there was a small library of his meticulous records, all entirely pointless after the first few weeks of the spill – but no-one had ever told him to stop.

I moved to ICI Billingham on Teesside, on England's bleak, industrial North-East coast, with a staff of four programmers, to put the Division's payroll and wages on to the local IBM 1401 computer. Stress and tedium prevailed, even though as 'a young executive direct from HQ' I was accommodated in another of the ICI-owned country houses, the nearby Norton Hall, which certainly lived up to its name: country house living at its very best, breakfast daily arranged buffet-style on a vast sideboard, with an equally enormous and delectable section of hot and cold fish, flesh and fowl of every conceivable and some surely inconceivable description. Dinners were of similarly impressive presentation and variety, with waitress service to rival that of a London club. However, Britain's largest chemical factory, impressive although it was, emitted such appalling acid and alkali pollution (never such as to mutually cancel, unfortunately), that washing rotted on clothes lines, and cars' Duco paintwork aged almost before one's eyes. One day I received an urgent request from 'Head Office' to entertain my boss, the Earl, when visiting Teesside with his sidekick, an elegant young man with tall, patent leather boots of a high polish. I decided to take them to a very ancient and beautiful pub, the Blacksmiths' Arms, splendidly isolated in the moors around the tiny hamlet of Rosedale. I had once taken a girl there, and the roast duck (wild, shot in the immediate environs) was of unbelievable quality. The meal was an outstanding success, and it being a fine summer evening, his Lordship thought a little wander on the moors would be 'good for the digestion'. However, his acolyte of the mirror-polished boots, angry after being squashed in the windowless back of my old blue van, refused to dare the mire, and stayed crossly in the uncomfortable vehicle, while I got to know the man behind the title in the best way possible – on a country walk.

I was never truly 'at home' in the business world, and fortunately followed the advice of another girl, Unity, who affected my life profoundly, at many levels, and more than half a century later still does. I wrote to my old Oxford tutor, whom I knew had recently assumed the chair in Experimental Psychology at Sheffield University, and he agreed to take me on for a PhD, the initial idea being that capitalising on my ICI computing, I should devise better ways to select appropriate would-be IT candidates in the profession of the future. That it worked out differently, and for the better, is the subject of a later chapter. Suffice it to say, I abandoned the sinking ship of computerising ICI's payroll, which was going nowhere fast, not least because of my incompetent inexperience, and arranged to commence doctoral studies in Sheffield in the autumn. In the interim, I set out on a six-week hitch-hiking trip to the Mediterranean, to visit major archaeological sites in Italy, Greece, Crete and Turkey – a mini-version of the eighteenth- and nineteenth-centuries' Grand Tours, sleeping rough in vineyards and on deserted beaches. A hippie with a mission, it was a wonderful way to expunge the bourgeois excesses of industry and the business world.

11

AN UGLY PICTURE IN A BEAUTIFUL FRAME

Sheffield, centre once for steel and cutlery, industry and grime, but surrounded by moorland and the beautiful Derbyshire Peak District, was on the cusp of a makeover when I loaded my old blue panel van with goods and chattels for a planned three years stint once again as a student. I stopped off briefly in the centre of Mold, the market town closest to my parents' cottage high in the ranges near the beautiful Vale of Clwyd, after a last nostalgic look back at the far Clwydian range defining their skyline. I had suddenly realised that I had no crockery or cutlery for my new home, wherever and whatever it may be, and it was Mold's market day. More than half a century later I still have one of the heavy yellow plates I bought on that first day of a new life.

After returning sick from something I had contracted in Istanbul, I had spent six weeks with my parents in their little Welsh retreat prior to commencing at Sheffield, and being qualified from prior employment for the dole, and not surprisingly not being able to 'find work for which I had been trained' (IT work, as it is nowadays known), I was eligible for a useful temporary allowance. My conservative parents would have been horrified that their Oxford-educated ex-businessman son was reduced to such a level, so I had to find an excuse for my twice-weekly visits to the Employment Exchange in Mold, on Wednesdays to 'sign on', and on Fridays to receive the hand-out. I kept a pair of old ICI overalls in the van to don on dole days, so as to fit in with the general clientele. The doctor's daughter also got me a part-time job at the local petrol station next door to the unofficial brothel (men's bikes would regularly appear propped against the wall, and after a short time disappear, to be replaced by fresh machines). However, after absent-mindedly filling a petrol-driven car with diesel, a disaster I shall NEVER again repeat, that position terminated, as did my relationship with the doctor's daughter; fortunately, I never had again to consult her father professionally.

With now some free time, I was fortunately able to occupy it in the unexpected and remarkably agreeable company of my second cousin, S, sent to stay with us by her grandmother (my paternal aunt), who I later realised probably did have something in mind for us both. Be that as it may, S, a buxom country lass and farmer's daughter well able to run down a sheep, as she demonstrated once or twice, and a little younger than me, greatly enjoyed our hill walks together in the historic Clwydians, and despite her far superior fitness and agility, she soon chose to hold my hand on these rugged perambulations – actually and actively taking the initiative – and subsequently of an evening we would lie romantically together on the softly glowing autumnal heather in the centre of one of the old, prehistoric Iron Age hill forts that crowned the Clwydian ridges. A truly golden autumn, with the spirits of the old-time Celts to watch over our amours from the ancient perimeter ramparts of earth, and a ruddy sunset dwindling above. Truly the gods of old Britain – and the weather – looked kindly upon us, and when the time came for us to go our separate ways, I, north by east to Sheffield and research, and S, south by west to Devon and the family farm, there were no tears or recriminations on either side, just happy nostalgic memories, as evidenced by our subsequent desultory and diminishing correspondence, and a happy and unexpected *rendezvous* some 20 years later.

Life's major moves, in this case across the Pennines, over the once-feared (in the winter snows) Snake Pass, past Kinder Scout (where a year later I was to come upon a beautiful flint arrowhead made by a Neolithic Briton) and the aptly named Featherbed Moss, and down the long descent into Sheffield's smoke – always involve a major hurdle: finding accommodation. A despondent Polish lady, known to the existing three single student inhabitants of her available single rooms as Ma Pagacz, presided over the slum property boasting a single bathroom-cum-toilet. A single gas ring on a hinged board which folded down over the grimy bath, or up for our ablutions, was the gesture towards supposedly-civilised 'Kitchen Facilities'. Back to the deprivations of my youth in Bebington, and a far cry from the sybaritic gentility of luxurious Norton Hall. But it was a relief to be free of the past, with an exciting future in prospect, whatever hazards might blow up over a distant horizon. And with a tatty, grease-stained copy of Katherine Whitehorn's *Cooking in a Bed-sitter*, a second-hand pressure cooker, and stackable pans (to keep the upper layers warm while simultaneously cooking on the lowest), I prepared passible, if not mouth-watering, repasts. Indeed, my pancakes were deemed by my colleagues sufficiently delectable that, on one occasion, a couple, which accidentally fell into the years of nameless grime behind the bath, were rescued and diligently washed under the ancient tap.

Apart from an unprepossessing teenage daughter, an invisible and presumably bedridden husband slowly dying of a serious lung condition (harrowing sounds of hacking coughing could be heard at night through the thin walls), and of course Ma P herself, we were all graduate or medical students. It seemed that the daughter from time to time went AWOL, and Ma P would frantically rush, unannounced, into our rooms, shouting, 'You got my daughter, where my daughter?', peer arthritically under the bed, and rush off to the next potential place of concealment or supposed villainy. It was never clear where she had got to on these occasions, or how or when she reappeared. We were just not interested, at 30 shillings a week, room unfurnished apart from a battered bed.

I bought basic furniture and furnishing from auction warehouses, transporting them precariously on the roof-rack of my old blue panel van, tied down with ropes through the windows, requiring entry into the vehicle, and egress, by climbing through the door at the back. Once the cargo, a better bed, began slowly to shift laterally, fortunately towards the right, and close to a roundabout. Quick thinking, and even quicker driving, clockwise round and round the roundabout a couple of times while simultaneously pushing sideways with my right hand through the open window, restored equilibrium sufficient safely to get back home. On another occasion, I found that my newly purchased bargain sideboard could not negotiate the narrow, steep and tortuous stairs up to my attic room; problem solved: I sawed off the legs, and later replaced them with bricks, covered by tasteful teacloths. In similar vein, a year or two later, as my name and fame became known in the student furniture-removal context, and I had acquired another elderly Land Rover for an archaeological expedition to the Middle East in the Long Vacation, I was asked by the husband of a musician who had purchased a piano, to help him move it home. When it proved far too heavy to lift it up on to the vehicle's tray, he said we could easily dismantle the heavy steel frame from the cabinet, effectively halving the load into two manageable portions. It was indeed surprisingly easy, but when the last and critical retaining bolt was slackened, all the ivories jumped joyfully up and out, with the release of key tension springs: the malevolence of natural objects. Surprisingly undaunted, husband collected keys and springs into a handy sack, and we delivered a now-stripped down, and once good quality piano to a tearful new owner. Any friendship failed to survive that move.

My room was lit by a single, fly-blown globe of low wattage in the centre of the ceiling. I bought a plug-in net of several extender globes to brighten the place; however, after a day or two they must have overloaded the old wiring, causing a rapidly expanding ceiling fire. A visiting friend, quicker thinking than I, seized an old-fashioned soda-water syphon I had on the table, and extinguished it. After I had hidden the incriminating evidence I informed Ma P that Janice had heroically extinguished a fire in the ceiling light point, and that an electrician should check matters over. Ma P was appropriately grateful that Janice had saved the whole house from conflagration, even although she normally greatly disapproved of visiting ladies.

Two of my male friends, on quite separate occasions, alerted me to the existence of a social and walking club, The Coffee Pot, which met weekly in one of our departmental lecture rooms. It was headed by a mild and bookish clergyman, with the air of one nevertheless possessed of certainty in matters of faith, who was generally referred to by our own professor and head as 'That bloody vicar'; these were terms identical to those which I was again to encounter years later in Australia when on a university science ethics committee, which was legally obliged to include in its numbers a minister of religion and a lawyer. Both of these members were of the expressed opinion that there was already far too much research going on, which was almost certainly inimical to matters of religion and public morals (it was the Swinging Sixties, and the Pill had appeared), and it was their role to slow things down. Anyway, my two friends went on to say that the club members were largely 'randy female teachers', and I really should give it a go. Eventually, unconvinced, I did, it was, and it changed my life after my one, first and only visit. I met my future wife, Judy, following her around at that meeting as she held the tray of refreshments; moreover, she reminded me strongly of Pip, one of my four London lovelies in our shameless share-house. So, within a remarkably short time I was equipped to commence my doctoral researches with both accommodation and a proper (if one may pardon any double entendre) girlfriend.

Although we often debated the matter, Judy's accommodation was definitely a little more upmarket than, and superior to, mine. She too had a single room, in a large and reasonably well-preserved Victorian house, in a more salubrious neighbourhood, a house which had been subdivided and was inhabited exclusively by single teachers. It was heated by water-filled radiators from a single, central, boiler, effectively a closed system. As a consequence of common constraints of design, standard bedheads in all six rooms pressed hard against their respective radiators, such that any activity in any of the beds transmitted a knocking noise throughout the network, just as is sometimes described as a communal communication system between cells in a prison. At weekends in particular, one or more sets of rhythmic knocking could be heard coming from the heaters, shortly after the arrival for the night of close friends or visitors. And to escape the ire of a suspicious cleaning lady, who had already expressed outrage at the evidence of apparently used condoms in the bin, I twice had to escape through Judy's ground-floor window, placed unfortunately close to the bus stop used by some of her senior science students who knew where she lived. One pest, however, which she had, in the cellar of the house, was rats, a pest from which at least in the wild state my place was mercifully free. Lab rats, however, were stock-in-trade for Judy, head science teacher with an honours degree from Durham University in botany and zoology; in fact, for dissection purposes she needed them – lots. And my Psychology Department always had lots to be got rid of, as there was a major research effort in animal learning and sensory processes. They were usually killed humanely by gas when no longer needed, and disposed of, but I was able to arrange their redirection to Judy for her High School labs. They would be handed over to her weekly in a paper bag when she came to collect them at the Animal House, but the trade was stopped when once, after inadequate gas treatment, the contents of the bag again became alive on a bus back to her place, which caused an unseemly commotion on their escape.

Over my three years at Sheffield I amassed a large collection of colour slides. Thus, in addition to my Business Computing lectures, I also ran illustrated travelogues with pictures of the exotic places I visited in my Land Rover archaeological expeditions which I organised during the summer vacations – not exactly the coolest time of the year for the Middle East or North Africa, unfortunately. Both sets of lectures were presented both for the university extension courses, and separately, weekly, for the local Workers' Education Authority (WEA). For the latter I would be collected, and returned, by a delightful Welshman in a grand old limousine of which he was inordinately proud. Every time, he would extol its virtues, running through a list of its wonderful fitments – a heater, windscreen wipers of variable speeds, fog and reversing lights, electric windows, etc., all in a liltingly lovely Welsh accent, as if they were a truly modern wonder. (I had fitted a windscreen wash to my old blue van consisting of a refillable detergent bottle on the parcel shelf beneath the dashboard, and a catheter donated by one of the London share-house sorority.) At the university I was once very urgently asked, on behalf of the Vice Chancellor, to stand in at the very last moment, when the hall was already filling for a major public lecture, to replace an eminent visiting speaker who was suddenly indisposed. I don't know what his topic was to be, but the Vice Chancellor himself collected and introduced me, and after my talk I got to know him as an eminent neuroscientist who had performed ground-breaking research into kuru, a neurological disease then particularly prevalent among women, widows predominantly, in New Guinea; they had all ceremonially eaten the brains of recently deceased tribal leaders in the hope of receiving their wisdom. So the world was introduced to what later would be known as prion diseases, which unusually can be caused by both genetic and infective processes. Prusiner much later would receive the Nobel Prize in Physiology for continuing the work on such related diseases as Creutzfeldt-Jakob and bovine spongiform encephalopathy (mad cow disease), which operate in much the same way. Indeed, there are disturbing indications that some other common neurodegenerative disorders like Alzheimer's may possibly behave similarly, if more slowly.

At another, departmental, talk, a well-known visiting psychiatrist down from Edinburgh gave an address on sublimation, a psychiatric rather than a chemical concept to describe a form of replacement activity, doing something trivial in lieu of something else more challenging. As an example, he proffered knitting, of all things, in place of masturbation. At this point a tall, serious graduate student put up her hand to interrupt, announcing to a stunned speaker and ribald audience, 'When I knit, I knit; when I masturbate I masturbate.' Incidentally, there was also present a senior staff member in the audience, male, who indeed was wont to knit during tedious meetings, etc., but who perhaps wisely refrained from contributing to the general hilarity. He also kept a small portable TV in a fridge; when asked why, his simple answer was just that it fitted.

Another 'character' in the university was a delightful, jolly lady, the wearer of heavy, prickly tweeds, who for a party trick when things were getting rather rowdy, would demonstrate that, with an appropriate stance, there was nothing in the female anatomy to prevent a woman from peeing standing up like a male. I believe she also could make her breasts rotate out of phase and in opposite directions, purely by appropriate muscular action, but unfortunately I was never able in person to verify this useful ability. But I am reminded of the professor of anatomy at one of the London hospitals who taught his class to waggle their ears, by what would come to be called biofeedback; he electrically stimulated the dormant muscles which we all have, and got the owner of the ear to concentrate on the resultant sensations as the ear waggled automatically on stimulation. Thereafter, most of the class could perform such (relatively benign) party tricks for the rest of their lives, and thereby came to be known as having been taught by this gifted teacher.

Within a month or two, Judy and I decided to marry, or at least legitimise our irregular union, as neither of us really felt the need for it also to be sanctified. In strict fact, she said one evening when we were returning from the theatre in her car (her new Ford runabout was far more comfortable than my van, and particularly well suited for back-seat canoodling), that for various reasons maybe that night I should perhaps not sleep over; without really thinking, I replied that perhaps we should marry – maybe not the most romantic of proposals, but it certainly provoked a very romantic acceptance response, and a memorable sleepover.

We were, in the end, some six months later married (her family would otherwise have been devastated) in one of the most romantic settings imaginable, the largely intact twelfth-century church of St Aidan, said to be where Christianity was first imported to Britain by that saint, and situated directly opposite her family home, in the beautiful old Northumbrian village of Bamburgh, once one of the three ancient capitals of Britain (Northumbria, the other two being Cumbria and Wessex). After the wedding, I, as the groom, had to leap over a stool, scattering handfuls of copper coins to the scrambling children, apparently an old local custom dating back centuries, and we retired on foot to a reception in a marquee set up in the garden. Like many family weddings, not everything ran entirely smoothly; I shall gloss over family misdemeanours, to recall the controversy surrounding one of my more dissolute friends, Pete. Invited and arriving late, my new mother-in-law asked him if he had been able to find accommodation. We had shortly (really, all too shortly) just returned in time for the wedding after our Land Rover archaeological expedition, and had slept under the vehicle at times for shelter. Pete caused shock, horror and consternation saying that it was a fine night so he had parked his little car over a conveniently dry ditch and slept there. He capped it all off by the next day eloping with Judy's chief bridesmaid, whom he had never previously met, to Labrador, where as an engineer he possibly had a job awaiting him. Nobody ever heard again from either of them.

Nature shortly after took control of matters, in the form of a pregnancy for which neither of us were ready, as we had plans after my PhD to travel and work, she as science teacher and I as lecturer, in one of the English-speaking countries overseas, with a preference for East Africa. In the golden 1960s, jobs and optimism were at their zenith for those with qualifications. We both agreed that something had to be done, at a time when that something was highly illegal, if regularly performed covertly. As it happened I shared an office with someone whose girlfriend had required just such urgent action, and it had been performed safely and successfully by well-qualified personnel acting underground and believing in what they were doing. The problem was I had to use the phone in the general office (no mobiles then) staffed by three motherly typing ladies, who always took an equally motherly interest in the telephone calls of 'their young men'. I had to arrange matters such that everything was clear at the other end, but not to the ladies listening in, or to any eavesdropping police should the line happen to be monitored. Not easy, but a date was fixed. Even the drive down, in Judy's Ford, was beset with difficulties. We filled up at the local service station, or rather, significantly, the owner did it for us – driveway service – and we set off on the long drive. After a while I noticed that the fuel gauge was no longer going down, and then, surprisingly it commenced ascending slowly. As in those days we always carried a spare can of fuel in the boot, I wasn't too concerned when we ran out at a likely distance covered. But I was concerned when only a gallon or so would go into the tank. When I inspected it, it had collapsed into a crumpled miniature of its former self. The old man at our service station had replaced the wrong filler cap, with an unvented one presumably as used in supercharged engines, and it had fitted, the atmospheric pressure collapsing the tank as the mechanical pump slowly extracted the fuel. We had to keep on stopping very 50 or so miles to top up, leaving the cap on loosely for air to enter. After the uneventfully successful 'termination' in London (a psychiatrist present deliberately made Judy cry, so that there was some evidence that she was indeed distressed), we slowly returned home, stopping at the garage to find indeed that the caps had been switched. I then had an idea; if atmospheric pressure had collapsed the tank, we should be able to re-inflate it on the airline. Judy and the owner took cover, I wrapped the airline nozzle with a rag to make a seal of sorts, and successfully re-inflated the tank with a series of metallic popping sounds. Afterwards, although thankfully leak-free, it never had quite its original capacity. The whole bizarre event reminds me of another, when we bought a nearly-new Land Rover and whenever we descended a steep hill the oil gauge showed low levels of lubricant, even though the dipstick showed full. Under warranty, the garage performed a number of expensive tests and replacements, but the problem obstinately persisted. In desperation, I said to the garage folk that the problem must be the dipstick – the wrong one. This was decried, but fortunately there another vehicle, the same model, so I swapped dipsticks – and found that indeed someone, some time, had replaced ours with the wrong one for some reason. Who was it who said that when all but one explanations have been tested and found wanting, the remaining one, no matter how unlikely, must be accepted?

I shall very shortly come to the serious side of my doctorate, what I actually did, why, and what I found – and the associated triumph and glory of having my very first paper published in that respected journal, *Nature*.

12

THE GOLDEN ROAD, OR A SHOT IN THE DARK

Mathematicians extol the beauty of an equation that simply and economically captures otherwise complex phenomena; theories may be elegant when they meet William of Ockham's demands of simplicity. There is an emotional quality and satisfaction in good science that is every bit as inspirational as good literature and art – and, dare one say, perhaps even some forms of religious ecstasy. Creativity in the arts and the sciences, if not maybe in religion, has many commonalities, be they its nurturing, flowering or realisation, or the associated subjective states and emotions.

It is 50 years since C. P. Snow, baron, novelist and scientist, wrote on the Two Cultures, Science and Literature-cum-Religion. (Interesting that he, too, included religion, although as an awkward adjunct to literature.) Both are intensely human pursuits, with all the subjectivity and personal investment of the human condition. Sympathetic non-scientists like to appeal to the ideal of an objective universality in the goals of science – hypothesis formation, observations, empirical testing and theory building. But what we believe, see and ultimately conclude are as much influenced by our personal, emotional and historical baggage, as by an ever-receding 'objective reality', of the sort envisaged 2,500 years ago by Plato, in his famous simile of the cave, and as reflected in the Fitzgerald version of *The Rubaiyat of Omar Khayam:*

> For in and out, above, about, below,
> 'tis naught but a magic picture show
> played in a box whose candle is the sun,
> round which we phantom figures come and go.

It is also 50 years since I played the part of a beggar in my school's production of James Elroy Flecker's *Hassan, or The Golden Journey to Samarkand* (1913). It was set by this, the last of the 'Parnassian' poets, in the Baghdad, capital of Harun al-Rashid, of the late eighth century AD. This period was the apogee of the political power of the Abbasid caliphate, a time of peace and a burgeoning of the arts and sciences before the successive waves of destruction by Turkemans, Mongols and various nomadic pastoralist hordes, to say nothing of current events:

> Have we not Indian carpets, dark as wine,
> turbans and sashes, gowns and bows and veils,
> and broideries of intricate design,
> and printed hangings in enormous bales?
> We have rose-candy, we have spikenard,
> mastic and terebinth, oil and spice,
> and such sweet jams meticulously jarred
> as God's own prophet eats in paradise.
> And we have manuscripts in peacock styles
> by Ali of Damascus, we have swords
> engraved with storks and crocodiles,
> and heavy-beaten necklaces for lords.

And this was the Baghdad, under the Abbasids, which inherited, preserved, translated and handed on the science, mathematics and literature of the Greeks, Romans, Indians and Chinese. It also added its own theoretical and technical contributions in medicine, biology, agriculture, mathematics, astronomy, optics, geography, geology, meteorology, physics, mechanics, chemistry – and of course, the pseudo-sciences of astrology and alchemy, itself an Arabic word.

It was coincidence that first introduced me to the mystical magic of the East, although seen through the eyes of Flecker, a Western poet. Fitzgerald's (1859) translation of the *Rubaiyat* fed my nascent romanticism:

> Awake! for morning in the bowl of night
> has flung the stone that puts the stars to flight:
> and Lo! the Hunter of the East has caught
> the Sultan's turret in a noose of light.

Ten years on and more than 50 years ago, during two successive summers and in two very second-hand Land Rovers, with five other like-minded postgraduate expeditioners, I finally set off for those fabled cities of Iraq and Persia, shortly before pointless and internecine conflict ravaged both countries. The 1960s were a golden period for the young; there was a brief window of relative prosperity and stability, when vehicles, medicine and communications had achieved a reliability not always matched today, and countries were accessible which have recently become decidedly off-limits.

In two Grand Tours in the Victorian tradition, we crossed in our Land Rovers most of Communist Eastern Europe, several Soviet Asian republics, the USSR,

Turkey, Syria, Iraq, Iran, the Lebanon, Jordan, Egypt, Libya, Algeria and Tunisia, along with deserts in North Africa, Syria and Iraq, and Iran. Our primary aim was to explore archaeological sites, in the T. E. Lawrence and Gertrude Bell tradition, and we slept rough every night around the vehicle from which we hung our mosquito nets, and suffered numerous breakdowns which we fixed ourselves, using the complete set of spares which we carried, as in those days one could hire, on a use or return basis, such kits. I had the requisite mechanical knowledge practically to rebuild the engine and suspension of the sturdy, Lego-like vehicle which is the classic Land Rover. One of our number, always based in London, had the job of arranging all our visas, and another wrote to food companies to sponsor us with packaged supplies.

An unexpected contribution of enormous value proved to be the girls' tampons, requisitioned to separate containers of fuel and water from mutual abrasion when the going got rough; a big 'thank you girls', although sadly you are tampon-wielding girls no longer. Your sacrifice, although resented at the time, was indeed invaluable. The tampons were as if designed for the job, down even to their terminal tags whereby to secure them in place. In similar fashion, we designed an 'automatic washing machine', from a wide-mouthed container containing water, washing powder, and two smooth round stones; the vehicle's motion did the rest.

Following Xenophon's precept, which as general and classical Greek historian, he recorded in his *Anabasis*, the march, in 401–399 BC, of his 10,000 back from Cunaxa in Asia to Greece, we always sought to camp the night atop a hill. For Xenophon, these were typically breast-shaped (mastoi) hills, often likely of volcanic origin, giving all-round views as from a defensive position. One night, in disputed Kurdish territory, we were fired on by what we believed to be separatists. We sent the three girl members of the expedition down to swim for safety in the warm hypersaline volcanic soda lake adjacent to our refuge. There followed an agonising period, during which one of our party, Pete, armed only with a rusty First World War bayonet from his grandfather's wartime souvenirs, and which we used as a general-purpose tool, got close enough to the 'enemy' to be able to identify himself, without, fortunately, being shot on the spot – an extraordinarily brave action. It transpired that they were young Turkish army recruits, sent to avenge a recent massacre of their number, and as scared as we were. I shall never forget the bitter taste of fear that affected us all that night. On another occasion, crossing the Syrian-Iraqi desert from Damascus to Baghdad, initially following a line of indistinct marker poles which soon gave out in a dusty wilderness, we adopted a compass course, and with relief sighted a low hill on the flat horizon, roughly corresponding to where on our pencil-drawn 'mud map' a place labelled as Jebel el Tanf should lie. We were mightily relieved – Jebel means hill, or mountain, and there was only one on the horizon. On that crossing we were stopped at a well by a local tribesman, who wanted us to carry with us to Baghdad the corpse of his just-dead wife. In North Africa, sighting a salt lake in the distance, we drove down to it, and decided to continue onwards to cut off a section of our journey – to find we had stumbled into a Second World War battlefield from 20 years ago, strewn with the rusting hulks of burnt-out vehicles; with fear of mines foremost in our minds, all but one of us (the driver) followed in the vehicle's wheel marks in the sand, so that we should not all be blown up – a real hazard in that region, we were later to learn.

On another occasion, probably then among the first Westerners to travel the Georgian Military Highway, we were arrested in the Russian Caucasus for illegal camping, waking one morning to find ourselves surrounded by military vehicles. After eventually establishing friendly relationships, we were taken for a ride in a Russian armoured personnel carrier, while soldiers searched our cargo. It was the box of putrefying snails, with their appalling smell, and collected for the zoologist doctoral supervisor of one of the girls, which secured our release. When camped on the shores of the Caspian, we all contracted a nasty skin infection, which I successfully treated with penicillin tablets ground up into one of the girl's face cream. It worked, and later, when talking to a Russian doctor, I told her the story, she asked us for any left-over penicillin, as the people's paradise apparently had little at their disposal.

An amusing incident was our encountering a broken-down British personnel carrier somewhere near El Alamein (or was it Tobruk, or Benghazi – I forget which of the, then British, military bases it was in Libya); we towed it back to base, and were in due course greeted by the Commanding Officer, with a Terry Thomas moustache and diction straight out of a movie parody. We were 'splendid fellows, who had put on a damn fine show'; when the phone went, he responded with, 'I say, you really have got your knickers twisted, old chap, quite in a knot.' We were then sent to the NAAFI and told to eat as much as we liked (we did!), while the transport section serviced our old Land Rover – basically the same model as then in use in the British forces. They also gave us some old copies of *Playboy*, which with its high-quality gloss paper made excellent material for shims (distance pieces) when, after replacing a worn wheel bearing, I had to adjust the clearance in one of the axles. I don't know what the eventual purchaser might have thought of it when we eventually sold the vehicle back in the UK. However, we did have a very lucky escape at the Dover customs; we had bought leather goods in Egypt, and, fearing heavy duties, had put them in polythene bags at the back of the luggage area, having poured some sticky treacle over the bags to discourage manual investigation. It very fortunately worked, as later on our final unloading I found someone had also secreted there, and totally forgotten, a bag of marijuana, purchased in Libya – which could have earned us all jail sentences.

On another occasion, arriving in Tehran, we perhaps foolishly held a mock auction in the main square of our rather pointless stock of lemonade powder; we mixed up free drink samples to hand out. Then a policeman arrived, to our consternation. However, when it became clear what we were doing, and we had given him some, he took two of us to the main brothel, where he said there would be good custom as it was 'very hot work'. The building was of an unprepossessing and unadorned concrete, inside and out, and the madam little better, but maybe the 'staff' did not need unnecessary frills. We never found out, but sold the lot.

We often wondered why the long, black, loose-fitting and generally unisex djellaba, as worn by the Bedouin, was coloured black; surely it attracted the heat? Some years later I read in *Nature* that an intrepid English doctor had asked the same question, and somehow persuaded tribesmen to carry thermometers attached to their nether regions, and recorded temperatures inside and out; it seemed that the apparel acted like a cooling tower, funneling a draught up over the body and out – a bit like the very ancient house 'cooling towers' we saw in Iran – forms of simple air conditioning. (*Nature* also once reported that someone had measured increases in the rate of male beard growth in polar expeditioners as a function of how soon they expected to be returning on leave to the remembered and longed-for arms and charms of wives and girlfriends.)

In our travels we were generally treated with amazing hospitality in the Eastern tradition. We fell under the spell of the desert – which eventually brought me to Australia, although that is another story. I shall never forget cresting a series of dunes at a golden sunset and seeing spread out in a basin the oasis of Palmyra, in the wastes between Damascus and Baghdad, with its groves of palms and the perfectly-preserved ruins (also, alas no longer intact) in the classical Graeco-Roman style, of Queen Zenobia's fabled city.

> Away, for we are ready to a man,
> our camels sniff the evening and are glad;
> lead on, O master of the caravan,
> lead on, O merchant princes of Baghdad!
> Sweet to ride forth at evening from the wells,
> when shadows pass gigantic on the sand,
> and softly, through the silence, beat the bells
> along the Golden Road to Samarkand.

Palmyra became the Baghdad of my imagination, as even before the days of Saddam Hussein the reality of Baghdad was sadly disappointing – a sorry mixture of the tawdry and the modern, with none of the charm or history of, say, Turkish Istanbul. Similarly, Egyptian Alexandria never for me even remotely approached Lawrence Durrell's city of enchantment. But on our journey, Palmyra was followed by Jordanian Petra, the nineteenth-century poet John Burgon's 'rose-red city, half as old as time', carved, literally, by the Edomites and Nabateans more than 2,000 years ago in Wadi Musa, out of the living rock deep in the desert mountains. Visited constantly now by tour buses, in 1965, at the time of our visit, it was deserted, except for a solitary goat-herd and his flock. In exalted mood we explored its every hidden nook from our base in an empty rock-cut tomb. Palmyra and Petra were followed by the virtually-intact Roman port of Leptis Magna on the Libyan coast, and the following year by Persepolis in the Iranian Dasht-i Marv. Built by the Persians as a capital during the Achaemenid dynasty by Kings Cyrus and Xerxes, in the fifth century BC, it was destroyed by fire a couple of centuries later by the Greek adventurer (and vandal) Alexander the Great. The ruins are imposing, and the perfectly-preserved carved panels on the grand ceremonial stairway are both magnificent and of immense historical value, telling of the nature of the peoples subject to the King of Kings.

These historical sites were to me iconic emotional experiences to rank with the Inca ruins of Machu Picchu, perched high above the Peruvian rainforest in a loop of the River Urubamba. Should we neglect or ignore the emotional drive that leads as much to archaeological exploration, interpretation and understanding, as to the lightning progress currently being made in my own research field, the neurosciences, in our attempts to understand that most complex of all known structures, the human brain?

> We are the pilgrims, Master, we shall go
> always a little further: it may be
> beyond that last blue mountain barred with snow,
> across that angry or that glimmering sea.
> We travel not for trafficking alone,
> by hotter breaths our fiery hearts are fanned;
> for lust of knowing what shall not be known
> we take the Golden Road to Samarkand.

What a splendid metaphor, from Flecker's pen, for the practice of science and the scientific method. Why then, when the West's apparent supremacy in technology, innovation and general living standards so clearly derives from the application of scientific principles, is science so much under attack from the political left and right, from intellectuals and anti-intellectuals, from the media and angry protesters and activists, from Bible-bashers and New Age gurus? Is it because we are unwilling to admit to the powerful forces of personal subjectivity and pure chance in asking certain questions, in the unfolding of discovery and in the construction of explanatory theory? Is it because as scientists we are somehow ashamed of the all-too-human side of our work, with aspects both 'good' (curiosity, excitement in the search, pleasure at discovery) and 'bad' (power, fame and self-advancement)? Are superstition, magical processes and blind faith the only alternatives to incomplete understanding for those of low scientific literacy? Is science somehow demeaning of humanity, dehumanising even? It can never, of course, disprove God's existence, but an enhanced understanding of our own puny survival in a vast, uncaring and ultimately pointless universe surely provides its own inspiration. And poetry and the arts provide other such sources. What price the two cultures? They are beyond price. To cite Aristotle over 2,000 years ago, '*Ho anexetastos bios ou biotos anthropo*', 'A life without enquiry is not worth the candle.

13

EYES, A WINDOW TO YOUR THOUGHTS

> *Sumuntur duo cylindri tenues, eadem crassitidine, alter albus, alter vero non, et ante oculum ponuntur, iter ut albus ab eo aliquantum absit; qui autem albus non est, oculo quam proximus sit, ita ut etiam contingat faciem.*
>
> Take two thin cylinders of the same thickness, one white, one not; place them before the eye so that the white one is some distance from the eye, while the non-white one is put as close as possible to the eye, so that it may even touch the face.
>
> When the cylinders we use are narrower (than the pupil) of the eye, the cylinder nearer the eye will be surrounded by it, and the white one seen by it; if they are much narrower, the whole, if less so, parts of the white cylinder will be seen on either side of the cylinder nearer the eye.
>
> With these cylinders, if well chosen, the one will just cover the other, with nothing to spare.
>
> In this way, then, the value equivalent to the thickness of the cylinders having this relationship to each other, certainly is no less than that of the (pupil of the) eye.

These words were written by the famous engineer, polymath and empirical scientist Archimedes of Syracuse, born 287 BC, in his work *Psammites/Arenarius/The Sand Reckoner*, when demonstrating how best to represent enormous numbers – in this case the (hypothetical) number of grains of sand in the cosmos. The abstract above is probably the very first, and very elegant, geometric way of determining pupillary diameter, and in fact when I published my PhD research and very first scientific paper, in the respected science journal, *Nature*, in 1967, hardly anything else had been done on the topic of pupillary dilation until then.

A, who was a compliant and rather credulous female cousin of my age, like me, had to attend regular family gatherings at Grandma's, to celebrate Christmas and similar festivities. The early 1950s coincided with renewed public interest in the lie detector, which recorded observable and measurable changes in such physiological variables as heart rate, blood pressure and skin conductance, although such newsworthy scientific concepts were not in A's normal ambit. It had not escaped my early-adolescent notice that monitoring her pulse, with my fingers lightly resting upon her wrist while asking provocative personal questions, would be an interesting empirical diversion while at the same time impressing her on my apparent omniscience. I was not wrong. The crude procedure was surprisingly robust, A was indeed deeply impressed by my seeming ability to tell whether or not she was telling the truth, and the technique lent itself to possibly developing a closer personal acquaintance, which was aided by the heavy Victorian drapes of Grandma's 'best room'. This room, with its dark uncomfortable furniture, was normally kept under dust sheets, to be removed only on very special occasions. Family get-togethers did not normally qualify, unless there was a christening, marriage or death, so we could safely escape there to do our 'research'. I even noticed that A's pupils also fluctuated in size at certain questions, especially when she blushed, both additionally useful and rewarding proxies (although I did not then know the term) for unease. The only immediate consequence of this Christmas tryst was the apparent loss of a tassel, supposedly attached to an upholstered sofa as beloved by the Victorians, a loss for which we were afterwards blamed, most unfairly – we were occupied in far more interesting matters than fabric tassels, after all – something which still rankles on recall.

Many years later I remembered those clandestine investigations, when A was more or less happily married, and I, although equally happily unmarried, was rather desperately trying to develop a PhD project in the broad area of physiological psychology. Cognitive processes were just emerging from the Behaviourist embargo on anything which could not be directly observed, and words like stress, arousal, attention and information processing were belatedly acquiring a modicum of respectability.

Just as I was recalling those pseudo-scientific trysts behind the drapes, and the particularly striking changes in the sizes of A's pupils at certain leading questions, I also fortuitously happened upon a copy of *Scientific American* to which a colleague subscribed – and in it there was an article by one Eckart Hess. He described his pupillometric measures of the autonomic correlates of people's aesthetic responses – like or dislike – to various patterns, using a special eye-camera. It essentially consisted of a Bolex ciné fitted with special lenses, drive and infra-red film. The eye was filmed at a few frames per second under infra-red illumination. The resultant film of hundreds of images was then projected and the pupil diameter hand-measured with a ruler. There was little automation in research in those days.

Why should pupillometry be of interest? The pupils are reciprocally innervated by the autonomic nervous system, contraction (myosis) being under parasympathetic control, and mydriasis, dilation (or 'dilatation', as preferred by Americans, who also seem to have a similar pleonastic predilection for 'transportation' over 'transport'), under sympathetic influences. They might therefore sensitively and accessibly reflect changing balances in arousal, stress, and processing load – a veritable window into the soul, mind, brain – of which the eyes are indeed external outgrowths.

At this point, a series of very fortunate coincidences intervened on my behalf, without any one of which I would not now be penning these words, or probably living in Australia, or maybe even enjoying the fruits of a lifetime of rewarding scientific research. The first coincidence was that in the Department's workshop a new Bolex was lying, unused. The second was that a girl I knew had a father who was an accomplished amateur photographer with rare infra-red experience. These two circumstances motivated me to seek the next sine-qua-non, a still, dark place where I could set up, undisturbed, a lab for filming my subjects' eyeballs in absolute quiet.

The Department had just taken over from the adjacent German Department an old Victorian building – where, incidentally, my girlfriend with the photographic father had worked. At the back, stairs descended below ground level, to a door fastened with a rusty padlock that clearly had not been opened for decades. Partly out of curiosity, I drilled off the lock and found a cellar, complete with a stone slab raised on a pedestal where meat and other perishables had in the nineteenth century been kept cold and away from rodent interest. There were also stacks of dusty, cobwebby old examination papers dating from the early 1900s. A perfect place for a lab. Brashly, and without consulting anyone, I arranged with the Maintenance Department to remove all those old documents – probably by now precious archival material! – and ran power lines down from the room above, which was about to become the new Departmental General Office.

The fourth indispensable coincidence was the presence in the workshop of an elderly Yorkshireman, slow and suspicious until he got to know you, and maybe eventually even came to approve of you. In my case he did, and took me under what turned out to be a rather amazing wing. Also a very keen and knowledgeable amateur photographer, he helped me experiment with a range of rare chemicals, which we mixed and diluted in old cordial bottles, and eventually came up with a special, prolonged, dilute-development procedure which raised the effective film sensitivity to really rather phenomenal levels by any standards. I bought a crude but indestructible and totally indispensable Russian ciné developing tank which accepted on its coil 33 feet of film. I then found a way of doubling its capacity by loading it, in the obligatory total darkness, with twice that amount by doubling over the exposed film, back-to-back, emulsion side out. As in the Minotaur's labyrinth, I followed Ariadne's precepts and employed string guides to orient me to reach for key items for my recipe for developing and fixing. This process took many hours on each occasion, with continuous agitation and frequent changes of chemicals. We even published an account of our process in a radiology journal, as it could greatly reduce exposure times in potentially hazardous X-radiography in the days just before new CT-scan procedures made it all obsolete.

Finally, I still had many of the remains of my childhood Meccano sets, and there was an Aladdin's cave of a War Surplus store in town, a real Boy's-Own delight.

From a growing pile of lenses, rods, connectors, electric motors and assorted nuts and bolts – many still in my own workshop to this day – I built a complete recording and projection system. Pupils, greatly magnified, of eyes of all shapes and sizes – although brown, like those of my then long-suffering fiancée gave the best contrast – were projected onto graph paper, a far better method than laboriously measuring by ruler. I pulled my 66-ft-long strips of developed film through my Meccano film guides, frame by frame, laboriously reading off and recording the changing pupillary diameters. The eyes were illuminated at a very low level as the participants viewed a back-projection screen (no computer monitors in those days) upon which I presented prepared slides detailing a variety of tasks or problems. Also recorded on the film was the illumination of several tiny event-marker lights, which told me about the various stages reached by the subjects at that point in the various cognitive tasks.

My parents happened to be visiting when I was ready to run some test participants. When Mother was comfortably (?) in place, and the makeshift apparatus commenced running, I casually mentioned that afterwards we would be lunching with Judy (of whom she had never even heard), and that we were to marry in the summer. Mother's dilatory response was the biggest I ever recorded.

At night, after a successful experimental run filming the eye of a co-operative participant, I would develop the film, preparatory to doing the laborious measurements and data recording the next day. In those non-automated days there was the undoubted advantage that at all times and at every stage of an experiment you were very close indeed to the data, and knew immediately if something might be amiss, and so could if necessary initiate corrective action. This situation probably held true for many branches of empirical investigation and for many scientific disciplines, and in these days of high speed computers it is something which we have lost, and can ignore potentially at our peril. Was it not one of the recent Mars Landers that was lost when someone forgot to convert between imperial and metric measures? Because I always like to have data manually checked to see if a new procedure is working correctly, I once noticed that the recording computer was regularly coming up with the same series of repeating numbers in a particular calculation – which reflected a feature of its own cyclical processing operations, rather than our actual data.

The fun part of research, then and now, was dreaming up interesting and novel experimental paradigms and procedures, and issues and questions which no-one until then had thought about in the context of human information processing and autonomic arousal. The eye, or more correctly the pupil, was in truth a window onto the soul – or, rather the brain, of which it is of course a direct extension. I learnt at all times to carry a notebook to record ideas – theoretical, new approaches, new ways of analysing data, new interpretations of findings. I still do, and beside the bed lies a ballpoint pen with a tiny light at its tip, a novelty item given to me one Christmas by a member of the family for fun, never anticipating how extremely useful I would find it.

Fortunately, I also learnt a great deal during this PhD period, over 50 years ago, about the physiological correlates of arousal and information processing, and how various task requirements, background light intensities, drug states and levels and response modes or requirements modulate autonomic indices. Nowadays there are no such war-surplus stores, and departmental workshop facilities have either disappeared or have been contracted out to indifferent outside organisations operating for profit rather than to support the researcher at every stage. Everything is automated, and so we have lost a lot of 'ecological validity' – we have lost realism and entered an artificial world ruled by the twin demands of speed and convenience. We have also lost what should still be a key element of a graduate student's education – getting your hands dirty in building your very own apparatus, which you know and understand at every stage of its use.

And another moral? Chance can play an enormous role in scientific investigations, and opportunities should be grasped whenever they appear. It was the great French biologist Louis Pasteur in the mid-to-late nineteenth century who observed that chance favours the prepared mind. It is not just the Boy Scout whose motto should always be 'Be prepared!'

Oh – and I wonder if A still remembers, or is still around to do so, the dark room with the Victorian drapes?

14

AOTEAROA

A year in the land of the long white cloud

In the golden 1960s, the world was one's oyster. Where next to head when the PhD was wrapped up? Africa? Makerere (now Uganda) still was highly regarded, and Unity's legacy was a lust for African adventures; or maybe Canada, or the United States? I never even thought of New Zealand until I chanced upon an ad for the University of Otago deep down in remote South Island – but in fact it was New Zealand's best, and is still a world ranker. Interviews were held in the High Commission offices in London, a city with which after a year there I was fairly familiar. I took the unusual (in those days) step of checking up on the Head of Department's credentials, research interests and publications (before Google, there was a very useful printed compendium, published annually). I soon found myself interviewing *him*, always a profitable move. The position was offered, Judy and I celebrated with apple crumble and custard at the local pub, for which it then was famous – we always resorted to the East End for this sweet, whenever rejoicing or seeking solace – and I went into top gear writing up my thesis. My supervisor and Head of Department, a nice, busy and vague gentleman of the old Cambridge school, knew little and frankly cared even less about what I had been doing, as long as I kept out from under his feet – how very different from today's graduate supervision which manages every stage of the student's progress, often, I fear, stultifying initiative. After checking some recently successful Sheffield theses for format, I asked the Professor's secretary to type it up for me (nowadays secretaries are anyway an extinct breed – you do your own typing unless very senior, and therefore almost certainly a keyboard incompetent), and duly presented him with a copy. 'Oh, a thesis, how VERY interesting' was his initial comment, 'What is it all about?' I patiently told him, and how to my immense chagrin, a very, very recent paper in the journal *Science*, after its rival *Nature*, the world's second most prestigious journal, had stolen my thunder. He then made one of the two most useful suggestions he, or indeed anyone else, could ever have made: 'Oh, that's no problem, send something to *Nature*.' I did, and it, my very first paper, was duly accepted, and was published by the world's top journal after all, to my surprise and delight. Pretty good for anyone, let alone a graduate student just starting off in the research rat race! His second suggestion was that he would ask a friend of his to act as external examiner in a viva voce examination; the internal examiner was to be the departmental statistician who had come on my most recent archaeological expedition by Land Rover – the only academic among a mob of students. That just left the need to pack up our meagre possessions, and to arrange a flight to New Zealand, paid for by the University of Otago. My supervisor's final comment, on learning my destination, was an aghast 'New Zealand! That's just academic suicide!' from a man, nice as he was, whose academic horizons barely stretched beyond Oxbridge. I just had to prove him wrong, and I did.

Although booked to fly to New Zealand, we were allowed to ship a standard tea-chest of personal and domestic possessions, and, unbelievably, our nearly-new, midnight-blue VW Beetle 1500. Most cars in New Zealand, which financially functioned at the time on a near-wartime level of economy, were old or very old British models; a new car was almost out of reach, being subject to 60 per cent import dues (if British, or assembled there), or 120 per cent if continental. However, resale values were considerably, but not correspondingly, higher. We believed ours to have been in the former category. Tax was also levied on the distance the car had travelled, and as ours had almost attained a critical milestone (literally), I jacked it up, started the motor, put it into gear, and let the counter – count! Everything was booked to sail on a ship of (I think) the Union-Castle line, but a foul-up resulted (most fortunately, as it turned out), in missing the boat (again literally). The ship sailed without our stuff, the Six-Day War broke out, and ships, including what was to have been ours, were stuck in the Suez Canal for years, with no insurance redress as nothing was deemed missing. Our beloved Beetle, as deck cargo, would have quietly rusted into dissolution. That said, a nasty shock awaited us on arrival in New Zealand; despite papers to the contrary, an officious official, after spending hours nosing beneath Beetle, emerged to announce triumphantly that he had at last found evidence that the car was one of a rare batch, much prized in Britain because of better Teutonic workmanship, to have been assembled you-know-where. We had to raise a crippling loan, on the spot, to release our wheels.

Judy had never flown before; I had once, in a small plane, when invited to address industrialists in Germany, with their sights on my pupillometric system as a possible device to assess customer interest. The visit was chiefly memorable for the Germanic formality of address: I instantaneously became an impressive 'Herr Professor Doctor Bradshaw'; I was treated to an excellent meal, my expenses met, and a valuable gift 'for my dear new wife', was presented with much pomp and circumstance. The journey east, over the Alps, in a new Boeing 707 jetliner, in late summer 1967, was literally an eye-opener.

We had tailored our itinerary by air to be as adventurous as possible, stopping off briefly in Tehran, which a year previously I had visited by Land Rover while passing through Persia. Thence, the only passengers apart from a mob of sheep with feet tied together, we boarded an Ariana Afghan Airways Second World War DC3, unpressurised, canvas deck-chair seats … At one point, navigating it seemed by sight and therefore flying low between the massive mountains of the Hindu Kush, cloud resulted in our getting lost, as we seemed to be flying in circles, passing and repassing an unusually memorable landmark. Kabul, then untouched by the usual, interminable tribal and religious quarrels, was an exotic eye-opener for Judy, particularly so since town was full with the *Loya Jirga*, the annual get-together of the various tribes and factions. Result: our pre-booked room in the only presentable hotel had been given to someone else who presumably beat our deposit. Solution: the manager was suffering from an unpleasant facial infection, which I knew antibiotics would fix, and I offered him a course from our travelling stock. Amazing, as Trump would say – a very superior room miraculously appeared; presumably someone else lost their booking. The rest of the journey, although fascinating, was largely uneventful. We spent some time in the Punjab (Amritsar), Delhi, Fatehpur Sikri (out in the desert in Uttar Pradesh, the Mughal emperor Akbar's old capital), and the Taj Mahal, all reached by train, Thailand (where we explored the *klongs*, and hired a car to go north), and Singapore.

After a brief stop in Darwin, then a small town largely, it seemed, of corrugated iron buildings in those pre-cyclone days, our flight continued over the seemingly endless plains, sand dunes and gibber country of the great Australian deserts, veined by grey-green creek lines and watered by occasional flooding rains, over chains of ancient mountains eroded down to crumbling stumps, crimson and fractured by years beyond count, in this the world's oldest and driest continent. I vowed that we would one day return and explore it by four-wheel drive. Although we did not know it at the time, within a year it was to be ours to wander in, wonder at, enjoy, and make our home.

Dunedin, on the edge of the green Otago plains, looked from the air depressingly like any small English town, until in the distance we saw the wondrous, snow-capped, jagged peaks of the New Zealand Alps, with beyond the remote rainforest fastness of the West Coast, with its unique botany and names such as Cannibal Creek, and Mounts Aspiring, Misery and Despair, and then the equally evocative Fjord Country, with Dusky and Doubtful Sounds reflecting the windjammer voyages of exploration, really not so very long ago.

Dunedin, named by Scottish immigrants 100 years ago after Edinburgh (both names signifying the fortified settlement of 'Eidyn'), was reminiscent of a British early-post-war town of medium size, with still a very-present feel of Scottish heritage. Shops had limited stock, 'until the ship comes in', and this was particularly true of most kinds of produce, particularly manufactured. And down where the ships did come in, it felt, not unpleasingly, rather like the ends of the world, with discharging vessels with names of origin on their sterns signifying distant and more familiar horizons, and the wider world beyond. In the city centre, The Octagon, was the Star Fountain, a complicated structure with presumably programmable modes of playing, which were announced regularly in the newspapers. Of an evening, one wandered down to watch.

Our rental home, alarmingly converted from what once had been a hen hotel, where chooks (as is the common Antipodean parlance) used to be raised, although now extended and suitably modified for human habitation upstairs, perhaps not too surprisingly turned out also to have rodent lodgers already in residence. Nocturnal noises in wall cavities and roof spaces kept us awake at night, and rat traps set therein were simply dragged away. But until we actually caught one as proof of infestation, the neighbours simply parroted 'It's only possums.' When the exterminators were brought in, they positioned me on the roof with a .22 rifle, to 'pot' refugees emerging from the poison gas released below, and which would also escape around my own feet. It also seemed a thoroughly bad idea to use a gun when on a flimsy 'tin' roof, so fortunately that particular scheme was dropped, and we camped for a few days in the garden with our hiking tent, until the place was deemed safe to enter – and of course decomposition of the corpses then commenced.

The garden itself turned out to be another problem; said to have won numerous horticultural prizes for roses and other blooms, our contract stipulated that it must be kept pristine, free of weeds and in show condition. This task clearly required some lateral thought. So from a timber-mill just upstream of a delightful little rivulet which meandered enticingly through our property (itself, although we did not know it, soon to be our next burden), we bought several dozen sacks of sawdust, to smother all exposed areas where weeds might grow. Unfortunately, this turned out to be a delightful playground for the local birdlife, in particular blackbirds, immigrants like ourselves, and generally unwelcome. They happily dug little pits everywhere, looking for whatever edibles might be concealed, and the weeds rapidly followed aplenty. Too late we realised what a bad idea it had been.

Then, on April 10, 1968, came ex-tropical Cyclone Giselle, a very rare and extremely severe event, in fact, the worst disaster in New Zealand's history on record. It sank the inter-island ferry *Wahine* in Wellington Harbour, with 53 of the 734 people on board drowning. Flooding was enormous, our idyllic little brook rose very rapidly in the middle of the night, and after having earlier sand-bagged the front door, we had to rapidly climb out of the lower-floor windows, as we could hear the roar of boulders washing down the big river a few hundred metres away on the other side of the valley, and escape before the bridges went. We got out in our VW Beetle just in time, and to the later delight of the local press, 'This newly arrived English couple took refuge from the elements in our new Olympic-size swimming pool.' We had nowhere else to go! Insurance covered the flood damage to the lower half (the bath therein contained several refugee crayfish among the sewage and detritus), and all vestiges of the prize-winning garden, along with the problematic sawdust, vanished downstream.

We loved our New Zealand stay, and most weekends and all holidays we took off camping; it was after all a botanist's delight, with its rare exotica, and we travelled on foot and by car almost everywhere in South Island, revelling in the drama of the southern Alps and their snowy, jagged, glaciated fastness, the sombre, barren majesty of Central Otago, and the vast, tawny-brown sweep of the Mackenzie Country in the rain-shadow of the Southern Alps, to say nothing of the Fjord

Country, the western rainforests, and their rare, exotic parrots, in particular the Kea, Kaka and Kakapo. Then there was the wild coastline south of the Otago peninsula, itself home at its tip to breeding albatross. I was invited to participate in a rescue dig before the building of a controversial aluminium smelter at Bluff, South Island's most southerly town, and where with a (then) red beard and a red shirt made by my mother, I was shunned as a communist. There I unearthed some beautiful Maori hand axes, and lots of Moa bones, giant birds like scaled-up ostrich, upon which they had feasted centuries ago, so hastening their extinction. Afterwards, we were invited to come out on one of the pilot boats that escorted the meat ships arriving at and departing from Bluff; we asked why they displayed no lights, and were told there was no need. Two weeks after, we heard that one of the pilot boats had been cut in two by a meat ship, with loss of all on board.

Then, one day, the Department was visited by a couple of speakers from Australia, dressed alike in dirty white raincoats, and one wearing the tie of the Brigade of Guards, recognisable as it was near identical to that of my old school, just when we had a camping trip planned. I therefore nearly didn't attend the talk, but for some reason felt I should, a decision which was to change our lives. I attended the talk, I must have asked a sensible question, I was offered a job at Australia's newest University, Monash, established with a biomedical and technological emphasis, and then (but no longer with the spread of urban sprawl) on Melbourne's outskirts. Indeed, it was built partly on the site of what according to the maps of the day was an 'epileptic colony', but which for a long time Judy for some reason insisted was a leper colony. We were very happy in our New Zealand idyll, but the wool clip prices were at record lows, funds and funding were badly stretched, staff were leaving in a brain drain, and only one year out of graduate school, without any postdoc experience, I was being invited to consider assuming the role of Head of Department; shades of the ICI debacle. Belatedly (I nearly missed the boat, as it were) and reluctantly I accepted. A boat passage was indeed booked, 1st class, just because we had some furniture, in fact, just a single woodworm-eaten cut-down bed for which we had paid $5 in an auction room; otherwise it would have been a far less interesting boat trip, Economy Class.

We had seen nothing of North Island, so we sent ahead to Wellington, whence the ship was to sail, a cabin trunk of camping gear, rented an old green bread van to travel and sleep in, and set off on our travels for three weeks. Apart from the beauties of Lake Waikaremoana, with its semi-tropical rainforest and a still active Maori tradition, and the fascinating volcanic pools and springs of Rotorua, to say nothing about the 'world famous blue pool' (I disturbed a man at midnight 'topping up' the 'wondrous natural colour' with a sack of copper sulphate), we were glad that we had seen so much of lovely South Island, notwithstanding plagues of ferocious sand flies on the Western side. In pouring rain, and on a particularly muddy and slippery earth road, edged with a precipitous ravine, I had to sit as far back as possible to add weight to the driving rear wheels; Judy had to take a steep and very tight corner at speed, and I momentarily stared death in the depths below, before the wheels again found traction. We spent that night in a celebratory motel.

Our ship to Melbourne was the *Angelina Lauro*, a passenger liner of 24,000 tons and built in the 1930s, then becoming a hospital and later a cruise ship, with a chequered history of fires and sinking, the latter while being towed for scrap in 1979. (Parenthetically, I believe that her sister ship, the *Achille Lauro*, might also have caught fire and sunk; if so, the line clearly had its problems, or a good insurance policy.) We shared a table with a young honeymoon couple returning to Australia, who rather shocked us, in our naïveté, by having a bottle of wine with every meal, and very large steaks and eggs every morning for breakfast. Is that what everyone does in Australia, we wondered. On the five-day voyage we were memorably followed by albatross, those wondrous tube-nosed ocean wanderers, rejoicing in their taxonomic name *Procellariformes*, roughly and appropriately translated as Spirits of the Storm. There followed the long journey just off shore of the uninhabited and densely forested East Gippsland coast; it was inspirational, except that Judy seemed to be an unexpectedly bad sailor. But she was pregnant, with our daughter-to-be Catriona. It seemed fitting that our first sighting of *Terra Australis Incognita*, the Unknown South Land as it used to appear on incomplete atlases and globes of old, should have been Point Hicks, so named for the lookout, Lt. Zachary Hicks, aboard Captain James Cook's *Endeavour* in 1770.

In Australia, to summarise the content of the next chapter, our first priority was to find accommodation, although for a few weeks we were put up in university flats built for the purpose. Renting cheaply from academics going overseas proved easy for three years, and a small family legacy enabled us to buy a tiny place out in the country, with no sewerage (septic tank only), no piped water (we collected rainwater off the roof, and 47 years on I still rely thereon), no gas (except bottled), dirt road access … but delightful views that more than compensate. Built as a 'spec-home' by a builder who put it up and then tried to find a buyer, it gave us a lot of trouble since he had got his distances all wrong, and had built across the boundary between two properties, but I won't go into that saga. It survived the devastating Ash Wednesday bush fires which took the houses, and lives, of neighbours, and over the years we modified and enlarged it, installing proper tanks in place of the initial swimming-pool water storage system. Our other priority was a vehicle, and having had VWs, and vans, in the past, and a baby on the way, we bought a new VW Kombi van for off-road camping with the next best vehicle to a four-wheel drive.

Thus began the next half-century of our lives, as Australians, and I was to disprove the dire predictions of my dear old supervisor; there was no academic suicide, not even a long slow death, although at 77 I don't know quite how long that particular ending can be postponed.

15

TERRA AUSTRALIS (NOBIS ADHUC) INCOGNITA

New country – now our next need was indeed accommodation. Our first month was spent initially in a bleak motel on a main highway adjacent to a huge new shopping development under construction, paid for by Monash. There, we had our second wedding anniversary, and Judy celebrated by vomiting (she didn't know she was pregnant, something which of course had explained her unexpected nausea while crossing the Tasman on our old liner). She also cried, in response to Australia's heat, dust and apparently American lifestyle, after the relaxed New Zealand country-town living. Then we moved to the university flats reserved for new appointees and family, and became friends with our neighbours, a friendship which has lasted until today, as we all age together.

Having bought wheels, in the form of the Kombi van, a vehicle next-best to a four-wheel drive, and within which I carpentered a luxurious double bed, beneath which was a large storage space for planned outback exploration, our next challenge was to arrange rather more permanent housing. We had both been used to country living, and feeling unready to commit to something as permanent as house purchase, over the next three years we rented three small properties out in the Dandenong Ranges east of Melbourne, each from academics going overseas for a year on sabbatical leave. By the time we were moving to the third and last of these properties, we had accumulated enough possessions to need seven Kombi-full trips to make the move. Durations of stay at all three were largely uneventful and pleasant, except for a small problem with the 'House with the Cats'; the owners had found homes for all seven of their erstwhile pets, except for one that continued to return, yowling outside all night and making sleep impossible. Even a good hose down from the garden hose proved unsuccessful, so I had resort to a gun (.22) which we were looking after for a friend, who at the time was experiencing certain difficulties with his wife and therefore did not want a firearm around the house. I had no intention of hitting the cat, merely to aim low into the dust and give it a good fright to hasten a departure back to more accommodating pastures. The cat promptly jumped up on to the top of the galvanised rainwater tank (the source of all our water out in the country), and I'll swear gave me a sardonic Cheshire-cat grin, as if it knew I wouldn't dare such a hazardous shot. But it got the message. However, it, or another of its mates, weeks later somehow sneaked into the house, and got locked in while we were away for the day. On return we found it in the bathroom, and it clearly had been relieving itself down the plughole, a remarkably percipient feline. The cats anyway did leave us one more unfortunate legacy; cat fleas, seemingly in millions, emerged from the carpets, to bite us, and our new baby, as proxies for pussy. Just as in New Zealand, we again had to have the house professionally fumigated, but fleas were a better target than the rats across the Tasman. We had now experienced floods and fleas; shortly we were to win the trifecta with fires, bush fires, terrifying, house-destroying bush fires. But that was to be a few years in the future, when by then we owned our own property.

We had by then become very friendly with the owner of the .22, and we all went together on numerous outback camping and photography trips, as he too had purchased a VW Kombi like ours. We often explored the romantic 'billabong' country of creeks, swamps and lakes, abounding in wildlife in the otherwise harsh semi-desert conditions around. Once V, an outstanding bushman from years of malaria patrol around Papua New Guinea, was catching European carp for his cat. Totally naked, covered in the black mud of the creeks, with a native fish-spear over one shoulder and a huge carp over the other, he clambered up on to the bank, disturbing a group of nuns who had set up a table, white cloth, crucifix, candelabra and all, for a retreat. The appalling apparition appearing like Satan made them flee in terror. Some time later, he was visited by his aged father from Czechoslovakia when the Iron Curtain momentarily lifted. Concerned at his son's single state, on return he advertised for blondes, and interviewed some 20 or so, chose one and put her on a plane to Sydney. Initially V refused to meet the plane, until Judy applied pressure, and the arranged 'marriage' proceeded apparently satisfactorily.

When not using his fish spear, V would shoot at the surface of the water to stun what lay below. He once took a young Chinese colleague along, who was so impressed by the technique, that thinking bigger could only be better, he bought a large-bore repeater, almost a machine gun. Peaceful angling waters were for a while disturbed by what sounded like mechanised warfare, until he was taken aside and told: 'It just ain't Aussie, mate.'

Before we came to own our own place in the country, we rented a tiny cottage near the hamlet of Emerald, named after the gemstones that used to be found by fossickers in the local creeks. Its medical needs were 'met' by the (very) old Irish doctor, 'Doc Murphy', whom I first encountered in his professional capacity when I developed a severe allergic reaction to an unknown precipitant, and he called to give me an emergency adrenaline injection. He had a gigantic syringe, which looked as if its usual employment was for administering nostrums to horses. When he charged it, I noticed an equally large air bubble – never the best 'adjuvant' in any injection. When I alerted him to it, he squinted blearily in its direction (his breath also suggested the possibility of a recent 'wee drop of the hard stuff'), and said, probably quite correctly, that he couldn't see it personally – and rammed it home. He then presented me with it, and said it was excellent if you charged it with whisky and injected best steak with it before cooking. I survived to tell this tale, and one other about our dear local doctor, who was in fact in most other respects held in high local esteem. There was a traffic accident outside the house; a pedestrian, possibly also having imbibed recently, was hit by a vehicle while wandering along the narrow, unmade and unlit lane, and the driver had driven off, leaving an unconscious victim lying where he had fallen. We summoned Murphy, who duly arrived, inspected the scene, and commented that as there was broken glass further along the roadway, the offender must have been going in that direction. Pleased with that deduction, he set off further down the road looking for additional clues. I had to go after him to remind him that the person lying on the road was not looking too good, and perhaps, just perhaps, should be attended to first, which he agreed.

The birth of Catriona, not surprisingly, was not without incident. The hospital was in Melbourne, at least an hour's drive away, and Judy one evening in the middle of a bacon and eggs dinner (I clearly remember the meal – a nice instance of so-called flash-bulb memory), noticed some regularly-cycling discomfort. We called the hospital and were instructed to come in at once. Judy lay stretched out on the double bed of our Kombi (no safety-belt regulations then), groaning out instructions as to our best route. When we arrived, the obstetrician was away, and being allowed to attend the birth anyway, I unexpectedly found myself delivering our daughter entirely on my own, which added a certain piquant significance to the occasion. A nurse did subsequently turn up to cut the cord, the obstetrician eventually arrived, and it was agreed by all that the birth had been unexpectedly easy.

We did our first outback journey, on lonely tracks in the Flinders Ranges, when Catriona was three months old. At a year I noted she had a developing strabismus (squint), and had just read Colin Blakemore's classic study, just published in *Nature*, on critical periods in the development of binocular vision. Nowadays I expect that there would be ethical issues in the conduct of this very important study: newborn kittens had one or both of their eyelids sewn together for varying periods, and at the end of each duration, and thereafter, they were tested on their ability to see depth in full 3D. It appeared that if the two eyes were not able appropriately to interact after a certain critical developmental period, they would never be able subsequently to experience depth, with one eye permanently suppressing the other, instead of seeing in full inter-ocular 3D. I pushed very hard, but unsuccessfully, to have our daughter's strabismus surgically corrected immediately, in the hope that we would beat the critical period, but we were too late; she looks fine, but cannot see in 3D, or use a binocular microscope, a problem in her career in medicine.

During an eventful outback journey on desert tracks ending at Ayer's Rock (now Uluru) in the very centre of the continent, extreme corrugations wrecked both of the Kombi's rear shock absorbers. We limped slowly to the petrol dump under the shade of a solitary tree, close to the iconic 'Rock' – in those days (1970) there were absolutely no facilities, just 44-gallon drums of fuel on planks, hand-pumped, and in attendance a mechanic, with a rough airstrip adjacent. We had a couple of rear 'shockers' flown out from Alice Springs, the nearest settlement, and made our way there, but by the time we arrived, the replacements had also failed. In due course we put ourselves and the vehicle on the train to the railhead south at Maree, then routed via the old Ghan line, named after the Afghan camel drivers, who until a few decades earlier had been the only mode of desert transport. The old route had little in the way of bridges over the creek lines – the track descended to the dry stream bed (rains in the centre are rare but torrential, leading to long delays if stuck between two creeks, before the new Ghan line replaced the old), and the old steam train creaked its way across, and laboriously ascended the other side. The memorable journey took more than two days, but we shared a compartment with a nurse returning from Alice to her people's property at Leigh Creek Station; we became very friendly, subsequently, with the family, and would stay with them en route inland.

Another outback family with whom we became friendly ran Nundora station near Packsaddle, South of Tibooburra, in outback New South Wales. Someone with an interest like me in rock art had heard that recently some interesting sites had been found in its vicinity, so we made a journey up there, intending to pass through Nundora. It turned out that the track on to the area was beyond the capabilities of our Kombi, but we were invited to tea, then dinner, then to stay the night … and ended staying a week, as rare rains had set in, making the tracks hazardous, and visitors anyway were rare then, and to be savoured. Len Halfpenny apparently had, as a boy, overlanded stock with his father and set up the station properly. There was a meat house close to the homestead – a small stone structure with open, fly-wired 'windows', within which temporarily to hang meat away from flies, before cool-rooms or freezers were available or could be run. The meat house was peppered with bullet holes, marking the last day of a 'bushranger' (robber) who had holed up and taken his final shelter therein. On Len's property there were two lakes, one salt and one fresh; on the far side of the fresh-water lake a group of illegal duck shooters had set up camp, together with an automated duck-plucking device. Len, a farmer but also an ardent conservationist, loathed duck shooters. We were with him when he drove his old Second World War jeep up behind a sand dune, unstrapped his First World War Lee Enfield .303, and deliberately fired a magazine of five rounds low over the water, so that the bullets hit the water, bounced up and tumbled, emitting an eerie howling. The shooters fled immediately, leaving behind their fancy gear.

Some years later, when we had bought a Toyota Landcruiser four-wheel drive, and we planned an expedition to the very remote Cobourg Peninsula North West of Darwin in the Northern Territory, Judy was asked by the Botany Department at Monash, where she was working, to collect certain rare plant specimens, reported to be present by the last scientific expedition to work there in the 1920s. After Cahill's Crossing, on the East Alligator River, one headed up towards Murganella, a fisheries research and monitoring post staffed by just one man, and then, following the tides, undertook quite a bit of hazardous shoreline driving in the absence of tracks. We were required to take a gun in the not improbable event of getting stranded, plus stores and fuel, in a four-wheel tandem axle trailer we had had specially made, and which we had to leave for a time part-way along as the going became too rough. In the event we did not get stranded, and had no need of the gun, which we were still 'looking after' for our friend. However, it proved unexpectedly useful in other, seemingly more benign circumstances. We were parked temporarily on a pull-in on a roadside in an area where, despite being a relatively busy highway, was at that time rather notorious for hold-ups and robberies. A car pulled up just in front of us, an old, dilapidated model, and a couple of somewhat unsavoury-looking characters got out, leant seemingly nonchalantly against the car, and eyed us up. We always carried the gun in the cab, and Judy got it out in its canvas bag she had made for it, and I laid it on top of the tarpaulin covering our gear in the trailer, and without looking or saying anything, rather ostentatiously extracted and loaded it. Our 'friends' immediately got back into their vehicle and drove off. Later on down the road I reported the car registration number at a police station. I don't know what happened, but the police seemed to indicate that it was not an infrequent event, and that we had done the right thing.

Before we left on this expedition, Zoology asked us to look out for a reputedly enormous 'bird-eating spider', reportedly noted in a certain cave deep in the Kimberley. Although the information was scrappy, they were said to build large and very strong webs, more like nets, and in this instance were strung in front of a faded Aboriginal representation of the creation-myth Rainbow Serpent, painted on the back wall. The cave we found exactly fitted this account, but our captured specimens showed they were merely large Orb-Weaver spiders.

Turning now to another occasion, many years later, when I was now a full professor, holding a personal chair in Behavioural Neuroscience, there occurred a very different kind of experience. We had been experiencing heat, dust, flies and sand, yet tempered by a haunting, nameless beauty, the magic of the remote Australian outback that to be experienced must be sought, even learnt. A month had passed for Judy and me into a 12-week four-wheel drive camping trip into the wilderness, the bush which we had so come to love, the nights under the brilliant antipodean stars, the days exploring creeks and gorges, sand dunes and rocky outcrops, looking for rare botanical specimens and art work left by the First People on their eternal migrations, during long-ago ceremonies whose only vestiges nowadays are faint petroglyphs in forgiving rock surfaces, or faded pigment stains depicting hands (Kilroy was here?), weapons, lizards or birds. It was time to refresh, to reconnect, in the welcome shade of an isolated outback pub, solitary at a junction in the bush tracks leading to nowhere in particular, incongruously adjacent to a modern telephone box. 'I'm going to call our daughter', I said, 'to see if all is well'. By then, Catriona was a young medical student, at Monash, like her father and mother.

'Yes, Dad', she replied, 'but there is an urgent message from the secretary to the Dean of the Faculty of Medicine; would you write a reference in support of your old friend and colleague, Dr C J, for a Personal Chair?' I had long thought that C was indeed worthy of a professorship, but without computer or even old-fashioned typewriter (this all took place considerably before the Millennium), how to achieve this? We went indoors, into the cool, beer-and-smoke-scented atmosphere of the quintessential bush pub, and ordered drinks and meat pies. The publican's daughter had an exercise book, with lined pages, for her School of the Air education by radio with a distant mentor. I was given a couple of pages, roughly torn, which were immediately smeared with traces of tomato sauce, together with an elderly, temperamental ballpoint, and immediately set to work. The completed reference, within a faded envelope, sellotaped shut as the glue had long ago denatured, was put in a pile of items to be taken to the nearest mail outpost in 10 days' time.

When we eventually returned to civilisation, and to the university, I learnt that C was indeed now a full professor, the proud occupant of a personal chair in Neurology, which would undoubtedly be good for garnering grant support for our growing research into Parkinson's disease. I was also told that my stained and tattered reference for him was to be framed and displayed as the most unusual document of its type ever to be received in the Faculty. As his 50th birthday fell about then, he decided to celebrate by hiring a couple of chalets at Dinner Plains, a ski resort up in the High Country of the Great Divide. Family, friends from Medical School when he was once a student, and select colleagues were invited for a sybaritic weekend of festivities and walking. On the first night I found myself at dinner seated next to the elderly mother-in-law of another eminent guest. She was a lady whose cognitive and inhibitory processes were distinctly impaired by the synergy of ageing and alcohol. I had to repel the advances of a wandering hand that would repeatedly land, light as a feather, upon my knee, and by degrees advance in a 'northerly' direction towards dangerous territory. A memorable if difficult dinner.

The next day we were to hike in a long crocodile file to the junction of two ridges, and turn right along the intersect to a magnificent lookout, where a four-wheel drive would arrive with an exquisite spread, to be set out on tables with immaculate white cloths, along with choice wines; the *pièce de résistance*, the culmination to a memorable weekend. But it didn't turn out that way. Whoever was deputised to head the line of hungry hikers, and turn right on the short final ascent, failed to do so, and while Judy and I were at the rear with C, the majority followed their leader, their *faux guide*, and continued on along a rough track, disappearing into the void. By now it was noon, with a blazing sun and no shade, and many of the valiant participants were far from fit. A delightful dining experienced had almost instantaneously morphed into a mountain rescue scenario. And while not the youngest, I was probably at that time the fittest and with most experience of the bush. I commandeered the four-wheel drive, and set off, only to find that the tank was near empty; and as a steep descent at one point was facing us, I feared that with the vehicle's angle the remaining fuel would no longer reach the exit pipe from tank to motor. So I continued on foot, at a half run. By a piece of extraordinary good fortune I soon met another four-wheel drive labouring uphill towards me, and stopped the driver. 'Yes', he said, 'there was indeed a group of very hot and fatigued walkers under a solitary tree who looked in poor condition'. I said that if he would ferry the most affected back up to the lookout, he could partake of the exquisite spread which waited, spoiling in the summer sun. But that was not the end of the matter. Another even more eminent medic, who had parked his very large and opulent Mercedes last in a line of cars in the driveway of one of the chalets, left his bag with car keys in the stranger's vehicle; the stranger then, all unknowing, drove off into bush obscurity with the only key which could release all the other cars. It took nearly a day to trace the four-wheel drive, using radio communications, and retrieve the errant key. 'The best-laid plans of mice and men ...'

Probably our most horrific experience was the occasion of the 1983 Ash Wednesday bush fires. We lived out in the country, deep in the Dandenong Ranges, with a beautiful series of National Parks and Nature Reserves adjacent; and on a day of 44 degrees Celsius baking heat, and a truly howling north wind straight out of the sweltering centre, some youths deliberately lit a fire. In no time at all, houses were bursting into flames all around us, and Judy and I, along with many others, had to hurriedly flee to the comparative safety of the local store, where the police and emergency services established a command post. There we heard that all houses were lost in our road, although this later turned out not quite to be the case; in a blackened landscape of stark tree trunks, twisted roofing iron, charred ruins of what had once been serene family homes, and burnt-out vehicles, our own house stood out relatively intact, although we had lost much of what had been an attempt at a garden. Somehow it had survived the firestorm, even though in the roof space we found piles of burnt leaves which had entered via gaps beneath the roof tiles, any one of which could all so easily have ignited a fire within. Had it gone up in flames, along with all my lecture and lab notes, I doubt that I would have continued in academia, and there were many who didn't. We later learnt that what saved our place was the fact that a fire truck became stopped at the fire front adjacent to the dam at the bottom of our garden, and spent some time spraying our place and the next door neighbour's. However, not far away two fire trucks and all their crews were engulfed in the flames, and all perished. Subsequently, we bought a couple of fire pumps, petrol-driven because power is the first thing to be lost in such circumstances, to direct water from our rainwater tanks, as no one had a mains water supply in the area, and every summer Judy and I would set them up and practise directing jets on to roofs and deck. Nowadays, on my own and with Judy in Aged Care, I vacate the property on bad fire days, and along with many others hope that the huge tanker aircraft nowadays maintained for fighting fires will manage any emerging situation.

On another occasion, planning to do some bushwalking in the Little Desert in north-west Victoria, we heard that there had been a lightning strike somewhere in the area, so we checked with the local authorities, to be told the fire was safely out. The next day we began walking along the summit of an ironstone ridge, and stopped for lunch where it ended, overlooking the burnt area below. We had barely started when Judy noticed a thin plume of smoke suddenly arise below with the breeze, and within seconds the unburnt area caught alight. We were downwind, on top of an exposed, vegetated ridge. We had no option but to do the one thing one never should do, try to outrun the bushfire, as the fire would come up from below and trap us. It was a terrifying trot back to the safety of a saltpan.

Fire, flood, fleas – our next plague was termites, the bane of owners of wooden buildings. Termites eat out the wood without betraying their presence, by never breaking through the surface until structural integrity fails, and the timber collapses. That happened to us one Christmas party time – a guest's chair leg suddenly went through the floor. However, the termite eradicator did a good job, not least with his entertaining but presumably fictitious accounts of how he had been employed by US government security agencies to advise on intelligence gathering. Delusions of grandeur?

Lest it be thought that all our anecdotes worth repeating took place away from our lab and place of work, work itself was not always such a serious matter, or entirely devoid of funny moments. We had a certain reputation for devising novel, complex electronic devices, which our very excellent electronic and mechanical workshops, and burgeoning IT section, constructed for us. Some such items, of unusual sensitivity, were easily vulnerable to electrical interference from ambient sources. We thought we had one particular problem beaten, until it became evident that while our male participants generally operated more or less flawlessly from the point of view of unwanted transients, spikes and other forms of electrical interference, the same most definitely was not true of our younger females. It was a female research assistant who commented that that particular demographic was likely to be wearing nylon knickers, unlike cotton briefs as sported by our males. Static-generating knickers were the problem! Solution: change into lightweight disposable cotton drawers, such as Aunty might sport. Problem solved, although some of the less technically minded young ladies worried about what might be happening within their knickers.

As research scientists, as well as clinicians, many of us were used to having temporarily to leave an experimental situation, at short notice, suddenly to see a patient requiring urgent attention. Quite often we might be trying out electrophysiological recording procedures on each other, and it was very inconvenient to have to disconnect numerous electrode leads laboriously affixed to the scalp, in the days before the 'shower-cap' method. Consequently, the leads were often gathered together into a harness, which could be disconnected *en bloc* as necessary. On one occasion our neurologist was hurriedly disconnected, and rushed in to an adjacent consulting room to see a patient, who was horrified to see his doctor appearing with what looked like a small forest of wires sprouting from within his brain.

Then there was our study where participants were to wear inverting or laterally displacing or deviating prisms over their eyes, along with a custom-built eye-tracking device we had developed, to displace the perceived ambient geometry of the surroundings, while walking a set route. Initially this required being guided around a tortuous course in a stroke-rehab centre for about half an hour, to adapt or habituate to the altered visual geometry. Once, while I was testing out the complex and impressive visual array, with my research student close behind me, steering me by my shoulders, we passed a group of patients who stared at me in horror, and one said, 'My God, poor, poor chap, what's wrong with him? At least we are spared that!'

My contract, on first employment at Monash in the golden 1960s, was that I was expected and required to take regular sabbatical leaves in overseas laboratories, to bring back to Australia, perceived victim in those pre-internet days, of the 'Tyranny of Distance'. Nowadays only the very fortunate, eminent or conniving can hope occasionally so to be paid to leave these shores for six months every fourth year. My contract so stood, inviolate and sacrosanct, until I retired in 2002, and I, my lab and the university stood I believe greatly to gain thereby. I spent much time in Oxford and Cambridge, also with professional visits of varying durations to Edinburgh, Reading, Exeter, St Andrews, Lancaster, Newcastle, Stirling and other UK seats of learning. I wrote a number of text books while there, set up mutually profitable collaborations, exchanged graduate students, learnt and taught many things. It was also of course an opportunity to visit research institutions and universities in many other parts of the world, as for shorter or longer periods I spent time in Canada (University of Victoria, British Columbia), Italy (Parma), the USA (Oregon), Chile (Santiago), South Africa (Rand Afrikaans and Witwatersrand Universities). Santiago we visited, rashly, in the very last days of President Allende's regime, in 1973. It was spooky, with machine-gunning in the streets at night, 'congrio' (a kind of eel) the only protein available, and in the complete absence of glass for some reason, all commodities, like jam, etc., being sold only in plastic bags. I could change money in the hotel lift at incredibly favourable rates – indeed, the Hilton, where we stayed, charged us US$1 per night, all meals included.

The Head of Department, on my first day of duties, met me at the door of the Hilton in his car; in the passenger seat at the front there was sitting one of his students; Head of Department summarily ordered him into the back seat to make way for his 'distinguished visitor'. Very fortunately (for me), I demurred, and immediately climbed into the back. Just as we entered the university precinct, via gates with a central stone column dividing the roadway, he misjudged the turn, and rammed it, quite hard, and the unfortunate student hit his head against some internal structure, and slumped unconscious and bleeding profusely. Head of Department jumped out to inspect the damage to his car, completely ignoring the unconscious student, so I had to summon help, using the rather basic Spanish which I had learnt before leaving Australia. I delivered my first lecture blood-stained. Very shortly afterwards the university was in fact taken over by the army, and the Head of Department (a self-professed communist, but with a house seemingly full of expensive artworks and multiple maids) became one of *los desaparecidos*, 'the disappeared ones' or missing persons; he did, however, re-emerge years later at Humboldt University in the old East Germany. So I guess he was lucky after all. And so were we.

It was now time to see something of Latin America, especially as I had acquired a basic ability in Spanish, aided by a good knowledge of Latin. (Hitherto, I had found it possible to cobble together an intelligible, if not intelligent, Spanish sentence using Latin, with truncated ablative endings and changing terminal 't' to 'd'; for Italian, in which I later became quite fluent, at least for reading, the trick was just to use the unchanged ablative ending.) As it was considered very unsafe to travel south out of the capital, we went north, renting a little Citroën Deux Chevaux, with its curious umbrella-handle-like gear shift (somehow whatever posture or angle you adopted, it still seemed to work, or to 'know' where to go). We drove north, up into the Andes, experiencing our first Chilean earthquake (we had felt a few tremors while in New Zealand), in a crazily sloping little hotel in the village appropriately named Los Andes. On our way up the steep pass at the foot of Aconcagua, the highest mountain in South America, we were stopped by a soldier who insisted we gave him a lift. It was fortunate, as in fact the road deteriorated greatly near the summit of Cristo Redentor, needing someone outside to help push, at which point, surrounded by frozen lakes and impenetrable banks of snow, we had to turn round, first letting our Australian daughter build her first Latin American snowman by the roadside. This was when we found that our brakes had stopped working (I decided it was the extreme altitude, causing the brake fluid to vaporise). We gingerly descended in low gear, to find as we got down and back to more temperate climes, that the brakes had, as expected, resumed working.

We flew north to Antofagasta, and conceived the desire to visit San Pedro de Atacama, deep in the Atacama desert, close to El Gran Salar (the Big Salt Lake) de Atacama, and reputably where no rain had fallen for 400 years. We rented a taxi and drove past long-deserted nitrate mines, complete with 1930s trucks lying abandoned as if yesterday except for the dust, and through a moon landscape with exotic names like La Valle de la Luna, and La Valle del Muerto (the valley of the moon, the valley of death), to San Pedro de Atacama and Toconao, where the snow melt of distant Andean peaks provided water. There I conversed, in a mixture of Spanish, Latin and French, with a Belgian monk who had assumed the job of safeguarding the mummies continually emerging from eroding sand dunes – an experience very similar to the one I had had, also with a Belgian monk, years previously in Corfu.

On returning to Antofagasta, we next took the incredible train trip over the high Andes to La Paz, Bolivia, crossing the Altiplano. En route we shared with a group of American students a third class carriage (hard slatted seats, peasant women wearing multiple petticoats – 'hay muy frio', it gets pretty chilly up here, in reality to conceal contraband), and with legs of llama, dripping blood, on the luggage racks above. Not good places to sit beneath. At the halt and border post on the summit, one of the students was found not to have an appropriate visa, and was about to be summarily ejected and dumped in the cold, when an Israeli on the train, who had been in their secret service, offered his services. Carrying an emergency forger's secretarial kit, in less than 15 minutes he knocked up a very passible, and completely acceptable, imitation of the real thing, as per the valid ones possessed by the other students. Inevitably the train broke down, and we were glad of our sleeping bags and child's potty strapped to our packs, as we had to spend a night awaiting a replacement engine.

In La Paz, we heard of an extraordinary road over la Cumbre (The Summit, 4,650 metres), down to the tropical settlement of Coroico, in the Yungas. This road was later officially designated the most dangerous in the world, with several hundred vehicles each year falling off the precipices which accompany the route, and was closed. Because of its extreme narrowness, the muddy surface, hairpins and landslips, unlike all other roads in Latin America one drove on the left, so that the precipice was beside you on descent, and descending vehicles had to give way at all times to those ascending. (Another idiosyncratic Bolivian road requirement was that generally on approaching intersections one had to hoot, and the first to do so, had right of way; town was a noisy place.) The scenery, from the high Altiplano and snow-capped peaks, down to the steamy jungle at the foot was and is incredible. We hired a vehicle and driver, and passed innumerable wayside shrines in memoriam to those unfortunates who never made it. Our descent fortunately was uneventful, and we lodged in a pleasant little accommodation place, and were given a bedside lamp, with no plug on the end of the wire, for illumination. 'Just poke the wires into the socket', we were told, and we did. Unfortunately whenever we did so, all the lights went out in the tiny township, and the generator stopped, presumably to avoid shorting out. We had power in our hands in both senses. On return, our (different) driver was less cautious, and we hit a large newly fallen rock in the road, bending the track rod connecting the two front wheels, which thereby assumed a pronounced 'toe in'. Fortunately this occurred at slow speed on the last section of our ascent, so we were never in any added danger, and we got back slowly and even more safely.

We then were taken with the further desire to see the pre-Inca archaeological site of Tiwanaku, sixth century, with the Gate of the Sun and probably constructed by ancestors of the Aymara people. So after returning from Coroico, next day we stopped the first taxi, and made a family day of it, as our driver also brought along his wife and daughter. It turned out that he had never been out of La Paz, or off the bitumen, and drove ever faster on rough, potholed roads, with me calling out to him to slow down, otherwise my daughter would be sick all over his nice new taxi, but he took no notice, doubtless showing off to his family. The inevitable happened, we hit a huge hole in the road at speed, fortunately without losing control, but smashed the suspension. So the rest of the trip we proceeded at a nice leisurely pace with a very cross driver. But the beautifully excavated ruins did not disappoint.

We lodged in La Paz in the Indian Quarter, with our American student friends, who had played cards with and fed chocolates to our daughter in the train trip over the Andes. We had to make a very early departure to catch a ferry across Lake Titicaca, and I was assured by the management the night before that the massive street door would be open in time for us; it wasn't. I pushed, battered, shouted – and in desperation took a running jump at it. It opened all right – the entire front façade, bricks and all, came down in a cloud of dust into the street, like an avalanche. As we climbed out over the debris, a furious management came boiling out of nowhere, but so came the students, who told us to flee one way, and they would lead the management in the other direction. It worked, and we all eventually caught the ferry with no further problems.

Our other major experience in South America was seeing Machu Picchu shortly before it became the modern tourist mecca. We alighted from the train at Aguas Calientes ('Hot Springs'), and ascended the winding approach road in a cattle truck, which felt somehow curiously appropriate. The site is so well known, and just too extraordinary, high above the loop in the nearly surrounding Urubamba, with lofty, jungle-clad Andean peaks all around, that further comment is superfluous.

After nine months spent rather miserably in Edinburgh (strikes and other problems meant a three-day working week, and with power outages, candles were dangerously offered in book shops), I was to lecture in South Africa. At times, in the big medical schools where formal attire was *de rigueur*, I was embarrassingly the only person without jacket and tie. The contrast between the left-wing politics of Allende's Chile, and the fascist, oppressive, right-wing regime in South Africa, could not have been more glaring. We were put up by the Head of Department, in a beautifully converted and appointed one-time garage, in a leafy suburb of Johannesburg. My contract was six weeks of lectures, and thereafter we were to be (and were) lent a Kombi van, camping gear, and all expenses covered for a few weeks travelling in the splendid, and massive, Kruger National Park and game reserve, where in those days one camped more or less unprotected from any inquisitive or marauding wildlife, although sometimes there would be assigned to you as protection an African guard, complete with rifle, whom you fed. One night, when all we had for all of us was a couple of cans of bully beef, our African guard showed unmistakable signs of displeasure and disappointment. Visits to and hikes in the magnificent Drakensberg mountains, followed by the Karoo, with its botany, so reminiscent of dry-country Australia, with so many closely related plant species (e.g. the Proteaceae), were no less memorable. We even got up to the stupendous Victoria Falls in what was then Rhodesia, and took a nostalgic sun-downer paddle-steamer boat trip with the locals up the Zambezi, even although visitors had been shot and killed recently in both areas.

The other memorable, and sad, experience was the result of us going away with the family one weekend up into the Northern Transvaal, to stay with a relative, Oom (Uncle) Phlip (Phillip) who had a delightful, high-country ranch. Sadly, an African maid, much beloved by the family, in our absence was assaulted, raped and severely injured by an ex-boyfriend. She had been taken to Baragwanath Hospital in Soweto, a location doubly no-go for whites. The Head of Department was unwilling to risk going, not so his wife, and I consented to accompany her. It was an enormous, but well-run hospital, staffed by and for Africans, with huge numbers of assault victims each weekend. We managed to ensure her continued medical treatment, and apart from being an extraordinary and tragic insight into a situation unfamiliar to most whites, it proved otherwise uneventful.

Although otherwise memorable, we had no such adventures in our other travels, at different times in the Canadian and the American Rockies, although bears were a potential problem when hiking. (One always carried when in the bush an empty can with a pebble in it, to rattle and warn the bear of one's proximity.) I was invited to give a course of 12 lectures in Italy, in Parma, for quite a substantial reimbursement, to be paid at the end. However, it was to be two years before a very large number of small-denomination postal orders started to arrive in dribs and drabs, sometimes three a week, then a pause of a week or two, by which time I had anyway put the talks into a very profitable book and published them. I can only assume it was some kind of Italian tax dodge. But that was Italy. One never mailed material to the UK; I was told to go down to the station, where on a certain wall there was a *pulsante*, a button to press. An adjacent door would open and one would drop in one's packet. It was apparently more reliable, faster, and at no cost. Typical amiable anarchic Italy! And every Friday I was dispatched to a different university in northern Italy, by a wonderful, efficient, clean and reliable rail service. At the end of each lecture, without fail, I would be surreptitiously taken aside and secretively (I never discovered why) handed a *busta*, an envelope containing a more or less substantial honorarium. This would pay for us to go somewhere interesting for the weekend. Such a country of happy contrasting paradoxes!

One weekend, the professor and head of Physiology with whom I was collaborating in Parma, Carlo Umiltà, invited us to his family's country castle, more properly a fortified tower, 'Il Torre di Carlo', in a beautiful area across the Apennines. The only entrance was from a trap door in the floor of the family home farm, a couple of hundred metres away. One then followed a dank, winding underground passageway, emerging through a similar trap door in the floor of the tower, which was without windows or doors to the exterior, but was equipped with a spiral stairway up to the battlements above. There are many similar such defensive structures in Italy. A couple of generations earlier, the roof had been replaced, and medieval tiles removed. One bore an inscription, in dialect, detailing rather luridly the sexual misdeeds of a local girl of the times, details which were not otherwise widely known: something like 'though she unstoppered her body, she cannot stopper the truth'. When the 'news' from the tile emerged, it reawakened old clan hostilities, which had otherwise long been simmering. Dangerous places, roofs!

16
COMMISSURAL CONNECTIVITY

So here was I, with a near-new PhD and just I arrived at Monash University, itself recently established in a paddock on the then-edge of Melbourne's suburban sprawl. Not any more. The paddock continued for a while to appear on maps as the site of an 'epileptic colony', an unfortunate and nowadays politically most incorrect, but some said not completely inappropriate term for the new tenants. I was soon asked to prepare a course of lectures on Memory and Learning, about which I knew little. The term 'business speak' was then an abomination way below the temporal horizon, and 'problems' had not yet been euphemised to 'issues', much less to 'challenges'. Nevertheless, I decided in accordance with that sorry modern cliché to make an opportunity out of a problem, to turn a necessity into a virtue. I would lecture on the Biological Bases of Memory and Learning, an approach with which I felt rather more comfortable. Because I soon recognised that in no way could the currently available material fill a standard 13-week lecture series, I expanded the course to cover Biological Bases of Behaviour generally. As no-one seemed to notice and the students seemed happy and interested, which in those halcyon days seemed to be the chief criterion of successful teaching, the following year I simply rebadged the lectures as Biological Bases of Behaviour, and these continued, with annual updates, for two decades.

Research is rightly said to inform teaching; there is nothing more stimulating for a class than to tell them, breathlessly, about the latest hot new finding, especially if you have just made it. However, curiously, less is usually said about the equally important reverse process, *teaching* informing your *research*. Here I was in Australia, claiming on apparently good text-book authority, in a lecture on the neural commissures interconnecting the two sides of the brain, that these commissures are far less evident in Australian marsupials than in other mammals. Could there possibly be some kind of adaptive 'reason' (read 'consequence') for such an anatomical omission? Surely it wasn't just because Antipodean native fauna were simply more 'primitive', in the Victorian vernacular?

Maybe a bright young spark did ask me about the possible functional consequences of such an Antipodean anomaly, or maybe I even asked myself – I forget! But I do remember wondering, while drying the dishes one morning in our rented house in the country, whether there are consequences for us humans when a visual stimulus is obliged to cross, from its receiving hemisphere, over the commissures to the other hemisphere where a response must be elaborated and initiated. Memories of what you were doing just when an important idea, or a news item such as a significant assassination hits one, are nowadays called 'flash-bulb memories', but that would definitely have been another story for my aborted course on lectures on Memory and Learning!

So would there be an actual measurable cost in, say, response speed, when pressing a button to a visual stimulus received, by the exigencies of the experiment, on one side of the brain, when now the other side of the brain was obliged to initiate the motor response? Any such increase in response latency, compared with when both stimulus processing and response initiation could occur within one and the same side (hemisphere) of the brain, should reflect transmission time across the commissures.

In theory, it was easy to arrange such a comparison: a flash of light received by either eye in the left periphery of the field of view is initially received in the brain's right visual cortex; a right flash is similarly elaborated in the left half-brain or hemisphere. I have previously discussed possible evolutionary reasons for such a curious situation. So, in 1969, I set up a situation to compare button-press choice reaction times to lights briefly flashed randomly to one or other side of a central fixation point, with responses by one or other finger of the hand anatomically on either the same or the opposite side of the body as the light flash. The latter, crossed, arrangement should be the slower by an amount equal to the time taken for information to cross the commissures, or, possibly, should similarly reflect the cost of signal degradation over a channel (the commissures) of imperfect fidelity.

But this was in 1969, and I needed a computer to run such an experiment, with millisecond accuracy, as only a few thousandths of a second might differentiate the two stimulus-response configurations. Again, I was lucky; a colleague had one of the very first such behavioural-lab computers in Australia, a PDP-8S. He agreed to collaborate with me on the project, and we got a reaction-time difference of 20 milliseconds, almost an order of magnitude greater than what might be predicted from knowledge of the neural pathways and number of synaptic connections involved. In a way, this was fortunate, as it stimulated us to an extensive programme of research on brain-behaviour relationships that lasted for decades; without such a stimulus I doubt whether we would have embarked upon such an ambitious and ultimately profitable programme. It was also unfortunate, in a narrower, shorter-term sense, as many years later, after much further research in many centres around the world, it became evident that the smaller figure of a few milliseconds was closer to the mark; our values, and those of others who varied our paradigm, were partly an artefact of additional attention-switching processes of which at the time none of us, or indeed anyone else, were really aware.

Shortly afterwards, my colleague in this initial enterprise died under rather unusual and certainly tragic circumstances, and the research grant which we had now won on the basis of early success, along with the all-important computer, became mine, to do with as I liked. Indeed, many years later Digital-Decus, as I think the firm manufacturing our computer was called, bought it from me for their museum of original, iconic IT equipment. We got much more than the original purchase price, and moved the lab rapidly into the computer age proper.

It was in the early period of my work at Monash that studies became widely disseminated of war-wounded veterans, always a sad source of neurological information on the basis of discrete deficits subsequent to localised penetrating brain lesions. It was clear that while certain language processes, at least in right-handed individuals, are largely elaborated in the left half-brain, face processing may similarly be a province generally of the right. Could we demonstrate this behaviourally with healthy, intact individuals, using a similar subtractive reaction-time technique to laterally-presented face stimuli? These would have to be matched to other, memorised, target faces which varied in specific ways from the test items. Could we similarly flash up numbers, letters, words, shapes, patterns, drawings … all to one or other visual field, and record our participants' discriminatory reaction times? Could we in this way get a handle on where and how in the normal brain all such information-processing systems operate?

At this point I was approached by two graduate students, one of whom had previously studied faces in memory experiments. We needed stimuli with ranges of features over which we had firm experimental control, as in the forensic IdentiKit system used by police for identifying possible felons by witnesses. It consisted of a huge library of varying feature overlays. We wrote to the distributors in California and hired the system. Like all equipment coming at the time from overseas, it had to pass through the hands of our University Customs Officer, a wily, knowledgeable and accommodating gentleman with a finger in every import pie, and believed by some to be able to supply anyone with anything they might at least half reasonably ask for. At the time a flasher was upsetting female students, and it being known that we had just taken delivery of an IdentiKit, we were asked to provide professional identificatory help. However, the victims were uniformly unable to say anything useful about the perpetrator's facial features, one even facetiously suggesting we should develop a system based on certain rather different principles.

Strangely, most of the faces we constructed from the system did possess a rather sinister aspect, maybe somehow reflecting the original source material. However, we showed that a right-hemisphere (left visual field) superiority for faces – and likewise for certain displays constructed from elements constituting other meaningful objects like bugs, car and cottage fronts – only occurred with easy, rapid comparisons, where all features or elements differed between any two items. With confusingly similar configurations which differed minimally from each other, the opposite, analytic or language, side of the brain proved pre-eminent. Was this why language had apparently evolved in the left hemisphere, because complex, feature-discriminatory processes common to many operations resided there, with simpler, global comparisons operating in the right? Indeed, we later showed that certain aspects of language itself, such as humour and context, were in fact also handled in the 'non-language' hemisphere.

Still unresolved was the question as to whether there might be a specialist face processor on the right, perhaps as recent imaging studies suggest, in the fusiform gyrus; alternatively, does that region also handle all complex patterns which are of a generic and significant nature to the individual, like makes of cars and so on, of which faces are just one, if a major, example? It was an exciting time, with similar split-brain studies now going on in the United States, under the Nobel laureate Roger Sperry, involving patients with severe and otherwise intractable epilepsy, whose commissures had had to be surgically divided to control the spread of seizure activity. Also, in Italy, a group which we fondly came to refer to as the spaghetti mob was simultaneously publishing almost identical studies and findings to our own. We soon entered into a happy and mutually very profitable collaboration with them.

I still don't know in truth if the marsupial brain is indeed 'commissurally challenged'; maybe it is not too late for someone to find out, but our early study does illustrate how a possibly unsound premise can still lead to useful and enlightening consequences. And teaching can indeed inform research, not just the other way round.

Nearly 200 years ago, an otherwise obscure English physician, cognisant of the two apparently mirror-image cerebral hemispheres within our skulls, speculated upon the possibly duplex nature of consciousness and volition, noting that each cerebrum is a distinct and perfect whole as a potential organ of thought, and that a separate and distinct process of thinking may possibly be carried out within each hemisphere separately.

Then, in 1860, the German pioneer of psychophysics, Gustav Fechner, argued that if it were possible (which he doubted) to cut the commissural nerve fibres connecting the two hemispheres, without killing the patient, it should be possible to duplicate a person. This commissurotomy operation has in fact until recently been a last resort for controlling the spread, within the brain, of otherwise intractable epilepsy. Indeed, as noted above, the Nobel Prize in Physiology and Medicine was shared by the physiological psychologist, Roger Wolcott Sperry, in 1981 for his study of the behavioural consequences of the operation. At the turn of the nineteenth century, the psychologist William McDougall, made a bargain with another Nobel laureate, the great physiologist Charles Scott Sherrington, that if he, McDougall, ever became incurably ill, the experiment should be performed on him; we have, however, had to await the invention of sophisticated experimental procedures to demonstrate what turn out often to be very subtle effects of commissurotomy. Indeed, in the 1950s, such pessimistic jocularities were heard as that the only function of the commissures seem to be keep the hemispheres from sagging, or instead to facilitate the spread of seizures.

As early as the fifth century BC, the Hippocratic writers of medicine in Greece had observed the occurrence of convulsions contralateral, or on the opposite side of the body, to the side of brain injury:

> For the most part convulsions seize the other side of the body; for if the wound be on the left side, the convulsions will seize the right side of the body, while if the wound be on the right side of the head, the convulsion attacks the left side of the body.

We still do not really know why there is this contralateral or crossed arrangement between a controlling cerebral hemisphere on one side of the head, and many sensory and motor functions, on the other side of the body. However, as I have already noted, an early ancestor, perhaps transitional between something resembling an early worm and a chordate, possibly underwent a 180-degree torsion or twist half-way along its body and nerve chord, rotating previously ventral structures to a dorsal position, and resulting in a cross-over between much of the body and controlling brain regions. Certainly the octopus and squid, with an enormous brain and behavioural repertoire, comparable to many a vertebrate, operate very satisfactorily with an uncrossed, ipsilateral arrangement.

So, if we cut the connecting commissures in humans, do we duplicate consciousness? This is not the place to describe or define what we mean by consciousness; many books have appeared on this matter, authored by philosophers, psychologists, physiologists and the occasional mathematician and engineer. All ultimately seek solace in metaphor; consciousness is like something else with which we can more easily come to grips. We can, however, note that we only become conscious of those action sequences which, under attentional control, are deliberately selected from other alternatives, and which require monitoring or executive overview, unlike other possibly concurrent activities which are so over-learnt or automatic that we may not even notice that we are doing them. Volition and attention are therefore clearly associated concepts, and just as we normally cannot easily undertake two deliberate action sequences, each of which requires monitoring, without at least alternating attention, so too we cannot attend easily to more than one stream of events, self or externally generated. Indeed, we now know that conscious, deliberate, volitional activity is largely under the control of cortical regions in the prefrontal lobe of the brain, while highly familiar or over-practised action sequences come to be mediated largely by subcortical structures which include the basal ganglia. The latter region is affected in Parkinson's disease, and consequently it is the practised, familiar behaviour which those patients find difficult, rather than more novel, attention-demanding activities, which often still, with attention, can be undertaken.

We can also invoke a further level of consciousness, awareness of the self as an individual separate from but among others like oneself. Such an awareness can be inferred from behaviour observed when an ape encounters its image in a mirror; some form of self-recognition (surprise, dismay or otherwise appropriate responding), rather than simply treating the image as a conspecific.

When unable easily to make sense of a situation, we tend to confabulate; confabulation is not deliberate lying, but rationalisation. A dementing patient with Alzheimer's disease forgets daily encounters with her neighbours, and when questioned may reply that everyone has sold up and left the neighbourhood. Someone instructed under hypnosis to open a window at a certain point in time may do so, and when asked afterwards why she did it, may reply, 'It was getting stuffy in here.'

We can flash a picture of, say, a chicken claw exclusively to the left hemisphere of a commissurotomy patient, where language is largely elaborated, and a snow scene exclusively to the non-verbal right side. When such a patient has to choose from an array of alternative related pictures, one by each hand, the left hand appropriately may tend to choose a shovel, and the right a chicken. When asked why, the verbal left hemisphere, oblivious of the snow scene perceived by the disconnected and non-verbal right hemisphere, may confabulate and reply, 'A chicken claw goes with chicken, and you need a shovel to clean out the chook shed.' Thus, each hemisphere may be privy after commissurotomy, to its own discrete information, when that information is fed exclusively to one side.

There are claims that certain kinds of categorical or general information may nevertheless transfer between hemispheres, despite severance of all commissures other than those subcortical connections necessary for the maintenance of life. Thus a patient was able correctly to respond 'yes' or 'no' to questions such as, 'Is it a film star/family member/politician, etc.?' when faces were projected exclusively to the non-verbal right hemisphere, even while unable to say exactly who it was. In the early post-operative phase, moreover, the left hand may occasionally try to pull down the trousers which the right hand has just pulled up, or the right hand may try to restrain the left from performing an inappropriate or unacceptable action, just as in Stanley Kubrick's amazingly prescient film, *Dr Strangelove*, shot in 1964. All are examples of inter-manual conflict, an issue to which I shall shortly return.

Such 'alien hand', or '*main étrangère*' behaviour is, however, commoner, although still rare, after a stroke or tumour damages both the commissural connections and the supplementary motor area on the medial (inward) side of one prefrontal lobe. The supplementary motor area, as we have found, is responsible for initiating sequences of volitional behaviour, while on the outer surface of the prefrontal cortex, the premotor area may initiate externally driven motor sequences in response to environmental events. The consequence of such damage is that now the patient becomes over-responsive to external events on one side of the body, such that the hand and arm seems literally to have a mind of its own. The syndrome may range from automatic grasping of any object touching the hand, via groping for such objects, to 'utilisation behaviour' such as picking up and operating tools and so on, in a complex and anarchic fashion, often to the consternation of the poor patient. Thus there is a classic instance of a woman with commissural damage along with damage to the supplementary motor area on one side after a ruptured aneurism, who was swimming up and down quite normally, got out of the pool, dried herself, then handed the towel to an assistant. At this point, trouble started because her left hand reached out and tried to grab the towel back from the assistant. A tug-of-war continued between the two hands until finally the assistant pulled the towel away. Other examples include the left hand closing doors and drawers as soon as the right hand has opened them; the left hand undoing buttons that had just been done up; the left hand removing pieces that the right hand had just placed in a collage; the left hand repeatedly removing items that the right hand had just packed in a suitcase, and so on. There are perhaps instances of conflicting emotion between the hands. Thus, a woman would pull her husband towards her with her right hand while the left hand simultaneously tries to push him away. On other occasions the left hand may cause inadvertent mayhem by appearing to try and co-operate with its fellow. In living skills, a woman was making good progress with an omelette when the left hand 'helped out', first throwing a couple of additional uncracked eggs, then an unpeeled onion and a salt cellar into the frying pan. There were also instances where the left hand deliberately stopped the right hand carrying out a task. In one instance the examiner asked a woman to put her right hand through a small hole. Nothing happened and then she said, 'I can't, the other one's holding it.'

Other instances include the right hand purchasing an object in a shop while the left tries to keep back the money, or even to steal something else; one hand taking something from a drawer, which is suddenly and violently closed on that hand by the other; and conflict between hands for dishwasher or television programmes. Patients may refer to the 'alien' hand as if it belongs to another person. Indeed, patients with a slightly different syndrome, unilateral neglect, may even claim that their left arm or leg really does belong to someone else, and shouldn't be in bed with them.

I am also reminded of the compulsive behaviours of some Tourette patients, behaviours which can nevertheless be inhibited (probably by structures at the base of the prefrontal lobes) in really important circumstances. Damage in these regions results in poor impulse control, social disinhibition, tactlessness and apparent lack of insight. Questioning can, however, reveal that such individuals still know what should or should not be done at an apparently theoretical level, but in real life will nevertheless go on to do the wrong things. *Video meliora proboque, deteriora sequor*, as Ovid commented 2,000 years ago, 'I know what's good and right, but still take the other path.'

It is possible to mimic certain aspects of pathological compulsive or utilisation behaviour in normal individuals. When distracted, we may pick up objects and play with them appropriately in terms of the object but inappropriately in a particular social context. When ready to execute a grasping movement, moreover, if we are suddenly flashed a drawing, such as of a saucer, which although irrelevant to the task to be executed nevertheless is visually congruent with the object (a cup) to be grasped, the latency to execute the grasp may be markedly reduced.

A lesson from all these findings is that attention, consciousness and will are all interrelated, and that a number of brain regions combine to form a network to mediate such essentially human behaviours. Damage to regions of this network can make us perform sins of omission, or of commission, with or without our knowledge. So are we really free agents? And when a commissurotomy patient's two hands sometimes seem to compete, is it fair to say that each hand's controlling hemisphere is operating under its own, unique, stream of consciousness, or might one hemisphere, temporarily or permanently, be operating 'zombie fashion' as an automaton, almost as when lost in reverie we doodle, or play with an object, apparently unthinkingly? Do apes, rats, lizards, fish … all have their own versions of consciousness, or do they also always act in automatic mode in their own best interests? That is definitely not as how it seems when we watch apes recognising themselves in a mirror, or interacting socially, each as it were with its own 'theory of mind', knowing what its conspecific must be thinking or knowing; nor is it how crows and parrots seem, solving complex problems with apparent insight. The only feasible alternative to such a viewpoint, that of human uniqueness, must take refuge in a claim such as that consciousness, unique to ourselves, is the accidental by-product of our uniquely complex minds, a kind of fast route to efficient problem solving.

A related question, also bearing upon the issue of interhemispheric integration of awareness, which, however, may merely serve further to muddy waters already teasingly turbid, relates to the privacy of our percepts. Philosophers have long held that one's percepts are necessarily private and inaccessible to anyone else; I can never experience the rose that you are examining, smelling or touching in exactly the same way that you do. I may of course judge that our experiences are essentially similar from our common behaviours. Given the success of the same patterns of animal camouflage and deceptive mimicry against a wide range of potential predators – birds, mammals, even certain insects and of course ourselves – there clearly must be certain commonalities at a perceptual level. Thus with its cryptic coloration a moth may blend with its chosen background, and be more or less invisible to ourselves, a hungry bird, rodent or dragonfly. There are innocuous butterflies that avoid predators by closely mimicking, Batesian fashion, unrelated Monarch species that harbour toxins culled from the poisonous vegetation upon which they feed. In Müllerian mimicry, two or more predator-resistant species that are distasteful, poisonous or perhaps stinging, may adopt similar warning coloration. There is even an Amazonian caterpillar that looks extraordinarily like the head of an alligator, right down to the tiniest detail. Presumably predator bird species are poor judges of size-distance relationships – they must have what vision scientists call bad size constancy!

That said, because two or more species are subject to similar deceptions, do they necessarily therefore see the world in exactly the same ways? Do two people, both of whom respond similarly to an array of visual illusions, inevitably share identical perceptual experiences? Can I ever *know exactly* what you experience? Can I in fact experience your tickle or your pain? I once viewed a fascinating documentary on conjoined twin girls; briefly, I wondered whether this extraordinary experiment of nature might address the issue or hold the key. Abigail and Brittany, joined from the navel down, inhabited the same body, although otherwise they had separate hearts, lungs, spines and digestive tracts from and including the stomach. These delightful, personable and insightful 11-year-old girls shared a pair of legs and arms, but of course had separate and fully independent heads. They could run, ride a bicycle, play volleyball and baseball. At school, they were necessarily treated as a single person at most games, but as two intelligent and separate individuals at their academic school work. One girl was said to control one arm and leg on her side, and the other the other pair, but their ability to coordinate, seemingly seamlessly, in catching, throwing, piano-playing and running, with no inter-brain connections above the waist, was, frankly, quite phenomenal. The experimental neuropsychologist in me longed to run some of the complex, computer-controlled tasks of bimanual coordination we have developed in the lab, and also to see whether limb coordination was affected when one girl was blindfolded.

Can Abigail and Brittany help us address the question on the privacy of one's individual percepts? If they were to sit on a sharp stone, both girls would, separately, experience the sensation arising from their shared, common buttocks; would it feel the same to both of them? It is after all a single sensory event. For a moment I thought this was indeed the 'philosopher's stone', as it were, to address the issue of perceptual privacy. However, the situation is as if I could somehow tap into your ascending sensory nerve fibres – while of course my interpreting brain with all its individual differences in organisation and personal history would remain separate and distinct from yours. Thus we must distinguish between sensation and perception, and note that privacy is more a function of brain processes, where sensations are elaborated as percepts, than one pertaining to the more distal skin receptors, where sensory events initially occur. Indeed, the whole issue of experiential privacy and sharing should rather be addressed at a higher level, in the performance of complex integrative acts and behaviours – such as ball and piano playing. And there, as we saw, the girls *did* seem to act as a single unit, making conjoint lightning-fast decisions to move this way or that, to catch, to throw, or to take evasive action. How could one brain possibly coordinate in this fashion with the other, given the complete absence of any high-level connections? Is each girl exquisitely and immediately sensitive, maybe even at an unconscious level, to behavioural cues emanating from her conjoined partner?

Upon further reflection, I realised that the very similar situation had in fact already been investigated for some years in that small, select and special clinical population – split-brain patients whose two sides of the brain had been surgically separated. This last-resort operation of course effectively results in two half-brains within a single head; there are, however, unlike the twins' situation, still deep midbrain and brainstem connections that can convey some gross perceptual and motor information from one side to the other. Such acallosal individuals, although still able largely to coordinate the two sides of the body – some would say in part by one half-brain unconsciously responding to bodily cues triggered by the other half-brain – do nevertheless, as we saw, at times show interesting dissociations, one hand trying to pull down the pair of trousers that the other hand is laboriously pulling up, and with sophisticated testing it became apparent that the knowledge-bases of the two half-brains did not always exactly mesh. When Abigail and Brittany played the piano, was it really 'just' a highly practised duet?

Indeed, with simultaneous damage to certain frontal regions of the brain, and via torsion to the band of callosal fibres interconnecting the two cerebral hemispheres, as can even happen in a simple vehicle accident, any one of us might suffer from that seemingly bizarre, complementary neurological condition: the alien or anarchic hand syndrome. Here, it will be remembered, the unfortunate individual may have to watch, alarmed and disbelieving, his non-dominant (i.e. the left, in right-handers) hand acting all unbidden and engaging in its own, often inappropriate, behaviours; it had become disconnected from the currently conscious volitional centres in the dominant hemisphere, to be briefly under the control of the other, minor, hemisphere.

Are we *all* of us, as it were, a composite of separate individuals united and unified by a common background of experiences and linking nerve fibres? Are Abigail and Brittany somehow analogous to 'split-brain' patients who, right from their very beginnings, have each been *also* endowed with complementary and completing half-brains, to make them whole individuals? And is it a kind of alien-hand experience, for Abigail, when Brittany makes a sudden unexpected (to Abigail) move?

No, we *don't* all perceive the world in exactly the same way. Synaesthesia, for instance, is a rare, inherited, neurological condition – not a disability, but maybe instead an unusual *ability*, over-represented in females – where certain sounds may almost instantaneously trigger the simultaneous perceptual experience of particular colours, or even tastes; where certain tastes may invoke particular colours or tactual sensations.... Synaesthetes we have studied all differ from each other idiosyncratically in how their particular, simultaneous 'cross-wired' experiences manifest – and yet all are entirely consistent, over long periods of time, in their own peculiar linkages. I shall shortly return to the fascinating problem of synaesthesia in Chapter 24.

Nor need we be in any way abnormal or rare, psychologically, in experiencing, as in synaesthesia, percepts that simply 'aren't there'. Lose a limb by misadventure or deliberate surgery, and you are very likely to experience a compelling phantom of that limb – the phantom limb phenomenon of amputees – so 'real' that you may be obliged to try to scratch its intolerable itch, or even try to stand on it when arising from a chair. Phantom breasts, and even phantom penises, have also been described by amputees. Such individuals may therefore vividly experience sensations which have no external physical basis or reality. Nor are such experiences delusional or hallucinatory in a psychiatric sense. Again, see below for more on this topic.

Conversely, damage to certain regions, typically of the right side of the brain, can cause the clinical phenomenon known as unilateral neglect; you may come to deny the very existence of an arm or leg on the opposite side of the body, even though it is clearly visible. Sane and sensible in all other respects, you may even claim it belongs to someone else! Indeed, there are cases which combine a phantom limb experience with neglect, with additional claims by the patients that they possess a third, centrally-located arm, or even a paired penis! Are such neurological disorders of body schema ultimately the source of body-dysmorphic syndrome? Such individuals may strenuously seek amputation of a perfectly good arm or leg 'because it doesn't really feel right or belong…' And what about the anorexic's distorted image of her body shape and size?

If only you could see through my eyes!

17

HARRY McGURK, READ MY LIPS

Ventriloquism

As a very young child towards the end of the Second World War, I was often taken for summer holidays to Llandudno, a staid 'watering place', as such resorts were then commonly known, to distinguish them from the more-raunchy holiday venues like Blackpool. On the 'Welsh Riviera' – yet another euphemism? – Llandudno was noted for healthy and bracing air, which meant that it was often cold, wet and windy, and for its imposing Victorian hotels with palm courts where the orchestra played while you partook of genteel afternoon tea. Forbiddingly large, impassive and unwelcoming landladies ruled the cheaper end of town, with boarding establishments boasting inappropriately optimistic nameplates such as Costa Bella, Mira Mar, Ozone House and of course Sea View. Redolent with the ubiquitous stale smells of overcooked meat and the obligatory three veg, they were almost an enticement in a period of general wartime privation.

On the pier, beside the Dodgem Cars, stood the Punch and Judy show. Children loved it, before TV came, and I could never get enough of the knockabout puppet play, with its fascinating and convincing ventriloquistic effects, whereby the characters continually abused each other. How did the puppeteer make the speech appear to originate so naturally and appropriately from the wooden mouth of each little doll, the right one in the right place at the right time?

Some 20 or so years ago I was faced with a similar research problem. But first, let me take you back again to the closing days of the Second World War. It was the beginning of automated warfare, when equipment operators were faced with the problem of too many things happening too fast all at once, more than could be coped with. Nowadays we call it Information Overload, but a young researcher, Donald Broadbent, later a Fellow of the Royal Society, was studying our 'channel capacity', or ability to follow simultaneously more than one message through earphones. Apart from the obvious relevance of such applied research, the studies demonstrated much that was not then known about attentional holding, switching, focusing and sharing. They also showed that when two messages went simultaneously via earphones, separately one to each ear, the message content in the right ear tended to dominate, although other features such as emotional aspects or personal identity may be better identified from the left ear. All this agreed with neurological observations from the period's many war-wounded; the brain's left side or hemisphere, to which the right ear preferentially sends its input – although exactly why the cross-over is still debated – is where language tends to be elaborated.

From the 1950s until the 1980s it was held that Broadbent's 'Ear Effects', as they came to be known, depended upon the belief that right ear inputs, in addition to projecting more strongly to the opposite, left, half-brain, also suppressed the left ear's weaker, uncrossed, signal direct to that same destination on the left. Similarly, the left ear input, in addition to projecting strongly to the right hemisphere, also suppressed the right ear's weaker, uncrossed, signal to that same side. This account also seemingly explained why ear asymmetries were at best very weak without competition between ears.

In the 1980s, with my student Jane Pierson, I wondered whether such ear asymmetries really needed pathway competition between the ears; could it instead be a matter of *attentional* competition? We first showed that ear asymmetries were in fact even more striking if *both* signals went to a *single* earphone, the messages being spoken by a male and a female voice to facilitate channel separation; the right ear clearly dominated the left in this purely *monaural* language-related task, as long as two messages competed for attention.

(Jane, our elected Departmental Sexual Harassment Officer, either despite or maybe even because of her own striking good looks, was once falsely accused by a vindictive male staff member of sexual harassment. The case was dismissed by our own Head of Department on the grounds that any red-blooded young man would 'give his eye-teeth to be so harassed' by Jane.)

A clincher for an attentional explanation would be the demonstration of an *apparent* right ear superiority when both signals in fact went equally to *both* ears, from directly in front and behind, but when ventriloquistic deception made it appear that they instead came from one side – the right. Note, first, that the location of a sound source which lies directly in front of or behind a listener is systematically ambiguous. We automatically judge direction of origin of a sound partly by very slight differences or asynchronies in times of arrival of a signal to the two ears. There is no such asynchrony with sound emitters lying on extensions, fore or aft, of our midlines, and our ability to localise improves as the sound emitter moves to an ever-more-lateral position.

So, we hid the loudspeakers, one directly in front of and the other behind the listener, who was led to believe that the signals instead came from a *third, highly visible*, speaker on the left or right, which continually emitted buzzes, hums, crackles and pops, thereby ventriloquistically 'capturing' the apparent location of the male and female voices. As before, the listener tried to follow and report on one of the two voices, and performed far better when they seemed to come from the right. The ventriloquistic deception thus proved extraordinarily compelling, indicating that Broadbent's ear asymmetries were attentional, rather than anatomical in origin, depending little or not at all upon pathway suppression, or where listeners actually received the message (left or right ear), and more on *attentional* processes and where they *thought* the message came from.

Visual capture of an auditory channel, the basis of ventriloquism, was demonstrated in a different way in the 1970s by Harry McGurk, in studies on speech recognition. The eponymously named McGurk illusion arises when speech sounds and lip movements are incongruent, failing to match, as in a badly-dubbed movie. Thus, if on a videotape the sound 'ba' is dubbed over the mouth movements of a speaker saying 'ga', listeners tend to report hearing a sound 'da', which is exactly intermediate between the two, in terms of where and how in a speaker's mouth the speech sound would be made. We therefore see that visual processing affects auditory experience in normal listeners, another form of visual capture.

But let me first digress again and note some other interesting and relevant neurological phenomena manifested by normal healthy individuals. The left side of the face, controlled by the right or more 'emotional' half-brain, tends to express emotions more strongly than the right side of the face. In contrast, the right side of the face, particularly the mouth, seems more important in the expression of speech, as shown by measurements of photographs of speakers' mouth and lip movements; this of course again reflects control of the speech apparatus, predominantly by the left half-brain. Watch a newsreader on television; eight out of ten show noticeably more extensive speech-related mouth movements or gestures by the mouth or lips on the speaker's right-hand side. (Remember, the speaker's right side is from the observer's viewpoint on the left side of the screen, and there is also a crossed relationship between side of brain control, and corresponding side of body, with the left half-brain tending largely to mediate language functions, and the right cerebral hemisphere to manage spatial, emotional and face-processing aspects.)

So, might mouth movement asymmetries also impact on our ability to lip read? Here, with my friend and colleague Mike Nicholls at Melbourne University, we employed the McGurk effect. With an electronic mask we exactly covered the left or right halves of the mouth in video recordings of the full face of speakers, or as a control, we left both sides uncovered. As expected, with incongruent visual and auditory signals, the speakers apparently saying one thing at a visual level, and something different at an auditory level, we found McGurk-type errors; people's reports of what they thought they had heard were influenced by what they simultaneously had seen. These errors were particularly prominent when both sides of the mouth were clearly visible in the control condition. The McGurk effect was, however, considerably attenuated when the right side of the mouth (from the *speaker's perspective*) was electronically masked, demonstrating that this side is more important to lip reading than is the mouth's left side; again, it is presumably the more expressive side during normal speech. The fact that the McGurk effect was no stronger when both sides of the mouth were visible, than when the left side was covered and the right side visible, suggests that the visual information provided by movements of the right side of the mouth is just as informative as that provided by movements of the full, unmasked mouth. So, in principle, we can lip read from someone with only half a face as well as from a normal person, as long as the unfortunate individual's mutilation spares the right side of the face.

We also mirror-reversed the images to test the possibility that such asymmetries may additionally be affected by an observer bias towards the left side – as seen by the observer – of images like the face. We do know that we attend somewhat more to the left sides of faces, seen in full frontal view, from studies employing so-called chimeric or composite faces. Photographs of individuals smiling or frowning are cut down the midline, and recombined so that the smile is on the left and the frown on the right, or vice versa. People tend to judge such composites as appearing overall more or less happy, or unhappy, on the basis of whether the particular emotion is represented on the left side, as viewed. The emotion is generally more strongly developed on the face's actual, physical, left side, that is, from the perspective of the *owner* of the face, due to that side's direct access to emotional centres on the right side of the brain. However, mirror-reversing the composites shows that a leftwards perceptual bias is largely independent of any motor differences in generating the expression. A leftwards bias, of course, directs attention towards the more expressive right side of a speaker's face, where lip reading may receive a boost. Is this one evolutionary reason why we tend to look slightly leftwards at a speaker during conversation? Or is it just a by-product of the perceiver's own emotional arousal, whereby activation of emotional centres in the right half-brain 'overflows', to cause a slight leftward shift in the focus of attention?

I wonder whether children watching a puppet show – although I now fear that Punch and Judy has followed the dinosaurs and the Tasmanian Tiger into extinction in the television age – tend to look more towards the left when watching the puppets' faces? We do of course still see 'speaking' puppets on children's TV; maybe there is a lesson to be learnt in trying to make as congruent as possible the relationships between the seen mouth movements and the soundtrack, to avoid unwanted McGurk effects. And the puppet masters should perhaps play particular attention to the right sides of their charges' faces to achieve maximum verisimilitude. Isn't that what ventriloquism is all about? And if you find totally confusing all this left and right business – brain, side of body, and side of a viewed image, whether or not mirror-reversed – please don't worry! Even after many years I still do too!

18

MIRROR, MIRROR ON THE WALL

Symmetrical stimuli and bimanual responses

You are standing before a full-length mirror; why is it that while your left and right sides are reversed, flipped, this is not true of your top and bottom, your head and feet? This question has exercised some very acute minds for hundreds of years, and there is room still for more debate. I won't answer it here, except to comment that the top-bottom axis or coordinate is determined by external, physical constraints, including gravity, while left-right is more a matter of human convention. A related issue is the question as to why, if you hold your knickers or underpants at the sides as if about to step into them, and without letting go, flip them inside out, left and right don't change, but the front now becomes the back. And if you turn a left-hand latex glove inside out, it becomes a perfectly serviceable right-hand glove. Next, and for obvious reasons this demonstration may be more readily performed on the male torso, get someone to stand, topless, with eyes closed, and trace, with a blunt stylus (a 'dead' ballpoint will do just fine), on his chest a cursive lower-case letter p or q, or b or d, which are left-right ambiguous, and ask him which letter it felt like. Do this several times, noting his answers, and repeat this time on his back. If you can, persuade someone else also to contribute, this time start on the back and then 'do' the chest. Even better, maybe, randomly alternate front and back and p, q, b, d. Then do the same but now on the hand – palm and back of hand when hand is held up, as if in salutation, with either palm or back facing forward. Maybe do all of this, as a party game if you like (kids and even adults will be intrigued), under three conditions: when the hand is in a plane further forward than the rest of the body, when it is further behind the plane of the body, and when it is in exactly the same plane as the upright body. Have fun at your local night club, and I won't spoil it by boring explanations!

And staying with parties and a desirable state of *deshabillé*, why is it so hard (as kids often seem to know) simultaneously to perform circular rotations on your belly with one hand while simultaneously patting (or tapping!) the top of your head with the other? What might this task or game have to do with bimanual coordination?

Why do we have a left and right? Why aren't we like certain echinoderms (starfish and sea urchins), which exhibit what is called a radial (or pie-shaped) symmetry? If we wish to navigate unidirectionally, there may be some advantages in having a leading edge with head, vision or other sensors and mouth at the front, and a propulsive system further back along with excretory apparatus. Like a worm, or lizard, fish or granddad, who after all is just a very advanced worm standing on end. Obviously, radial symmetry can also work (maybe not spherical, like an orange, if you want to get anywhere fast, and are bigger and better than a bacterium). And the octopus' ground plan has aspects in common with radial symmetry, and it can certainly go places, and fast. Although it must be a problem coordinating all those 'legs' – a problem at least addressed in evolution by giving it a semi-decentralised nervous system.

I once had an even more than usually brilliant honours student, who wrote to me from Hobart, Tasmania, asking to do an honours project in my lab. He had excellent credentials and I took him on. As he had nowhere to live, Judy and I took him in as a lodger. He bought an old banger of a car, which needed an oil change, and he asked me how to do it. I explained, as in my younger days I used to do all my own car servicing, before I got older, stiffer, wiser and wealthier, and cars became impossibly complicated. He stood at a loss, and with some embarrassment asked me if I would do it for him. My first thought was that this is going far beyond what might normally be expected of a professorial supervisor; my next one was, 'what the hell, he is a worthy young man', and I did it for him. I'm glad I did, as from his honours thesis emerged no less than five research papers in top neurological journals – more than many consultant neurologists over their lifetimes have to their names. One achievement, particularly germane to the present argument, was unbeknown to anyone in the lab; he took apart a complex device we had constructed to measure sequential choice reaction times, with programmable levels of stimulus and temporal uncertainty, and which we had designed for unimanual operation. He totally reconstructed and reprogrammed it so that he could design and run a very neat bimanual task, and found that Parkinson's disease (PD) patients have great, inordinate, difficulty with bimanual coordination. We now know that the supplementary motor area in the brain receives input from the basal ganglia, a movement hold, release and sequencing system, and one or both of these neural systems become defective in PD. Did it matter that he did not know how to do an oil change? I bet he can now, although as a top consultant in a major medical discipline, I doubt he will ever need to.

On the strength of his findings, I designed a custom-made device to accommodate a more complex combination of bimanual demands, a device which with modern touch-screen technology would nowadays probably be superseded by a more elegant design of finger tracing, although the principles would remain. A pair of hand cranks was set up before a participant, whose task it was to rotate them, at various speeds in time with a metronome, either in phase with each other, or out of phase by 180 degrees, and either both in the same direction (both clockwise, or both anticlockwise), or, the easier condition, symmetrically in opposite directions. We could thereby quantify the extent to which participants deviated from the target phase in degrees. We confirmed our original findings with PD, and extended them to Huntington's disease (HD), major depression and schizophrenia, all conditions which in several other aspects suggested frontostriatal (basal ganglia – supplementary motor area, BG-SMA) involvement. Additionally, we found that the schizophrenia group resembled the HD group more than the PD group. It is interesting that there have been other reports, including our own, that people with schizophrenia, and also with autism or Asperger's, may be clumsy and awkward, with, as we have shown in the last two groups, problems extending also to gait – where it is still of course a matter of limb (now lower limb) coordination. Indeed, we have found that various other BG-SMA (frontostriatal) deficits are widespread in neurodevelopmental disorders, including also Tourette, obsessive-compulsive (OCD) and attention deficit (ADHD) disorders and depression. The problem would seem in part also to be one of transcallosal interhemispheric integration of limb movements, on opposite sides of the body, and separately mediated by the two halves (hemispheres) of the brain, in company with the BG-SMA axis or system. Please note that the next paragraph summarises material from a previous chapter, and can be skipped if already familiar with it; otherwise it is included for explanatory purposes.

The corpus callosum, that massive tract of interhemispheric connections, used sometimes to be surgically sectioned, before superior control measures were developed, so as to limit the spread throughout the brain of otherwise intractable epilepsy. Then, under extreme and contrived laboratory conditions, sometimes the patient would behave as if controlled by two separate minds, with two separate streams of consciousness. Thus there are reports of the right hand seeking to complete a task being performed by the left, or trying to pull down the pants which the left is pulling up (usually it was the dominant, right, hand exerting control over the other). Then there are reports of 'alien hand' behaviour, after anterior callosal damage or commissurotomy, with (usually the non-dominant) hand making seemingly purposeful but quite unintended movements, sometimes to the alarm of its 'owner', who cannot inhibit it; indeed he/she may try to restrain it with the other hand – just as in that extraordinarily prescient movie *Dr Strangelove*, where the owner is trying with one hand trying to hold down the other which seemingly is wanting to give a Nazi salute. We all of course can be 'in two minds' – a form of mental modularity – undecided, but at any one time with only one line of thought accessible to full introspective awareness, maybe via unifying attentional switching and selecting mechanisms in the prefrontal cortex. And again, we are all sometimes guilty of unthinkingly 'playing' with an object, usually appropriately for its intended purpose, but inappropriately in a current context – as with doodling.

Nearly three decades ago, while visiting Cambridge, I was browsing obscure journals in a neglected corner of the library; I chanced upon an article on motor overflow or synkinesis, a term used to describe uncontrolled or unconscious movements, associated with intentional movements, but themselves unintended and without a definite purpose, and generally not associated with any defined neurological condition. These unintended movements often seem contra-laterally to mimic intended movements made by the other limb or hand. They may be more common in the very young and in the older person, and when the task is effortful, or the performer is fatigued or stressed. I had in fact recently encountered an elderly Chinese gentleman, shortly after a major frontal stroke, whose arm would uselessly but exactly and symmetrically mimic every intended movement performed by its fellow, to his evident concern, rather after the fashion of a flying bird's wings. Be that as it may, the experimental procedure employed in this paper I had encountered was theoretically interesting, but in practice very crude: participants had a weight (of various values) attached to a cotton loop over the extended index finger, the downwards pressure of which they had to resist, while the corresponding finger of the other hand was monitored for any movement. I thought how much better we could design and develop such a paradigm! We constructed a pair (one for each forefinger) of force transducers, to measure the force exerted, on command, by the active finger, and any corresponding pressure exerted by the other, 'alternative' or passive forefinger. We measured the maximum force that the participant could produce, and then required them to generate and maintain, for a set period of time, a percentage of that value, thereby controlling for individual strength differences. In some conditions participants could see, graphed on a screen in real time, their moment-to-moment pressures, so as to try to keep within target range. We found that children and the elderly had most trouble inhibiting overflow, and everyone likewise when there was fatigue, stress or attentional demands, or when the non-dominant hand was active. This spread of activation between hands must at some level involve the interhemispheric commissures, such as the corpus callosum, such that activity in the controlling hemisphere is generated, and presumably inadequately inhibited, in the other hemisphere, perhaps through incomplete developmental commissural myelination in the young, and callosal degeneration in the elderly. It is interesting to note that there are reports of elderly patients also having difficulty with bimanual coordination as in our cranks task. There are also reports that children with ADHD, a neurodevelopmental disorder involving the BG, itself necessarily involved in motor overflow, also exhibit raised levels of overflow.

An animal or even a person needs to recognise an object, another person or a face irrespective of whether it is seen from the left or right side; and subsequently it is usually unimportant whether or not we remember the orientation in the original encounter. Given the largely symmetrical nature of the vertebrate brain, questions have long been asked as to whether in some way visual memory traces, if transferred or compared between hemispheres and thereby across the commissures, are somehow mirror-reversed during that process. Children have particular difficulty, while learning to read, with letters such as p and q, b and d, and may even mirror-write, especially if left-handed, and consequently, as it used to be said, poorly lateralised and presumably thereby 'reading from' the other hemisphere. In the early 1970s, when there was a vogue for invoking hemisphere problems of this sort,

I generated left and right profiles, differing from each other by various features (shapes of chin, nose, forehead, and so on), oriented so as to face left or right, and flashed them up in pairs for comparison as to same or different. They were thus sequentially flashed, in pairs, either both to the same hemisphere (left or right, via the opposite visual field, as the optic pathways cross from eye to brain), or one each to different visual fields/hemispheres, and in either case oriented left or right, same orientation in both, or reversed in one. We found that judgements for mirror-reversed profiles were performed overall more slowly and less accurately than when both profiles faced the same way, but this performance decrement was less when the two members of each pair went to different, opposite sides (hemispheres), offering at least partial support for some kind of interhemispheric symmetrisation process.

The left side of the face (seen from its owner's perspective) tends to be more emotionally expressive, and it seems that portrait painters may be (perhaps unconsciously) 'aware' of this, as there is a preponderance of left side profiles over right. And if we construct 'chimeric' faces composed of composites of a left-side-smiling and a right-side-frowning face, or vice versa, the one with a smile on the left, as viewed, is generally seen as happier than its fellow. The same situation applies if you construct chimeric faces, one set composed of two original left halves (with one half reversed to abut its unreversed fellow), and another set similarly constructed from two original right halves. Now, you ask which chimera more closely resembles the original, whole, uncut face. Invariably it is the face constructed from two left halves.

And it is not just faces. If you construct a horizontal grey-scale strip, with the dark end to left and light end to right, and place it directly above the same strip now left-right reversed, so that its dark end is now on the right, and its light end on the left, and ask people which of the two strips LOOKS darker overall, they will tend to choose the one with the darker end to the left. The same applies if you ask them which of the two SEEMS lighter – again it tends to be the one with the lighter end to left. Wedges, similarly constructed, with a reversed copy placed above or below, will produce analogous effects, when you instead ask which wedge SEEMS overall the larger/smaller.

Maybe get a new mirror if you don't like how your face looks to (or at) you!

19

CONSCIOUSNESS, WILL AND TIME

Hosting a party, I had soup accidentally spilt on my lap by an ageing friend sitting beside me. I retired to the bedroom for a hasty exchange of trousers, and while pondering the unwanted changes, including increasingly careless movements, which accompany our advancing years, I glanced at the full length mirror to check I had done up my flies – a possible error of omission (not, I would emphasise, one of commission!) that at least extends back to my middle years. But, no flies; and no trousers! Good God – I had completed quite automatically a full bedtime swap, and was now wearing pyjamas. Thank God for mirrors! We all need protection from our own unwanted automatisms.

'I did not know I loved you till I heard myself telling you so: for an instant, I thought "Good God, what have I said?", and then I knew it was the truth', or something to that effect is said to have been the account by the great British philosopher, Bertrand Russell, of one of his not inconsiderable number of romantic encounters.

All too often we may act semi-automatically, autonomously even, often even in response to our 'gut' feelings, before becoming consciously aware of what we may have said or done, and whether or not it was in fact appropriate to the context – social or practical.

The world's great golf players seem to have overlearned, through repetition over thousands of ever-changing instances, the stance and swing appropriate to each next stroke, whatever the varying environmental details. Many have noted that too much introspection can screw up their shot. 'Go with the flow, and don't think about it too much', may be the best mantra.

Consciousness and will have long been the playground of philosophers, like our amorous and eminent Lord Bertrand; only recently have psychologists, often of a philosophical bent themselves, dared to play on the same dangerous playground, and then often only when they have gained security of job tenure. Indeed, ventures into the hot topic of consciousness and will seem often to be a favourite diversion, in every sense, for eminent, retired Nobel laureates, whatever the relevance or otherwise of their original discipline. It is widely regarded as the Hard Question, and it is only a minor exaggeration to comment that there seem to be as many books written on the topic as the proverbial sands of the restless seashore.

Is there a consciousness centre somewhere in the brain, and if so, where does it reside? And how are its arcane processes realised? When, and where, between perception and action may they operate? Is there perhaps more than one centre, handling different aspects? Is there maybe a state of mind, possibly managed by a widespread brain system, even to be identified with if not identical to what has come to be labelled the default network, which is particularly active during periods of quiet introspection or even when we 'let our minds wander' or daydream, as well as during active attentional thought, or when remembering, problem solving or planning for the future? Current thinking suggests that there is indeed such a network of interacting brain regions whose activity tends to synchronise or correlate, each with each other. Is it perhaps the neurological correlate of the self? It is surely no accident that the widespread brain damage in dementia, especially of the Alzheimer's type, destroys the very personality, the ability to remember, plan, imagine the future, reflect upon oneself, all generating with loss a kind of emotional widowing. Three main networks or hubs have been proposed, on the basis of clinical and experimental findings, for such a default network: (1) the posterior cingulate cortex; (2) the medial prefrontal cortex; and (3) the angular gyrus. The posterior cingulate may mediate involuntary perceptual and attentional aspects; the medial prefrontal may be more concerned with personal and autobiographical aspects, planning for the future and decision-making; the angular gyrus, given also its strategically located linking position, may interlink perceptual, attentional and spatial processes.

Is attention inextricably linked with consciousness? Of the four identifiable attentional processes, orienting (typically to something new or important), selective (latching on to it), sustained (hanging on to it, resisting other siren calls) and divided (multi-tasking), clearly the third is the most likely attentional candidate for a link with aspects of consciousness. In what is called 'the vegetative state' after major brain injury or in a coma, with the patient apparently unresponsive to speech or other forms of stimulation, might there nevertheless sometimes be a residual level of conscious awareness? It is no good just examining changes in brain activation patterns when appropriately interrogated, as any such changes may merely reflect automatic decoding processes associated with language. If, however, you ask the patient to imagine playing tennis, or walking through her house, and you find characteristically different and appropriate activation patterns, extended in time, this may indeed suggest some level of consciousness. Indeed, in a further step, some few such patients could even answer 'yes' or 'no' to personal questions, such as 'Is your name Felicity?', or 'Were you born in 1990?', when the affirmative answer was to be given by imagining playing tennis, and the negative by imagining walking through the house. Such recent demonstrations suggest we should not prematurely 'write off' comatose individuals, or those deemed sunk in an insensible vegetative state. Vagal nerve stimulation, moreover, of such patients with long-standing 'unresponsive wakefulness' recently led to a regained ability to respond to certain commands, and a sustained recovery to a 'minimally conscious' state. The vagus nerve modulates the heart rate and lung function, and is also involved in memory, arousal, alertness and emotion.

Thomas Willis, the putative father of neurology, argued way back in the seventeenth century for a multiplicity of what he then called 'souls'. I would argue that we, too, nowadays, experience many different facets or even types of consciousness, all simultaneously operating, in parallel, and involving a number of different brain regions or systems. When one or more of these systems 'goes down', or is temporarily or permanently defective, then we are in thrall to a temporary or permanent psychiatric syndrome. Our concept of an object or class of conceptually related objects may similarly depend upon 'binding together' a range of attributes relevant to the idea or definition of that object or concept – a silver candlestick has a characteristic or generic shape, colour, weight, value or context within which it is relevant. A particular band of frequencies, around maybe 40 Hz and originating in the thalamus, is thought by some to act as a temporary 'label' whereby momentarily the neural correlates of these 'qualia' or qualities for a particular situation or occasion are labelled or tagged. Each of these qualia might of course on other occasions be combined with others to characterise or identify some other object or situation: a silver coin, a brass candlestick, and so on. Consciousness may operate along analogous or possibly higher-order lines involving synchronisation.

Considerations such as the above invite questions about timing, in particular, whether consciousness, rather than being a kind of continuous flow, like the river of time metaphor, is instead like a series of sequential snap-shots or 'takes', and, if so, the possible duration of each of these momentary and successive conscious 'experiences'. I once showed introductory students how to perceptually disconnect the glowing lit end of a moving cigarette from the rest of its body, by using rapid strobe illumination. When the cigarette, so illuminated in the dark, is rapidly moved, the lit end seems to proceed somewhat ahead of the rest of the moving tube, only to immediately recombine on cessation of motion. We can continuously sample the continuously burning end, but only intermittently see the strobe-illuminated body, such that it seems to lag the former. Careful control of rates of movement and of strobed illumination can throw light upon important temporal constants in visual awareness. We can thus study the 'flash-lag effect', as the phenomenon is grandly known, and the 'psychological moment' (a term first used, although in a rather different context, in 1871), when we might feel we experience the occurrence of an instantaneous present.

If there is such a phenomenon as a psychological moment, how long might it be, or might there be more than one such 'moment', depending upon the context? One possible context relates to the 'flicker fusion rate', as in cinematography – the frequency at which an intermittent light stimulus appears to be completely steady, or, with a succession of successively-projected frames of a moving object, when the latter is seen to move in a smooth rather than in a flickering fashion. Another everyday instance is the 50 Hz or 60 Hz mains-driven flicker of a light source which is in fact seen as continuous illumination. However, experiments show that the critical flicker fusion threshold is far from constant, depending on colour, brightness, light/dark adaptation, the exact position on the retina of the eye where a stimulus is placed, and so on.

When a signal is presented rapidly (a very brief flash or click) to a waiting and ready subject, who does not know exactly when the stimulus will occur so cannot predict and anticipate, there is a 'simple reaction time' of around 120 msec. When there may be more than one possible signal, each type requiring its own, different response (choice reaction time), with maybe a different button for each type or location, reaction time increases as a logarithmic function of the number of possible, different, alternative stimulus-response pairings. Thus, a straight line graph, with a characteristic slope emerges. It is as if, plotting the graph to logs to base 2, the participant makes a series of successive halvings of the array of available or remaining alternatives – if it is not in the first half of possibilities, it must be in the second half, and so on until there are no other possibilities left – when it must therefore be the last, residual, remaining possibility. Either way, simple or complex, it might suggest that there is an associated psychological moment of around 100 msec.

However, there is yet another experimental paradigm possibly relevant to the issue – that involving use of delayed feedback. If speakers are prevented, with sound-attenuating earphones, from hearing what they are saying except with a very short delay, they can be reduced to (to them embarrassing) stuttering incoherence and/or silence. The critical delay is around 250 msec – much above or below that, and the 'delayed auditory feedback' paradigm is less effective. My group found that the effect, and the 'best' delay of a similar value, are even more striking with electric piano playing, where of course it is easier than with speech, totally to eliminate instantaneous auditory feedback, electronically, with an electronic keyboard. And delayed visual feedback while writing something, or tying your cravat or a knot, gives us the same value. It is as if there is a loop involving the sequence of respond, then monitor correctness, or if otherwise, then modify response sequence, with a loop value of around 250 msec.

So is there perhaps a whole set of different psychological moments, of different values? This might not be so strange or necessarily inefficient; we now know that there are in fact a whole series of 'biological clocks', monitoring the passage of time important for various biological functions, both within the organism as a whole, and at an intracellular level. Maybe the same is true for the 'psychological moment'.

We can also investigate the apparent simultaneity or otherwise of two events occurring in different sensory modalities, such as a click (auditory) and a flash (visual). Electrical activity in the auditory and visual areas of the brain is not simultaneous (the retina of the eye requires more time to perform a slower chemical transduction than the rapid electromechanical process in the ear), even when the two stimulus events are simultaneous. Nevertheless, our perception of the two events is one of simultaneity; the faster auditory process must somehow be 'slowed' for the slower visual signal to complete transmission; the two end states then appear simultaneous.

A controversial finding is that motor activity in the brain seems to precede our awareness of intention – we seem to do something before we decide or intend to act! If true, where is there room for freedom of will? Thirty years ago, in an experiment, Benjamin Libet's participants watched a slowly rotating clock hand, and voluntarily made hand movements at times of their own choosing. Sometimes they were to report the perceived instant, as shown on the clock, when they made the decision to move; other times, they were to report when they felt they had actually moved. In this way he ascertained when people formulated an intention to move, and when they actually did so. At the same time he determined onset of changes in electrical activity over motor areas in the brain, and in the muscles themselves. The electrophysiological correlates of movement preparation preceded those of actual conscious awareness of intention by nearly half a second. He also found that people's judgement of each movement's beginnings shortly preceded the onset of movement potentials in the muscles themselves. As it happens, it is known that all intentional movements are preceded, in the brain, by the generation of a prior copy of the expected sensory consequences thereof, what a successful completion of that movement should feel like, against which the actual sensory consequences can be compared – what it did in fact really feel like; in this way, with any discrepancies, a correction can then, if necessary, be initiated. This is all known as the theory of efference copy or reafference. So do we construct for ourselves an illusion of free will by linking, in time, the neural correlates of intention, action, and the consequences of action? Perceptual or motor events may have to occur within a finite window of perceived time for them to seem to be associated. Indeed, appropriate electrical or magnetic stimulation of the brain's supplementary motor area can generate a desire to actually make a planned movement, a feeling of imminent intention, facilitation, initiation or even inhibition of such a movement. Intriguingly, such brain areas can be affected in schizophrenia, when unfortunate patients may behave inappropriately, lose control, or even invoke an external agent to explain their inappropriate emotions' thoughts, actions or speech.

In a scientific world where we are rapidly moving to where amputees may be able to control the movements of artificial or prosthetic limbs by thought alone, from potentials generated over motor areas, it is possible to address some of the problems and phenomena described above by measuring the intervals in time between the onset of such potentials, and actual responses. Thus, if the task were one of choice between two types of movement – maybe go left, or go right – can we predict, from the nature of the potentials, and before the subject actually responds, whether with a normal or a prosthetic limb, which of the two responses will be initiated? Again, it seems that these potentials do allow an observer to make such a prediction at an accuracy well above chance level.

One possible answer to such apparently paradoxical challenges to our vaunted and aspirational autonomy of freedom of will and action is, of course, that the earliest moment in the cascade of events unleashed with the initiation of a voluntary action, corresponds to when a decision process commences, and that our judgements of time and priority of event occurrence are both highly subjective and flexible. Thus, participants may click a mouse, and a light then flashes after a short delay. The procedure is then repeated for quite some time to strengthen the expectation that the mouse click causes the flash. Then, unbeknown to the participant, the interval is substantially reduced, and participants now, paradoxically, *perceive* the light to occur before the click.

If a vibrator, as used in physiotherapy or as purchased in some 'adult' shops, is applied to the elbow, its stimulation will affect muscle stretch receptors, producing an illusory Pinocchio effect when at the same time the participant is holding his or her nose. Thus, the stimulation of the elbow stretch receptors causes an illusory bending outwards of the forearm; since the latter is anchored via the hand's fingers grasping the nose, the illusion is resolved by the nose seeming to stretch, as in the myth and puppetry of Pinocchio. A related 'tunnel effect' exemplifies how such illusions of space interact interestingly and meaningfully with speed and therefore time. When adjacent locations on the skin of, say, the forearm, are repeatedly stimulated, perhaps with a brush, at about the same time, the brain comes to represent them adjacently. The more times this coincident stimulation occurs, the stronger the neural connectivity. In one experiment, a soft paintbrush was moved back and forth along the forearm at a constant slow rate, except for a middle, covered, 'tunnel' section of its trajectory where it moved at ten times the rate, but was not felt, being covered. The sensation of the brush in this middle, unstimulated section was perceptually filled in from the traversing motion, and the participants reported that they felt that the brush was continuously moving along the whole arm, which then felt shorter – the opposite of the Pinocchio effect.

Then there is the oddball effect; the image of an object A (maybe a coin) is flashed on and off, flickered, on a screen, and participants judge its perceived duration, a value which tends to decrease over time – object A seems to be 'up' for progressively shorter durations. But if object A is suddenly replaced by B, maybe a bottle, the perceived duration jumps right up again back to baseline.

Moral: linear extent and temporal duration, which jointly determine speed, are flexible and labile in the human (and doubtlessly also animal) mind. There is no such thing as *the* psychological moment; there are many. And free will? We are yet convincingly to disprove its aspirational and possibly illusory existence. Maybe there really is no such thing as freedom of will – or maybe, just as with the psychological moment, we may be buffeted by several conflicting wills. Is that what can happen in psychosis or states of disinhibition, or obsessive compulsive disorder? Or when I simply say, 'One part of me wants to do A, while another, C.' Indeed, how blurred can be the boundary between wish and will? I wish I knew, but won't pursue the matter.

FIGURE 1 1958 Birkenhead School, Speech Day prizes

FIGURE 2 1960 The Old Forge for sale

FIGURE 3 1962a Oxford graduation

FIGURE 4 1962b Arctic expeditioners, Tundra. I am at the front on the right

FIGURE 5 1965a PhD researches in my cellar lab. I am in the chinrest, Eric Eagle to the rear right controls the apparatus

FIGURE 6 1965b Sheffield, Africa, expeditioners. I am on the front jerry-can rack

FIGURE 7 1965c Sheffield, Africa, Palmyra, still intact before destruction by IS

FIGURE 8 1965d Sheffield, Africa, route to Baghdad, by compass across endless dusty plains

FIGURE 9 1965e Sheffield, Africa, Sahara camp. I stand guard

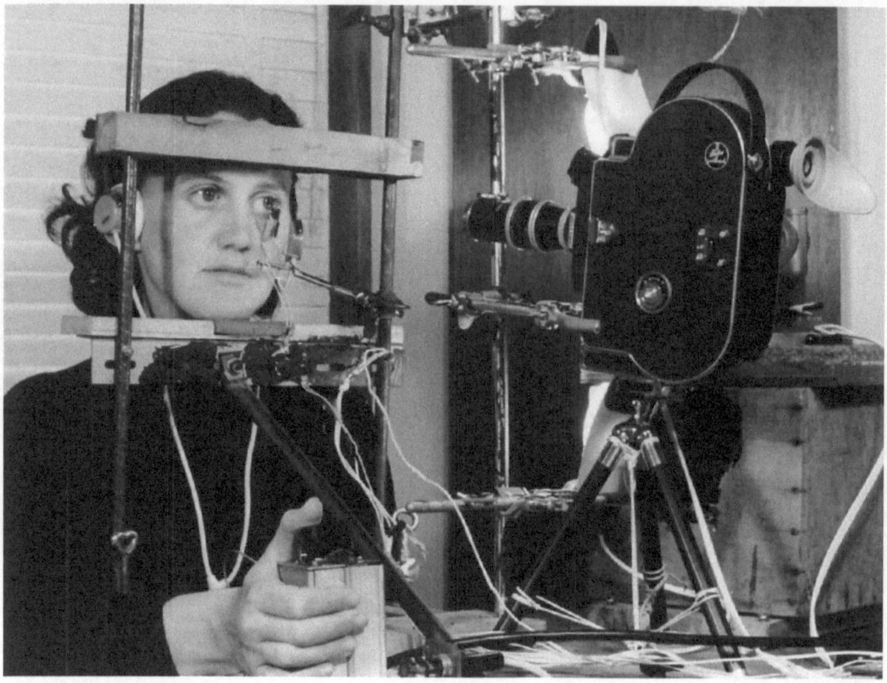

FIGURE 10 1967 My wife Judy in my pupillometer

FIGURE 11 1988 DSc award, with my daughter Catriona simultaneously graduating with a First in Medicine

FIGURE 12 2006 My official portrait

20

WHEN IGNORANCE IS BLISS

Not long ago I came across a box of my old possessions, containing a picture book of farmyard animals entitled *My Farmyard Friends*. My mother had sent the material years earlier, when clearing out my juvenilia, and it had long languished until the time came for another generational spring clean. *My Farmyard Friends* immediately evoked vivid recall, in the finest detail, of its pictures. It also brought back a much darker memory, but more of that shortly. I was particularly struck by the fact that it was only the physical presence of the actual book itself which apparently could provide sufficient context or cues for the re-emergence of long-inaccessible associated visual memories, memories which probably could never have otherwise re-emerged, no matter how careful and extensive the verbal prompting. Indeed, we all know how finding an old theatre ticket in a long-disused suit pocket can bring back many a long-forgotten emotional memory. Maybe we should hoard all life's trivia, fully to recapture old loves, triumphs and disasters! Maybe it is some such similar subconscious 'awareness' of the potentiality of inanimate objects which underlies the phenomenon, and pathology, of the clinical condition nowadays known as 'hoarding', where real pain on parting with collected and assiduously accumulated junk is experienced.

What was the dark secret associated with the children's bestiary? Around the age of three, I acquired a severely infected big toe from some minor trauma, accompanied by exquisite pain and impressive swelling and discoloration. In those late-wartime years in England, the family doctor visited you, rather than the other way round, a visit which was as social as it was therapeutic. The toe was to be lanced, and to distract me, I was presented with this wonderful new book to look at during the procedure. Not only do I remember that the procedure climaxed exactly at the page where a friendly old cart horse was hanging his head over a stable half-door, but also that I had felt absolutely no pain whatsoever, and that even that realisation itself puzzled me, and actually made me naïvely aware of the power of distraction.

Fast-forward, now, to a few years ago, and exactly the opposite situation, when I had to undergo a largely routine esophageal endoscopy. This involves the examiner passing a scope down the patient's throat to the stomach – potentially a thoroughly unpleasant experience requiring a level of 'conscious' co-operation by the patient. In a world where date-rape drugs apparently permit sexual predators to make their victims co-operate to some extent, while subsequently retaining little or no awareness of what transpired, we can at least be grateful for the fact that similar partial anaesthesia permits the endoscopy patient to co-operate with the examiner, while subsequently remembering mercifully little or nothing about the procedure. In the anxiety-provoking minutes just before 'going under', I tried to distract myself by carefully reviewing a complex experimental design associated with a new research project. The room I was in, although fairly featureless like most such places, nevertheless possessed drapes of a certain shape and colour, and one or two obvious fittings. Suddenly, in the midst of my ruminations on experimental procedure, I became sharply aware of a complete change in the room's layout; in fact, with a shock I saw that it had immediately become a totally different room, while my thought processes had seemingly continued in an apparently seamless way across this instantaneous transition. It was this last observation, rather than the realisation that the operation had been completed entirely without my knowledge, but presumably with my full or partial co-operation, that most impressed me. Nor was I at all groggy on coming round – it was literally as if a section of my life had been neatly excised, and all cognitive processes equally neatly continued across the closed-up gap.

These two personal, almost everyday, instances illustrate two rather opposing memory phenomena – the power of context to cue the recall of very remote and otherwise inaccessible memories from extreme childhood, and the power of modern drugs selectively to inhibit memory formation without leaving a subsequent 'gap' in the stream of awareness. Indeed, some experimental success is recently being reported on possible procedures retrospectively to delete pre-existing and unwanted memories, but that is another story for another time.

There is a clinical condition known as 'dissociative fugue state', whereby an individual may perform often quite bizarre (or even perfectly normal) acts, in an apparently purposeful fashion, with subsequently total memory loss or amnesia for the episode; alcohol, physical or mental trauma may play a precipitating role. The state may or may not be accompanied by sudden loss of personal identity, and all autobiographical memories. Significant distress, not surprisingly, may be experienced during or after such an episode. As this section is an attempt to illustrate clinical memory and attentional phenomena with relatively benign examples from everyday life, let me recount something superficially similar, in my own experience, to the clinical fugue state. In my mid-twenties I used daily to drive to and from my place of work along a featureless series of three-lane roads running through equally featureless countryside, the roads being punctuated by a regular series of roundabouts. In one direction, I had to continue straight ahead across three such roundabouts, and turn left at the fourth. One day I suddenly realised, with something approaching terror, that I was in totally unfamiliar territory, without the faintest idea where I was or how I had got there. I knew nothing then about fugue states, not that it would have helped me. Pulling up in a panic, I gradually realised that the most likely explanation was that somewhere along the track, while preoccupied, I had inadvertently turned either at the wrong roundabout, or in the wrong direction, or both.

It seems almost a truism to claim that memory is a reconstructive process, rather than something akin to making, storing and rerunning a video clip. However, this was forcibly brought home to me some years ago when I participated, as a supposedly healthy control, in a study of individuals suffering from memory problems. The actual procedure was not exactly novel, being borrowed from one developed by Elizabeth Loftus in her classic studies on the powerful effect of suggestion in recall. A video clip was shown of a minor traffic incident involving some superficial damage to a vehicle. The participants were subsequently asked either 'How fast was the car going when it hit the lamp post?', or, instead, 'How fast was it going when it hit the road sign?' In fact, it had only hit one of these obstacles, but participants, myself included, were quite sure, when subsequently asked, that it had in fact hit the obstacle mentioned, apparently almost parenthetically in the seemingly far more important context of its speed. We concentrate upon certain key features in a scene, and fill in, creatively, the subsidiary context.

I actually had a real-life experience which bears on, parallels even, the above account. Driving with my 10-year-old daughter down a steep, narrow and winding back road in Wales, round a corner we unexpectedly and without advance warning came upon a group of roadmen making repairs. As I was driving at a rate appropriate for the conditions, I had no problem pulling up in time; not so, a car that came up behind me at too fast a speed. The driver (very fortunately for us, not so the roadmen) somehow drove between us and a massive roadside wall – and killed two of the men outright, in front of our eyes. I won't dwell upon the horror of the situation, and getting help in a remote region; suffice it to say that when later interviewed by the police, and asked how fast the car was going, I gave a figure (I forget what it was, but far too fast for safety); months later, as a witness in court, I was again asked about the offender's speed, and quite confidently gave a somewhat different speed. There was a fairly considerable discrepancy (I forget the direction) between the two figures, both of which I gave in good faith. Fortunately (but not for the offender), it made no difference to the verdict. Memory in a forensic situation is notoriously unreliable.

Truly amnesic patients, and those suffering from dementia, may take this a stage further with frank, unintentional, confabulation. I once studied aspects of short- and long-term memory processes in patients suffering from Korsakoff psychosis. This condition, commonly caused by prolonged and excessive alcohol intake and associated thiamine deficiency, affects memory circuits such as the hippocampus and temporal lobes. Old memories typically remain largely unaffected; not so the formation of newer memories for events occurring after the illness onset. The patients all seemed entirely rational – almost excessively so – and when questioned as to what they were doing in the hospital ward, invariably confabulated that they were merely visiting friends, and soon would be returning home to dinner with their spouses.

Similarly, my mother, in her final years living in the family home, regularly claimed that all the neighbours, and in fact everyone in the street, had left, either permanently or on vacation, and that she was some kind of survivor in an otherwise empty world. And, indeed, that was probably how it was for her. When we showed her the neighbour on one side washing his car, and the one on the other side mowing the lawn, she would rationalise that they must have come back for a while, although in a few minutes she would have again forgotten she had seen them, and return to her solipsistic and lonely world. Thus, confabulation involves the generation of 'fabricated' accounts of events or experiences, not necessarily deliberately, or with conscious intent, to compensate for and make sense of the paucity of retained information in memory. As a form of 'honest lying', it illustrates the constructive nature of autobiographical memory – something which, in this era of 'recovered memories' in the context of possible child abuse, we should always be aware of from a forensic viewpoint.

It is not just memories which may be selective and reconstructive. At a purely perceptual level, we see largely what the context leads us to expect; hence the difficulty in picking up errors while proof reading. There is a phenomenon known as 'change blindness', a dramatic demonstration of which involved aficionados of a ball game watching a particularly exciting stage in the proceedings, at which point someone dressed in a gorilla suit strolled across the field; few of the avid spectators even noticed the intruder.

Many years ago, during my doctoral research, I was measuring pupillary changes in the human eye which typically accompany cognitive processes and variations in information processing load, superimposed upon various background light intensities. We had an eminent visitor to the Department, a specialist in hypnosis and hypnotic suggestion, and we thought it would be interesting to 'suggest' to experimental participants that the brightness of the background illumination was rhythmically fluctuating, up and down, in synchrony with a rising and falling tone. In fact, it remained constant. In those to whom the hypnotic suggestion was made, pupillary dilations tended to track the auditory tone. I often regret not having followed up that 'quick-and-dirty' pilot study with a properly controlled experiment, but unfortunately our eminent visitor, who alone could make the hypnotic suggestions, did not stay long enough.

Suggestion, however, may have a powerful influence, for good or even ill, in the clinical context of the placebo effect. A placebo is an assumedly inactive substance or procedure, as a control to serve as baseline for comparison with an active treatment of interest. Thus, a new drug is typically trialled, blind to both patient and administering physician, with half the patients merely receiving an inactive placebo. If the patients subsequently shown to have received the active substance improve, compared to those on the placebo, the drug is deemed to be potentially efficacious. The problem is, even placebos can have positive and beneficial effects, if the patients believe in them, as they usually do. (A recent study surprisingly showed that placebos can still work even if the patient is informed as to the true nature of the prescribed 'medication'; maybe they still harbour a secret hope as to the pharmacological efficacy of the 'sugar pill': homeopathy?) Thus, there can be both behavioural and brain-activation changes indicative of cognitive and emotional benefit in depressed and obsessional patients on a placebo. Moreover, in a study of Parkinson's disease, where the neurotransmitter dopamine is produced in insufficient quantities in certain neural circuits, placebos temporarily improved both dopamine levels, and clinical state. This situation may partly underlie recent concerns that expensive antidepressants, sometimes with unwanted side effects, may be no better than placebos. Thus, depression is indeed notoriously susceptible to at least temporary amelioration by suggestion, cognitive behaviour therapy, and other non-pharmacological interventions.

If placebos can benefit, what about the possible powers of suggesting the opposite? This is the 'nocebo' phenomenon; while the Latin *placebo* literally translates as 'I shall please or help', *nocebo* means exactly the opposite. Indeed, as we all know from everyday experience, telling someone that a procedure may lead to unpleasant consequences often leads to self-fulfilling prophecy, at least in the eyes of the beholder or victim. Maybe that partially explains the curious findings reported in a Christmas number of the eminent medical journal *The Lancet*. To determine the efficacy, according to those of faith, of prayer, seriously ill patients in a hospital were divided into two groups, one of which was repeatedly prayed for. That was the group that actually did worse in the end – maybe the prayers made them think they must be doing – even worse!

Plato was undoubtedly correct when two and a half thousand years ago he cautioned against blind trust in the simple evidence of our senses. The evidence is rarely simple.

21

I DIDN'T THINK I HAD NOTICED IT

Unconscious processing

It was 1974, and I had been lecturing in Chile, in Santiago, the very centre of the insurrection against Salvador Allende, that within days of our rather hurried departure erupted into total mayhem. We had then travelled, fairly roughly with our 4-year-old daughter, up along the line of the Andes, through Bolivia and Peru. At the end of five or six weeks we were faced with a very long flight across the Atlantic via Paris to London, where we discovered that at some point our baggage had gone missing. When eventually matters were sorted out, and we were hurriedly reading various immigration information sheets and forms in a state of considerable fatigue, I noticed something rather strange; I seemed to see items that were not really there, or rather, were elsewhere but reasonably adjacent to where I was actively reading on the sheet. It was as if I was taking in information extrafoveally, away from the immediate point of fixation. This made me wonder whether normal readers, in a normal state rather than acutely fatigued, also might partly process material beyond their current point of fixation, perhaps subconsciously, but in a way such as to influence or bias whatever they at that very moment were directly attending to. So when I was established at Edinburgh University, where I was to spend six months sabbatical, I devised a simple experiment. It was in the days before personal or office computers, and if one wanted to flash material to a particular part of the retina, one used a device called a tachistoscope, a massively expensive device replete with lenses, timers and switches to project material, maybe in controlled sequences, to known retinal regions (as long as the experimental subject was fixating a central fixation point), for known durations. There was no such device, analogous to an electron microscope in a biology department, at Edinburgh, so I used an ordinary slide projector, with a carousel-type magazine, fitted over the lens with a solenoid-operated shutter. Stimuli, which were converted into transparencies, consisted of a centrally located word of ambiguous meaning (e.g. palm – tree or hand; bank – river or cash; box – container or fight…), with on one side a disambiguator (tree, cash, fight…), and on the other a meaningless string of consonant letters matched in length to the particular disambiguator on the other side. I flashed several hundred of such triplets for a duration too fast to permit any eye movement. The task was to report the central, ambiguous word, along with any word which would identify its immediately perceived meaning, and with anything else they had been able to see on the displayed stimulus. I ignored all trials where they reported the disambiguator itself. It emerged that even when unable to report the disambiguator, the meaning the participants tended to attribute to the central, ambiguous item was in line with the unreported disambiguator. I published the findings in the then very prestigious *Journal of Experimental Psychology*, noting that what one understood, during reading, was influenced by unconsciously processed material beyond the immediate point of fixation, the fovea. Fortunately, I added a caveat, that an alternate possibility was that very rapid forgetting might instead or additionally be operating. I say 'fortunately', because my main conclusion ran counter to the strongly espoused belief of a then very influential psycholinguist that nothing outside of fixation had any effect, conscious or otherwise. A good friend and colleague of mine then at Cambridge replicated and extended my findings, but neglected to invoke that little, critical caveat, and such were the professional jealousies that life was made very difficult for him thereafter.

But was the finding so surprising? Ten or so years previously, subliminal advertising was made illegal. Flashing, during a movie or TV programme, of pictures too fast to reach conscious awareness, perhaps showing a deliciously frothing favourite brew, was thought unfairly and immorally to promote its purchase by covertly influencing our behaviour. But we now know that the latter is in fact continually being moulded and redirected by subtle influences of which we are largely or even entirely unaware. And we subsequently may justify such directed behaviour by frankly confabulatory explanations in which we may firmly believe, while they are nevertheless quite unrelated to reality. I am reminded of those nineteenth-century stage demonstrations of hypnotic suggestion where a volunteer is sought from the audience: 'When I snap my fingers, you will forget everything now that is happening, but will nevertheless go and open the door.' And that is apparently what often happened, whether or not it was in fact stage-managed by an accomplice masquerading as the volunteer; the individual would seemingly justify his action by commenting perhaps on the heat in the room.

Another demonstration of such confabulatory phenomena comes from the lab of Nobel laureate Roger Sperry; certain individuals, as a consequence of surgical intervention for intractable epilepsy, had had the tracts severed which interconnect the two halves of their brains. When a command such as 'walk!' was flashed to the visual field which exclusively projects under such circumstances to the right, non-verbal, hemisphere, the patient could not say what the word was, but would nevertheless obey it, justifying the action as a need to stretch the legs.

Unconscious behaviour per se is not strange or unusual; we are all familiar with the problem that our reflex actions, automatic orienting responses and complex motor skills can be disturbed by introspection. 'Don't think too much about your golf shot,' say the professionals. And if I concentrate on writing my signature, it invariably seems to come out distorted in some way. Similarly, intuition, according to the *OED*, is 'the ability to understand or know something immediately, without conscious reasoning'. Thus, we continuously, without conscious attention, are able to recognise patterns or consistencies in the stream of incoming sensations, leading to gut feelings or initial broad guesses which subsequently bias our thoughts, actions or expectations. We even *hear* ambiguously-pronounced words differently if, while listening, our mouths are mechanically stretched into different positions representative of the various interpretations; and a mechanically-induced smile may even make us *feel* better. While conversing with another, it seems that we again, quite unconsciously, come, both of us, to mirror each other's patterns of expression and gesture. At a more visceral level, we respond immediately and appropriately, without further thought, to a threatening facial expression, and only later can rationalise as to why we took such rapid evasive action. The subcortical amygdala is seemingly prewired to detect such possible threats. Moreover, tasks, where we have to detect hidden rules or regularities in sequences of letters or numbers, show that even those who claim incompetence may gradually improve with practice, even though they don't know why, and swear that they are only guessing. Importantly, concurrent brain imaging shows that the amygdala, along with other structures, is active in such acts of gut-wise intuiting. When students ask me about possible courses of action, I tell them to follow their gut instincts, and am myself continually surprised how accurate my own initial impressions of a situation or person tend to be.

Knowledge can therefore be acquired intuitively and implicitly, as insight, gut-wise, as well as from deliberate, explicit hypothesis testing. The former, possibly the default mode, may precede more explicit, conscious, deliberate and slower thought processes. It clearly relates particularly to the more primitive and immediate emotional aspects of behaviour – fear, anxiety or desire – requiring simple general tendencies of approach or avoidance. Thus, in many social interactions, it is important that we know whether or not to trust the other person. Indeed, there are numerous small, fleeting cues which typically escape our conscious awareness, but which research shows can betray the liar – brief, barely perceptible flickers of the mouth or eye musculature.

Nor need the signalling be mainly visual. In a recent German study, absorbent pads were placed under the armpits of students about to take a major exam, and again when they simply socialised or exercised. Other students sniffed the sweat samples while their brains were scanned. None claimed actually to perceive the difference between the two classes of sample, but the two versions had quite different effects on brain activity. Such olfactory signalling probably involves volatiles known as pheromones, others of which may also synchronise the menstrual periods of girls sharing a dormitory, or bias choice behaviours in sexual contexts. Pheromones may therefore modulate hormonal or neurotransmitter systems common to all mammals. Thus, a nasal spray of oxytocin may enhance a person's tendency to generosity or willingness to share money; a related hormone, vasopressin, is known to strengthen pair bonding in rodents. It is now being asked whether individuals, perhaps with severe autism and lacking the ability to empathise with another's feelings or viewpoint, might possibly benefit from similar treatment.

TV viewers will remember a few years ago an angry Iraqi journalist hurling his shoes at the then US president, and also at the Iraqi prime minister. The former quickly dodged the missile, such a novel threat leaving no time for cognition, while the latter barely flinched; presumably he already intuited that shoe missiles were of little real significance compared to the all-too-familiar bombs. Thus, there seem to be two independent pathways in the visual system, one for rather more leisurely and thorough perceptual recognition, and the other for immediate or emergency action, with the latter pathway permitting placement of the focus of attention on threats before they are consciously perceived and fully comprehended.

Forty or so years ago, the paradoxical-sounding phenomenon of blindsight was first described. Under certain circumstances, some clinically-blind individuals, with total destruction of their visual cortices, were found able to make visually-guided pointing or fixational eye movements quite automatically, while vigorously denying that they could see anything at all. More commonly, when forced to guess the location, orientation, velocity or direction of movement, they scored considerably above chance, despite complaining about the unreasonable bizarreness of the request. Since then, such apparent preservation of lower-level visual information has been ascribed to the operation of the undamaged dorsal (space-processing) visual stream, or 'where' pathway, despite the total loss of the ventral (identifying, or 'what') mechanisms. Blindsight can even be temporarily induced in intact individuals by briefly subjecting the visual cortex to a localised strong magnetic field. Such transcranial magnetic stimulation blocks conscious perception of a visual stimulus, even though the individual can still correctly reach towards it.

Thirty years ago I unexpectedly experienced striking personal confirmation of the operation of fairly complex cognitive processes to which I apparently had no conscious access. If you attach small lights to people's major joints, and film them in the dark so that only the lights are visible, the latter do not appear to constitute a meaningful pattern, such as a person, at least until the individuals commence to move. If they walk, sit down, stand up, act to throw something or to pick it up, the separate and apparently randomly distributed lights immediately seem to assemble and constitute someone performing a meaningful and recognisable activity. I wondered whether we could interpret such biological motion, as it is called, as being generated by a male or a female walker, when filmed on a treadmill. Trying it with some colleagues, I was at first very disappointed; we all felt that our forced choices, 'male' or 'female' for the various walkers, were entirely random. Yet later on analysis, it seemed that our scores were very often correct, well above chance. Presumably such a discriminative capacity is of major evolutionary or adaptive significance!

In one version of the serial reaction-time paradigm, there can be an array of, say, eight stimulus lights. When one suddenly flashes, the participant has to press as fast as possible the corresponding button immediately beneath it. Then another light will briefly illuminate, requiring a corresponding response, and so on in a seemingly random sequence. But in actual fact there is a repeating sequence of, say, 12 lights and associated responses, a sequence which is itself repeated, seamlessly, over maybe 10 cycles. Gradually, participants get faster, as if becoming increasingly familiar with an underlying pattern, but not so, of course, if as a control all 120 trials are truly random, without any underlying pattern. Nevertheless when questioned, participants usually deny all knowledge or suspicion of any such inherent sequence. Unconscious, automatic pattern learning, divorced from all awareness?

The clinical literature is of course replete with accounts of apparent preservation, at a more automatic and unconscious level, of cognitive processes lost to more direct conscious operation or introspection. Deep dyslexia, an acquired reading difficulty consequent upon localised brain injury to regions in the left cerebral hemisphere, is characterised by the individual often substituting a word of closely related meaning. Patients may say 'boat' when shown the word 'yacht', or 'sword' for 'dagger'. With unilateral neglect, consequent upon right-sided brain injury, patients may deny being able to see anything odd about the left side of an object, but if asked to choose between two bank-notes, one torn on the left side, they will invariably choose the intact one, without apparently knowing why. With form agnosia, we typically lose the ability to discriminate between objects with different shapes, while still being able to perceive colour and motion. Nevertheless we can pre-form our grasp and orient the hand appropriately to grab and pick up the particular object, even though denying being able to tell one shape from another. This old observation strikingly supports the recent hypothesis of *affordances* as underlying object perception. We recognise a cup in terms of how we would manipulate and use it – perception as implicit action. I am reminded of Roald Dahl's horrifying short story of a disembodied human brain and associated eye floating indefinitely in a nutrient solution. Could it continue to perceive, in the absence of any possibility for resultant action? But that story itself could even be seen as a metaphor for the tragic and frighteningly real neurological condition, the locked-in syndrome (motor neuron disease, MND), where all voluntary and involuntary skeletal action or movement is gradually lost.

Finally, I must mention those controversial EEG studies examining the time course of decisions how to respond in a choice situation; it seems that the patterns of electrical activity in the human brain can predict which of two (or more) choices that individuals will make, when there are alternatives, quite some time before they actually think they have made the decision or respond. We seem to become aware of our decision afterwards; at a subconscious level, the 'die has been cast'.

22

WHEN RECOGNITION FAILS

Agnosia

We take far too much for granted our wonderful ability to visually recognise, rapidly, effortlessly and accurately, people, objects, instances and events, despite an enormous range of often very degraded viewing conditions. We can recognise cups, cars, cats and caterpillars far better than any computer. It is amazing that things so rarely go awry, with failure to recognise someone or something, or occasionally falsely recognising them as someone or something else, or very rarely indeed, firmly continuing to believe that things are really very different from reality. Such delusional beliefs will be the subject of this section. All acts, however, of recognition, or of delusory misidentification, involve the interface between perception – seeing the presence of something – and memory – recognising something for what it is in the context of past experiences.

At least three brain regions participate in recognition: the occipital cortex mediates perceptual processes, the parietal cortex locates objects in space, and the temporal cortex is where object identification and recognition largely occur. With localised parietal damage we may no longer be consciously aware of an object or events in certain spatial locations, for example, on the left, while unconsciously still apparently taking account of them in our voluntary actions. With temporal damage we may pick up and appropriately handle an object without consciously knowing what it is. A doctor, after a stroke which caused such an agnosia, could only describe his stethoscope as 'some kind of tube with a bright disk at the end', and surgical gloves as 'bags with out-pouchings attached'. Strangely, at an unconscious level, much knowledge seems to be tacitly preserved, as agnosic patients can often still appropriately and correctly handle objects they deny all knowledge of; they may even try to work out with some insight the objects' identity. Thus, shown a picture of a bus, a patient said, 'It's a wagon, public transport, stagecoach? No, no, it must be a cab.'

Sometimes, with category-specific deficits, knowledge is apparently lost for certain discrete categories of object: foodstuffs, small tools, items of furniture, man-made objects, as if the neural access routes to related concepts cluster together and can be simultaneously lost. Thus, a patient who could still differentiate between hundreds of different species of orchid could not cope with small mammals. A squirrel and a cat must both be mice because they both have whiskers! Another patient, no longer able to recognise pictures of vegetables, including carrots, correctly understood the concept of bribery and encouragement in a drawing of a donkey being led along by a carrot, while not apparently knowing, at a conscious level, what the carrot actually was.

When we view an object, such as a silver candlestick, we see it as an entity, not as a collection of disparate qualities: metallic, of a certain hue and brightness, of a certain shape suitable for supporting a candle in a particular orientation, upon a particular substrate, and of a certain value. However, all these qualities are separately processed in different brain regions before being combined into (so as to characterise) the object in question. How, and where, are these characters 'bound' together? It looks as if the neural activity, corresponding to the separately-analysed and processed sensory qualities of an object, is tagged or coded in each case with a characteristic frequency. Cases occur where such binding partially breaks down, and where, with several simultaneously present objects, their respective qualities may be misattributed or interchanged: a blue pottery plate and a silver candlestick are seen as a blue pottery candlestick and a silver plate. Any more disruption of course, and we experience a completely agnosic inability to recognise either object. Conversely, with simultanagnosia, while qualities may be correctly attributed to an object, we may only ever be able to attend to or even see a single item at any one time, in the visual field, all others being perceptually invisible or apparently non-existent.

In one classic instance, the patient viewed a boxing match, and reported that he could see only a single participant, who seemed to be inexplicably knocked around by an invisible opponent, just like the random Brownian motion of pollen grains when we see them in a microscope as buffeted by invisible atoms in thermal motion. With considerable attentional effort, he could switch to the other participant, whereupon the first would vanish.

With metamorphopsia, alterations in an object's customary perceptual quality lead to apparent changes in size (micropsia or macropsia) or in orientation, or distance (teleopsia) or three-dimensional quality. There may be a frank hallucinatory quality, for example, a woman who sees a poodle on a bus, whereupon all the passengers seem to acquire poodle faces; or where the patient sees a Father Christmas beard on everyone at a Christmas party. With polyopsia, a visual image may be multiplied repeatedly, rather like the multiple after-images we may experience when repeatedly glancing at the sun. Finally, with palinopsia, an image may persist or recur long after the stimulus is removed, often in a blind part of the visual field.

Prosopagnosia is a category-specific form of object agnosia which seems limited to faces; patients can no longer recognise previously-familiar faces, although they may work out who they are from the possession of a mole, or a moustache, or from the sound of the speaker's voice. Again, a startle response to certain faces indicates that knowledge may be tacitly preserved at an unconscious level, despite the patient denying any knowledge about the person whose face it is.

Faces provide an enormous quantity of information on, for example, personal identity, age gender, emotion, expression, personality, intention, attention, and, of course, in interpersonal communication. Identificatory processes may vary for familiar (recognition) or unfamiliar (discriminative) processes. We may process them via whole-face gestalt recognition, or via piecemeal feature-by-feature analysis, which from electrophysiological evidence may be the way monkeys recognise human faces. Faces may be familiar or not, such as the recognition of famous faces or family members, or may be unfamiliar, and requiring discriminating one from another. They may be blurred or clear, upright or inverted, presented as photographic positives or negatives, or drawn from a familiar or an unfamiliar race or people. They may be caricaturised to enhance their recognisability. At one time or another, my lab has been involved in many aspects of research such as this.

Faces are of course unique, we encounter so many every day, and they are all basically very similar. Is it this property of mutual confusability between the category instances that underlies prosopagnosia? Some prosopagnosics certainly may also develop difficulties discriminating between members or instances of other similarly overburdened generic categories. A Belgian farmer could no longer individually recognise his cows; a tailor developed problems recognising different cloths; and a vet could no longer correctly diagnose variants of different skin diseases. Likewise a motoring enthusiast developed problems identifying different makes of cars. Other prosopagnosics, however, do seem only to confuse faces. So the question remains, is there a unique, dedicated, face processor, maybe in the right ventral-occipito-temporal regions including the fusiform or lingual gyri, or is there a more general-purpose system, maybe disseminated throughout the brain, for all such complex, generic configurations? Thus, house fronts, insects and even 'greebles' (artificial objects designed to be processed holistically, as may be usual with faces) may be substituted.

If, as seems to be the case, there is a right-half-brain (hemisphere) bias to face processing and spatial aspects generally, along with the well-authenticated and much stronger left-hemisphere lateralisation for language processes, we can ask what might happen if early in life the left side of the brain is extensively damaged, to the likely decrement of speech and language. If the injury occurs early enough, it is as if language, as a dominant function or faculty, invades the intact right side, to the disadvantage of the latter's normal spatial and facial bias.

One woman lost only the ability to recognise her own face in the mirror, something that even chimpanzees can do. She nevertheless called the mirror image 'my friend' who 'likes doing what I do'. Visitors were asked to 'speak quietly, so as not to disturb my friend in the other room over there'.

While much more is known about acquired (after injury, etc.) prosopagnosia, somewhere between 2 and 3 per cent of the population may be born with developmental or congenital form or forms – recognition failure, or problems in discriminating between apparently similar faces or individuals. So are there perhaps critical periods for the proper development of face recognition capacities, maybe in the first few months or years of life, or is there some opportunity for plasticity throughout life?

I believe I may myself be one of the few percent who have problems with faces; I often find certain faces very difficult to distinguish. Once while on sabbatical at Edinburgh University, for months I could not consciously distinguish between the faces of a particular janitor and a cleaner. However, I still somehow knew which face belonged to which occupation, so to greet them by name in the mornings I had to mutter the mantra, sub-vocally, 'Jolly Jack the janitor, dour David', personalities which characterised the two individuals. Also, I sometimes see people coming towards me who, impossibly, seem to be the same as individuals whom I passed just moments earlier.

Just as some of us are born with, or instead acquire, prosopagnosia, a very small percentage of individuals seem to have instead a quite extraordinarily superior capacity to recognise faces, maybe only seen once, fleetingly, and years ago; such individuals are now sought for forensic purposes in several of the world's major jurisdictions. And face-recognition systems using machine learning are being developed: the system is asked to guess if a face is male or female, old or young, happy, angry, sad or disgusted, Japanese, Chinese or Korean, even (believe it or not) with or without criminal proclivities. The system is given feedback as to correct/incorrect, and learns to be highly accurate with new material. The criminality aspect is particularly interesting, as 100 or more years ago the Italian criminologist Cesare Lombroso made similar, nowadays derided, claims on the basis of studying lots of mug shots. He was likely borrowing concepts from the equally suspect 'science' of phrenology, where personality was believed to be mirrored in and interpretable from characteristic 'bumps on the skull'. However, even in that outmoded context, it has been known for a long time that individuals suffering from such developmental disorders as schizophrenia, Williams syndrome and Friedreich ataxia tend to present with a typical facial configuration or facies.

With respect to judgements of female pulchritude or male handsomeness, it was found that if one averages, mathematically, all the different feature dimensions and separations, the faces corresponding to such averages are rated as most beautiful of all. So beauty is just minimal deviation from the group mean.

There is a collection of disorders known as delusional misidentification syndromes, characterised by the belief that people or places are not what they seem, but are substitutes, with small but definite differences from the real thing. In 1923, Jean Marie Joseph Capgras described Mme M, a 53-year-old housewife who asserted that her children and husband had been replaced by doubles, near-perfect duplicates or imposters; she sought a divorce on the grounds that her husband had been murdered by the double who was now living with her. Since then, there have been many similar cases, with claims that various relatives, friends or doctors are imposters, usually with evil intent. One Capgras case even believed that his cat had been swapped, and another that he himself was an imposter. It may be that while the perceptual processes of recognition remain relatively intact, the usual emotional context or reactions towards the person or object are somehow disturbed, such that the percept 'just no longer feels right'.

In 1927, Paul Courbon described a 27-year-old female, passionately fond of the theatre, who believed that the famous actresses Robine and Sarah Bernhardt were disguising themselves so as to persecute her; the disorder was therefore named after the great contemporary Italian mimic Fregoli, the Fregoli delusion, and typically involves the delusional misidentification of individuals as being familiar persons in disguise. So the patient claims persecution by someone who has assumed the guise of the mailman, or the milkman, or the doctor.

Courbon described the condition known as inter-metamorphosis in 1932; people are seen to change physically and psychologically into someone else. Thus, Sylvie saw other children looking exactly like her own, while her husband could alter his appearance to look just like the neighbour. All this differs from the Fregoli syndrome where the patient is confused by the identity, but not the appearance of the stranger.

With the delusion of inanimate doubles, the patient may believe that places or things have been replaced by near exact replicas. Examples include household furniture, pills and possessions. One 74-year-old man kept, over ten years, a meticulous record of more than 300 personal items he believed stolen and replaced (as inferior doubles) by his wife and nephew. The patient may puzzle as to why his garden has been so successfully duplicated outside the hospital. Usually the double is seen as just detectably different, and slightly older, shabbier or inferior. In one case the patient believed that her two young hens with small combs had been replaced by two old ones with large combs.

Finally, with the delusion of subjective doubles, described in 1978, one believes that one's own double is abroad, either as an independent individual (perhaps a clone) or even as oneself. This may well be the origin of the Germanic belief in the *Doppelgänger*.

Very often patients with these delusory misidentification disorders also show signs of prosopagnosia, although both conditions can appear in pure form. Face recognition may involve both the feeling of personal relevance or familiarity (an emotional response) and an act of conscious identification. The former but not the latter may be preserved in prosopagnosia, while with delusory misidentification disorders, one or the other may be differentially affected. We have all had feelings of 'déjà-vu', that we have experienced some contemporaneous event some time before.

We must distinguish delusions (false judgements or beliefs held with extraordinary subjective conviction) from hallucinations, which are false perceptions, often vivid, occurring in the absence of an external stimulus, but recognised as such. Many of us may experience hypnopompic hallucinations, fragments of speech or shapes, just as we drift off to sleep. These, and even clinical hallucinations, may in part stem from our brain's normal strategy, in visual or auditory perception, of automatically filling in expected predictions as to the likely progress of incoming information flow. In hallucinatory processes, normal or pathological, there may be reduced input, so we fill in missing material, in line with our attenuated or provisional expectations, and tend to see what we expect to see, such as faces in clouds or in rock formations, a phenomenon known as apophenia. This condition should not be confused with its kind of opposite, aphantasia, where maybe a few percent of us just cannot see what is normally 'in the mind's eye'. Generally speaking, hallucinations will tend to occur whenever input is faulty, missing, or deviates in some way from expected, typical or actual reality.

I enjoy reading novels in a number of languages, and when relaxing after an hour or two of this, I often seem to hear odd, random phrases as if actually spoken in the relevant language. Again, after prolonged typing, on closing my eyes I may see random bits of text in a matrix of indecipherable surrounding letters.

Deafness, blindness or limb loss can lead to hallucinations. Charles Bonnet, the Swiss naturalist, described in 1769 his blind grandfather's visual hallucinations, while amputees often experience, extraordinarily vividly, the presence of a phantom leg, with apparent feeling and movement, upon which they may even be tempted to try to stand. However, it is only with the delusions that we get attempts at rationalisation. One patient, questioned as to her claims of possessing two identical sets of children replied, 'Well, my husband was a sailor, you know, and anyway with all the moving around, we did have trouble keeping track of things.'

With the Cotard delusion, the affected person holds the erroneous belief that he or she is in fact already dead, or has ceased to exist, or is missing certain vital organs, or even may already be putrefying. While there are clear links and similarities to the delusional misidentification disorders, in particular, the Capgras delusion, the locus of the psychopathology has been variously ascribed to anomalies in the fusiform face area, the amygdala (associative emotions), or the parietal lobe (spatial interrelationships between body parts in the overall body image).

It really is a wonder that things go wrong so rarely, and I guess it will be quite some time before we understand exactly how our marvellous recognition system operates.

23

PHANTOM LEGS AND NEGLECTED ARMS

When I was a child, a local man would often cycle past, with his wooden leg clipped to the crossbar; before dismounting, he would unclip and re-attach it to his stump, all that was left from his war-wound. But he said he would still get 'a terrible itch' where his leg had been, which, surprisingly, he could temporally and partially alleviate by scratching the wooden prosthesis.

Mr A once suffered a horrific industrial accident: his left arm was caught in the machinery he was operating, and was torn from his upper body, 'avulsed', in the bland medical jargon which seeks to drain the emotive connotations of everyday terminology. He survived the event, but is now faced with an unexpected problem, unexpected by him, but not uncommon in such circumstances. He suffers continual discomfort in his missing limb. Indeed, the latter seems somehow to have survived in a distressingly real, if disembodied form. He can feel it beside him, sticking out, in fact, in an unnatural, dystonic posture, with the fingers painfully clenched. Because it is not really there, he cannot unclench the fingers, try as he will, imagining himself picking up objects with the phantom fingers. Moreover, he finds himself walking sideways through doorways, to avoid catching the rigid, raised, phantom on the doorposts. His equally down-to-earth friends are beginning to wonder about him.

Mrs B lost a leg to cancer years ago. She has long had arthritis in her good knee, but is also plagued with discomfort in her missing leg, pains which are resistant to powerful analgesics. The phantom limb is so real to her that sometimes, unthinkingly, she tries to stand on it and topples over, to her embarrassment and her family's concern.

All three experience what is known as the phantom limb phenomenon, whereby a missing appendage seems somehow still to be in place, often assuming awkward, dystonic postures, and experiencing unpleasant, uncontrollable pain or discomfort. The phenomenon was first described in 1551, by the French military surgeon, Ambroise Paré.

Mrs C recently had a stroke which affected the left side of her body; she can no longer use her left arm, but because the right side of her brain is involved, her speech is intact. Language, of course, is largely represented in the left side of the brain, which controls the right side of the body. She knows she has had what her doctor euphemistically calls a cerebro-vascular accident, but is surprisingly unconcerned by it. Indeed, she is quite anosognosic, which blandly, and roughly, translates as ignorant of any disability. This too, is not uncommon after right-brain injury. Although well past middle age, she has always used make-up liberally, and continues to do so, but the result is little short of horrific. She puts eye shadow under her right eye, and lipstick only on the right half of her mouth. Her left cheek is devoid of the rouge and powder which she liberally applies to the right. Always fond of her food, she finishes every morsel on the right side of her plate, often leaving more or less untouched her favourite delectables on the left, and asks for more. Her carers quickly learned to rotate her plate 180 degrees, to everyone's satisfaction.

Mrs C has what is clinically known as left hemi-inattention or left neglect. There is nothing wrong with her vision, it is just that she no longer notices things on the left. Whereas the phantom limbs of Mr A and Mrs B don't really exist, but feel as if they do, the left side of Mrs C's world continues to exist, but is no longer noticed. If we give Mrs C a horizontal line to bisect, she places her transection far to the right, as if large extents on the left either don't exist, or are of very small value. When Mrs C draws a clock face, or copies a picture of a flower, she omits much or all of the left side. If her attention is repeatedly drawn to this, she might reluctantly add the odd extra detail.

Mr D had a tumour removed some time ago from a region of the right brain, the parietal lobe, similar to where Mrs C had her stroke. His drawings of clock faces also omit the numbers 7 to 11, like those of Mrs C; unlike her, however, he includes them in his drawing – on the right. His clocks have the full range of numbers, 1–12, all down the right side. He clearly knows clocks run from 1 through to 12. His drawings of the map of Australia, moreover, have Perth placed just above Sydney on the right-hand side. The latitude is correct, but not the longitude. He has had his neglect for much longer than Mrs C, who might subsequently come to draw clocks and maps like Mr D, and exhibit what is known to neurologists as allochiria: 'getting the side wrong'.

In northern Italy, my old friend and colleague, Professor Edoardo Bisiach, with Mediterranean flair, asked his Milanesi neglect patients to imagine they were standing in the grand Piazza del Duomo, the Cathedral Square, somewhere they all knew very well indeed. He first asked them to imagine they were facing the magnificent façade of the Duomo, and to describe all the buildings, from memory, on either side. They all had had damage to their right parietal lobes and suffered from left neglect. (Right neglect, after left-side damage, is much rarer.) They all faithful reported all the buildings on the right side of the square, omitting all the buildings on the left. When, however, they were asked to imagine themselves with their backs to the Cathedral's façade, they again faithfully reported all the buildings on the right, the buildings which they had previously omitted from the other imaginary standpoint. Neglect therefore involves mental images, as well as real scenes. Why usually the left? Just as the left side of the brain mediates many aspects of speech and language, so too the right side of the brain seems to handle spatial awareness and attention on both sides of the body, while the left only mediates attentional awareness of what lies to the right. Damage the left half-brain, and apart from severe speech and language disability, there is little or no spatial dysfunction on the right, as the right hemisphere can take over that side of space from the damaged left. Damage the right hemisphere, however, and while there is little or no language dysfunction, as these processes are managed by the intact left hemisphere, there is now, however, acutely severe compromise of spatial functions on the left side, as the left (language) hemisphere is unable to take over spatial functions from the damaged right hemisphere. Note, however, that the early, acute, phase of spatial neglect may often tend to resolve to some extent over time.

Mrs C and Mr D, although unaware at a conscious level of what is happening on the left, still seem to be processing some information at an automatic level. When shown two banknotes, one above the other, with the left side of one note torn or disfigured, they will choose, if asked, the intact note, while denying that there is any real difference between them. The experiment has not been done, but I suspect that the gourmandising Mrs C, if given the choice of two plates of her favourite fare, with more or better serves on the left in one plate, would choose the latter, even though she might never get round to finishing it, and would probably claim that her choice had been random.

If I am placed on an office chair and rapidly spun, on stopping, my eyes will track in a direction determined by the original rotation, and I shall feel dizzy. My vestibular or balance system has been stimulated by the rotary motion, and it has the effect of momentarily reorienting the direction of my focus of attention. If you put cold water into one ear canal, and warm water into the other, the effect upon the vestibular system, whose receptors lie close to the surface, is similar to that of spinning. Back in Milan, Edoardo Bisiach wondered whether he could, with this technique, override the effects of brain damage, and redirect attention to the left, in a patient whose neglect was so severe that she denied the very existence of her left arm. This surely is a syndrome exactly opposite to that of the phantom limb, physically absent but psychologically present, with which I started this chapter. The interview with Professor Bisiach (Bisiach, Rusconi and Vallar, *Neuropsychologia*, 10 (1991): 1029–1031) describes how the patient believes she found the arm, apparently 'belonging to her mother', beside her in the bed. She did not know the whereabouts of her 'true arm' until given vestibular stimulation with hot and cold water, when she suddenly 'found' her left arm, and could not locate her 'mother's' arm. The effect, of course, soon wore off, and once again the patient claimed that her left arm belonged to her mother.

In addition to vestibular stimulation, following a suggestion of mine, more or less successful attempts at ameliorating hemineglect have been made by fitting patients with laterally deviating prisms to spectacle frames.

V. S. Ramachandran, perhaps aware of Edoardo Bisiach's success in compensating for the effects of unilateral neglect with so simple an intervention as caloric irrigation, attempted something similar with a particularly intractable, and painful, phantom limb. The patient complained that his phantom left hand felt as if it was painfully clenched and could not be relaxed. Ramachandran arranged a mirror so that the patient saw his good right hand mirror-reflected, and in the exact position that his missing left limb would have occupied. The patient was then told to try to clench and unclench *both* hands, while watching his phantom hand, really of course, his good right hand reflected to the left. In this way the patient immediately seemed able to gain control of his phantom, and the sensation disappeared! Judicious use of a mirror subsequently permitted the patient to continue to maintain adequate control of his phantom limb.

It seems certain that the parietal lobe, where the brain maps the skin and muscle senses of the body, is deeply implicated in both the neglect and the phantom limb phenomena. The parietal lobe codes position in space, with respect to the direction of gaze, the orientation of the head and of the trunk, all three of which may at any one time be out of sync with each other due to eye, head and body turns, and the direction of the gravitational vertical, should one lie down on one or other side.

Neglect and phantom phenomena of the limbs may not always be all-or-nothing experiences. There is a report of a lady with a parietal cyst, who said her arm and leg seemed to drift from conscious awareness and fade unless she could see them. While we are all in a sense only aware of our body parts while we are for some reason thinking of them, or they are painful, the patient noted that while lying in bed she might suddenly realise that she had lost her arm; only when she looked at it did she know where it was. This led to unfortunate incidents such as her tripping up fellow passengers walking down the aisle of a bus in which she was sitting; her foot, unbeknown to her, was sticking right out.

Another of my friends and colleagues, the late Professor John Marshall at Oxford, told me of a patient with right-brain damage, who developed the belief that he had acquired a third, supernumerary arm 'in the middle', in addition to losing the use of his left arm.

And then there's the patient with a right parietal meningioma who had the uncontrollable and distressing feeling of having four legs, in the absence of any delusional belief about their real existence.

Is the phantom phenomenon necessarily restricted to limbs?

A man has been described as experiencing a phantom penis, complete with phantom erection. It also happens that the part of the brain which maps the genitals is adjacent to the part for the foot. An intense orgasm may indeed spread electrically to the foot area, causing rhythmic contractions of the toes, a phenomenon to which I can personally attest. The male foot amputee, you guessed it, has now described intense orgasms extending to his phantom foot. Maybe it's the case of the man who mistook his foot for his penis.

While visual neglect (hemineglect and hemi-inattention are also alternative terms) is most clinically obvious in the visual modality, it may occur also, or exclusively, in the auditory modality. In reading and writing, only the right side of the page may in some instances seem to be processed, while in others it may be the initial letters, on the left sides of words, which are seemingly ignored, wherever the words occur on a page. Thus LORD and WORD may be confused, or DOVE and LOVE, but not DONE and DOVE. Yet again, near or peripersonal space may be unattended on the left, with more or less intact performance for far or extrapersonal space. While lesions in either or both the frontal and parietal lobes may contribute to the syndrome, the motor or action components may be more compromised with frontal damage, and the more perceptual and attentional aspects with parietal involvement, although this may not be a hard and fast rule. Generally, the syndrome is associated with problems in *disengaging* from events to the right, hence the phenomenon of extinction, where symptoms are more pronounced when there are also events occurring and requiring attention on the right side. With the analogue, pseudoneglect, in normal healthy adults, the tendency instead is to *attend* slightly more to events or material on the left. Thus, while navigating a maze while seated in a wheelchair, patients will tend to collide with obstacles on the left, while healthy individuals may graze objects on the right.

Maybe if your life is troubled by phantom problems, such as intractable itching where your left leg used to be, it will be alleviated by following up with a right hemisphere stroke resulting in left neglect. But be careful what you wish for!

24

IS YOUR TUESDAY GREEN?

Synaesthesia

A penetrating, insistent phone ringing, from a caller who would never give up, in fact, what one might expect from a senior, successful journalist; but I am getting ahead of myself. Barbara was a graduate student from another university, but then I did seem to attract the attention of certain such external individuals, determined students who wanted to spread the net for knowledge and possible guidance widely, beyond the immediate confines of their own institution. She was older than most, shy, diffident even, but definitely very determined, and possessed of some fluency in several languages, which appealed to my own long-standing and extramural philological and linguistic pursuits. She wanted me to act as an associate supervisor for her research into brain areas that might mediate second and third languages in polyglots – as a function of the number, proficiency, age-of-acquisition, whether spoken, heard or read, etc. – using electrophysiology. In particular, she planned to use the various wave forms present in the EEG during a language-related task, and associated evoked potentials. We had gone over her findings in my room, and lunch was calling; I had locked my office door and we were waiting outside for the lift that never came. Then I heard my office phone ringing.

After a minute or two, Barbara said that maybe I should go back in and answer; at first, I refused, then curiosity overcoming my usual lunch-time pangs, I returned and picked up the phone. The caller was the editor of a well-known and quality Australia-wide newspaper, weekend edition. 'What', he asked, 'did I know about synaesthesia?' His boss's daughter apparently 'had' it. At first, I demurred, not wishing to get involved in what might easily become a protracted issue, but as it happened I had very recently given it as a research-review topic for some very bright third-year students, who unearthed some quite remarkable observations from the pitifully few then extant studies; indeed, it was at that point considered to be very rare. What if I could avail myself of the might of the media, as we were always encouraged to do by our university and funding masters? We could do a feature in the weekend edition, which would reach many people, a captive audience, in the jargon. We could appeal for research volunteers, and maybe run some of the same technologies as Barbara was using, and maybe have a world-first in documenting the condition's (if that was indeed the correct way to characterise it) natural history.

We arranged a conference, to include also a very bright post-doc student who had done his PhD with me and later gone on to Cambridge for his first post doc. We also enrolled an Honours student, partly to manage the research as her chosen topic. Anina at first was reluctant – what if we could not get any participants? At this point, Barbara, who had also attended out of interest, diffidently and to our intense surprise and some relief, volunteered that 'actually, I am in fact a synaesthete'. So we had at least a 'single case', and hopefully we might unearth some more.

Very shortly after our meeting, we had drafted an article for the press which in fairly simple terms explained the nature and what was currently known about the phenomenon, and which appeared very soon after. It provoked a veritable storm of correspondence, such as 'Synaesthesia is such a beautiful word, it is itself a shimmering green shot through with white flashes.' Others wrote that they were delighted and relieved to learn that they were not 'different' from other people, or simply crazy, but that there were other individuals who also vividly experienced colours to certain sounds, numbers, days of the week, months of the year, or even cities. Yet others wrote that they had long thought that everyone had such experiences, and it was perhaps only in their teens that they realised that they were in fact somehow different. Some were even surprised that the phenomenon had a name. 'Such a nice name, in fact.' One girl said that she had first learnt of it when her sister asked, 'Is your Friday green like mine?' (It wasn't.)

Thus, synaesthesia is characterised by an *inducer* stimulus or experience triggering an additional or *concurrent* experience. It is automatic, requiring no conscious effort, and is difficult to suppress. It is unidirectional, in that, for example, if Tuesday is perceived as 'grey', the experience of encountering a grey stimulus does not provoke the thought of 'Tuesday'. A synaesthetic experience may arise sometimes from the mere thought of the inducer. There is even the report of a colour-blind synaesthete who nevertheless somehow saw certain monochrome letters in a kind of private 'colour' of his own. Conversely, a jumbled matrix of monochrome letters to be searched for a target letter may be easy for some synaesthetes, as the target letter may 'pop out' in its synaesthetic colour, although the mechanism and maybe even the evidence are somewhat disputed. Conversely, a search among a jumble of coloured letters may be slowed if the target letter is of a colour incongruent with the synaesthetic experience, or facilitated if congruent.

Synaesthesia means, in Greek, a linking of the senses. It represents an unusual ability, a 'positive' sign, rather than a disability, loss of function or a neurological defect. Some such individuals may see Tuesday as pale grey-green, Thursday as steely blue; Sunday 'may be like Monday, deep burgundy, only paler'; Wednesday may be the colour of a Red Delicious apple in a faint mist, but the pairings are highly idiosyncratic, from person to person, even within the same family. And synaesthesia definitely tends to run in families, perhaps inherited as an X-linked autosomal dominant gene. Nevertheless, for a given synaesthete, the associations are usually permanent and lifelong – in fact, an extremely high test-retest reliability over extended periods is a criterion for belonging to that class.

One synaesthete's grand-daughter 'is a faint, silvery red, quite different in fact from her actual name', while her son 'is a pale lemon yellow'. Colours in response to sounds, words or even people themselves are not uncommon manifestations, and are typically seen as a film before the eyes, or as a surface coating or shell, or even as a coloured flash. Some may hear sounds in response to colours, and even feel or taste music. The composer Scriabin, a synaesthete, in an attempt to share his experiences with the uninitiated, wrote *Prometheus, the Poem of Fire*. Coloured lights were linked to the keyboard to illuminate the room in time with the musical notes.

Several hundred people wrote to say how they experienced synaesthesia. They, and as was later found to be the case in subsequent studies, including our own, were very often female, sometimes with a poor sense of direction, maybe a tendency to emotionality and also perhaps to occasional feelings of unreality or depersonalisation, of déjà-vu, and of psychic or paranormal experiences. It was all somewhat suggestive of temporal lobe involvement, a brain region notorious for the experience of 'psychic', hallucinatory or religious phenomena ('the God spot', it has been suggested!), and one where inputs from the various senses may be combined in object recognition, and in finding one's way about. Many synaesthetes claimed or later were shown to be highly creative in the arts, and to find that the phenomenon was often of considerable assistance whether in creativity or in remembering things, people or places.

Thus, some synaesthetes say that they can easily memorise strings of numbers, letters or words, from the vivid colour coding evoked. Others, that it helps their spelling ('vowels all have colours, which are then modified by the colour of the following consonant'), while yet others say that they can easily memorise telephone numbers or car registrations. One girl said that while waitressing, she automatically colour-coded the diners, when they placed an order at a table, an experience which was far more vivid than the colour of their clothes, thereby being able to match up meal orders quite easily for up to 20 patrons. A teacher colour-codes her students, while a woman who sees numbers uniquely disposed with respect to each other in space (a phenomenon now known as 'spatial sequence synaesthesia'), wrote:

> An anticlockwise circle represents 1–10, 11 and 12 go upwards from 10, while 13–20 lie along a horizontal line to the right from 12. From 21–30 it is then straight up vertically, and from 30–100 a straight line to the right. After 100, the same pattern follows. In the 6th grade our teacher used to get me to go to other classrooms and add up rows of numbers he had written on the blackboard; I was lightning fast. Perhaps this was the normal way of adding – I had no way of knowing.

With my friend and colleague Professor Mike Nicholls, then at Melbourne University, I have studied rather analogous situations even in non-synaesthetes, who often see numbers distributed linearly in space, often from left to right in terms of magnitude – the so-called number-line phenomenon. We probably all of us have a predisposition to some form of spatial synaesthesia; maybe the same is true with respect to colour, which is either more pronounced or developed, or less lost over development, in lifetime synaesthetes.

Indeed, childhood is now known to be a period not just of the forming of new neural connections, but also one of controlled or programmed pruning, apoptosis, of now maybe redundant connections. This is of course analogous to sculpting, where unwanted material is chipped away from a block of marble to reveal, as it were, the desired statue 'hidden' within. Maybe synaesthesia is simply the retention of wider inter-sensory connections, long past their 'normal' use-by date, and maybe we all once had a similar potential. Mind-altering or hallucinatory drugs, such as mescaline, which affect the serotonin pathways in the brain, may in fact activate a latent system of this sort. Thus, LSD users spontaneously comment upon synaesthesia-like experiences. Maybe during development we normally acquire alternative and apparently more sophisticated ways of coding reality, such as by language, which are incompatible with more 'primitive' synaesthesia. Indeed, preliterate societies are often said to have far better visuo-spatial memories, so-called 'eidetic imagery', than their literate researchers. Moreover, an autistic girl, Nadia, with savant capacities, could draw at a very early age with extraordinary virtuosity, while quite unable otherwise to communicate. When after much effort she was taught to speak, her artistic capacities rapidly regressed. It was as if language had somehow competed for, or inhibited, her capacity for artistic expression. At the other end of the age spectrum, there are accounts of elderly individuals with developing dementia whose declining language capacities unmasked hitherto-hidden artistic talents.

Might the possession of synaesthetic potential predispose certain such individuals to additional savant-like capacities, such as abnormal memory or computational ability? As portrayed so effectively in the movie *Rainman*, autistic individuals with savant abilities may possess startling computational skills of mental arithmetic or calendrical computation. They may be able to give the day of the week which corresponds to 23rd July in the year 2253, after only a moment's hesitation. The very rare capacity for absolute pitch, present in very few musicians (although there are recent reports of it being present in many more children below a certain age), may have its counterpart in what we might call 'absolute colour'; one woman wrote to me that she could carry colour accurately in her head, and did not need to take samples of cloth or thread to the milliners. I should, however, hasten to add that no link between synaesthesia and autism has ever been found or even suggested.

There may of course be a downside to such extraordinary feats of memory; in his classic study, *The Mind of a Mnemonist*, the great Russian neurologist Aleksandr Luria reported the capacity of someone who could effortlessly recall masses of arbitrary material, but who afterwards would complain of the resultant 'buzzing, blooming confusion' of past and present. It is of course just as important to be able to forget as to remember. Some of our synaesthetes admit being occasionally confused by their spontaneously-evoked colour experiences; and then there is the apocryphal tale of the professor of fisheries, who refused to learn his students' names, because every time he mastered one, he would forget the name of a fish. Indeed, I wonder whether the apparent decline in memory capacities which we all seem to experience with advancing age is in fact as much due to functional competition and confusion between members of an ever-expanding 'lexicon' of experiences, as due simply to a failing neurology.

Might synaesthesia simply be the result of having experienced in childhood certain pairings of colour with number, shape or sound? While, generally, synaesthetic pairings (perceived colour with an initial letter or sound, e.g. of day of the week), may seem largely arbitrary, differing between individuals, when we later did a fine-grain analysis we did find that there was a statistically significant correlation between the initial letters of the colour and those of the days of the week. Several synaesthetes, however, who learnt maths with the notorious system of Cuisenaire rods, whose length, numerical value and colour were matched, bitterly complained that the rods' colours seemed all wrong to them. The same comments came with respect to teaching reading by using coloured phonics.

Synaesthesia may, as discussed, extend to touch, tastes and smells; foods may be described as 'pointy', 'spiky', 'curved' or 'flat'; and don't wine-tasters tend to use similar descriptors with respect to wines? Is there a hidden synaesthesia here? One woman said that the quality of her period pains evoked corresponding colours, while another noted that with acupuncture, the locus and depth of the needle evoked different colours. Yet another said that different words evoked smells such as of bushfire, cooking meat, incense, tobacco, stale beer, sour milk, rotting fruit, and old metal handrails.

Is synaesthesia somehow related to the hypothetical mechanism of binding, whereby all the disparate qualities of an object, or 'qualia', as termed by philosophers, are tied or bound together in the evocation of that object? This may be achieved by labelling, with a characteristic frequency of around 40 Hz, the various patterns of electrical activity corresponding to the perception or conception of all the qualia of a currently attended object. Thus a silver candlestick signifies or connotes value, a certain colour, metallic properties, a particular function, romantic meals, etc. The thalamus, deep within the brain, a locus of convergence, may briefly 'label' the neural correlates of all the component qualia so that they are transiently and functionally brought together, to represent the momentary idea of – a silver candlestick!

Brain-imaging studies have been performed on volunteer synaesthetes, finding abnormally-increased neural activity in, for example, visual association areas in response to certain sounds, which agrees with the idea that such individuals may have retained connectivities, lost perhaps during development in the rest of us, between the senses. We have investigated the timing of synaesthetic experiences, and the extent to which their evocation may or may not interfere with or facilitate other decision processes. However, once again, each synaesthete may be unique in her experience. One in fact wrote that colour was immediately and vividly evoked, others that it is much more subtle, tacit or implicit, although it does seem that a finite period of time, maybe reflecting processing or attentional aspects, has to elapse for the synaesthetic experience to develop or to influence other aspects of perception. The fact that some synaesthetes have spontaneously commented that in addition to being left-handed, they can also mirror write with either hand, would suggest that there are as yet unknown motor manifestations.

While earlier studies suggest a prevalence in the general population of between 1 and 4 per cent, in a study of 192 adult synaesthetes, we found the figure to be considerably less, with approximately six times as many females as males, and with a strong familial effect; contrary, however, to other reports the incidence of left-handedness was within normal limits. Synaesthetes, as in earlier anecdotal reports, were more likely to be involved in artistic or creative pursuits. The fact that there was a significant consistency in the colours induced by certain letters and digits, for example, the elicitation of red by 'R', just as in non-synaesthetes, does suggest that the development of lexical-colour synaesthesia may incorporate early learning experiences common to everyone. The fact that colours were only experienced for letters, days of the week or digits, suggested that inducers were typically part of conventional sequences, such as Monday, Tuesday, Wednesday…; A, B, C…; 1, 2, 3,…, and that the learning during an early critical period of such sequences may be particularly important in the development of such synaesthetic induction, determining the particular pattern of lexical-colour links, a pattern which then may generalise more widely.

In summary, the synaesthetic colour experience may not be exactly like that with 'true, objective physical' colour. Disagreement between synaesthetes as to the nature of the experience, and the fact that it may only arise *after* the inducer is consciously recognised, suggest that the phenomenon is more *conceptual* than *perceptual*, requiring deeper levels of cognitive and probably memory-related processing, maybe in the anterior temporal lobe. Synaesthesia may thus be an exaggerated form of 'normal' cognitive processing, personally idiosyncratic, but with certain commonalities arising from sometimes similar early childhood experiences. It may arise either from failure to inhibit certain such associations, or from incomplete developmental pruning at a neural level, or maybe from a combination of both mechanisms.

An important conclusion to be drawn from the history of our investigations into synaesthesia, is that chance and random events, in this case a phone call that was nearly missed, can alter the trajectory not just of research topics, but also that of people's entire lives. Anina happened to be looking for a project; Barbara happened to be present, as our very first synaesthesia candidate, providing validity for the likely existence of an adequate pool of synaesthetes without which we would not have dared proceed – our own later data suggesting the probability of such a proband being at hand as being very low. Anina, a girl from the Australian bush, ended up with a stellar career – several papers in the august journal *Nature*, a post-doc in Harvard medical school, and is now a university professor … You just never know your luck in research, 'Chance favours the prepared mind.'

The last word should go to observations by the unique, gifted, and unusually warm-hearted and empathic individuals who took time and effort to contact us:

> The colour for a particular name may change in different people with that same name.
>
> The first letter dominates the colour of the whole word, but if I read slowly I get colours emerging for each letter.
>
> Vancouver tastes like rice pudding but with raisins.
>
> Of course Wednesday is green; it just is.
>
> Six should be an odd number, but like all the even numbers it does lie to the left.
>
> Love is a buttery yellow … love is yellow with bubbles emerging.
>
> I hate the new phone numbers that now start with 9; such a depressing, dark-grey colour.
>
> I once saw a woman who went a lovely silvery blue.
>
> I avoid playing middle C and nearby notes because of their earthy odour and mud-brown colour, which I dislike intensely.
>
> If I happen to see a red or scarlet object, I hear its high-pitched sound.
>
> If I have difficulty remembering certain phone numbers, I realise the colours are incompatible.
>
> Bradshaw is a pale luminous shade; xxxx (a senior politician) is a dirty brown.

25

BODILY INTEGRITY AND IDENTITY

Is it really me?

Nearly 50 years ago, when just beginning student life, I had two curious experiences, which bear in an interesting way upon certain phenomena relating to one's personal or corporeal identity and individuation.

In the first, I was looking out of the window of a sixteenth-century building wherein I shared a sitting-room with a fellow undergraduate. We gazed idly down into the Fellows' Garden and saw the eminent philosopher and head of our college, Warden Mure, strolling pensively, presumably deep in metaphysical thought and with hands clasped behind his back, among the famous limes where Tolkien had composed The *Lord of the Rings*; sadly, these same trees are now felled because of fears of litigation and liability. We wondered whether, by force of united but silent will-power, we could get him to stop, turn and look up. The very moment we commenced willing, he indeed stopped, turned abruptly and looked back up to our very window. Such was our instantaneous embarrassment, guilt even, at the apparently successful transfer of thought processes that we immediately dropped down out of sight, and only later wondered whether it was coincidence, rather than a successful demonstration of the occult. And yet, as sceptical scientists or credulous commoners alike, I'm sure we have all experienced the powerful and disturbing sensation of someone watching us, or standing behind us, whether or not there is really someone there.

Later that year, on a winter vacation walking with a friend on the fells of England's Lake District, we found ourselves early one frosty morning high upon the exposed ridge of Striding Edge. The sun, at head level, had only recently risen over an adjacent valley to our left, while to our right was a bank of fog rising high above the next valley. On the edge of this fog bank I saw an image of myself, surrounded by a beautiful halo, purple radiating out in concentric bands through all the spectral colours. In this uncanny image I could not see my companion, nor could he see me. When I raised my camera to capture this doubly-spectral image, the image did the same. This was the rare phenomenon of the so-called *Brocken Spekter*, named eponymously after the highest peak in the German Harz Mountains, a range renowned in Teutonic folk lore. We had each met our *Doppelgänger*, our double; however, this uncommon meteorological circumstance of precise alignment of illuminating sun, viewer and a projection screen of fine water droplets (which provided the prismatic effect) did not of course lead to instant mutual annihilation, as the fable foretold, like the meeting in modern physics of matter and antimatter. After all, the phenomenon had a sound basis in meteorology and optics. Can we similarly explain our apparent sensation of being watched from behind?

In a very recent article in the august and usually sceptical science journal *Nature*, the authors note that the anomalous sensation that someone is nearby, when there is nobody, has often been described by psychiatric and neurological patients, as well as by healthy individuals, but the exact mechanisms of this illusion – or is it really a hallucination? – are not well understood. The authors describe the repeated induction of this sensation in a 22-year-old woman, of normal psychiatric history, who was undergoing focal electrical stimulation of the left temporo-parietal junction of the brain, as evaluation for possible surgical treatment of epilepsy. The illusory person apparently just behind her closely shadowed or mimicked changes in her own posture or body position. Temporo-parietal regions are known to be involved in the integration of multisensory body-related information, the self-versus-other distinction, and other illusory own-body perceptions. Interestingly, the patient did not recognise that the apparent being was an illusion of her own body, projected into extra-personal space. Similarly, many patients with schizophrenia, with hyperactivity in these same temporo-parietal regions, may misattribute their own actions to some other individual or agency, and suffer from delusory feelings of alien control.

There are accounts by adventurers and others finding themselves *in extremis*, suffering, exhausted, fearing for their lives, or labouring to extricate themselves from terrible situations, of being accompanied, often close behind, by a 'ghostly' mentor, maybe proffering profitable advice. This feeling of a helpful companion or presence is sometimes called the Third Man Experience, guiding unfortunates such as the great Antarctic explorer Sir Ernest Shackleton to safety on his epic escape from near disaster. The term (the Third Man) may take its name from T. S. Eliot's poem *The Wasteland* where he interrogates his interlocutor about the latter's apparently constant hallucinatory companion.

One of my early graduate students, who later progressed to a cabinet position in the Federal Government, once described to me an out-of-the-body experience she had had during a prolonged and painful dental procedure. As so often in such accounts, when the individual has been exposed to a period of great stress, threat or pain, she seemed to be looking down upon herself lying in the dental chair. Rather than there being an illusory shadow person lurking behind her, she seemed, from a different vantage point, actually to be looking *at* herself. A prominent Swiss group of neurologists recently proposed that such *autoscopic* hallucinations and *heautoscopy* (literally, in Greek, 'seeing yourself') are two variants of an apparent reduplication of one's own body and self. In the former, an exact mirror image of oneself, occasionally only of one's face or bust, is perceived visually. In heautoscopy proper, one is confronted by one's own double, or *Doppelgänger*, which may or may not exactly mirror one's immediate appearance, but is nevertheless *felt* to be one's double. Frequently, *heautoscopic echopraxia*, or the imitation by the double of one's own bodily movements, gives the impression that one's real identity actually resides in the double. Focal brain lesions of the temporo-parieto-occipital junction may precipitate the phenomenon, as may extreme pain, discomfort or stress in the otherwise healthy.

Maybe we should in fact distinguish between classical out-of-the-body experiences (where the individual has the impression of seeing a second, own, body, out in extrapersonal space), from autoscopic hallucinations (where one sees a double of oneself, not necessarily looking or behaving completely identically, out in extrapersonal space without leaving one's own body), and from heautoscopy. In the latter, one again sees oneself out in extrapersonal space, but cannot easily decide whether or not one is disembodied. In fact, such individuals may claim that they experience seeing the world from two simultaneous or alternating perspectives. In all such instances, there are varying levels of failure at integrating visual, tactual, vestibular and kinaesthetic or proprioceptive information. Thus, the various senses no longer agree as to bodily position and posture.

While there is no reason to suspect psychiatric disturbance in instances of heautoscopic hallucinations, or out-of-the-body experiences, this is not usually true of the group of syndromes collectively known as *subjective doubles*, where someone else is believed to have been transformed into oneself, or another person is believed to have taken on the physical characteristics and identity of oneself.

If, under certain circumstances, it is as if our personal or corporeal identity can somehow be copied, can the opposite occur? Clearly, the complete phenomenal disappearance of one's entire corporeal self would be extremely counter-intuitive, although, with Cotard's syndrome, patients may claim that they are already dead. However, patients with *asomatognosia* typically describe parts of their body as temporarily or permanently missing from corporeal awareness, generally with the preservation of full insight; thus they are surprised and disturbed by the experience. A middle-aged woman, without neurological or psychiatric antecedents, described how when sitting in front of her computer she unexpectedly felt dizzy and found that the lower extent of her left arm was no longer to be seen. Indeed, much to her surprise she seemed to see the table *through* the arm; she could see her arm only above the elbow, with a clear-cut demarcation or border at the apparent termination. Gradually, after some minutes, there was progressive restoration of the whole limb. Such asomatognosia, or failure to perceive parts of one's own body, is to be contrasted with the phenomenon of unilateral neglect, where it may be more a matter of failure to recognise one's body parts, typically on the left, although both syndromes seem to involve similar parietal lesions. Both conditions, however, have as their phenomenological obverse the common experience of many amputees – the 'phantom limb phenomenon', which my group has been investigating. Here, there may be a powerful illusion of the continuing existence, complete with pain or itching, of an amputated and no longer present member.

Asomatognosia may therefore be considered a loss of embodiment of a real limb, and the phantom limb phenomenon as the persisting embodiment of a missing limb. Motor mechanics using such tools as a screwdriver often describe sensations of roughness or vibration as being localised at the very end of the tool – as a sort of extended embodiment of the actual hand or arm – while functional brain imaging confirms that in such expert tool users there is indeed an apparent extension in the brain map of the limb, so as to encompass the tool as an actual part of that limb. Illusory embodiment may also be experienced by everyone with the 'rubber hand' illusion. If one's right arm, say, is concealed from view and replaced by an apparently identical rubber replica in full view, and which adopts a position (perhaps via a mirror system) and posture as similar as possible to that of the real, concealed, arm, and if the rubber arm is seen by the subject to be gently stroked by the experimenter, then there is often a powerful illusion of touch or tickle. And apparently even mice can experience a caudal version – when shown a rubber replica of their tails being threatened!

Then there is also the phenomenon of *apotemnophilia*. The Greek literally translates as 'a desire for amputation', and is best illustrated by a typical case report of a male, married with a child, who successfully sought to have his leg surgically amputated above the knee, as he had always felt somehow incomplete or 'wrong' (*xenomelia*) with two normal arms and legs, and believed that the amputation would paradoxically make him more 'whole'. According to a recent survey of 34 individuals recruited from the internet, most, who now have their own web site, are male, and often report a sexual component. They are frequently well-educated, involved in an ongoing intimate relationship and have long harboured hidden desires, often back to childhood, for an amputation, 'so as to restore my true identity'. In a substantial minority of instances, they may have attempted self-amputation via a variety of dangerous procedures, such as use of shot guns, chain-saws, wood-chippers, dry ice (as with one of our own correspondents), or lying on railroad tracks. Those desiring a leg amputation far outnumbered those wanting an arm removal; amputation was typically sought on the left side, although some wanted it done bilaterally. Given the close proximity in the brain of those cortical areas mapping and controlling functions of the lower leg to those representing the genitals, while the upper-limb mapping is adjacent to that of the face, one wonders about the underlying role of possible emotional and sexual drives. However, it is noteworthy that the majority of the individuals displayed no significant psychiatric symptoms, apart from a preoccupation with amputation. The condition may be conceptualised as an extremely unusual dysfunction in the development of one's fundamental sense of corporeal identity or integrity, with the label 'Body Integrity Identity Disorder' (BIID). Certainly, those who have somehow succeeded in securing an amputation under proper surgical conditions typically report themselves as delighted with the result.

Incidentally, the other side of this integrity coin relates to an apparent predilection (usually in males, but I do personally know of one such female) for sexual or romantic partners who are missing – again usually a lower – limb. There is even a website for such aficionados, declaring themselves to be 'devotees'.

BIID clearly resembles another body dysmorphia, anorexia, which predominantly may affect females. And then there is the newly identified condition, muscle dysmorphia, increasingly manifesting in males who obsessively exercise, adopt harmful diets, and abusively bulk up on steroids to increase muscle mass, often to grotesque proportions. Females, however, are not immune.

Bodily integrity and identity clearly may be disturbed at various levels, wholly or in part, with or without psychiatric or neurological involvement. The French philosopher, René Descartes, over 300 years ago, declared '*Cogito, ergo sum*', 'I think, therefore I am', in his existential search. However, our corporeality is clearly fragile and potentially easily disturbed; so too, of course, is the apparent unity of our mental and cognitive processes, whatever the views of Descartes. How often do we say, 'One part of me wants to do this, while another wants to do that'? But that is another story for another time.

26

EMPATHY FOR PAIN AND MIRROR NEURONS

After giving a talk on ABC Radio National, I was contacted by someone whose deceased husband used bitterly to complain of severe pain whenever he witnessed injury to another. About this time the neuroscience literature was reporting, in monkeys, a new class of nerve cells, mirror neurons, adjacent to motor regions (controlling movement) in the brain's prefrontal cortex. Such neurons activated – fired – not only when the animal executed a goal-directed action, such as reaching for a piece of food, but also whenever another monkey, or the human experimenter, was observed to perform the same goal-directed action. They did not fire when just the food item was seen, or when a meaningless action was observed. In a published article I wondered whether we could explain the deceased husband's experiences of pain, on observing another in distress, through a similar, pain-related rather than motor-related, mirror system. Since then, emotional regions of the brain have also been shown to exhibit mirror neuron activity, firing not only during the experience of an emotion, but also when one observes another person apparently experiencing such an emotion.

A few years' ago, my daughter had a prolonged and very painful delivery. She told me that ever since, whenever she observes or even merely hears about someone's injury or pain, she experiences sudden 'electric' pain shooting down both legs from the pelvic regions and terminating at the knees. About this time, with my doctoral student Melita Giummarra, we commenced investigating the natural history of the phantom limb phenomenon, whereby many amputees may continue to experience the often very compelling illusion that their missing limb somehow is still there, as if in a phantom form. Of our 300 or so such amputees, many of whom also suffered from constant and intractable associated pain, some eight volunteered, unprompted, the observation that, like my daughter and our original, deceased patient, they experienced further sudden sharp pain whenever exposed to another's trauma.

There are also a few reports of *synaesthesia for touch*, whereby someone observes that whenever they see another touched on a particular location, they too seem also to feel a corresponding touch. Why then don't most of us usually feel another's such sensations? Are these mirror sensations normally kept below threshold? Can we perhaps invoke an analogous mechanism, *synaesthesia for pain*?

The original mirror neuron concept, involving observation in another of an intentional, meaningful, goal-directed action, is clearly motor, unlike synaesthesia for touch or for pain, and may play a key role in action-understanding and imitative learning, even perhaps the acquisition and evolution of language, skills and tool manufacture and use. Thus, to understand the goal of another person's behaviour, we must not only match it against our own motor system, but also covertly imitate the other's action. Indeed, 40 years ago the motor theory of speech perception proposed that we understand another's speech by covertly and sub-vocally recreating, in real time, the speaker's likely mouth movements, rather than by merely following the speech sounds. More recently, dramatic support came from the finding that what you hear when listening to ambiguous samples like 'head' and 'had' is influenced by externally-induced experimental deformations of the skin around your lips; you almost literally hear with your mouth! The old motor theory of speech perception clearly anticipated features of the mirror neuron hypothesis. It is also compatible with the widely-held belief that verbal language evolved from gestural communication, rather than from earlier primate patterns of vocalisation. Chimpanzees share many of our gestures, and can communicate with us quite efficiently by means of gesture; we ourselves fall back on gesture when words fail; and individuals in profoundly deaf families very rapidly develop their own 'language' of deaf signing. A mirror neuron system may therefore have originally evolved to facilitate communication, and it is interesting that such a system has just recently been found to underlie song acquisition in songbirds.

When we wish to improve a skill, such as a golf swing, clearly repeated practice helps. Even watching a skilled athlete in action can facilitate our own progress, while observing another making responses incompatible with those which we wish to achieve can prove disruptive. It is not, however, so widely known that simply *imagining* oneself repeatedly performing such practice can be almost as beneficial as practice itself. Are we perhaps here repeatedly running the motor programme for our developing skill through our mirror neuron system, with the actual motor output turned off or inhibited? Something analogous to this does actually happen in dreams, where we are normally prevented, by a kind of descending paralysis, from acting out the dreams' content and possibly injuring ourselves. And maybe dreams themselves are part of a mechanism for consolidating or covertly practising, during sleep, significant motor programmes constituting our repertoire of skills.

The part of the monkey's brain originally identified with a mirror neuron system, in the premotor cortex, corresponds to our own motor speech region. The latter is closely interconnected with a more posterior, parietal, region. These two regions, while active during *observation* of another's action, are even more active during the *execution* of one's own actions, and most active of all during *imitation*, that is, both observation *and* action. Such observation and covert imitation of another's observed experience, through a mirror neuron system, clearly evokes representations of what another person *is* doing, what he or she *ought* to do, and what you yourself *may intend* to do. All this is beginning to encroach upon another, current, 'hot topic', social cognition and in particular, *theory of mind*.

We cannot ever prove that our fellows have perceptions, thoughts, feelings, desires, fears, knowledge ... just like ourselves. However, a solipsist life, to use the term beloved of philosophers, whereby we each believe that everyone else is a robotic zombie or automaton, is clearly not going to get us very far. 'I *know* that you *think* that my daughter *fears* that your husband has designs upon her...' We all impute a range of beliefs, knowledge and emotions to our fellows. So too do chimpanzees; if a chimp is in the presence of two handlers, one of whom was seen to go off to hide a piece of fruit, the chimp will solicit help only from the handler likely to know the fruit's whereabouts. Such a theory of mind may be defective in autistic individuals, who typically have problems understanding what others may know, fear or believe. Do mirror neuron systems enter into the acquisition and deployment of a theory of mind, and are autistic individuals deficient in the operation of certain, or maybe all, mirror neuron systems? Such people certainly have major problems with imitation, language, appropriate social interactivity and empathy, emotionality, attributing intentionality to others and certain forms of motor behaviour.

Mirror neurons may therefore play a key role not only in understanding another person's goals, but also their emotional and cognitive state. An important element of communication is to interpret and understand the meaningful behaviour of others, and empathically process their associated affective and emotional states. As with action understanding, the observation or imagination of another person in a particular emotional state may automatically activate a representation of that person's actions, goals, intentions or feelings, in largely the same neural networks that are involved in actually experiencing or doing, oneself. By evoking the other's inner state, the observer is in a better position to predict the other's future actions, and at a social level to interact appropriately with him or her – a notoriously difficult problem for someone with autism.

Mirror neurons may therefore play a major role in action understanding, imitation, communication and empathy. Pathological imitative behaviour, which clinically is associated with prefrontal damage, is related to *utilisation behaviour*, where an individual may employ disinhibited, stereotyped and situationally inappropriate use of an object. Clinical patients exhibiting such imitative behaviour automatically imitate the gestures and behaviour of others, even if asked not to do so, and if, in fact, it is highly inappropriate. When asked to stop, they either continue to imitate, or recommence when their attention is diverted. Importantly, however, for our argument, rather than merely performing an action identical to the one observed, they tend to perform largely similar actions that *achieve the same goal*. The prefrontal damage probably releases the parietal regions from the inhibition normally exerted by the prefrontal lobe.

At a much more benign level, we all of us tend to match our behaviour to that of our peer group, or people with whom we are interacting, a phenomenon known as the chameleon effect. Such empathic synchronisation of complementary modes of behaviour, posture, mannerisms and speech patterns undoubtedly smooths interactions, and leads to feelings of empathy and rapport, and may account for claims that married partners (and maybe even the family dog!), tend to grow to appear ever more like each other. It probably justifies (if that were ever possible) the use of 'canned' laughter in TV comedy shows, to promote at least the semblance of audience hilarity, and may explain the well-known contagion of yawning. Indeed, once on a mountain top, I was visited by a large skink while lunching; perhaps finding my presence tedious, it yawned – and so did I!

Facial mimicry is already apparent in one-month-old infants, who may smile, stick out their tongues and open their mouths when seeing someone else doing the same. They soon also, unless autistic, follow the direction of another's gaze, thereby sharing and synchronising attention; there is currently debate about the extent to which other primates, and perhaps even the domestic dog, may do the same, although the adaptive nature of such shared behaviour, in the context of food sources or potential danger, is obvious.

So in this scheme of things, where comes empathy for pain? Can it have a possible adaptive significance, with benefit at least to the observer, if not also to the victim? Our eight amputees who volunteered that they experienced, in their phantom limb or stump, pain that is triggered by observing, thinking about or inferring that another is in pain, had all lost a lower, and never an upper, limb. It so happens that unlike the upper limb, whose cortical representation is adjacent to that of the face, that of the lower limb is adjacent to the cortical representation of the genitalia, a region with major emotional involvement of a sensory nature. Emotionality, if expressed by the face, is of course more a motor than a sensory phenomenon, and is unlikely to be as intense as that experienced genitally. Foot or shoe fetishes are in fact far commoner than hand or glove fetishes! Each of our cases, moreover, all had one thing in common: they had all endured intense, traumatic or chronic pain. Perhaps such an intense experience had disinhibited the normally restrained tendency in all of us to match our emotional reactivity, empathically, to our conversational partners.

If there is a moral to the story so far, always look away when someone is in pain! That's difficult for my daughter, she is a physician.

It was at this point in Melita's work that fortuitously, and fortunately, we were approached by another potential doctoral student from New Zealand, with outstanding electrophysiological credentials, wishing to extend Melita's published findings to a study in depth of mirror sensory synaesthesia (or empathy) for pain. Bernadette O'Loughlin proposed the above term, as a parallel to mirror (or synaesthetic) touch, to describe the unfortunate gentleman with whom I began this chapter. Empathy, of course, is generally construed as a good quality, referring to how we perceive and understand sensation, mood and feeling in others; an ability, as it were, to put oneself in another's place – theory of mind. Unfortunately it can, of course, go wrong or prove counterproductive, as in instances of social contagion, mob behaviour, and empathy for pain. The latter can be caused by or result in real physical, or hardly less real, psychological or emotional pain. Indeed, similar brain regions seem to be activated in both situations. With respect to empathy or social pain, the superior temporal sulcus (right hemisphere, with abundant serotonin receptors), the anterior insula (on the left, representing internal body states), the inferior frontal gyrus (emotions, inhibition), and the cingulate cortex (decision-making, particularly with respect to affective aspects), are prominent, along with the amygdala (emotion, particularly negative). With respect to true synaesthesia for pain, activity in the mirror somatosensory cortices, insula and rostral cingulate are prominent, promoting somatosensation. Additionally, the parietal cortex, along with the supramarginal gyrus mediating the overall body plan and the location of body parts relative to each other, may be involved, just as it is also in out-of-body experiences.

Mirror sensory synaesthesia may be acquired, as in amputees, where there is a relatively high incidence of around maybe 30 per cent, or developmental, where it may be less than 2 per cent. Mirror pain responders tend to have relatively high scores for empathy, and therefore by extension, for theory of mind. Since people with autism typically score low on the latter, it may perhaps be predicted that they would experience mirror touch or mirror pain infrequently. Such individuals do tend to score low in terms of shared attention, looking where others look, a capacity well represented in bonobos ('pygmy chimpanzees').

Mirror neuron activation occurs also with disgust. I remember a colleague with whom we used to go camping; he tended to vomit whenever his infant son did so, and if rather cruelly the rest of us fabricated a 'disease of the day', he would soon claim similar symptoms. In carers, emotional burn-out is not uncommon, a form of synaesthesia for pain maybe, and is associated with abnormal serum cortisol readings; such readings can occur even in non-carers exposed to gruesome videos. Maybe they would be poor candidates for the caring profession. Surprisingly, even diagnosed psychopaths, usually showing little concern for fellow human beings, nevertheless show raised cortisol levels under such circumstances, suggesting absence of abnormalities in their mirror neuron system itself.

Interestingly, lower limb amputees with mirror pain synaesthesia experience a pain response when seeing physical threats (a knife with unobserved retraction of the blade, or hammer) to their embodied 'rubber hand', where the latter optically occupies the position of, and closely resembles, their real, obscured hand. (Even mice, apparently, with an embodied rubber tail visible where their concealed real tail should be, show fear.)

Mirror pain may be related to echopraxia, the compulsive imitation of another's actions even when inappropriate. It clearly involves a positive symptom, an additional experience, whereas most pathologies involve a negative symptom or loss of function. Its exact mechanism could involve either disinhibitory processes, or instead one of somatosensory remapping, just as in our studies of musicians' dystonia. In any case there may be increased vigilance towards any potential threat, and as so often, both processes may contribute synergistically.

27

STOP IT, IT TICKLES

Why you can't tickle yourself

I have vivid memories of reading, many, many years ago, two quirky little studies that piqued my interest then, and have repeatedly bubbled up into consciousness in such contexts as children's parties, and while looking at myself for some reason or other, in the mirror. The experiments were trivial, downright silly, you may say, but the theoretical implications may be profound. I have also often thought of them as possible research projects for students. One of the studies asked why, as many party-going children know, we cannot simultaneously tap our heads with the flat of one hand while with the other performing circular, rotary motions on the stomach, a different movement in another plane. I won't waste much more time on this study, except to say that decades later I devised a complex, computerised system to measure our ability to rotate the two hands, in or out of phase with each other, and in two modes, mirror symmetrical (perhaps left hand clockwise, right hand anticlockwise) or congruent (that is both in the same direction). Importantly, we found theoretically and clinically interesting differences in the abilities of various patient groups with damage to the motor systems of their brains.

The other study, about which this section is concerned, still worries me; I feel there are interesting things yet to be done, possibly with neurological patients. It was written in 1975, with the delightful and intriguing title, 'Why can't we tickle ourselves?' , and much of what follows was the subject of my talk under the Australian Broadcasting Corporation's Ockham's Razor series hosted by Robyn Williams, to both of whom I offer my sincere thanks. (Parenthetically, this observation, that one cannot easily experience a full sensation when tickling oneself, dates back at least to the time of Aristotle.) But before you all go off to try it, go first and look at yourself in the mirror. Gaze deep into one of your eyes, if you can bear to, and move fixation from one eye to the bridge of your nose, to the other eye, and back again. Can you see your eyes moving? I'll bet you can't! If, however, you get a friend to stand beside you, he or she will have no difficulty seeing your eyes move;

nor will you, if you look at your friend's. (Incidentally, while doing this, take time off to notice how asymmetric your friend looks, in left-right mirror-reversal from normal, but that is another story, to which I'll return later.)

So why can you not see your own eyes move? The fact that you can see your friend's eyes move shows that it is not merely a problem of visual resolution, in that we cannot pick up movements so fast or so small. We still don't know the full story, but a phenomenon known as saccadic suppression is probably responsible. Thus, just before we move our eyes, a signal is sent, probably from the motor system, to suppress visual processing during that, upcoming, movement. Presumably there is some kind of filling in, as we do not experience a black-out, or blank-out, whenever we alter fixation, as in reading word-to-word along a line of text. Indeed, experiments have shown that our thresholds for perceiving visual events whose occurrence is coupled to a voluntary eye movement, are greatly raised during a saccade, a refixational eye movement. In this way, maybe, we are protected from experiencing rapid 'smearing' of the external scene across the retina in the back of the eye.

Now, look at something and gently press the corner of your eye with your finger, or even better, with someone you can trust, get him or her to do it for you. You should see the world apparently move for you, in the direction opposite to that of the finger pressure. The interesting question, however, is not why the world moves with such external pressure on the eyeball; it should, as images on the retina are moving in the opposite direction; but rather when you voluntarily move your eyes through the normal, internal, oculomotor system of nerves and eye muscles, why don't you see the world slip by? The oculomotor system, just before an eye movement, sends a signal forward to the visual perceptual centres to cancel such apparent movement, a process, known in the trade as reafference or efference copy, which we shall shortly see may help explain why you don't feel ticklish when you tickle yourself, but you do when getting someone else to do it for you.

A very few people, and I am one of them, can train themselves to slowly and smoothly run their eyes along a horizontal contour, for example, the top of a page, as if tracking an imaginary ant running along the contour. It must be done smoothly, without the usual series of discrete, saccadic, jerks or re-fixations, such as we normally employ in reading, jumping from word or word cluster to the next. If you can do that, you can beat the suppression system, and experience the background slip smoothly past in the opposite direction.

There is an important principle in neuroscience, of relevance to engineering design, whereby a copy of a motor command is used to generate, continuously, predictions of the sensory consequences of the ongoing motor act. This prediction is then compared with the actual sensory feedback from the movement. If there is a discrepancy, the action can be modified or corrected appropriately to reduce that discrepancy, and so efficiently achieve an intended goal. This process explains why, if your car's brakes fail suddenly as you depress the pedal, the car seems to speed up, even though it merely fails to slow down. Similarly, the process can attenuate the sensory effects of self-produced movement, leaving us free to respond to the flow of external events, uncontaminated by the immediate consequences of our own actions. Such a process goes some way to explaining why a self-induced tickle is less satisfactory than the real thing, produced by someone else.

Since the original 1975 paper, all manner of ingenious tricks have been employed, including 'tickling machines', operated directly by the 'ticklee' as both one and the same tickler and ticklee, or by someone else. Generally, the quality of the tickle is better (or worse, depending upon how you view it) when someone else operates the handles. It is also stronger if the ticklee operates the system with a slight, imposed, delay, such that his or her movements are less directly linked to the resulting sensations. All this suggests that the tickling sensation is attenuated or lost with a direct link between the ticklee's movements and the resulting tactile experience. Of course, we still don't know why, in an evolutionary, adaptive sense, we experience the sensation, any more than why we laugh, or yawn, or indeed, why infants and children in particular, and even the apes, laugh when tickled, although I shall shortly return to this issue. Nor do we know why laughs and yawns are themselves 'infectious', triggering similar responses in others; I once observed a lizard yawn, and even found myself following suit!

A slight imposed delay in the loop between self-generated tickling actions and their consequences upon the skin surface can thus restore the tickling sensation. This is reminiscent of the fascinating old phenomenon of delayed feedback. Speak into a microphone, continuously record your speech on tape and play it back, via close-fitting earphones, almost immediately, so that all you hear is your own speech, delayed by 1/5th of a second, and you stutter, stammer and prolong your discourse in a most distressing fashion. If you are deaf, such delayed auditory feedback has no effect on you; I once sadly discovered this during a University Open Day demonstration, when an elderly hard-of-hearing ex-Army Officer triumphantly departed. Delayed visual feedback, such as seeing yourself write, or tie your cravat, through a similarly-delayed video loop, leads to 'motor stuttering'. It can be very disturbing.

Delaying is one way of altering the feedback loop and affecting both the quality of a sensory experience and our capacity for motor control. At the beginning of this account, I asked you to look at a very close friend's face, beside your own, in the bathroom mirror. You may have noticed how grossly asymmetrical he or she now looks. You have, of course, left-right mirror-reversed your friend's normal appearance; that appearance is no more or less asymmetric than normal, but now is merely asymmetric in the direction opposite to what you have come, over time, to expect. You have learned to compensate for such incidental asymmetries in your friend's face, while now, in the mirror, the reversed asymmetries work against this normalising process, and your friend can look quite horrific. Similarly, if you view yourself in a doubly reversing system, your now-unfamiliar asymmetry will seem doubly pronounced and odd.

The point of all this is quite simple. We perceive, generally, what we have come to expect, and we do, normally, what we plan to do; such expectancies can be frustrated by delaying or altering feedback. It is clearly maladaptive to feel a tickle whenever, by chance or design, we self-stimulate, for example, the soles of our feet, perhaps when walking barefoot over dry leaves, so it is adapted-out. Similarly, we don't normally want to see the world move when we move our eyes, or be distracted by irrelevant asymmetries in our friends' faces. Motor plans, and expectancies, can accommodate the regular, unwanted, consequences of our actions; frustrate those expectancies, and a whole world of interesting or disturbing experiences awaits you! More generally, our capacity to process information in real time is limited, especially when performance is non-automatic. Processing speed and accuracy may be made more efficient by a system of continuously updating predictions of what is to be expected in terms of what may happen and where and when it may do so. The most accurate predictions can be made when the input represents sensory feedback from self-generated actions, as there is precise information on all aspects, including when the next upcoming event will occur. The predictions are more uncertain with respect to externally generated sensory input, as in a tickle by someone else.

Why do we laugh, when tickled? Francis Bacon in 1677 observed that when tickled, 'men even in a grieved state of mind, yet cannot forbear laughing'. In 1941, Lenba found that tickle-induced laughter occurred in his own children, despite his having deliberately refrained from tickling them during playful situations, and having always hidden his face behind a mask so that they would not associate tickling with smiles and laughter. I don't know what else this did for his children. Some years ago a group built a tickling machine. Their subjects thought they were being tickled by the machine, although in reality a real person lay hidden within to perform the act, however, the subjects laughed just as much when tickled by what they thought was a machine as when tickled by a real person. So we are still no closer to knowing why we laugh when tickled.

The rare, clinical phenomenon of gelastic epilepsy shows that an electrical malfunction deep within the brain can trigger unwanted laughter, although even then a patient, when asked why she was laughing, replied, 'I don't know, it must be that funny machine of yours, doctor.' We call that type of explanatory response 'confabulation', yet another way that we continuously try to make sense of the confusing, changing world in which we live!

I just must add two afterthoughts: rumour has it that if you sit on your hands to make them numb, you can successfully self-tickle, although I can't confirm this. Second, it is reported that people with schizophrenia can also self-tickle; they too, because of a general deficit in the capacity for monitoring their own internal cognitive processes, may tend to attribute internally generated brain activity (their hallucinatory voices) to external sources.

28

HUNTINGTON'S DISEASE, THE LADY OF THE LAKE AND THE HUNT FOR THE GENE

Early in the nineteenth century, there lived a woman in Venezuela, in a stilt village on the shores of a large lake, with an outlet to the sea, Lake Maracaibo. She died of a then unknown, and what was to prove to be a comparatively rare, slowly developing, devastating and ultimately fatal neurological disease. More than two centuries later it would be shown to have genetic origins, and would be passed on to a Venezuelan kindred, as an abnormal autosomal-dominant allele, where the prevalence nowadays is extremely high. The lake, and surrounding villages, would become a natural genetic laboratory. The first cases may have occurred in early seventeenth-century Europe, and debate continues as to whether all present-day cases are direct descendants, a founder effect, or whether any new mutations have since occurred, or can occur. Be that as it may, the Lady of the Lake, who bore nine children, is thought either to have lived with an affected European, possibly a Portuguese sailor who found his way into this natural and pleasant retreat, or to be the daughter of a woman who had done so.

The first clear and perceptive account of this disorder was given by one George Huntington, after whom it is eponymously named, in 1872.

> The hereditary chorea, as I shall call it, … is confined to certain and fortunately few families, and has been transmitted to them, an heirloom from generations away back in the dim past. It is spoken of by those in whose veins the seeds of the disease are known to exist, with a kind of horror, and not at all alluded to except through dire necessity when it is mentioned as 'that disorder'.
>
> *(Huntington 1872)*

He then went on to describe three main peculiarities of the disease: (1) its hereditary nature; (2) the fact that it manifests usually in adult life; and (3) a tendency in its sufferers to insanity and suicide.

Estimates of the prevalence of Huntington's disease (HD) vary, ranging from up to 10 per 100,000 in Northern Europe and the USA, to 17 per 100,000 in Tasmania (again, probably from a single female immigrant), and 700 per 100,000 around Lake Maracaibo, although in some villages it is nearly universal, and is known locally as '*el mal de San Vito*', or Saint Vitus's dance. As the average age of clinical onset (around 45, but with wide variations) is typically post-reproductive, it is unlikely to be 'selected out', although relatively rare and rapidly progressing (up to 10 per cent of cases) instances of juvenile or adolescent onset do occasionally occur. Such unfortunate individuals often show regression in cognitive and other skills.

A progressive neurodegenerative disorder, it is characterised by the insidious onset of mild personality changes and minor motor incoordination, followed by uncontrollable choreiform (dance-like and hyperkinetic) movements, cognitive deterioration (especially the 'executive functions', which include cognitive flexibility, abstract thinking, rule acquisition, initiation of appropriate and inhibition of inappropriate actions, and attentional processes), and affective and psychiatric symptoms. A form of dementia typically develops, along with a range of neuropsychiatric, emotional and personality changes. Aggression and a range of compulsive, delusional, frankly psychotic and inappropriate behaviours, including alcoholism, gambling and hypersexuality, may manifest. Memory and speech deficits appear, along with abnormal saccadic (eye movement) control. There is no cure, and treatment is at best palliative, with symptoms progressing relentlessly to death, typically from aspiration pneumonia or cardiorespiratory failure, about 16–20 years after onset of clinical symptoms.

Family studies showed that having one parent with the disease gave you a 50/50 chance of developing the disorder, and a certainty with both parents, before the causative gene was found. With my students, knowing that movement sequencing was particularly affected in HD, we developed a programmable sequential reaction-time device, with varied amounts of advance information provided for each rapidly sequential choice point. We found that a number of individuals known to be at risk (from having a parent with the disorder, but at time of testing being themselves clinically intact), were two or more standard deviations outside (slower than) healthy controls. We believed that they were probably destined to develop the disorder, and our predictions sadly proved correct. The device has since been developed for international use in testing movement control in the disorder. Shortly afterwards the causative gene was identified.

Some two decades ago, Nancy Wexler, born in 1945, visited Melbourne, and her public lecture was a quite extraordinary experience, not least because born of a kindred, many of whom, including her mother, had had the disorder, she nevertheless made it her life's work to work out its genetics. She led the research team to Lake Maracaibo, and they successfully located the causative gene, on the short arm of chromosome 4, making this the first autosomal disease locus found using genetic linkage analysis. It thereby permitted creation of a chromosomal test to identify carriers – possibly herself. However, she knew how much happier she, and her sister, would both be if they were to take her own test and it proved negative – and how personally devastating it would be if it proved positive in either case. (One of our own patients, having seen a parent and another close relative die of the disease, and feeling he was already himself experiencing preliminary symptoms, decided to spend his remaining days in the fast lane with an expensive and irresponsible lifestyle; then when the genetic test became available, on a whim he took it – and found he was in in fact in the clear, but financially bankrupt, and with nothing now left to live for. He was, paradoxically, devastated at the 'good' news.) With her lecture delivered as a most striking and authoritative figure, along with fascinating illustrative material of the lives and environs of the unfortunate inhabitants of this exotic location, I was enthralled by both speaker and talk, and have often wondered since why no one has made a full-length documentary movie; it seemed to possess everything needed, and more.

The disease-associated mutation, discovered in 1993, is an expanded and unstable trinucleotide (CAG: cytosine, adenine, guanine, together normally coding for the protein glutamine) repeat sequence within the causative gene. Such unstable repeats (e.g. CAGCAGCAGCAG...) are like a kind of genetic stutter, and involving different protein-coding genes, may occur in other disorders such as fragile X syndrome and Friedreich's ataxia, upon both of which, like Huntington's disease, my group has worked, and myotonic dystrophy, spinocerebellar ataxia type 1, and spinobulbar muscular atrophy. Unaffected individuals have less than 26 CAG repeats; between 27 and 35, the individual will never be affected, but any offspring might suffer, since there can be a tendency down the generations for the number of repeats to increase: 'dynamic instability'. Between 36 and 39 repeats, the carriers may or may not be affected, while with 40 or over, they definitely will be, should they live long enough; indeed, the odds shorten, the more the repeats. In these cases, with 36 or more glutamines, a mutant protein variant, huntingtin, is produced. Interestingly, many other mammals, including primates, have CAG segments that differ in length among individuals of the same species, but humans may have the most.

What other roles, possibly beneficial, may the gene play, bearing in mind that since age of onset is usually post reproductive, it is unlikely to be selected out? Expanding numbers of the CAG codon may actually assist in the development of the nervous system after birth, as long as the rise does not surpass the disease threshold. Thus, the Huntington's gene may be involved in neural tube development and protein binding, thereby increasing the number of neurons in the globus pallidus which is part of the basal ganglia, a brain region central to my group's research for the last 30 years, with its control of planning and movement sequencing. Indeed, carriers of the gene who are destined to become affected may, before illness strikes, show high levels of cognitive functioning.

What exactly are the deleterious effects of the gene on the brain? The corpus striatum within the basal ganglia, and the cerebral cortex, are regions, particularly controlling cognitive and executive functions and movement initiation and sequential control, where a class of neurons is particularly targeted. The basal ganglia ordinarily inhibit circuits that generate specific movements; movement initiation involves a signal from the cortex causing the inhibition to be lifted and the movement released. Damage to this region may cause inappropriate release of the movement (as in Tourette's syndrome, TS, another of our areas of research) or inhibition, as in Parkinson's disease (PD), where we also have been working. Our colleague, Professor Bob Iansek, developed the explanatory set and cue model to account for awkward initiation of movements as in PD, and the erratic movements as in HD and TS. Indeed, shortly before death, a patient with HD tends more towards the inert, akinetic and PD-like end of the spectrum.

The constant and unpredictable choreiform jerks typically flow across the body like complex fragments of normal, intentional behaviour, and are often referred to as 'premotor synergies', reflecting an origin in the premotor cortex. They are idiosyncratic to each individual, and slowly evolve over time, giving purposeful acts a baroque quality, almost as if the patient is trying to smuggle in and conceal unwanted activity among and amidst normal voluntary movement – a situation very similar to that other, more benign, hyperkinetic disorder of the basal ganglia, Tourette's syndrome. They can also be briefly suspended at will, and if deeply concentrating upon a difficult puzzle, they may, we noticed, even disappear. We also found that patients have particular difficulty with controlling such movement parameters as direction, force, extent and duration. Loss of automaticity results in problems in performing concurrent tasks. On the other hand, the brain's amazing spare capacity can preserve normal function for some years after electrophysiological, structural and functional imaging shows clear pathological changes. However, in the final stages, movements slow down, with continuously changing features (athetosis) and akinetic (rigid posture), as in PD.

In one very unfortunate and local family we studied, a mother and all her three children, by a sad 'deck of cards' dealt by fate, suffered from the disorder; only the father was, of course, unaffected. He daily fed his helpless wife and the eldest child three times a day, directly through a gastric 'peg', waiting for them to die, as by then they were in the terminal stages. At the same time he had to watch, helplessly, the other two children advance to a similar state of total, akinetic, dependency.

It would be nice if we could predict exactly, based simply on the number of repeats, when a carrier would become ill, although as there is no cure yet, intervention would be palliative at best. However, research is showing that other genetic and environmental factors, such as activity and possibly diet, just as they can help in staving off dementia in the elderly, may interact with the calendar of genetic inevitability in HD. One of my old doctoral students has been involved for some years in trying to develop a predictor equation, with the main variable, number of repeats, modified by other adventitious variables, genetic, lifestyle and environmental, in the hope that early intervention might, as in mouse models of the disease, postpone the inevitable.

Part of the difficulty in predicting exactly when clinical symptoms might appear, on the basis of the number of CAG repeats, may stem from epigenetic factors – environmental influences turning on or off certain genes. Thus, some time before the role was known of epigenetics modifying the expression of genes, we studied a pair of identical male twins. We found that they differed markedly in a range of behaviours and performance.

While it is certainly true that as yet there is no known cure for HD, nor even a reliable way of halting or markedly slowing its relentless progression, very new genetic advances, such as CRISPR genome editing, may, I suspect, offer a totally new way forward. This new technique allows existing genes to be removed and new ones added, resulting in permanent modification of genes within an organism. Maybe, with gene testing at birth of at-risk individuals with a parent suffering from the disorder, his or her CAG repeat sequence could be appropriately shortened; however, I have not as yet heard or read of such a suggestion.

It has been a rare if sobering privilege to study such a uniquely horrible disorder; I always tell my students that behind every fascinating new finding, there invariably lies a personal tragedy; nor have I been personally immune from such a sombre scenario with my own wife's massive stroke.

29

PARKINSON'S DISEASE

When go turns to slow

Among the ambulant poor of my childhood on the post-war streets of bomb-blasted Birkenhead, I vividly remember (in my mind's eye I can see them now) old men. They were never, for some reason, old women; maybe the latter were just less adventurous and stayed indoors, or were not obligatory bread-winners – unlike those fast-shuffling old men, blank of face, semi-stooped and bent forward, as if half-running so as not to fall over, so short were the steps they took. Sometime later, when old enough to appreciate the turning wheels of industry, I would occasionally be allowed to visit my father's place of work – 'The Works', the Stork Margarine Works, where he was a maintenance engineer. Everywhere, huge tanks and pipes, the hum of pumps – and a choking smell of escaping ammonia, presumably a refrigerant. What might be the toxic connection?

In 1817, an English doctor James Parkinson, born in 1755, described *paralysis agitans*, a disorder, he noted, characterised by tremor and alterations in gait, posture and speech, with, he believed, relatively unimpaired intellect and the senses, although we now know that such impairment is not uncommon. And we now also know the disorder eponymously as Parkinson's disease (PD):

> Involuntary tremulous motion, with lessened muscular power, in parts not in action … with a propensity to bend the trunk forward and to pass from a walking to a running pace, the senses and the intellect being uninjured … The first symptoms observed are a slight sense of weakness, with a proneness to trembling … most commonly in one of the hands and arms. These symptoms gradually increase in the part first affected, and at an uncertain period, but seldom less than 12 months or more, the morbid influence is felt in some other part … or limb.
>
> *(Parkinson, 1817, pp. 1–3)*

If medicine was Parkinson's career, fossil collecting and the nearly nascent discipline of palaeontology was his true passion. For this he achieved eminence and the award of the Royal Society of Surgeons' first gold medal in 1823, shortly before his death, to recognise his 'distinguished labours and discoveries', and for his 'splendid work on organic remains'. Indeed, his book, published in 1804 with the title, *Organic Remains of a Former World* made him internationally famous.

Even earlier, nearly 2,000 years ago, Galen described 'the shaking palsy', and similar mention is made in the Ayurvedic texts of India of 1000 BC. As the disorder is primarily one of ageing, there would not have been very many such elderly individuals around.

PD is a nasty degenerative neurological disorder mostly striking in middle to late life, like Alzheimer's, although some might regard both maladies as 'merely' a form of accelerated ageing, and inevitable if you live long enough. It has a mean age of onset around 60, and steadily increases in prevalence thereafter, although around 7 per cent of cases classified as young onset begin between the ages of 20–50. Around 13 new cases per year are reported per 100,000 persons, with maybe a preponderance of males – maybe accounting for my childhood observations on the streets of Birkenhead – although this difference is disputed. Unless appropriately managed and treated, death can be expected after about 12 years from initial diagnosis.

This neuromotor syndrome is characterised chiefly by a resting tremor (5 Hz, disappearing during voluntary movement), stiffness (muscular contraction), slowed movement (bradykinesia), and postural instability with associated difficulties with walking and gait. Thus, just as I remembered, the patient tends to shuffle rapidly (festination) while leaning forward, with loss of balance and a propensity to fall. While walking, there may be a tendency to freeze, often when passing through a doorway, but ascending/descending stairs, or riding a bicycle or dancing may often be unimpaired. My group believes that these paradoxical observations reflect the fact that it is often over-learnt and normally semiautomatic functions which are worse affected, while actions requiring continuing adaptive responses to changing and externally cued situations, employing different and largely intact motor pathways, are less impaired. There often also occurs dementia, with difficulties in cognitive, attentional, planning and other executive function, while sensory (particularly visual), emotional (anxiety and depression), memory and sleep disturbances may even precede motor symptomatology. Tremor seems to underlie a characteristic 'pill-rolling' type of finger movement, involving thumb and forefinger; a ratchety cog-wheel rigidity, when a stiffly-held limb is passively moved, may replace the alternative 'lead-pipe' stiffness. The face acquires a mask-like expression, due to muscular stiffness; writing tends to progressively reduce in size along a line (micrographia), and speech becomes higher in pitch, lower in volume, and, as we reported, often inappropriately 'pitched' as a function of interpersonal distance during conversation. However, prognosis seems better for patients initially presenting with tremor (often regarded as a 'positive' symptom, with excess of function, like chorea in Huntington's disease, rather than rigidity, a 'negative' symptom of functional deficit). Interestingly, while tremor increases while PD patients attend to a difficult problem, we have noticed that chorea in Huntington's tends to decrease. These are all phenomena with which my research group has been intimately concerned over the last two or three decades.

Parkinson's disease may be primary (idiopathic, and of no currently certain cause), or secondary, typically the result of some insult to the brain, whether from a toxin such as pesticides (particularly the organochlorines), or herbicides (and farmers do seem to be rather more prone), or possibly even recreational methamphetamine. Did, I wonder, years of exposure to possibly toxic levels of ammonia 'down at t'works' bring about, or hasten the onset of, my father's PD? Alternatively, it may result from repeated blows to the head as with certain sports, especially boxing. In the 1980s, various users of 'recreational' drugs consumed a contaminated batch of a synthetic opiate, MPPP, which brought about a permanent Parkinsonian state from the toxic action of the metabolite MPTP. This incidentally proved to be a way to generate PD or something very similar for study in animal models. A novel hypothesis is that prion particles may be implicated in PD. Prions are unusual infective agents which may be acquired, rather like viruses, or even be inherited directly via one's own genome, and either way cause protein misfolding. Examples are bovine spongiform encephalopathy (BSE, 'mad cow disease'), Creutzfeldt-Jacob disease, and kuru (New Guinea). Recent evidence suggests that a runaway self-propagating cascade of misfolding proteins may be operative in AD – and maybe also in PD – the alpha-synuclein protein being vulnerable thereby to aggregation. Where PD appears to develop from a genetic inheritance, prion-like activity may thus be responsible, and where there seems instead to be an environmental cause, an infective route, possibly via the nose (the olfactory system is an open portal to the brain, and olfaction is an early casualty of PD), or via the gut so as to disturb its normal and beneficial bacterial flora, is being considered by some. It is certainly the case that there are neural similarities and interconnecting pathways between gut and brain, with suggestions of changes in the gut being an early aspect of PD. A new slant on the adage 'follow your nose and trust your gut feelings when making decisions'.

In some instances of primary PD, there can be a clear genetic link, in particular with respect to the gene coding for parkin or for alpha-synuclein. The latter may be particularly significant in that it is also operative in Alzheimer's dementia (dementing processes are common in advanced PD), a source of personal concern as my mother died of Alzheimer's, and my father with PD, a genotype in my own instance unpleasantly likely to 'give' me one or both disorders.

Motor symptoms (usually the most initially salient) in PD stem from the death of cells in the substantia nigra within the basal ganglia (BG), thereby reducing the availability of dopamine (DA), a very important neurotransmitter, intimately involved in voluntary movement and mood, especially pleasure. Indeed, the best diagnostic procedure for the disorder is a 'challenge' with DA (or, rather, a precursor such as the drug, levodopa); if improvement is immediate, however temporary, then PD is very likely. There is also a number of loosely related and generally very similar disorders, known as Parkinson's plus, such as multiple system atrophy, progressive supranuclear palsy, corticobasal degeneration and Lewy-body dementia. The progressive cell death in PD may in turn stem from the build-up of toxic proteins in the neurons, exactly analogous to the build-up, in Alzheimer's disease (AD), of similarly toxic tau protein elsewhere in the forebrain.

Analogously as with Huntington's disease (HD), where we saw the importance of the normal healthy BG in automatically initiating each next movement subroutine or sequence as soon as the previous component is executed, or inhibiting it if/when no longer appropriate, the BG in PD now come to exert excessive cortical inhibition. In HD (a neurodegenerative disorder) and Tourette's syndrome (TS, a neurodevelopmental rather than a neurodegenerative disorder), there is instead excessive and inappropriate motor release. There are five major pathways connecting the BG with the rest of the brain, all operating through the medium of DA, and responsible in turn for motor, oculomotor (eye movement), cognitive, emotional and attentional aspects of behaviour; very little else is left to chance! Motor output from the BG is largely to the supplementary motor area in the frontal lobe, from where my group has been recording the electrophysiological *Bereitschaftspotential*, a 'readiness' potential, signalling the release of each next element of a largely automatic or overlearned motor sequence, a potential which we find is greatly reduced and abnormal in both PD and HD. In a complex serial-reaction-time task with PD patients, we have tried artificial augmentation of this signal as a possible therapeutic measure, using carefully timed transcranial magnetic stimulation (TMS), simultaneously with when each next move is due, but without success. We know that PD patients have most difficulty with routine sequences like walking on the flat, but cope much better when there are additional cues present, as when ascending or descending stairs and each step needs monitoring; consequently, in a journal article I once speculated whether a device could be made and worn which projects a bar of light in front of the patient at an appropriate point in the stepping cycle, like the tread of stairs, for the patient to step over. I since heard that an engineer with PD himself was successfully trialling my idea. Of course, the famous neurologist Oliver Sacks reports the ingenious carpenter with PD who crafted a walking stick with a short horizontal bar near the base, over which the user had to step when freezing, simply by rotating the stick 90 degrees so that it became an obstacle instead of just pointing forward and out of the way. The moral of all this is that automatic sequencing is lost in PD, and all such complex sequences have to be consciously performed 'on line', instead of automatically.

Treatments with medications which increase the availability of DA work well for the first few years, but as the disorder inexorably progresses, like HD and AD, problems typically arise, often as an undesirable side-effect of the medications themselves. Indeed, DA itself, although essential, is nevertheless neurotoxic. Thus, apart from the drugs becoming increasingly ineffective, involuntary writhing or dystonic posturing tends to develop, along with problems with impulse control, hyper-sexuality, pathological gambling, hallucinations and delusions. There are also various autonomic nervous system problems (hypotension, sweating, oily skin, constipation, urinary incontinence, sexual difficulties...). Caffeine (high levels of coffee intake) and nicotine (one of smoking's few benefits!) may be neuroprotective, at least prior to clinical onset; so too, curiously, may be obesity, and the very commonly used anti-asthma drug Salmeterol! Oxidative stress along with iron has been implicated in the pathology, and it may be no accident that women, with heavy monthly bleeds, and regular blood donors may also be advantaged. Curiously, the disorder's relentless progress may be slowed by exenatide, a drug used to control diabetes.

When medication starts to fail, and/or unwanted side effects develop, one of two surgical procedures may be adopted; both depend upon the fact that the BG consists of a complex interactive network of excitatory and inhibitory pathways. Deep brain stimulation (DBS) involves a device, analogous to a cardiac pacemaker, being carefully implanted deep into the BG and associated circuits, in a position so as to either inhibit structures inhibiting the cortex, or further excite intrinsically excitatory regions. Similarly, with the lesional approach, regions with inhibitory effect upon the cortex may be destroyed.

In a world seemingly fixated upon the apparently unlimited clinical potential of stem cell treatment, after an initial burst of seemingly exciting progress, the early promise seems to be fading, although research continues into possible regeneration of the substantia nigra and/or related structures. One problem may be that even with new cells developing in the right places, they will still be vulnerable to whatever caused the disorder in the first place, although it might be a way of buying some extra time.

How did my group first become interested in researching PD? After our earlier success in devising new approaches to studying HD, I casually mentioned to my daughter, then a first year medical student, how appropriate it would be for us to move into PD, as a disorder with certain common and other interestingly different symptoms. She said, 'You should talk to one of my lecturers, Dr Bob Iansek, who is currently talking to us about PD.' I did, and a wonderful friendship and collaborative partnership developed which lasted for decades, with many grants and publications, until we both 'retired'. 'Chance', I always say, 'favours the prepared mind'.

30

MUSICIANS' DYSTONIA

A brain out of tune

'Chance favours the prepared mind' was my observation at the end of the account of our foray into the fascinating tragedy which is Parkinson's disease. We had some choice chances, choice in both senses, when opportunity offered us entrée into a seemingly related although far more benign disorder, musician's dystonia. As so often, the chain of personal choice and effect extends far back, to the early 1970s, when I was approached by a charismatic and talented Canadian girl, Anne Gates, with an unusually useful combination of qualifications, including physics (with acoustics), experimental psychology and music. She had come across some of my early publications, and wanted to do a PhD with me. Our collaboration proved amazingly fruitful, in no small part due to the wealth of electronic and acoustic gear we bought, invented or constructed, at a time when we were blessed with an enthusiastic and collaborative electronics workshop.

Later, by the mid-1980s, our expanding research group had gained a reputation for its work on Parkinson's disease, and I was then approached by the Professor of Music and Dean at Melbourne University to collaborate in studying musicians' dystonia, a neurological condition plaguing some of his players. I declined, not wishing to spread our research net too wide, and I knew little about it, even though it seemed to have certain relevant Parkinsonian features, but literally within a month or so I heard from a very well-qualified girl in New Zealand, Vanessa Lim. Her qualifications, otherwise very similar to Anne's, also included experience in electrophysiology; and she was strongly supported by my old friend and colleague at Auckland University, Professor Michael Corballis. I changed my mind, and took Vanessa on. It always helps to have a bright graduate student to join one in a new project, to clear away the brushwood, as it were, and to do the initial spadework.

The next unexpected node in the causal chain was the fact that our music professor, Max Cooke, wanted me to go to Hamburg to meet a friend and colleague of his, an eminent German neurologist Eckart Altenmüller, who as a talented musician himself also had an interest in musicians' dystonia. Again I demurred, but again, quite unexpectedly, I was invited to lecture for a fortnight at an important NATO summer school on Neurology, all expenses paid with an honorarium, at Delmenhorst, near Bremen, and not too far from Hamburg. But, surprise, surprise (although I do now wonder whether Max might have had a hand in it), Eckart was also contributing to the course! We became good friends, and after each day's sessions, Eckart would play one of his own compositions.

Eckart had an excellent electrophysiology lab, with better facilities even than we had back home in Australia, and he offered to take on Vanessa for a 9-month collaboration. It was extraordinary how everything fell into place, and she never let us down. In fact, as they would say in the part of the world, England's industrial North, from where I originally come, 'T'lass did us reet (right) proud, she did.'

Dystonia ('cramps') is a neurological disorder characterised by involuntary and sustained muscle contractions and abnormal, twisting postures, resulting in loss of fine motor control in highly practised movements. When focal, the dystonia only affects a single, circumscribed body area. When task-specific, the symptoms only manifest during completion of a particular activity or task, such as writing, or playing a certain musical instrument (musicians' dystonia) usually after massive amounts of practice. Initially, there may be increasing lapses in performance, which can of course also stem from other causes. Gradually, although often quite painless, symptoms may worsen, with string players, the problems typically affecting only certain fingers, usually the ones most used (hand dystonia). With woodwind, symptoms may involve hands, face or mouth, tongue or jaw (embouchure dystonia). Tremor and involuntary contractions of the face musculature may occur. Generally, precision is lost, and fingers may tend to curl, bow or 'stick' to the instrument or keys, freeze suddenly, or stick out sideways. Subtle modifications of posture or instrument may temporarily alleviate matters, and other activities using the same parts of the limb or hand may remain unaffected. Often, familial aspects seem to suggest a genetic link, and men seem more prone to the malady than women, although overall frequency rarely exceeds a few percent. Onset tends to be between 30 and 40 years of age, and there is no cure as such, although symptoms may be alleviated with injections of botulinum toxin (Botox) or anticholinergics.

The condition may easily be misdiagnosed as simple overuse or stress, but, being painless, the source and origin suggest a central rather than a peripheral origin, seemingly involving a kind of inappropriate remapping of key sensorimotor brain areas, and/or an inhibitory deficit from a possible genetic origin. Thus, co-contraction of opposing agonist and antagonist muscles, and excessive motor overflow (see the motor overflow section) is common. Interfering and inappropriate sensory input may fail to be 'gated out', as normally occurs during a rapid, practised and skilled movement. Otherwise, the supplementary motor area has been invoked, a region receiving 'release' or 'hold' signals (the *Bereitschaftspotential*, see Chapter 29 on Parkinson's disease), from the basal ganglia for each next stage in a complex, overlearned motor sequence.

Vanessa's own electrophysiological work supported the inappropriate sensorimotor integration and mapping approach, finding also that, in musicians' dystonia, there may additionally be abnormal sensory representation in quite different sensory areas of the brain and modalities, with patients who present with finger, hand or arm dystonia also showing evidence of abnormal *auditory-area* activity, and performance, when asked to discriminate or process simple auditory signals. This sensory viewpoint receives further support from the efficacy of certain sensory tricks ('*gestes antagonistes*') to 'unlock' an unwanted posture or response. Thus, with torticollis or 'wryneck', where the head is involuntarily held in an inappropriate and unwanted turn to one side, someone else grasping it and forcing it even *further* in the *same* (seemingly inappropriate) direction may 'unlock' it. And with blepharospasm, where the eyelid is involuntarily held open or shut, simply touching it may free it.

When I watch a professional pianist playing a fast movement over an extended period of time, I not only wonder at her ability to target successive keys so fast and accurately, seemingly never with even a single false note or timing, but now with an extended understanding of dystonia from working with Vanessa, I also wonder how very few in fact seem to develop this occupational hazard – of potentially disastrous proportions for their careers.

31

CLOTHES-PEGS, SEX, HOBBIES, ADDICTION AND GAMBLING

Liverpool, once a vital English seaport lying across the River Mersey from my birthplace in Cheshire's Wirral Peninsula, housed in my childhood some large department stores. Despite or maybe even to compensate for the many privations during the Second World War, my mother would regularly take me to visit the clothing departments. All I remember, as a 3-year-old, is obsessively collecting pins randomly discarded on the carpeted floors, doubtless to my mother's embarrassment – unless of course they went into her prized sewing repository, to join assorted buttons, tapes and other such useful paraphernalia of repair or construction in a period of great privation. But I think it was simply the urge to collect that probably drove me – a simple urge perhaps like graffiti, divorced from any subsequent aesthetic or utilitarian purpose. Later, as a 4- or 5-year-old, I specialised in collecting bus tickets, thrilling, I well remember, to such rare exotica as the spoils of a journey on an obscure local bus line somewhere deep in rural Wales during a family holiday. These particular tickets were rectangular, prized specimens with two smaller rectangles excised at diagonally opposite ends. It was a natural progression to stamp collecting, which had a number of advances, and advantages, compared to bus tickets. They were of a largely standard shape and size (although spiced with such rare and delectable prizes as the occasional round or triangular specimen, usually from some utterly obscure island country, seeking fame and financial fortune via philately as a last resort); stamps moreover could also be displayed by mounting in special albums with stamp hinges, and were eagerly traded among one's peers, or given as bribery or rewards by those in authority. Indeed, amidst the debris and junk of juvenilia, I still have my old stamp album, together with that of a friend, swapped for a large box of luscious if ephemerally shiny brown 'conkers', or horse chestnuts, which my favourite uncle had sent me. Graham's mother, son in tow, hot-footed it round to demand that the swap be annulled, but my mother, strangely, took my side; she asked Graham which he preferred; when he replied 'the conkers', the album stayed with me and the two mothers never spoke to each other again, although Graham and I remained friends. He even threw in a combination lock, to seal the deal, which has served me well for some 70 years.

A family holiday when I was 10 on Britain's south-west coast introduced me to the wonders of wandering along the cliffs and shorelines of the fossil fauna of the Jurassic Blue Lias – in those early post-war years collecting had not yet depleted nature's treasure chest. This powerful new obsession still holds me partly in thrall, and introduced me to palaeontology, taxonomy, evolution and the aesthetics of perfect preservation in a medium far more durable than the original living form.

Why do we collect things? Why are the things we collect generally so uniformly useless for our own lives' Darwinian struggles? That favourite old TV programme on ABC TV, *The Collectors*, illustrates the utterly bizarre pointlessness of so many obsessively assembled collections. All are meticulously displayed, from clothes-pegs of every conceivable design and colour to tin-openers, from car wheel disks to portable transistor radios. There are hardly any remotely similar behaviours elsewhere in the animal kingdom. The adornments of his mating bower by the Australasian bowerbird, generally conforming to the male bird's own particular predilections of colour and type, are carefully arranged and displayed, but at least he has the reproductive excuse of sexual selection in wooing a mate: she will choose to reproduce with the best male around, as indicated, proxy-fashion, by the quality of his bower display. Could that purpose, maybe far removed, sanitised and sublimated, possibly be the rationale behind a carefully chosen, exquisitely presented and meticulously displayed collection of late Victorian dressed dolls? But I doubt whether any twenty-first-century gentleman, however desperate for a mate, would fall, consciously or otherwise, for that particular form of sexual selection.

Collecting is typically an occupation, or, rather, a *preoccupation*, bordering upon an obsession. Clinically, however, obsessions (the underlying thoughts and drives), and the related compulsive acts, are largely unwelcome intrusions into one's life, which the sufferer from obsessive compulsive disorder (OCD) knows to be abnormal, and only indulges in them – be it hand-washing or compulsive checking, or almost any other bizarre and ultimately pointless act – in an attempt to reduce rising levels of anxiety; any relief is of course usually only temporary. (Curiously, seeing another perform your 'pet' compulsion, such as them washing their hands, may alleviate your own compulsive urges.) Rather than obsessive-compulsive disorder, collecting seems more to resemble a manifestation of the clinically-benign obsessive personality subtype, where the individual may typically gain a modicum of pleasure from always acting in a careful, methodical, meticulous and at all times appropriate manner. However, there is no evidence that collectors otherwise manifest aspects of the obsessive personality subtype. Indeed, the pleasure they gain from the exercise of their hobby is surely far more real and intense, and different in kind from the anxiety accompanying OCD. The concepts 'intensity' and 'hobby' may in fact be particularly significant; all forms of collecting can be characterised as hobbies – although other hobbies such as photography, travel or painting may involve little in the way of overt collecting per se, where it is perhaps the experience itself which is more important – the journey, rather than the destination. Maybe the only behaviour, activity or state which approaches the emotional intensity of collecting (the hunt, the find, the acquisition, the display), is perhaps the condition of being 'in love'. But the love lust we all yearn for and maybe come to regret at least has a potential reproductory justification. Love, however, despite initial-stage heady exuberance, can all too often end in bitterness, recrimination and regret, while with hobbies, the joy of acquisition may persist, or slowly diminish, but rarely ends, like love can, in emotional despair. Which brings us back again, of course, to sex. Parenthetically, it is noteworthy that the beautifully crafted, highly symmetrical 'hand axes' of the Acheulian Period, half a million years ago, as produced by our hominid predecessors *Homo erectus*, are exquisitely over-engineered, by a relatively small-brained creature, with respect to any possible utilitarian purpose. Maybe, as has been seriously suggested, like the peacock's ridiculously dramatic tail, their purpose was simply to woo the bashful local lasses on the plains: perhaps a kind of 'See how clever I am – come breed with me', and like the bower-bird, 'just' another instance of sexual selection.

To return to modern love; the intensity and obsessive quality of the experience, the pining unhappiness punctuated by brief periods of equally inappropriate exaltation, looking with the mind instead of seeing with the eyes, all seem more to relate to aspects of the woes of obsessive compulsive disorder, than to either the mild satisfaction of the obsessive personality in doing the job well and seeing it right through, or the happy hunting of the avid collector. Maybe the Roman poet Ovid captured best the painful, hopeless even, quality of the love obsession with his lines:

> *Sic pectore toto uritur, et sterilem sperando nutrit amore.*
>
> He burns with all his heart, feeding his fruitless love on hope alone.

Perhaps the purest and most obsessive form of collecting is that engaged in by the 'twitcher', with his (somewhat more rarely 'her' – and what might that tell us?) bird list of ticked and vacant sightings. And then there are also the plane and train spotters. Plane spotters can be found in the departure lounge of any large airport, and are immediately distinguishable in their manner from mere passengers. The first train spotter who came to my notice was when as a new undergraduate at England's oldest university I realised that a thin, earnest, bespectacled and appropriately bepimpled youth in my intake group had deliberately foregone the pleasures (possibly doubtful, as far as the post-war plumbing went) of a room in the romantic thirteenth-century college, in exchange for a grim and grotty little garret overlooking the city railway station. In this way he could be for ever on hand, at least during his leisure hours, to record engine numbers of arriving trains. Not inappropriately, he was an Engineering student, a discipline, according to Professor Simon Baron-Cohen of Cambridge, notably notorious for an over-representation of mildly Asperger-like practitioners.

In the brain, nerve cells, and indeed whole neuronal systems, communicate with each other via chemical messengers. While there are many such classes of neurotransmitter, dopamine is perhaps particularly significant in the present context. Low levels of dopamine, and/or down regulation of its specific receptors, are notoriously associated with Parkinsonian immobility – of gait, of manual actions, even of the facial musculature and expressions. It is also released in the limbic basal ganglia at moments of intense pleasure – which, indeed, it may mediate – or when receiving a reward of some kind, or when engaging in natural (sex, eating good food) or unnatural (e.g. drug-addictive) behaviours. Dopamine-lowering medications (to alleviate psychotic delusions) may diminish or eliminate pleasures to be gained from following a hobby, or the urge to engage in them; dopamine-enhancing medications, to control the tremors or rigidity of Parkinson's disease, may sometimes promote unwanted gambling or inappropriate sexual activity. An acquired addiction to sex or pornography, perhaps from an initial seemingly harmless introduction via the internet, is generally associated with a major dopaminergic contribution; the latter is of course also doubtless true of many aspects of hobbies, collecting and 'pure love' itself – if, indeed, in the end, despite poetical posturing, love is ever purely pure!

I have a colleague, eminent as both a clinician and as a neuroscientist, whose passion is wine. Not in fact an avid drinker, his 'cellar' contains mostly rare and expensive vintages, rapidly passing any half-reasonable use-by date. They are generally too special – too valuable even – ever to be opened and sampled. They have now become mere tokens to be traded or exchanged, or kept like gold bars as a hedge against difficult economic times – and to be inspected as objects to be enjoyed at a purely visual or cerebral, rather than gustatory, level. And isn't that what also happens with many of the great art collections, where the contents attract prices out of all proportion to their actual aesthetic value, however assessable? And where that inflated value suddenly collapses when against all odds and expectations the prized piece of artwork is suddenly revealed to be a fake, forgery or 'merely' the work of an obscure disciple.

I have another acquaintance, one of whose artistic and collecting passions is much darker, perhaps reflecting more clearly than most the possible linkages between the obsessive and the frankly scatological. He has a photograph album devoted to shots of dog turds, taken from a range of vantage points, and portraying a surprising range of shapes, forms and textures. Why does he do it? Why that particular choice of subject matter? Then, why do we also have within society those who suffer from kleptomania (more commonly females of a certain age, whose shoplifting felonies often encompass endlessly unnecessary additions to the underwear drawer), and pyromania (typically, but not exclusively, younger males who may somehow even gain a form of sexual pleasure out of their attempts at arson). These obsessions, for that is what they surely are, again seem to have an underlying scatological if not frankly sexual undertone or underpinning.

I have often wondered whether hobbies, including collecting, are exclusively a consequence of a modern, more leisured lifestyle, although several hundreds of years ago the ecclesiastically underemployed church minister in rural Britain (e.g. Gilbert White of Selbourne fame) was typically occupied and even well known for his contributions to natural history. Did the ancient Greeks have hobbies? Did they ever indulge in that extraordinary pastime, with so infrequent rewards, recreational fishing? They certainly had a considerable interest in entertainment, whether the theatre or early forms of board games, or athletic competitions (which had a major political and religious focus) from which we derive our modern Olympics. Their word that is the nearest equivalent to our modern concept of the hobby or pastime is probably *diatribe* (final 'e' sounded), whose original meaning, *a wearing away*, came in classical times also to signify *a pastime, amusement, waste of time* – and also, by a separate extension from the original significance, our modern derivative, *diatribe*, or *abusive interchange*. Clearly there is always an underlying history of the pejorative in the concept, from whatever angle we approach it!

What do we make of modern youth's recent fascination with IT 'tech' devices – mobile phones, iPads, social media, which appear to be generating major emerging psychiatric consequences of a most unwelcome kind – aggression, bullying, anxiety, depression, sleep problems ... with endlessly obsessive checking, monitoring, responding? From a neurochemical viewpoint, such behaviour, like love, seems to be closer to a true addiction (acute withdrawal symptoms if deprived of further opportunities to indulge), than the far more benign collecting, train or bird spotting, etc. behaviours, although they all do seem to operate at least in part, via the universal 'pleasure principle', dopamine. And then there is hoarding, where a lifetime's detritus and debris are obsessively preserved. While the scientific study of hoarding is still in its infancy, it somewhat surprisingly does seem that while hoarders do grieve if deprived of their accumulated hoard, their acquisition and guarding phase is seemingly pleasurable.

And what is my own passion nowadays? Chiefly books. Thucydides, the Greek historian, called a good book a *ktema es aei*, a possession forever. Of course there is plenty of scope for the scatological even in literature! And we all have at least a little of the frivolous, if not the downright obsessive in us; it's just that it may be a little more evident or bizarre in some!

Are you a good driver? Or, if you teach, do you reckon you are above average? How healthy is your lifestyle? Most people generally reckon that they score above average, and in a recent study 70 per cent of 1,000,000 high-school students rated themselves as above-average leaders, and 94 per cent of college professors claimed to possess above-average teaching abilities. How can that possibly be true, when by definition the average has to fall at 50 per cent? People seem consistently to overestimate their own abilities, as well as their vulnerabilities and extent of control over events, and they underestimate their vulnerability to risk. While the associated dangers (road accidents, financial loss in gambling, drug overdosing, sexually transmitted infections ...) are obvious and often inevitable routes to ruin, maybe it is adaptive to be somewhat over-confident? Is there some benefit in having others think that we are indeed superior? Recent games-theory simulations, as well as real-life competitions, do suggest it can be adaptive and beneficial to be overoptimistic; thus, instead of simply running away from the situation, or opting out of the contest, we may thereby learn more about our potential opponents, or the exact statistical properties of the particular situation. However, the dark side may emerge when we risk overtaking that truck on a blind bend, or having sex on a blind date, or we commence gambling or taking drugs. The problem is in identifying our own personal and potential vulnerabilities. With Jodie Feil and Felicity Lorains respectively, I have recently been studying some of the vulnerability aspects, from a neuroscience perspective, associated with addiction and gambling.

Would you like a salted peanut? Until you were asked just now, neither the thought nor the desire would likely have even entered your head, but once a peanut is consumed, you tend to continue eating them, until or even past satiation. The salted peanut phenomenon, as it is known, is a simplistic model of addictive behaviour. It exemplifies the separate roles of drive and reward, and possible failures of inhibition.

Drug dependence involves repeated drug administration and recurrent relapse. Over-activity or over-involvement of the traditional reward circuits, involving the neurotransmitter dopamine, have until recently been invoked as the main mechanism for drug-seeking and drug-taking, but lately frontal-lobe anomalies, involving failures of inhibition, have also been proposed. Chronically-exposed addicts typically exhibit executive, inhibitory and decision-making impairments. There is, however, the traditional chicken-and-egg problem: has drug-taking caused these maladaptive changes in brain and behaviour, or were they already present, leading one into the drug culture, possibly even initially as a form of self-medication for underlying anxiety and depression? The third possibility, of course, as so often in such apparent dichotomies, is that both mechanisms, initial brain anomalies and drug-taking, are operating in a mutually-self-sustaining, amplificatory and circular fashion. Indeed, a somewhat similar circularity underlies the salted peanut phenomenon, that simplistic model of a self-terminating and fortunately fairly harmless addictive behaviour.

Executive function is our conscious capacity to flexibly adapt our thoughts and behaviour towards a current goal, including the ability to plan, organise, direct attention and suppress or inhibit responses to powerful, prepotent yet inappropriate representations or stimuli. The dorsolateral prefrontal cortex, along with the associated, and subcortical, basal ganglia, is fundamental. The basal ganglia (NB: ganglion – singular; ganglia – plural, cf. bacterium, bacteria) inhibit unwanted actions, and release or allow to pass whatever is currently held acceptable or desired. Cortical systems associated with the dorsolateral prefrontal cortex include the orbitofrontal circuitry and the anterior cingulate. Dysfunction of the former system is linked primarily to inappropriate social behaviours such as impulsivity, socially anomalous activity and disinhibition. The anterior cingulate detects and corrects errors. Both systems are also involved, in subtly different ways, with motivated behaviours. Prolonged drug-taking may modify how these systems function, leading to further drug-seeking and drug-taking, even when it is no longer pleasurable.

Recent studies consistently demonstrate a relationship between prolonged drug administration, leading to structural and functional imaging changes in those three areas of the prefrontal cortex – dorsolateral, orbitofrontal and anterior cingulate – and the persistence of drug-seeking behaviours. Behaviourally, executive function, response inhibition, performance self-monitoring and decision-making are all impaired. These effects occur, to a greater or less extent, with stimulants such as cocaine, with opiates, and following alcohol dependence. Affected individuals become increasingly unable to inhibit the prepotent urge, especially when returning to cues or environments associated with previous drug-taking, to resume addictive behaviours; they exhibit a correspondingly diminished ability to monitor the potentially negative outcomes of their 'habit'. With chronic nicotine use, data are as yet rather more scarce, but generally similar trends seem to be appearing. In chronic smokers, acute smoking abstinence is associated with impaired executive function and response inhibition; conversely, acute nicotine administration may increase frontal activity and temporarily reverse deficits in response inhibition. Such an observation is compatible with my earlier suggestion, that acute nicotine administration could initially act as a form of self-medication in individuals with pre-existing inhibitory deficits. Over time, however, continued consumption may simply exacerbate reduced frontal activity and impaired executive function, and thus make it all the more difficult to drop the habit.

Novel brain stimulation techniques, such as transcranial magnetic stimulation and transcranial direct current stimulation, which can selectively stimulate or inhibit discrete brain circuits, can target the frontal regions so as to reduce craving and consumption. These techniques are additional to the more traditional pharmacological interventions tailored to address the particular drugs of choice. Clearly, it is better never to get exposed to addictive substances in the first place, but this may not be easy in those of us with particular personality profiles, temperaments or backgrounds, which we now know may include impulsivity and childhood difficulties in behavioural regulation.

For most people, gambling is a form of entertainment accompanied by a rush, when winning, which has been likened to a drug-induced high. However, for some, gambling develops into a serious problem. Pathological gambling is currently classified as an impulse-control disorder, alongside kleptomania and pyromania. Other researchers prefer to see it as closely related to substance and alcohol abuse, and define it as a behavioural addiction. Pathological gambling and substance abuse are more common in young males, and share clinical characteristics, symptoms, diagnostic criteria, neurobiology (particularly the ventral striatal reward system where the neurotransmitter dopamine is abundant), and genetics. Thus, substance abuse and gambling both include a higher frequency of a variant of the dopamine receptor. Both behaviours also tend to co-occur, along with other comorbid mental health disorders, with very low rates of treatment-seeking, and high rates of drop-out and relapse. Both are associated with similar symptoms of craving, withdrawal, tolerance, and recurrent thoughts. There is, of course, absolutely no reason why both explanations, poor impulse control and addiction, should not simultaneously operate, particularly if dopamine excess in striatal function impacts upon weak inhibitory control, in the prefrontal cortex, of subcortical impulses. The latter region, as we saw, is where we elaborate our decision-making in daily life. Deciding when to initiate, or desist from, gambling, how much to bet and what type of gambling to pursue all involve decision-making, while having yet another drink or 'line' of cocaine is just a simpler situation otherwise closely parallel to gambling. Nevertheless, just as drugs of addiction vary greatly – opiates, stimulants, alcohol, nicotine … so too are there various types of gambling which may differentially appeal to different personalities and demographics, and possibly even the sexes. Thus, dog- and horse-racing have maybe a strong masculine and social aspect, perhaps with a preponderance of younger adherents, while the more solitary and mechanical gaming machines may attract older females. There are many routes into the gambling culture.

Genetic and biological vulnerabilities to gambling include neurotransmitter genes and receptors, psychological impulsivity, cognitive and attitudinal biases, and gambling availability. Some may gamble to escape life's drudgery and demands, as perhaps with electronic gaming machines; others with low arousal levels may gamble on the horses or at the casino for excitement. Yet others, with no overt psychopathology, may develop problem gambling from exposure to the highly addictive reinforcement schedules associated with gaming machines. The various forms of gambling, and the different games, all vary in terms of pay-off, bet size, schedule of reward, and skill. High levels of depression, with or without anxiety, commonly co-occur in all cases. And the same is true with addiction. Neurocognitive and neuroimaging studies of gamblers indicate problems of inhibitory control, and reactive attentional and emotional biases to gambling-related stimuli, just as substance abusers may be turned on by drug-related paraphernalia. Such individuals also manifest deficits in decision-making, characterised by impulsivity, overconfidence and risk-taking, and insensitivity to delayed rewards. Thus, gamblers typically prefer smaller rewards if immediate, over larger, delayed ones; they are also more willing to sacrifice a small certain reward for one which is larger but uncertain. Pathological gamblers who frequent electronic gaming machines often perform worse on decision-making tasks than those who frequent the casino, perhaps reflecting differences between those who play games of chance and those who play games of skill.

Gambling tends to promote its continued behaviour through activation of the reward pathways. Thus, we see attempts to recover previous losses by continuing. And 'chasing losses' is strongly associated with impaired control and impulsivity. Chasing losses, 'near misses' (where a win is apparently 'just missed'), and outright wins all activate the dopamine reward pathways; gambling promotes dysregulation in brain areas involved in reward-based learning, decision-making and cognitive control and impulsivity. Indeed, high impulsivity is also associated with several psychiatric disorders, including ADHD. However, just as with addiction, we can ask whether these behavioural, cognitive and frontostriatal anomalies predate the development of pathological gambling, or are at least partly its consequence. High impulsivity in adolescents suggests that it might predispose one to pathological gambling, rather than be a consequence.

Cognitive distortions in pathological gamblers include exaggerated beliefs in their ability to win, over-confidence, a propensity to make risky decisions, superstitious beliefs such as that a particular position or machine is 'lucky', selective memory for wins and amnesia for losses, and the 'gambler's fallacy', where a win is thought to be due if a run of losses has occurred.

As so often with major social issues – and think of the hideous cost to so many individuals, their families, and third parties assaulted, killed or injured in alcohol-related incidents and traffic accidents – governments are ever reluctant to take even the smallest initiative. State and federal instrumentalities have themselves become addicted to the resultant revenue. And who can forget a certain Victorian state premiere trumpeting the virtues of a so-called 'gambling-led financial recovery'! Such considerations, the lobbying power of vested interests and greedy, selfish and immoral 'big business' (alcohol, tobacco, gambling…), and the virtuous bleating of self-professed libertarians parading the nanny-state arguments and appealing to the virtues of education and self-restraint, have all blocked any initiatives to protect the weak and vulnerable. What use, on its own, is education, when addiction involves innate and all-consuming compulsive tendencies channelled by environmentally available triggers and promoters? While the terminally and painfully ill must at all times apparently be protected from themselves and from selecting a gentle exit by suicide, assisted or otherwise, not so those vulnerable to destructive, all-powerful and frankly irresistible addictions, and their unwitting victims.

It's enough to drive one to drink!

32

FUN, FRAUD AND FABRICATION

What a tangled web we weave

Sixty years ago, when I was a schoolboy privileged to study the old Greek authors in the original, the world of classical scholarship was briefly shaken by the apparent discovery, somewhere in Egypt I think, of a new text; it seemed to be part of a tragedy by one of the three great poets, Aeschylus, Sophocles or Euripides. The fragment seemed kosher, with phraseology, vocabulary, metaphor, style and expression of apparent authenticity and verisimilitude. Runners were described as 'rowing their legs to a rapid tempo', or something of that sort, just the sort of improbable turn of phrase which was in fact beloved by the classical baroque. But so many even more outrageous expressions followed thick and fast, that it became evident as a spoof, a deliberate 'con'. The perpetrator was someone at the end of his career, who without malice aforethought, wanted some innocent fun at the expense of his too-serious colleagues.

Again 60 years ago, the intelligentsia were alerted by C. P. Snow to his 'Two Cultures'. He noted the strong parallels between the creative process in the Arts (literary, graphic, music) and the Sciences (Biochemistry, Physics, Mathematics). Sudden insights, the need to record plans for elegant solutions or designs before they slip from memory, the exhilaration of discovery or creation, all have closely similar counterparts in the 'Two Cultures'. The psychology too, whether playful or of ill intent, is very similar. How many scientists have 'massaged' their figures for a better fit to theory, or 'stolen' an idea from a co-worker without attributing it? How many writers have been guilty of plagiarism, major or minor, or of inappropriately borrowing a plot from someone else? Many of us remember, 30 or so years ago, the brief excitement occasioned by the apparent rediscovery of Hitler's diaries. And again, there is the still unsolved mystery of the lovely sixteenth-century Voynich manuscript currently held in Yale University library; replete with wonderful illustrations and composed in a truly beautiful 'script', it cannot be translated as from any known orthography or culture. Is it an elaborate medieval fraud, hoax, practical joke?

Ten years after leaving school, after a period as an undergraduate and later as a doctoral student, I began research in the neurosciences. I soon learned a lesson which has been lost, not only on most of the general public but sadly, even on the administrators of grants; that is, scientists only rarely 'try to prove' something. Usually, they want to discover something new, and their journey is like an eighteenth-century voyage of discovery along uncharted coastlines. Of course, whether seeking confirmation of a hypothesis, or embarking on a 'fishing expedition' in the sea of undiscovered facts, numbers are the bottom line, and numbers may be inappropriately manipulated, a theme to which I shall return.

One hundred and fifty or more years ago, the pioneering French neurologist, Paul Broca, wrote the dictum '*nous parlons avec l'hémisphère gauche*', we speak with the left hemisphere. He gave his name to a region of the brain, Broca's area, which, if damaged, leads to a characteristic kind of speech deficit, Broca's aphasia. An affected individual, after a stroke, tumour or wound to the area, loses the ability to construct grammatical sentences. With considerable difficulty he or she may endeavour to communicate by stringing together chains of words like someone who has a dictionary of a foreign language, but no knowledge whatsoever of its grammatical structure. When viewing a scene of a boy throwing a stick for a dog across a road, and causing its death in a vehicle accident, a patient may say, 'Boy throw stick dog road car hit dead.' Usually we have no great trouble understanding the gist, except perhaps for reversible sentences like 'The boy kissed the girl'; 'Boy kiss girl' is ambiguous, as girls also kiss boys, in a way that 'Boy bite oyster' is not.

A few years after Broca, the equally-pioneering German neurologist Carl Gustav Wernicke gave his name to an area and another speech disorder, Wernicke's aphasia, which is characterised by features in some ways opposite to Broca's aphasia. The patient is fluent and grammatical in speech which, however, is curiously devoid of content, meaning or substance; indeed, its jargon quality may even remind one of certain politicians on the hustings. Words may also be mauled ('loliphant' for 'elephant') or inappropriately substituted ('binoculars' for 'spectacles'). The patient also has problems understanding the speech of others.

Well over 100 years ago, the German neurologist, Ludwig Lichtheim, actually predicted a disorder which had not yet been described. He thus went beyond the voyages of discovery of Broca and Wernicke, although it was not for some time that his 'hypothesis' was 'proved', to use the popular term. Interestingly, Shakespeare would have understood 'prove' to mean 'test', rather than, as nowadays, 'confirm'. Lichtheim proposed that a break or lesion in certain pathways between Wernicke's and Broca's areas would result in 'conduction aphasia', the inability to repeat speech heard, and understood, in Wernicke's area, and transmitted, 'conducted' to Broca's area for articulation or reporting. Lichtheim proved prescient, and his hypothesis was confirmed (after being 'proved' or tested) in the great forge of empirical science and clinical observation.

Falsification in science can therefore occur at least two levels: trimming observations to make them more internally consistent, or fabricating entire data sets in conformity with a preconception of hypothesis. Could one perhaps come up with an entirely new syndrome (like Lichtheim's conduction aphasia, which incidentally has been confirmed, 'proved', innumerable times), and so gain kudos?

A year or two ago, I was joking with my students how one could construct spoof syndromes, disorders which could exist, maybe even do exist, but for one reason or another, happen not to have been described. It's all a bit like the Roman historian Livy's description of history: an account not so much of what happened, but of what might have happened; the historical novel view, I suppose.

Disorders can be 'acquired', like most of the aphasias, after an injury, or 'inborn', 'developmental' in the jargon. Some may be both; thus, dyslexia, problems in reading, may be acquired after injury, or present 'inborn' in children, as developmental dyslexia. In the 1990s, there were reports of a condition, termed 'horologagnosia' by the authors, where one or two patients, with a very specific, localised lesion, lost the ability to tell the time from old-fashioned analogue clocks or watches. In this instance the disorder was observed or noticed, rather than predicted in advance, a chance discovery.

It is clearly very unlikely that there is a specific brain centre devoted to telling the time from analogue watches, unlike the general situation with language with its clearly adaptive evolutionary role; presumably the 'watch' area has been involved in other forms of analogue judgements of daily life throughout the ages, and were appropriate tests to be devised, deficits would be demonstrated, 'proved', in the modern sense. Could one possibly predict other, hitherto unreported syndromes or deficits from a knowledge of general brain function and of modern life?

This is where my spoof syndrome comes in. For nearly 100 years we have known of a rare condition, prosopagnosia, where the patient loses, after brain injury, the ability to recognise people, even himself or herself, by the face. Faces are seen as faces, and emotions (happiness, anger, sadness, fear) are correctly recognised, but the patient has absolutely no idea whose face it is, even though other cues, such as dress, voice, step, hair or skin colour may be correctly and easily used for identification. As prosopagnosia is typically an acquired disorder, in hitherto normal healthy individuals, I jokingly proposed to my students that we describe a family of 'developmental propagnosics'. Members of my mythical family would all be born with the disorder, but otherwise normal. Like the spoof lost play of fifth-century Athens, dramatically unearthed, it seemed, from the desiccating deserts of Egypt, my family would emerge from out of the blue, as it were. Of course, we never did anything about it.

Imagine my consternation, years later, when I read a report in a very prestigious medical journal, of just such a family, two parents, three daughters and one son. The youngest daughter complained to the author that she had never been able to recognise familiar people in a reliable manner, and that her father, brother and middle sister had the same problem. Indeed, her mother always had to instruct them all beforehand about who was coming to visit that day. As Edward de Haan, the author, notes, there is certainly a biological and probably a genetic basis to the family's problems. Clearly, if I want to spoof my colleagues, I'll now have to come up with something else. Development horologagnosia would be one possibility, but it would be nice to think of a totally new condition, developmental or acquired.

Deliberate fraud, and I never would really 'spoof' my colleagues, even in temporary jest, is both fairly frequent in, and highly destructive of, the edifice of science. There is the notorious recent case of a professor of palaeontology in a developing country who is said to have bought fossils from rock shops and sent them individually to a range of eminent colleagues elsewhere, with the claim that they all came from a particular, rather unlikely but not entirely improbable locality. The eminent colleagues, scenting a free publication (and unfortunately the bean counters of science management reward by quantity, not quality) were happy to say 'how very interesting', and have their names added to the offender's latest paper, as a freebee – and thereby lending further credibility to the 'discovery', and providing a stamp of authoritative approval. How the mighty can fall! Yet he is said still to have retained his university post and local standing.

I have had two personal experiences of such academic fraud, both several decades ago. In one, a graduate student of mine had good reason to doubt someone's published findings, and wrote asking to see some of the original data. The reply came back that their research assistant had it all, but had (conveniently!) left to take up another position unknown. When my student contacted the university where the work had supposedly been done, the reply was that there never had been such a person working there.

In the other instance, my close colleague, on receipt of a major clinical research grant for a rare and very serious neurological disorder, employed a research assistant to do the testing. The figures seemed just a little too good, and also slightly odd, to another, experienced assistant working in the lab, who voluntarily chose to spend two weekends checking the data, and found that all the numbers were entirely fabricated, made up – something which could have had very serious clinical consequences. Again, it proved very difficult to dismiss the offender, who, we were told, could sue and/or otherwise bring great discredit and disrepute upon the University's good name.

A schoolboy colleague found the tedious business of memorising apparently arbitrary dates in history an unnecessary impediment to his creative interpretation of world events, and in examinations he inscribed key date sequences on his finger nails with a fine needle. In those days one's eyes were sharp, and fountain pens provided readily available ink! To view the dates, he would smear them with a blob of ink which made them stand out; just as readily they could be made to vanish with a quick lick. Another pupil, tending to subscribe to the views of the Roman historian Livy, that his discipline should record what might have happened, rather than what actually did, found it both challenging and rewarding to make up fictitious quotations and ascribe them to real authorities, safely assuming that if they sounded plausible the examiner would accept them as real. Simple schoolboy fun, or morally dodgy? Nowadays, of course, sophisticated concordance programs are available to search for possible fraudulent matches (content, style, grammar) between two pieces of writing to determine possible fraudulent plagiarism. Although designed for checking students' work, in a time when excellent essays upon almost any topic are readily available on the web, they can be used even in the context of suspected malpractice in the work of very senior academics.

But what do we make of the final-year dental students who, in their qualifying exam, cemented tiny radio transmitters into their teeth, to communicate questions to an outside accomplice armed with a text book? Would we entrust ourselves or society to dental procedures by such presumably ill-prepared individuals? Said one Arthur Clough:

> Thou shalt not steal; an empty feat
> When it's so lucrative to cheat.

And what about those medical scientists who falsify the reporting of techniques or findings simply to secure a publication, international notice and the possibility of lucrative funding – with potentially fatal consequences for unfortunate patients, if clinical medicine unwittingly adopts the technique? Where, if anywhere, is there a borderline between 'creative writing' and downright fraud? Does it partly depend upon potential consequences for third parties?

Administrators, an accursed bean-counting tribe which has escaped the confines of corporate big-business to 'manage' the creative process of scientific enquiry – an oxymoron if ever there was one! – now seek to impose quantal values upon its 'products' (another misuse of language), the research papers publishing the findings. Funds – institutional, salary, and for further research itself – and professional advancement and promotional opportunities – now depend critically upon 'productivity', or the 'research quantum', whatever that euphemism really means. It seeks to assess what, how much, and, increasingly, where, you choose to publish your findings, thereby often inappropriately influencing how findings are disseminated to the wider scientific community. Key indices are numbers of papers and the journals' 'impact factors'; crudely, the latter are held to reflect how many people subsequently quote, and therefore presumably have read, your work. Of course, the latter assumption is not necessarily true (all too often reference lists are simply copied from one paper to another), and a paper may often be quoted simply as an example of faulty design or erroneous conclusions. 'Letters to the Editor' rarely raise a single 'bean', leading, embarrassingly, to one university totally discounting such highly-esteemed contributions to that most prestigious of all scientific journals, *Nature*. Not surprisingly, we see young researchers being encouraged by administrators to chop up their work into as many as possible 'smallest publishable units' for submission to the least prestigious of journals, as it is seemingly important to get out as many papers as possible whether or not anyone is going to read them. Such 'spaghetti-publishing' may attract more institutional funding, but it is deadly for the reputation and future career of the aspiring young scientist. It doesn't help, of course, that the process of peer review is often so arbitrary, with any two referees often disagreeing violently as to whether a paper is acceptable.

A few years ago, the prestigious neurological journal *Brain* ran an experiment; recent key papers were 'rebadged' with a new authorship, title, and a few cosmetic changes, and resubmitted to referees as new. Woefully few were recognised as fraudulent, and the bulk of the rest were hardly more likely to be considered worthy of acceptance than an entirely new submission. Yet, as the authors and editors concluded, we really have nothing better with which to replace the peer-review system for vetting submissions. Who was it who said that democracy was the worst possible way to run a country, except that there really aren't any better ways?

Less worthy, and more foolish, were the efforts of a recent researcher who similarly took published papers from prestigious journals and resubmitted them, under his own name, to more obscure journals from his home country. Eventually his plagiarism was detected. And then there was the university vice-chancellor who resigned after his books, from concordance tests as mentioned above, were said to contain many lengthy unattributed passages apparently 'borrowed' from the published work of others. Where do you draw the lines between original thinking, rewording others' statements, and reproducing them wholesale without attribution?

Fraud can run the gamut from outright plagiarism, or falsification of data, to slight 'massaging' of the figures.

After all, a little inaccuracy can save a lot of explanation, said the satirical storywriter Saki or H. H. Munro. Why should a brute fact hinder my beautiful theory? Is it wrong if data from certain subjects, experimental conditions, or trials, are excluded from group means because they are somehow deviant? Maybe no, if properly constituted and recorded exclusion criteria would anyway reject such instances as deviant in a manner *unconnected* with the hypothesis in question. Or maybe if the data, while otherwise completely consistent with overall group means, were unusually erratic, 'noisy' or incomplete. But it is always a fine line, especially where there may be clinical consequences.

Gregor Mendel is one historical figure whose published data are said to be just a little too good to be true. It is as if he already knew how the numbers should ideally fall out, and wanted his to reflect a perceived underlying reality. An appropriate form of data trimming is widely employed by cognitive scientists who routinely measure very fine differences in reaction times. Any such times less than a critical minimum amount deemed necessary for decision processes are rejected as anticipatory responses, and any exceeding another larger figure are rejected as reflecting an attentional lapse or other unwanted event. All remaining times within a particular experimental condition exceeding, say, three standard deviations from group means (which defines them as statistically peculiar), are replaced with that value, thereby removing unwanted outliers and smoothing the data.

Totally unacceptable, however, was the behaviour of someone I knew who, when asked by the editor of the journal where he had submitted a paper, to run some more subjects under a new experimental condition, simply made up the numbers because he thought he knew what should happen. Sadly, the whistleblower in the lab was himself discredited, as all too often happens, and the university itself sought to suppress the matter lest 'it bring discredit'. Indeed, the university's naïve attempt at resolution was to require re-running of the offending condition under video-recording. And what happened? As in a bad spy story, the camera was mysteriously stolen! Nor did the matter end there; the offender promptly sought and was offered a very senior position elsewhere, just in case the whole sordid story should break. The new institution, however, had smelled a whiff of scandal on the academic grapevine, and wrote to a third party, who is said to have memorably replied 'I don't know what you might have heard, but the truth is far worse than you can possibly imagine.' End of story – end of career? Not quite. I did hear some time later that having fallen out in a big way with a colleague, he decided to get his own back by inviting him to a 'reconciliation feast' (in the treacherous tradition of antiquity) of his own devising; he was an excellent cook. He made a strong curry, and within his guest's portion he concealed an equally strong aperient; very soon after he took his friend on a longish walk, far from any 'bathroom refuges' or other forms of convenience, 'rest rooms' or places of personal concealment…

Henry Poincaré claimed that science, like a house, is built of bricks. Such bricks are said to be objective, value-free observations of unbiased, disinterested (although never uninterested) individuals. It isn't. It is an intensely human enterprise, subject to all the ambitions, jealousies, animosities, prejudices, and even sense of fun, of its participants. It is just like similar enterprises in the Arts. Witness the Surrealist artist Salvador Dali, and his painting of a watch melting in the sun. Perhaps, in my retirement, I should sculpt a statue of Venus, in the classical style, and bury it in the sands of Egypt, to await discovery. Didn't something like that happen with the Piltdown fraud? How do we in fact know the authenticity of many similar supposedly 'real' museum pieces? Or in fact, as is emerging nowadays, the authenticity of many pieces of acclaimed Aboriginal art? Maybe it doesn't really matter, if it is still good art, however judged, but good science requires verification for it to add a brick to the house of knowledge. And maybe there lies the difference between the Arts and the Sciences. Not in the sense of fun.

This section is about fraud, falsification and the spoof in intellectual endeavour. Clearly they all lie on a common continuum and reflect, and may be differentially motivated by pressures for personal advancement, malice, or a misplaced sense of fun. A few years ago an eminent Canadian colleague of impeccable credentials committed suicide when her ground-breaking work was repeatedly questioned on grounds that many of us strongly held were themselves of dubious merit. Science, and the arts, are intensely competitive. If I were ever tempted to end my career by inventing, and describing a joke syndrome, it would call into question all the publications of my colleagues to which over the years I have contributed my name, quite apart from those where I was sole or first author.

In psychiatry, there is a rare condition called Munchausen Syndrome, which involves repeated fabrication, or pretence of physical illness, usually acute, dramatic and convincing, by a patient who wanders from hospital to hospital seeking treatment, and attention. Patients may simulate many physical disorders, and bear the scars of repeated, unsuccessful, surgery; they are usually intelligent and resourceful, and differ from malingerers because, although their deceits and simulations are conscious, their motivations for forging illness and quest for attention, are largely unconscious. Munchausen Syndrome by proxy is an even more bizarre variant, where the individual's child may be used as a surrogate patient; the parent may even injure the child to simulate disease.

I wonder whether, one day, someone will turn up familial Munchausen Syndrome by proxy, perhaps even involving pets? Maybe it's no coincidence that Munchausen Syndrome is anyway, itself a kind of fraud.

I really must add a couple of postscripts. Some years ago I coined (as I thought) the term allodynia, to describe a case, reported to me, of someone feeling sharp pain, simultaneously, in the corresponding body part, when witnessing sudden injury to another person. Subsequently I read exactly that term being used for where a migraine sufferer felt simultaneous pain in a region distant from her head.

My second postscript relates not to fraud, but the current problem in several disciplines, maybe especially psychology, with replication. In the journal *Science*, the Center for Open Science reported attempts at replication of the findings of 100 studies published in high-ranking psychology journals during 2008; for 60, they were unsuccessful. One researcher, moreover, who openly admitted to bogus figures, found that researchers around the world claimed replication. It is of course possible that the original hypothesis, although not in fact tested at the time, nevertheless was in fact sound.

Great minds ...?

33

A GOD OF THE GAPS AND DENTAL DISTRESS

On the nave wall of the church in the village where I was born, Higher Bebington in the North-west of England, just across the River Mersey from Liverpool, there was a fossil footprint of an early reptile, *Chirotherium*. Shaped like a hand, and hence its name, 'hand mammal', it came from the adjacent, Storeton, desert-derived exposures of the Triassic New Red Sandstone, laid down 225 millions of years ago, and discovered by quarrymen in 1838. A bored and occasional member of the congregation, and sitting as a child through the tedium of liturgical theatre, I would seek relief by studying this wondrous relic of a bygone age of giants. How, I now wonder, did those early church fathers – or even mothers? – reconcile the likely geological antiquity of the fossil with ecclesiastical teaching of a recent creation? Or was it just further evidence of Noah's flood in England's green and pleasant land? Or can we see it as a metaphor for a rapprochement between science and religion?

'Religion', not surprisingly, comes from Latin *religio*, itself from the root **lig*, to bind, as in 'ligature', 'legal', and in Latin signifies a range of related meanings: scrupulousness, conscientiousness, piety, reverence for the gods. 'God', itself, comes from the root **ghu*, to worship; the Greek for God, *theos*, comes from the root **thes*, to place or offer prayers. The Latin for God, *deus*, derives from a root meaning 'bright', which also gave rise to the archaic Greek *diwos*, divine, and the names of the (bright) sun gods *Zeus*, and *Jove*. In antiquity, the twin concepts of breath (as of life) and spirit (as of soul), appear in such words as *anemos* (Greek, wind, as in anemometer), the Latin *anima* (soul, as in animate), and *spiritus* (spirit), along with *spirare* (to breathe). The Moslem *Allah* is in fact *al 'ilah*, 'The God', while the Jewish *Yahweh* can translate as 'He that Is'.

Religion, sport and politics are, sadly, the sources of more acrimonious and divisive debate, violence and even wars than almost any other totem. And religion may be the worst offender, for, as Voltaire said, 'Those who can make you believe absurdities can make you commit atrocities.' Why do we even need to believe in the so-called transcendental? The sci-fi writer Arthur C. Clarke observed that, 'Any sufficiently advanced technology is indistinguishable (to the rest of us) from magic', while Michael Shermer of *The Skeptic* magazine noted that 'Any sufficiently advanced extraterrestrial intelligence is indistinguishable from God.' So where do we draw lines between fairy tales, myths, superstition and religion? A recent poll in the UK found that more believed in God, fewer in life after death, fewer yet in Hell, and fewest of all in the Devil. And where nowadays do angels fit in the general picture? Or is there now no longer room in an overcrowded pantheon for such aerodynamically improbable beings?

Religion, as the 'opium of the people', may serve to allay fear of death; we do seem to be the only creatures to be aware of our own mortality. So is religion an institutionalised social placebo serving to generate an opioid inner peace? Or does it go further, to seek to explain ultimate reality in the current absence of any better empirical or causal explanatory system? As a species, we seem always to crave causality in coincidence and correlation – *post hoc, ergo propter hoc.* Just as we seem to perceive meaningful patterns in Rorschach ink blots or clouds, does a pervasive 'effort after meaning' extend all the way from basic perceptual processes to higher cognition and reflective thought? If science continues to find ever more satisfactory explanations for natural phenomena, will The Deity be relegated to occupying the backmost pew, or the remaining gaps in our knowledge, a veritable God of the Gaps? And where do we fit ghosts, spiritual healing, telepathy, astrology, alchemy, lucky numbers, reincarnation, Ouija boards . . . ? My mother, never a person to wear the divine on her sleeve, or to enter God into her life's equations, had a real thing about walking anywhere near ladders, or breaking a mirror, or seeing a single magpie (hours spent fruitlessly hunting for two more to put us right again), or having a black cat cross her path. So many potential obstacles to a truly lucky life.

The eighteenth-century theologian William Paley said, 'If one stumbled upon a watch, one would not assume it had always been there like a stone.' A watch, he felt, implied a watchmaker, and its intricate design, beautifully fitted to a particular purpose, implies a designer. In Western societies, there have historically been two polar positions of the kind:

> God created human beings pretty much in their present form at one time in the last few thousand years.

And

> We developed over millions of years from less advanced forms of life without any supernatural intervention.

Recently, attempts have been made at a rapprochement. The evolutionary theorist Stephen Jay Gould bought, some might say copped, out of the more general debate by comfortingly invoking two separate, non-overlapping 'magisteria', or domains, religion and evolutionary biology. Others, of a fundamentalist Christian persuasion, try for a blended position, invoking the argument from Intelligent Design:

> Humans developed over millions of years from less advanced life forms, but God always guided this process.

While Intelligent Design has been around in one form or another for many years, only recently has it started to impact upon the teaching of biology. Its advocates, seeking to bring a meaning to life and a purpose to 'evolution', argue that many biological structures or systems, like the eye or the immune system, are just too complex to result from natural selection, and so must have been designed by a creator. This is creationism in a new 'respectable' guise, but it is no more scientific, no more open to possible empirical testing, and of no predictive value. Again, there are plausible pleas for its inclusion in the scholarly curriculum on the grounds of even-handedness in a 'debate' (just as in anthropogenic climate change?) even though there can *be* no possible *scientific* debate about an unverifiable proposition. Indeed, the obvious imperfection in so many incompletely adapted organs, structures and life forms would indict any half-competent designer; there is nothing 'intelligent' in Grandpa's lifelong haemorrhoids, or my knackered knees. (The fact that they saw out my reproductive years means of course that they could no longer influence adaptive evolution.)

Proponents of Intelligent Design claim that the anthropic principle in cosmology is consistent with that approach, noting that if a whole series of physical constants had originally been 'set' slightly differently, when the universe began, neither it nor life itself could have either existed or persisted, so there must therefore be or have been an original designer, creator, or god, to set it all up, just right, in the first place. There is a basic circularity in this argument, of course, relating to the facts that we are here and able to perceive and interact with that universe, and that there may indeed exist an infinity of other possible universes; this, however, is not the place to debate that particular issue. In any case, as Richard Dawkins observes, such a designer much have been a sadist to construct, as a *tour de force*, plagues, parasites and the continuing predator-prey arms race. Some, of course, might say that this is just another version of the theological problem of the existence of evil. If, from an evolutionary perspective, God must have been Dawkins' blind watchmaker, in theological terms are we perhaps, even more, blind God-makers?

Evolutionary biology and molecular genetics have given us the genes; these are the fundamental units of biochemical variation, subject to selective pressures via the environmental vicissitudes to which are exposed the corporeal bodies under their control, and which may or may not survive to reproduce. So individuals survive or perish, and the taxon continuously adapts to ever-changing circumstances.

It is a common misapprehension that the unit of selection – in terms of surviving or perishing in a given environment – necessarily lies only at the level of the individual organism. Richard Dawkins argued passionately for the adoption of a different perspective, to be taken from the viewpoint of the gene, which can be seen to 'selfishly' manipulate expendable 'host' bodies in an ever-challenging and ever-changing environment. In 1966, more than 50 years ago, George Williams laid the groundwork for much of this new critique. Adaptation, he noted, the design feature of living things and a key concept in evolutionary theory, has its most fundamental and universally applicable understanding at the level of the gene. Genes, he said, have been designed by natural selection to exploit those properties of the world that promote their self-replication, to turn out more copies of themselves – more genes – just like viruses, in fact. They gain access to the environment's properties via adaptation. Over time, natural selection has exploited regular, stable, recurrent and dependable features so that adaptations may prosper. These adaptations can transform potential resources from a largely indifferent environment into one that is exquisitely suited to a particular species. In this sense the environment constitutes just those aspects of the world which are relevant for the gene; different species are themselves clusters of different environments, and different adaptations pick out different environments. For any adaptation, its environment consists of those regularities which are crucial, in terms of natural selection, for that adaptation.

Such concepts, of course, extend far beyond biology; evolving motor car and computer designs show similar, continuing, changes in response to perceived demand. Some may call this progress, but in the great pageant of ever-changing life forms from the earliest pre-Cambrian, we should perhaps be wary of invoking anything 'beyond' simple change. Dinosaurs were just as adapted to their habitat and generally as complex as modern mammals – and, maybe, even Mercedes motor cars.

Recently, Dawkins coined the word 'meme', by analogy with 'gene', to describe units of culture such as ideas, fashions, technologies, customs, and so on. These, he argues, evolve in much the same way as genes. Only the fittest memes survive, as selection weeds out less appropriate alternatives. Darwin himself wrote:

> A struggle for life is constantly going on amongst the words and grammatical forms in each language. The better, the shorter, the easier forms are constantly gaining the upper hand, and they owe their success to their own inherent virtue.

If a cell (or group of cells – an individual creature or person) is host to genes, the mind is host to memes; some will survive, some will change, some will go to the wall. Are the various religions, some static, some changing, some disappearing, just memes hosted by particularly receptive minds? Should we beware, lest like viruses invading ourselves, or taking over our computer hard drives, the dead hand of religion comes to dominate our minds? It exploits ordinary cognitive processes so that its adherents passionately display costly devotion to counter-intuitive worlds governed by improbable, supernatural agents.

Another slant is given by neuroscience. Some forms of temporal lobe tumours or epilepsy are associated with extreme religiosity. Recent brain imaging of devotees engaging in prayer or transcendental meditation has more precisely identified activation in such sites – God Spots, as Vilayanur Ramachandran calls them. Psilocybin from magic mushrooms contacts the serotonergic system, with terminals in these and other brain regions, generating a sense of cosmic unity, transcendental meaning and religious ecstasy. Certain physical rituals can generate both these feelings and corresponding serotonergic activity.

So, was Man made in God's image, or have we made Him – or should it be Her? – in ours? In modern middle revivalist America is He a WASP, a White Anglo-Saxon Protestant? Why does He intervene so little in answer to our problems, prayers or praise? How many undiscovered gaps in our evolving scientific knowledge are there left in which His faithful believers may find Him? And why should bigoted believers seek to impose their pernicious, ratbag doctrines upon the rest of us, on everything from abortion to euthanasia, from the curtailment of gay rights to that of stem-cell research, and from evolution to geological time itself? Evolutionary models are every bit as beautiful and intellectually and morally satisfying as the myths, stories and precepts of an ossified theology – and they can explain, predict and be applied in hosts of important and socially useful ways. We may have to fear more than Moslem fundamentalism alone.

Thus, we could contrast two extreme positions, religion against science:

> Evolution in the sense of common ancestry might be true, but evolution in the neo-Darwinian sense – an unguided, unplanned process of random variation and natural selection – is not.

And

> The church has always been opposed to the advances of science, but fortunately science has continued progressing, and thanks to that we live in better conditions.

A quarter of a century ago I experienced bad toothache while travelling in Utah, America's Mormon heartland. I sought urgent help. Despondent in the dental chair, and at the mercy of a young and charismatic practitioner of the drill and forceps, I was suddenly put on the spot – a quite unforeseen spot. 'To which church do you belong?' he asked. Maybe body language conveyed the idea that I just might not be a true or even part-time believer. 'Yes, I have heard that Australia is a godless country; afterwards you must give me your address, and I'll send you some literature.' It was a difficult situation, and I thought it advisable to go along with the idea, possibly with a slightly modified address.

Fast forward to a few years ago. My new dentist, young and charismatic in a different kind of way, turned out to be an aspiring thespian. She commented in the course of my treatment that she was appearing in a fringe review due shortly to open in the City, and as she had a few free tickets, would I like to come along to the show? It was, of course, this time much easier to acquiesce, and I went on to ask what kind of show it was, and what part she was playing. It was, she said, a review, a nude review in fact, and that was how she was appearing. In the buff. However, I never got there, not because I felt in any way uneasy about seeing my dentist in all her naked glory, unconventional although it might in fact be, but because I genuinely had other engagements at the time.

Reflecting upon the two situations made me realise that they had enough in common to raise questions about the implications of certain belief systems, conventions and tenets. I don't know what in his early days Darwin, the initially-reluctant sceptic, made of the biblical claim that we are all made in God's image. A modern theological and biological synthesis could, I suppose, see God as a kind of super alpha-hominid; or maybe the adaptive evolutionary constraints which moulded and optimised our general anatomy and bilaterally symmetrical ground plan (paired sensors at the front, along with food-intake system, propulsion units at the rear along with waste disposal facilities) also necessarily operated at a celestial level. Or maybe there are simply just a limited number of solutions to the problem of best practice and design, and God and Man necessarily share them as a kind of convergent evolution. So did God evolve? Biblical thinking, although notoriously driven by received wisdom and revelation dating from long ago, nevertheless does seem gradually to 'evolve', if with glacial slowness, and hardly keeping pace with advances in knowledge, or changes in moral thinking.

The alternative approach, that God is perhaps instead conceived of in our image, rather than the other way round, has maybe more appeal to anthropologists than biblical scholars and true believers. Whatever the situation, and whether or not he intervenes in our affairs and responds to our prayers (I don't intend to discuss the problems of evil, suffering, original sin or Intelligent Design any further), how should God be conceived of, seen, visualised or imagined? Dressed in the clothing of the twenty-first century, in biblical, Jewish or Arab attire? In unisex gear? Nude, like my daring young dentist? As a human male fully equipped for reproductive processes? They did after all debate in the Middle Ages whether Adam had a navel…! Maybe we should even view God as one of those frequent imaginary friends retained from childhood? And maybe that is exactly how the idea of an all-powerful deity actually originated – a hangover from a wistful, lonely, deprived or abused childhood, or even from fever-induced hallucinations.

Many might find such questions confronting, or at odds with their religious beliefs or inclinations; they can of course be asked, *mutatis mutandis*, in another guise. What then do we do with ghosts? Many cultures see ghosts as the spirits of the departed, unhappy, unfulfilled or unappeased dead. Indeed, there is a surprising uniformity, across often unrelated cultures, in how ghosts are conceived; does this make them any more likely or probable? (And similarly, is the existence of God more probable because of the near universality of belief in an all-powerful, omniscient, and often vengeful being who needs appeasing with prayers, incantations and the occasional sacrifice?) Ghosts may or may not equate with souls, although the latter may sometimes be conceived of as even antedating birth, and not just serving as some sort of requiem or post-mortem residuum. Again, souls, unlike ghosts which seem literally to frequent their old 'haunts!', may be destined for some other place, either of eternal bliss (the Judaeo-Christian-Moslem Paradise, or the Viking Valhalla), or where there is the possibility of eternal suffering and repentance. (Purgatory, however, seems capable of accepting both ghosts and souls.) A nineteenth-century experiment involved the continuous weighing of an unfortunate, moribund individual just before, during and after life's extinction; the experimenters concluded that, like the ether of similar notoriety, the soul, if it existed, had to be devoid of mass and substance. While the ether has vanished from modern physics, ghosts, spirits and souls of the departed still linger on in an uncertain conceptual purgatory or half-way house of the hereafter. Indeed, when, earlier, in our primate evolution, did we even acquire or evolve a soul? Where reside the spirits of all the departed Neanderthals? Of course, it would indeed be very nice if after the expiry of our mortal, corporeal bodies, there was some form of continuing existence, better than before, to look forward to as a disembodied soul, but the body/soul dichotomy is no more ultimately fruitful than that of mind/brain.

So, to return to our earlier discussion, if we meet up with our equally defunct relatives in the great hereafter, or encounter a ghost in the present Vale of Tears, what is the dress code? There are plenty of ghost stories to give us a lead – clothing as worn at the time of death, or a nice neutral shroud-like sheet, but to my knowledge there are no nudes or otherwise naked spirits or ethereal virgins. When we all meet again, will Grandma (young and pretty again, or old and crabby, as we remember her) be in the flapper gear of the 1920s, or wearing a kind of celestial bikini or even a G-string – and if so, where will it have been manufactured? Imported from an earthly factory, or home-made in heaven? A young Moslem lady, interviewed recently, stated that she was looking forward to paradise where she confidently expected to be able to don a burka, niqab, hejab or shadoor of the finest cut and silk. I foresaw certain practical problems with such aspirations, to say nothing about the predatory male aspirations towards a certain number of virgins always available for each lucky male; unless, of course, in heaven, virginity, like toenails, may be endlessly regrown.

Sir Thomas Bodley, founder of his eponymous late-medieval library in the University of Oxford, is said to haunt the far older library at Merton College, where he was a fellow, got up in the gear of his times. He is also said to be visible from the knees up when viewed on the upper floor, and just as a pair of ambulating feet protruding from the ceiling (which was raised after his death) when seen from below. So, in some sense, even floors leave traces of earlier incarnations. Why, statistically from theological market surveys, do more people feel more comfortable, or less uncomfortable, in espousing a belief in ghosts than in angels, saints or heavenly spirits? And in such beatific beings, rather than in devils and demons; and in a blissful heavenly eternity, rather than in a hell of endless torment and punishment? Is it wishful thinking, or just a natural optimism? Whatever the reason, to return to our earlier theme, how are angels and saints attired? Somehow the question seems more relevant, and associated with fewer practical difficulties of a combustible nature, in a heaven of temperate climate, than in an inferno (Jupiter, Mercury, Venus?) where we might even need asbestos undies.

Dress, of course, may be seen as a metaphor for other similar theological problems. Is there a *lingua franca* in the hereafter, or does an unearthly Tower of Babel perpetuate throughout infinite time? (The Jews are said once to have claimed with a certain Hebraic arrogance that God spoke Hebrew, the language of creation.) Do heavenly speech and modes of communication evolve in lockstep with earthly analogues? Will there be an ethereal internet and a heaven-wide web? Or is there a timeless *à la mode*? But why should we be so anthropocentric, in the light of a modern universe which is anything but geocentric? And in such a limitless universe – or, even more extreme, multiverse – is there a local God or chief for each sentient life form, each made in each other's image, with a celestial CEO for the whole wondrous creation? Is he/she/it/they carbon- or maybe silicon-based, or 'just' an ethereal force field? Or even, after all, a version of the elusive God-particle long sought by theoretical physicists, a super Higgs Boson? At least that would be a truly impressive title to worship.

Just as Greek mythology relates the time of the War of the Titans, and the bible describes fallen angels and similar past and future cataclysms, some more apparently realistic or probable than others, is continuing celestial warfare, in our own sorry human image, also on the cards of eternity? And, at a more mundane and prosaic but personally significant level, will there be dentists in Paradise, to help us manage the likely consequences of consuming too much heavenly (if not Turkish) delight? And, if so, where do dentists, those wielders of woe and purveyors of pain, go when they die? Was it Oscar Wilde who observed that if good Americans go to Paris when they die, bad ones must go back to America? As dentists again, in another round on Earth of an eternal cycle of endless dental reincarnation? Because that is an alternative, and somehow seemingly more economical, ecological and satisfactory approach, to a world or universe with its adjunct heaven and hell. As sinners or saints, we can inhabit our very own heaven or hell here back on earth; and that of course is exactly how it may actually seem to us, on good or bad days respectively. The Judaeo-Christian bible opted for a different solution to the problem of sin – a sort of version of the cometary extinction of the dinosaurs at the end of the Cretaceous; God erased, in a massive flood, his whole animal creation, and entrusted Noah with the job of saving the stock in his fabulous ark, for a brand new start all over again in a manner reminiscent of that envisaged in another context by Stephen J Gould. (Strangely, God seems to have forgotten about the vegetable kingdom, so essential as provender the herbivores he saved and upon which we all depend, which must somehow have managed to survive the cataclysm on its own. And where did all the water come from, and where did it go afterwards?) And did Noah also save samples of every insect, including biting purveyors of pestilence, every microbe and virus, in a maritime forerunner of a modern top-security microbiology lab? If so, it surely was truly miraculous in the original sense. And, if so, at least it was a miracle of decent proportions, unlike the rather tawdry, banal and pathetic modern versions, which rarely seem to go beyond weeping statues and fuzzy images of saints or Madonnas on such improbable backgrounds as pieces of cloth, or as shadows or impressions in evanescent sand or on deformed potatoes.

Indeed, in a hungry world bursting at the seams, it would be great to get the loaves and fishes scheme to work again. But a religious scientist must accept that while it is somewhat unscientific to believe in miracles, it is probably irreligious not to. Miracles are seen as extremely rare events that apparently contravene natural laws. If not rare, they aren't miracles (although natural laws may need rewriting to accommodate them). If rare, they may merely reflect the normal distribution of event probabilities from very low to very high. Religion *causes* some individuals to see certain merely rare occurrences as miracles, rather than miracles *promoting* religion. But what if it *is* the true word of God, being in the bible? But if the bible is true (because God says so – in the bible!), I'm reminded of the old circular self-referential paradox: '"All Cretans are liars", said the Cretan.'

So how do miracles differ from Harry Potter events? Maybe that's the question so disturbing to some churches, so much so that some excoriate J. K. Rowling. Anyway, I do have an upcoming appointment with the dentist; now *that* is where I *would* settle for a really mundane miracle – problem-free teeth for my remaining days on this lovely planet where, as Darwin puts it in his limpid and inimitable prose: 'From so simple a beginning, endless forms most beautiful and most wonderful have been and are being evolved.'

I'll drink to that, when my oral anaesthetic has worn off!

34

THE LITTLE BRAIN

In the early 1960s, I graduated from Oxford's cloistered shelter with a degree which included Experimental Psychology, then a fairly new discipline, and soon learnt, when asked at parties what I did for the proverbial crust, to avoid replying with anything containing the BBQ stopper 'psychology'. Otherwise I would receive queer looks, silence, followed by the statement that 'I suppose you are psychoanalysing us', or a hurried account of a supposed relative's neuroses, which led me instead to claim expertise in neural engineering. That brought the conversation to safer topics such as problems in bridge building. In the 1990s, the newly emerging discipline of behavioural neuroscience was a blessed relief.

Behavioural neuroscience is in many ways a rebadging of experimental psychology, along with clinical neurology, cognition, motor or movement aspects, linguistics, artificial intelligence and neuroanatomical approaches to behavioural manifestations of brain function. Add in the study thereby of neurodevelopmental and neurodegenerative disorders, common or rare, and you have a fascinating new approach offering seemingly endless questions to ask and technologies to employ, although as I always tell my students, behind every fascinating new discovery, there will usually lie a personal or family tragedy – as indeed I myself personally know all too well.

Be that as it may, the research neuroscientist can address two inter-related issues: first, how to further our understanding of the normally developing, functioning or ageing brain via the study of disease models which involve the occurrence of selective impairments, structural, functional or behavioural. Second, how better to understand the nature, signs, progress, assessment and management of particular neurodevelopmental and neurodegenerative disorders. And in my particular case at the present time, how better to understand two particular and specific brain circuits or systems, the frontostriatal and frontocerebellar, which are respectively involved in initiating and sequencing fine motor programs or movement sequences, and in accurately acquiring, achieving or attaining target endpoints in a specific movement element or trajectory.

There are just so many ways we can consider the brain's gross anatomy, so many joints at which its nature can, as it were, be carved: there are the two nearly mirror symmetrical cerebral hemispheres, left and right, each with subtly different functions. There are the largely cortical regions mediating higher levels of mood, cognition and movement, and there are the underlying subcortical and mainly regulatory structures. There are the grey matter (cell bodies), and the white, axonic or interconnecting fibres. And my own current patch, the cerebrum and cerebellum.

Did you know that at the back of your head you have a second or 'little' brain, the cerebellum, in addition to your much bigger or 'main' brain, the cerebrum? Resembling a cauliflower, surprisingly little, relatively speaking, is as yet known about it. Traditionally thought to coordinate voluntary movements, motor tone, balance, posture and gait, we now know it also plays a major role in cognitive, attentional, decision, memory, and even linguistic processes.

In the late 1980s, quite out of the blue, I was asked to supervise a graduate student's studies on Huntington's disease, an uncommon, inherited, autosomal-dominant disorder characterised by unwanted and intrusive 'choreiform' (somewhat dance-like) movements, and later by rigidity similar to that suffered by those with Parkinson's disease. Apart from these gross clinical features, remarkably little was known about the disorder. Maybe around 1 per 10,000 may inherit it, which is genetically characterised by an expanded and unstable trinucleotide (or triplet, in this case CAG) repeat sequence which codes for the protein huntingtin. Unaffected individuals have on chromosome 4 up to 35 copies of the triplet, people who will develop the disorder have 40 or more, with an uncertain grey area or future for those falling between these two values. The more the repeats, the more the (increasingly neurotoxic) associated protein, and the earlier the disease onset. Regions within the basal ganglia, part of the frontostriatal system, are particularly vulnerable.

With my students, particularly (now Professor) Nellie Georgiou-Karistianis, I devised a number of cognitive and motor procedures to characterise the clinical manifestations of the disorder, and success led me to apply what we had learnt to Parkinson's disease, a somewhat more benign and (for a while at least) pharmacologically manageable disorder typically of late middle age or later onset, where tremor and rigidity are two of the cardinal signs. Again, certain regions in the basal ganglia, different from those mediating Huntington's disease, are progressively damaged, in part, perhaps through continuing toxic action of the otherwise essential neurotransmitter dopamine, which is involved in mood regulation, learning and movement control.

Our increasing success with these two *neurodegenerative disorders*, largely involving various structures within the basal ganglia, led me to ask what might happen in the event of mal-development of that structure, but now in the *neurodevelopmental disorders* like Tourette's syndrome, obsessive compulsive and attention deficit hyperactivity disorders, schizophrenia, autism and depression. That work took us from the early 1990s to around 2005. Then it seemed time to adapt the techniques which we had so far developed to disorders of the *cerebellum*, both neurodegenerative and neurodevelopmental. This structure, far more ancient in an evolutionary sense, is more concerned with, among other things, a particular movement's end-point accuracy, fine-tuning and achieving in a smooth and timely fashion the specific action's original aim. We have been fortunate in being able to study relatively large samples of unfortunate individuals suffering from three relevant but rather rare disorders: (1) Williams syndrome, with my ex-student Dr Darren Hocking; (2) Friedreich ataxia, with my ex-student Dr Louise Corben; and (3) most recently, Fragile X, with my colleague Professor Kim Cornish and her student Claudine Kraan. It has been a particularly fascinating research period, and also an opportunity to employ a range of complex technologies: structural and functional magnetic resonance imaging to determine via brain scans possible areas which are anatomically abnormal or function differently from those of healthy control participants, and structural or functional differences in area connectivities, using diffusion tensor imaging.

Williams syndrome is a relatively rare, genetically based, neurodevelopmental disorder, with prevalence estimates of maybe 1 in 10,000 births. It is caused by a *de novo* microdeletion on chromosome 7, involving maybe 28 genes. The behavioural phenotype is associated with inattention, distractibility and hyperactivity, alongside social disinhibition and non-social anxiety. There is a unique cognitive phenotype of relative strengths in verbal activities and face recognition, alongside weaknesses in visuospatial processing and visuomotor control. Several components of higher-order executive control (decision-making, organising, planning, attention) are compromised, including difficulty in inhibiting unwanted, intrusive or automatic 'prepotent' responses. Individuals with Williams syndrome have a distinctive profile of increased social drive or gregariousness, with personalities verging on the hyper-sociable, and an unusual attraction to human faces, with an intensely focused attention to the region of the eyes. There is also an attractive elfin-like facial appearance, along with congenital vascular disease, both probably due to the disorder's association with the elastin gene affecting connective tissue.

Relatively little is known about dysfunction of the motor system in Williams syndrome, a system which in fact is far more easily accessible than the cognitive, and where we have largely concentrated our efforts. Anomalies have previously been noted in the basal ganglia and posterior parietal regions of the brain, regions handling visually guided actions, planning and movement control. Clinically observed dysmetria, or over- or under-shooting reach movements, suggests cerebellar involvement, as do subtle anomalies of gait.

Darren and I developed a research programme systematically to assess the upper and lower limbs (gait), employing sophisticated kinematic recording and measuring systems of movement in those with Williams syndrome. With gait, when individuals walked at various speeds, we found that those with the disorder typically displayed reduced speed and stride length, but like Parkinson's patients with basal ganglia deficits, they attempted disproportionately to compensate with increased cadence (stepping frequency). Their stride lengths were more variable and their posture more broadly based, perhaps as compensation for postural instability, all indicative of cerebellar impairment. When negotiating obstacles, affected individuals were late in adjusting to the spatiotemporal aspects of the walk, showing exaggerated and more spatially constrained visual guidance in placing their feet just before crossing the obstacle, again indicating cerebello-parietal involvement.

At the level of upper limb fine control, while aiming for discrete targets, individuals with Williams syndrome were particularly affected in the final kinematic components of target acquisition, slowing excessively in the last stages of movement, and with reduced and more variable end-point accuracy, again indicative of cerebellar problems. Increased stationary time before movement initiation suggested additional basal ganglia problems.

Dr Hocking is now completing imaging studies to verify these behavioural observations.

Friedreich ataxia, an autosomal recessive disorder, is the most common of the inherited ataxias, that is, problems in limb coordination, with a frequency of about 1 in 30,000. Onset typically occurs around age 10, and is progressive, with increasing spasticity, scoliosis (lateral curvature of the spine), absence of lower limb reflexes, foot deformity and cardiomyopathy as in Williams syndrome. The individual is usually confined to a wheelchair by 20, and may not survive beyond the late thirties. Shirley Hazzard's (2003) novel *The Great Fire*, set in 1945, gives a good description of it with one of her major characters, Ben, although when I happened recently to read it I wondered what was in fact actually known about it 75 or so years ago! Like Huntington's, there is an unstable expansion of a trinucleotide repeat, this time GAA, and on chromosome 7, with an increased repeat size leading to earlier onset. Its clinical features are due to a deficiency in frataxin, a mitochondrial membrane protein, which causes stress in cellular processes. Damage is noted in the spinal cord, spinocerebellar and corticospinal tracts, the cerebellum itself and its dentate nucleus.

In our group, Dr Louise Corben studied motor programming (using reciprocal tapping between buttons) and found that affected individuals were slower both in the preparation and the execution of each sub-movement, with a strong negative correlation between age at disease onset and performance, suggesting that the disorder affects neurodevelopmental stages. Using kinematic analyses and targets displayed on touch screens, she found problems both in movement initiation or planning, and in the final stages of target acquisition, and with error detection. This all suggests both basal ganglia and cerebellar involvement. When a series of automatic movements had to be made between two targets, with occasional oddballs occurring which required inhibition of the normal regular response pattern, and execution, instead of a totally different movement, those with Friedreich ataxia were particularly affected. They were similarly disadvantaged when required to respond in the presence of competing, interfering but irrelevant visual information, or when guiding visual cues were absent or conflicting.

Dr Hamed Akhlaghi followed up with confirmatory brain scans, showing that the volume of certain cerebellar structures, such as the superior cerebellar peduncle, is reduced in the disorder. Volumes correlated negatively with clinical severity and disease duration, and positively with age of onset. Our activation scans showed disruption of cerebello-fronto-cerebellar loops, leading to negative consequences in distal brain regions, including the basal ganglia, a phenomenon known clinically as diaschisis. Indeed, a structure like the cerebellum may malfunction in several possible ways – under-activity, over-activity, abnormal activity, or as noted just now via its effect on other downstream structures, such that they instead seem to malfunction – diaschisis again!

We have recently commenced work on yet another neurogenetic disorder with likely cerebellar malfunctioning, the fragile-X-related group, which is associated with CGG repeat expansion of the so-called fragile X mental retardation 1 gene. There are both developmental and degenerative neurological manifestations. Fragile X syndrome is said to be the most common single-gene cause of intellectual disability and autism, affecting approximately 1 in 3,600 males and maybe 1 in 5,000 females worldwide. As with Huntington's disease, there is a toxic gain of function from the effects of certain proteins, over-expression causing neural damage. Individuals within a certain range of repeats, considered insufficient to generate the full-blown syndrome, were long thought to be free of any deleterious phenotypic consequences, but we now know that a considerable percentage are at risk of developing late-onset neurodegenerative decline – the so-called Fragile X associated tremor ataxia. Often there are also reproductive problems, increased risk of dementia, and motor symptoms. With PhD student, now Dr Claudine Kraan, at Monash I have been studying early cognitive and motor changes as possible indicators or precursors of later neurological decline. There is, of course, a protective effect from the normal allele on the second X chromosome in apparently clinically normal female carriers (females have two X chromosomes, while males have an X and a Y), but evidence is now accruing of abnormal psychomotor ability, motor coordination deficits, increased postural sway and gait anomalies – all suggesting cerebellar involvement. However, there are very few imaging studies, although what exist so far do suggest abnormalities in cerebellar-cortico pathways and in the cerebellar peduncles. Parenthetically, another heritable disorder, cystic fibrosis, according to conventional wisdom, should likewise not manifest in someone with only one copy of the relevant gene, but members of my own family, including myself, can attest to the fact that, as in Fragile X, such carriers are not entirely free of symptomatology.

And this brings me to another point: the question of autism and Asperger's. Many readers will know that the latest edition of the psychiatrist's diagnostic bible, the *DSM V*, has, we believe wrongly, subsumed Asperger's under autism. My old student, now Professor Nicole Rinehart, and I have characterised a number of motor differences between the two disorders, which are particularly evident in gait, and we have good reasons to believe that they stem from different degrees of cerebellar and basal ganglia compromise.

Behavioural neuroscience, the offspring of parents such as experimental psychology, psychiatry and neurology, among others, has a lot to offer in the way of furthering our understanding of normal brain function, and of pathological processes in clinical medicine. It is in that golden period of expansion when every new discovery opens up a multitude of yet more fascinating questions to address. Truly it is one of science's most rapidly developing and exciting fields, not least because in addition it addresses one of our great and most fundamental mysteries – the nature of thought, consciousness and action, and the control of our behaviour. Although nearly 78, I do hope to be around for the next 20 or so years to see, and maybe even contribute to, some of the answers. Apart from Parkinson's, from which my father suffered, and Alzheimer's (my mother), I am at least too old to likely develop any of the syndromes mentioned here. And also too old to be useful as a healthy control!

35

THE MAGICIAN'S APPRENTICE

Back to basics

In Greek mythology, Narcissus, son of the river god Cephissus and the water nymph Liriope, was a beautiful youth, beloved by the nymph Echo, whom he cruelly repulsed. For this offence, Aphrodite, goddess of love, punished him by making him pathologically enamoured of his own image as reflected in a pool of water. His continuing and fruitless attempts to approach his beautiful self-image led to his despair and death. Are we not all just a little tempted by a similar fascination, an urge to understand, see even, something of the workings of our own minds, maybe to be glimpsed through a study of that latest of scientific endeavours, passions one might almost say, cognitive neuroscience? It can be no accident that the prefix 'neuro-' nowadays appears before so many other existing disciplines – neuroethics, neurophilosophy, neuroeconomics, neuroforensics … Can all these disciplines be better comprehended and mastered through the lens of brain mechanisms?

The human brain, that most exquisitely complex of all known systems, manages so much of what seems to render us human – possession of a mind, however defined with respect to a substrate such as the brain, consciousness, will, intention, attention, ethics, personal and legal responsibility, thought, emotion, cognition … the list goes on and on. And in the last couple of decades so many wonderful new procedures and technologies, 'boys' toys', one might call them, have been developed, whose operators can present to us dazzling images of brain structure (at both the macro and micro levels) and function, both of region and of inter-regional connectivirties, in colours and tones often so aesthetically stunning that a Renaissance painter in Italy would have given a limb for access to them.

Pictures may have launched a thousand ships, they may be worth more than a thousand words, but such pictures as come from the scanners of today must always be interpreted with caution, a caution which is not always observed in this brave new world which seems to open a window into The Last Great Mystery. Indeed, some say that ultimately it requires the brain to understand itself, a logically impossible and futile act of narcissism. Time alone will tell, but plans are currently afoot in several parts of the world to fully characterise and even build a brain in all its barely imaginable complexity. The new discipline, cognitive neuroscience, is now almost come of age, but it will require, were it to make any truly meaningful progress, a thorough understanding of experimental and statistical principles, and this I fear is where basic scientific training may nowadays be falling behind the rigour which was once deemed necessary for a thorough apprenticeship in understanding how to formulate hypotheses, rigorously design studies, collect, analyse and interpret data, and draw statistically and scientifically valid conclusions.

Fifty-three years ago I commenced my PhD in what was then known as experimental psychology. I chose a completely novel topic in the area called physiological psychology; I set out to measure the effect upon the oculo-motor system of cognitive, thought and problem-solving processes, as mediated by the autonomic or involuntary motor system. In those distant days, psychology encompassed such broad disciplines as learning (animal and human), sensory and perceptual processes, behaviour genetics, personality, skills and ergonomics, clinical psychology, and much of what in the popular mind was thought to be the true domain of a soft or inexact science, or simply descriptive common sense. I was able to conclude from my doctoral research that pupillometry, as it later came to be known, was a highly sensitive and readily accessible approach to measuring cognitive load and stress during information processing, sensitive not only in a quantitative sense, but also with respect to the temporal aspects – onset, duration and offset parameters.

Shortly after my doctoral completion, I was offered a lectureship at Monash, then a very new institution indeed, headed by a very far-seeing foundation professor, Ross Henry Day. He insisted that, as a biological discipline, psychology should be placed firmly within the Faculty of Science, and that the proper object of teaching and research should be the scientific analysis and description of behaviour – human and animal – with the understanding, of course, that we too belong to the animal kingdom. Not everyone was happy with this, and for years there would echo the occasional, residual student complaint, 'When are we going to do some real psychology?'

My professional career commenced in the golden years of the late 1960s, a period of near universal postwar optimism, and just before the full angst of Australia's adventure in Vietnam had taken hold. There were abundant funds to develop new lab-based courses, and I was asked to run the new first year lab classes (130 students), and to lecture in Cognitive Processes and Animal Learning. I knew nothing about the latter, except that there seemed to be a tedious Skinner-driven obsession with Classical and Operant learning in rats, and schedules of reinforcement, an arid characterisation which seemed to me to miss totally the full richness of behaviour change. So in the first year I surreptitiously dropped the 'Animal' qualifier in the designated course, Animal Learning, concentrating instead upon the biological bases or substrates which involve neurons, synapses, neurotransmitters, brain regions and the effects of lesions, natural and artificial and localised to certain structures, upon the acquisition of new behaviours. In the second year, as no-one seemed to have noticed the change of emphasis, I made a further change to the title, from 'Biological Bases of Learning' to 'Biological Bases of Behaviour', which enabled me to address such interesting topics as drive, motivation, sleep, language and other higher cortical functions.

Just before I had arrived in Australia, two seminal volumes had appeared, which enthralled and inspired me, and which I believe formed the substrate of the slowly emerging field of cognitive neuroscience. Aleksandr Romanovich Luria's magisterial *Higher Cortical Functions in Man* (published in Moscow in 1962, English translation in 1966) surveyed lucidly, systematically and comprehensively an enormous Soviet corpus of findings of the effects of Second World War wounds in discrete cerebral areas upon cognitive functions. The other book was Ulric Neisser's *Cognitive Psychology*, published in 1967. He described exciting new findings from a host of ingenious experiments where visual material (letters, numbers, words, patterns), singly, in a matrix or sequentially, were flashed to normal healthy individuals under tightly controlled temporal or spatial constraints, to determine how it was all processed and what was ultimately seen or reported. Absolutely nothing like it had ever been done before, and the conclusions opened up the emergent field of cognitive psychology. I based my teaching and research around these two works, which, I believe, combined to form the union later to be known as cognitive neuroscience.

In my first year lab classes, as a bow to the original 'Animal Learning' title of one of my lecture courses, I decided to go beyond the old, tired, tried and tedious lab rat; with my wife Judy, a biologist, I collected hermit crabs from the local shore line. These little marine crustaceans inhabit the cast-off, conical spiral shells of sea snails. With a blob of plasticine, the tip of the inhabited shell could be stuck to a substrate so that the crab itself could protrude from the open end of the shell in a jar of sea water. I placed a small light bulb above the creature, and two wires, insulated except for the tips, one on each side of the shell opening, such that a 6-volt current could briefly be passed across the animal, causing it rapidly to withdraw. The students were then free to determine how many exposures of a brief, low-intensity light flash alone, which had no effect upon the animal, or a pairing of light flash and current (in either order, and with various intervals) could 'condition' the animal to withdraw just to a light flash, and how many such light-flash-alone trials would suffice for the animal to 'extinguish' its learnt, withdrawal response.

It was, however, in the cognitive realm that I, and, I believe, the students, had the best time. Before computers, with monitors upon which all manner of material can be presented for controlled durations and intensities, and perhaps in particular sequences, cognitive scientists were reliant upon the tachistoscope, literally 'very brief or fast viewing'. This device became an essential tool analogous to the biologist's microscope; indeed, we had an enormous multichannel device occupying its very own room, with its lenses, mirrors, filters, prisms and electronic controls of exposure durations and sequences, via plug board and multiple timers. However, to do what I had in mind for teaching the students, I needed 12, for groups of three

– participant or subject, experimenter and data recorder – to devise experiments and presentation procedures and to collect and analyse data. I devised a beam tachistoscope, consisting of a pivoted arm, weighted at one end with a weight that could be changed or slid along the arm so that the other end, bearing a set of mirrors, would pass a viewing hole at chosen speeds. The mirrors, set at different angles, passed removable cards mounted so that their images would be reflected to the eye piece. Crude but effective, with later modifications based upon an adjustable pneumatic door closer, we were able to simulate and extend, maybe less elegantly but quite effectively, the 'classical' findings described by Neisser in his book. Colleagues somewhat enviously or even unkindly would sometimes refer to them as my Model T steam tachistoscopes.

Other devices I pioneered included sets of adjustable and filtered audio-oscillators to act as audiometers in studies on signal detection theory and auditory psychophysics, where we could apply appropriate mathematical treatments. We also devised and constructed sets of visual simple and choice reaction-time gear, to study the mathematical application of information theory in the context of various schedules of *a priori* and *a posteriori* probability series. I also found a way to modify and set up tape recorders to provide auditory feedback, delayed by various intervals between 100 and 400 msec, of the ongoing speech of participants reading from a prepared text; at a critical value of 200 msec, a fundamental interval within which we now know the brain continuously monitors and corrects ongoing speech and other complex sequential movements, speech typically breaks down into stuttering incoherence or is blocked. The procedure is known as delayed auditory feedback, and we were able to study the effect of different volumes, intervals and materials. Indeed, with such and other techniques and instruments, enthusiastically manufactured by our talented departmental workshops (mechanical, electronic and later IT), I was able to teach eager 18-year-olds sophisticated theoretical concepts and experimental procedures. While then considered as lying under the aegis of experimental psychology, they have now become part of a rebadged cognitive neuroscience, and I believe gave students a very valuable hands-on lesson in technique and how to improvise in what Neisser called an ecologically valid framework, unlike the often artificial and rather sterile procedures available nowadays to students from computer monitors. Indeed, apart from running rather artificial studies, pedagogically speaking, by computer, the other great 'laboratory' cop-out, based upon financial savings and economies of scale, is the substitution of a video for real hands-on experience. Apprentice researchers should get their hands dirty as soon as possible, if possible, to build, and certainly to operate apparatus which may be comparatively simple in realisation but sophisticated conceptually. They should collect, analyse, apply appropriate statistical tests to and interpret their findings, and present them clearly, concisely and coherently, in the context of prior findings and of any initial hypotheses driving the study, in a paper which in principle is publishable, and in practice is intelligible to unsophisticated readers or those from other disciplines. Similarly, web-based and online learning can never replace the stimulation of a real, live lecturer excitedly telling the class about her latest findings or those of a colleague, and who extemporises and answers interesting questions from a newly-informed audience. And that new development, the Massive Online Course (MOOC), to which often hundreds of thousands may sign up, but apparently fewer than 10 per cent ever finish, may turn out to be the proverbial flash in the pan.

We celebrated our department's 50th anniversary in 2014, and I do regret and deplore how, maybe universally, lab teaching in many disciplines has dwindled nowadays, supposedly for reasons of cost and efficiency, with the demise of those wonderful workshops with which I once worked, to devise simple, robust and ever interesting analogues of the cutting-edge techniques and concepts of yesteryear. Indeed, I have recently, and very profitably, resurrected a number of them, in updated form, to study patient groups suffering from inherited and acquired disorders of the motor system involving motor cortex, cerebellum or basal ganglia.

In summary, upcoming neuroscientists have some wonderful new toys – big, expensive and flashy generators of Big Data, to use the latest buzz word, but without a good practical grounding in experimental technique, it could all be an expensive waste of time. How else can we play Narcissus at his own game, without coming to a similar sad end of frustration and disappointment?

36

STROKE

The hour that struck

24 October 2010, 7.00 a.m.

'Bring out the black bag', she said. 'Which one?' I asked.

Since the recently celebrated 'Decade of the brain', an unprecedented public awareness has developed of matters of psychological or neurological interest. Many will remember hearing of, or even experiencing, the seemingly intrusive but usually unnoticed 'gorilla', the man in the gorilla suit who runs across the field of view at the climactic height of a hard-contested ball game. In the general excitement he is indeed ignored and unremembered. Then there are flash-bulb memories, whereby we can vividly recall exactly what we were doing when we first heard of an event of major or extremely news-worthy significance: assassinations or attempted assassinations of presidents or popes, or death and disaster. So, indeed, I vividly recall the exact conversation I had with my wife on that fateful Sunday morning of 24 October, 7.00 a.m. seven years ago, while camped in a remote valley at the foot of a mountain we had planned to climb that day. It was the very last conversation we were ever destined to enjoy.

Judy's rheumatologist, to whom absolutely no blame is attached, and whom she had consulted concerning some comparatively minor arthritic back pain prior to our planned week of strenuous bush walking, had recommended that she should commence a double dose of a well-known nonsteroidal anti-inflammatory. It belongs to a group of drugs (COX-2 inhibitors), one of which achieved fairly recent notoriety for a dose-related increase in the risk of adverse circulatory events (strokes, heart attacks), and was taken off the market. Other closely similar medications, some non-prescription and off the shelf, have very recently likewise been shown to considerably increase the risk.

Judy took her first-ever double dose at 7.00 p.m. on the first night of our vacation after we had set up camp and had our evening meal at the foot of Mt Stapleton, a rugged eminence in the Victorian Grampian ranges, and home to many spectacular species of orchids whose blooms at that time of year we had come annually to admire and photograph. Now, no more.

When exactly 12 hours later at 7.00 a.m. the next morning she seemed uncharacteristically unable to answer my question, I looked enquiringly at her, to see a face in the grip of savage contortions, and her right hand clawing ineffectively. In the 45 years I had known her, she had never had an epileptic seizure, at that moment the only possible differential diagnosis. When in dismay I asked her to firmly grasp my hand with her right, which I tapped, she could not do so, but shortly before lapsing into unconsciousness she succeeded with her left; then my very worst fears were confirmed. It was clearly a stroke, a major one, and apparently affecting her dominant left hemisphere which controls speech, manual dexterity and the opposite, right, side of the body. It was the worst possible scenario, and one on which we had both worked as researchers for many years. Fortunately she was in her sleeping bag on the bed I had constructed in our four-wheel drive Toyota Troop-Carrier/Land Cruiser. In the confusion I could not find my mobile, and when I found hers I did not know her PIN; fortunately when I tried her date of birth – a sequence we are all advised not to use – it registered. But there was no reception in that remote valley on the Coppermines Track.

I abandoned all camping gear outside the vehicle and drove to a ridge to use the phone, knowing that from now on our lives would be totally and irrevocably changed. Having researched in the area, I really knew too much. Emergency Triple O put me in contact with medical services and we arranged to rendezvous with an ambulance at Halls Gap, the nearest settlement, in about 40 minutes. They were there and waiting. Unlike my vivid memory of Judy's last words and the dire events immediately following, I now have little recollection of that terrible drive. I do know, however, that we greatly exceeded any speed limit, and the Troop Carrier was pushed to its near maximum. In maybe 30 minutes we reached the nearest bush hospital at Stawell. Remembering, as I thought, that with an arterial blockage, clot or embolism, the commonest form of stroke, there is a therapeutic window of five hours during which thrombolysis or 'clot buster' treatment can partially 'rescue' the dying oxygen- and glucose-starved neurons or brain cells, I had carefully noted exactly when it had all happened. Had I but known it, by a terrible coincidence the very next day on the ABC Health Report to which I always listen, thrombolysis was discussed in detail, and the window was noted as now not exceeding three hours. In any case I resolved to plead for its administration, while fearing that it would not be available in country areas, but only in the so-called tertiary hospitals. It is, moreover, strongly contra-indicated with the less frequent stroke variant, haemorrhagic, where it would simply exacerbate the existing bleeding which characterises that subtype.

To my admitted surprise and relief, Stawell did in fact have a partial dose which was promptly administered after a sleepy technician took a CT scan, to confirm that Judy's stroke was indeed embolic rather than haemorrhagic, when the drug would of course merely have exacerbated matters. We then had to locate and obtain the rest of the dose. Horsham, three-quarters of an hour's drive away, did have some, but the resident neurologist was understandably reluctant to part with such a precious commodity. Eventually, perhaps even because Judy had already had some administered, he complied, and it came by taxi, the minutes continuing to tick away. The drug must be administered slowly, by a special time-controlled pump, over 20 minutes. After 10 minutes I noticed that the gauge indicated very little progress, and I was asked to help check the calculations and settings. Despite my own emotional state and personal involvement in this unfolding Greek tragedy, I ascertained that we were out by a factor of ten (i.e. one decimal point, an easy error to make in an entirely novel situation). After rectification, and when the last drop was in, it was close to mid-day, outside either presumed therapeutic window, three or five hours.

I can only thank everyone concerned – paramedics, the staff at the two hospitals – for their valiant efforts, and for arranging for Judy to be 'medivac-ed' by light plane back to Melbourne, to my University's own hospital, Monash Medical Centre, while I drove back alone. Another horror drive, and this time I remember looking hard and long at that incomparable Grampians skyline, of 'unimaginable height', according to Major Thomas Mitchell, its early explorer, thinking that this would probably be the very last time that we would both have seen those beloved ridges, part of our lives now for nearly half a century since we first arrived in Australia.

I chose as her destination Monash Medical Centre (MMC) rather than, say, the Austin or the Alfred Hospitals, as Judy and I have together researched stroke and its neuropsychological consequences (together with a range of other neurological disorders, some rare like Huntington's disease, Williams syndrome, Friedreich ataxia … and some common, like Parkinson's disease), both at MMC and at Kingston Rehabilitation Hospital, where she was eventually sent for six months of intensive therapy. We have, and have had, numerous colleagues, students and friends at both institutions, from top neurologists to doctoral students, and I honestly just do not know how I would have survived, let alone coped, without their incredible and unfailing support – advice, management, help, meals, companionship, country walks … It has been truly humbling, and in a strange way wonderful and inspiring, and I have got to know and get close to them in ways I would never have done otherwise, giving me a profound faith in the underlying worth of human nature.

Another coincidence: 15 years before, one of my previous graduate students, with whom I had researched the spatial and other processes largely subserved by the right hemisphere of the brain, had come down to Melbourne to see me – in a wheelchair. She had suffered a massive stroke, probably haemorrhagic, as she was still young, in her right half-brain. Judy's symptoms, aphasia and apraxia, with right-side hemiplegia, were therefore the mirror image of Del's visuospatial and attentional deficits with left-side hemiplegia. It should, of course, be remembered that either side of the body is subserved by the opposite, contralateral, side (hemisphere) of the brain.

For relatives or carers of stroke victims there is a nightmare of bureaucracy, with seemingly innumerable competing organisations (federal, state, council, charitable) involved in providing care, funding, assistance, therapy, and a morass of acronyms and red tape. You come to dread mail drops or telephone calls, or the message on the answering machine. Sometimes you begin to think that you could do it all quicker, better and in a simpler fashion yourself, and that you don't need 'the system'. Indeed, after a 'training' and settling-in period, when the patient is discharged from hospital into your care, you may well be right. I was invited to apply for a carer's allowance, means tested. Lengthy queues, production (after considerable effort) of numerous documents as proof of identity and qualification, interviews, judgement that I had met all requirements, then later receipt of a letter saying that I did not qualify as I had failed to produce those identifying documents (which of course I had, and which had been judged at the time as more than sufficient). Return to the system, eventually to be told that the original clerk had misfiled the material and that I did indeed qualify. This sort of experience, with variations, sadly seems far from uncommon. Thus, on two occasions I have completed an organisation's paperwork as apparently required, returning it promptly, only to be told that in the interim they have reorganised, renamed and developed a new set of paperwork which replaces the old, and must instead be completed. Costs can be horrendous: a month's supply of Pregabalin (only one of Judy's entire pharmacopeia of medications) would cost $140 if it happened to be prescribed for stroke-induced *pain* of central origin, but was capped at about $40 if prescribed for stroke-induced *seizures* (from which she is fortunately free). Yet the neurological mechanisms, and the practical consequences for the patient, are nearly identical in the two cases. (Subsequently the cost was in fact very substantially reduced when it eventually went on the favoured Pharmaceutical Benefits Scheme list of drugs.) A wheelchair seat cushion, filled with gel to ease pressure, cost $764. And it goes on and on, haemorrhaging money. I just do not know how people, untutored in basic neurology and the hospital system, without friends in high places and an army of graduate-student acolytes, some also trained in allied health, and without a daughter herself a physician, could possibly cope in a system which is fundamentally flawed and needs redesigning from the bottom up, and radically simplified.

Judy, a slight and athletic 72-year-old when 'struck down', with no known risk factors (normal blood pressure, blood glucose, cholesterol and lipids), exercising daily all her life, a bush walker who was ever mindful of her diet, free elsewhere in the brain of all signs of cardiac or cerebrovascular abnormality (as ascertained by magnetic resonance imaging, magnetic resonance angiography, cardiac ultrasound, Doppler echocardiography...) had somehow experienced occlusions in both the anterior and the middle cerebral arteries on the left side of the brain, rendering her mute and aphasic, and paraplegic on the corresponding right side of the body. Did she experience a brief period of atrial fibrillation during the night, which interacted with the effects of the medication she had taken? She had no such prior history, and heart function proved entirely normal.

I became her sole carer, 24/7, for close on a year, for every bodily function, and my own scholarly and scientific research career had to be terminated. And Judy was, and still is, locked into a life of pain, discomfort and humiliation, with severely attenuated cognitive, language and motor function. While she can follow simple conversation, she cannot contribute anything substantial or useful. She can do none of the things that we all take for granted and enjoy. Her life, previously that of an active free spirit, is curtailed by the bounds of her wheelchair and where I can take it, and for that dreadful first year at home, the visits of rehabilitation specialists and carers. How meaningful is her existence for her? Would she have preferred not to have pulled through? Should we dare ask such questions? I know that in my own case I could not bear such an existence, and like many others would choose a gentle exit when there is no longer any light at the end of life's tunnel. I can already hear outraged howls from the religious right, from self-appointed ethicists, assorted bigots and do-gooders of various persuasions. But in the meantime I did everything possible for my mate of 45 years, who still knows and loves me, largely helpless although she is. Given the enormous extent of loss of brain tissue, her inability to say even one word or to move her right limbs, it is frankly amazing that her personality was and still is largely unchanged, apart from some very minor frontal signs (a tendency to perseverate – to continue with a previous response now no longer relevant). Although slow, she could even at one time produce from a pile of coins and notes a target sum such as $7.75, but sadly even that little window has since shut. An interesting observation, but which underlines my maxim to students that behind all such empirical and clinical novelties lies someone's personal tragedy.

I wondered; will there be some slow continuing improvement, given her indomitable spirit, or is she now as good as she will ever be, with maybe even a slow continuing decline? In the meantime, I am reminded of the Ionian-Greek historian, Herodotus, who reported 2,500 years ago, in his *Histories*, an old sage's observation that no-one can be called happy, or indeed otherwise, until they are dead.

As her sole carer, dressing, feeding, washing and toileting her, I gave her a bell to awaken me the three or four times a night that she needed the commode in our room. My sleep was disjointed and badly broken. The house was modified in bathroom and toilet areas, and I experimented with various ways of washing her. In the end, the only practical way, I found, was to strip myself naked and after bringing the wheelchair to the edge of the bath, to manoeuvre her over the raised border, into the bath, and on to a stool appropriately placed therein for showering, and to ignore the other expensive and extensive modifications that had been made elsewhere. Likewise, I gave up using the collapsible ramps I had purchased at considerable expense for getting her up and down the entrance steps, and came to rely upon my still adequate physical strength to manually lift the wheelchair, with her in it, up and down each separate step. And despite instructions never to leave her unattended, life without shopping, hair-cuts and visits to the doctor, dentist and bank just proved impossible. There was, however, one truly useful skill I had learnt during her earlier rehab: how to get her out of her wheelchair and into the car, and vice versa. Such transfer is not at all easy when there is such a degree of physical impairment, and where some physical strength is required by the operator. The sequences of movements are not dissimilar to those involved in manhandling a small wardrobe, and great care is necessary to avoid ever holding the patient by the flaccidly paralysed right arm, which can so easily dislocate at the shoulder. Indeed, after several failed attempts by various crafts people, without the eventual manufacture of a truly workable AFO (ankle-foot-orthotic or leg brace), walking of any sort, or car transfer, would just not have been possible. For the latter, I had to employ some ingenuity, modifying one of her old boots high enough for her to perch her bottom on the edge of the car seat, on to which I had laid several sheets of slippery polythene so that I could slide her across sufficiently far into the vehicle.

Judy is locked into a life of discomfort, pain and humiliation, with severely attenuated cognitive, linguistic and motor functions. To ascertain her moment-to-moment needs, I always have to ask a series of progressively more specific 'yes'/'no' questions, but an inappropriate early response would easily derail the entire subsequent process of her often ambiguous nods or head shakes. I was left wondering whether there would be any slow or small improvements to come, or whether she had reached a plateau, or maybe just a slow, continuous decline was likely. At one point, during rehab, Judy was able to stand, almost unaided, and pat back a balloon tapped towards her, in a kind of slow-motion tennis; not any more. There followed a succession of urinary tract infections, falls (with fractures of femur and humerus, followed by surgery and more rehab), and another neurological event (almost certainly another stroke, rather than as at first thought, a seizure, as she was left with additional deficits). The last again occurred during the night hours, with facial convulsion and rapid loss of consciousness. As I followed the ambulance to hospital I wondered whether this event was likely to prove terminal, and if so, whether it might even be a blessed release for her from an unhappy existence. I know that were the situations to have been reversed, that is what I would have wanted for myself, and whatever the opponents of euthanasia might say, it is most certainly NOT the case that modern medical and hospice practices can promise a pain-free existence of dignity and quiet surrender. Wishful thinking, or deliberate blindness to the unpalatably true realities of our final months? In any case, Judy was back in acute care for some weeks, and one morning I was told she was ready to be released back into my home care. I got her into the car and we set off home. However, we had only been going five minutes when I noticed that she was again losing consciousness and slowly slumping down to the floor of the car. I immediately turned round and returned to the hospital where I was informed that I would have to join the triage queue – some two to three hours long. At this point, semi-deliberately, I 'lost it' and refused to move. I even managed to get her, in the wheelchair, into the admissions office, whence, after making a sufficient commotion, I succeeded in getting her back to the ward from which she had been discharged. Sometimes a carefully controlled and titrated outburst can achieve far more than politely playing by the rules. There, it was agreed that she was indeed not ready for discharge, and after another fortnight, with the help of a really sympathetic social worker, an excellent facility offering the requisite high-level of care was located. I had spent much time checking out some eight institutions, which ranged from the splendid to the execrable, from nineteenth-century Dickensian to the latest ultramodern, from the heartless but efficient to the shambolic but caring, and in fact everything in between. I was eventually very fortunate to be directed to the one which seems, over the last six years, to combine the best of all qualities. But it is still a gilded cage, and a personal destiny which I intend at all costs to avoid if possible. Dying with dignity should be everyone's birth right, and I carry with me several cards all saying DO NOT RESUSCITATE – maybe I should have that exhortation tattooed on my bare chest. When my seriously demented mother had to enter a nursing home in Wales, we found one run by a couple of Irish ex-hotel keepers, operating a shambolically cheerful if somewhat scruffy outfit, where the residents at least seemed moderately cheerful in a probably rather unhygienic atmosphere of barely-controlled bedlam.

Judy has been in her place now for a good few years, and at nearly $50,000 per annum, plus medications (some expensive), it is not clear what the future would hold should the money ever run out. On the positive side, her facility is close to home, and en route to Monash University, so on weekday mornings I can call in to the labs and have lunch with my students, ex-students and colleagues, and visit Judy in the afternoons; as one of my students said, it is partly a matter of establishing a new rhythm to one's life. I have been camping with the family of one of my old students, been for a week to Flinders Island in the Furneaux group near Tasmania with two other friends, and drove with them for a couple of weeks around Namibia in West Africa; and with other friends I even saw something of the remoter regions of the Philippines. Whenever I am away, I arrange a roster of our old friends briefly to call in and see Judy. I haunt sales at the various walking, hiking and 'bush outfitting' shops, to get clothing for her which is light, durable and easily donned given the extent of her disability. I have been taking her out several afternoons a week, to favourite local cafés, beauty spots and lakes or dams, and the veranda at home which is on the edge of bushland. This has itself led to a dilemma: by so removing her from the confines of the nursing home, she is missing out from participating in the often useful rehab programmes which they run. Which is the more important? Further rehab and exercise, or relaxing in the company of her life's partner? Many say I should push for as much rehab as possible, but more and more I have come to believe that what may after all be the shortish time remaining for us together should be spent in the way which she has come to prefer. Friends, family members, carers and specialists all have different views on such matters. As so often may be the case, I as major carer have come to believe that I may be in the best position to resolve this issue. I read to her daily, from light short stories, and from time to time I play simple games with her, such as asking her to point to what I am wearing or to point to its colour (on a chart), and so on. One of her old colleagues and best of friends visits her regularly, and with help she even seems somehow able to manage a simple game of Snakes and Ladders. She does not in fact seem to learn or improve much, and little seems to be of much real functional use, but it plays a useful social role and there may after all be some residual learning. Otherwise, TV is a real blessing, as is the wonderful mobile library, which every few weeks brings her picture books on botany, gardens, travel, history, and so on.

Until struck a few years ago by the seemingly ubiquitous blight, for folk of my age, of knee trouble, I continued my habits of 40 years, of walking an hour a day, up and down a 150 m local hill, and 'pumping iron' on the carpet of my study. I am nearly 78, and can just about lift her, in stages, should she fall; will I still be able to do this in three years' time, when I shall be over 80? Will I or Judy still be around? Will the money have lasted? What will happen if she is the sole survivor? We fear advancing age, yet dread the alternative, a premature demise. We seek the comfort and security of company, a partner for life or a part thereof, especially perhaps someone to share our declining years and save us from a lonely old age. Yet except in rare – possibly even fortunate? – instances, one or other will inevitably predecease the one who is left behind, who may thereby grieve the loss of a dear companion. The loss may occur relatively rapidly, as perhaps in earlier times, or nowadays it may be a more drawn-out process as with dementia or stroke, with greater possibilities for medical intervention to delay the inevitable. The longer our life expectancy, the more likely it will be that, paradoxically perhaps, the process of dying may itself become more lengthy and drawn-out. When we retire, it may be prudent to 'take on board' some of the skills, practices or responsibilities of the other partner, whether it be cooking or house maintenance, domestic finance or driving, so that the tribulations associated with continued existence are not compounded with grief at a sudden loss. I know, I have had to adjust, and my own initial partial incompetence added to my early woes. I had to learn, and, strangely, feel the better for it, and a lifetime working in trying to understand brain and behaviour helped me to distinguish between grief, depression and anxiety. If you survive a life trauma, you can be the stronger for it, but it will help immeasurably if you make early preparations, so as to manage to cope on your own, and if you also make and extend a network of mutual support. Such support, in times of need, can come from unexpected quarters and manifest in decidedly unusual, unconventional, surprising and really welcome ways.

There has appeared a whole new journey, an unexpectedly welcome silver lining in life's tangled tapestry.

37

I'M AS OLD AS I FEEL

That wonderful old weaver of tales, recorder of curiosities, facts, fiction and fantasy, Herodotus of Halicarnassus, wrote his incomparable *Histories*, in lovely Ionic Greek, around 460 BC. In them, he recalls the Riddle of the Sphinx, the mythical Throttler, who despatched in this fashion travellers unable to solve her eponymous riddle, 'What walks on four legs in the morning, on two at noon, on three in the evening?' The answer was 'man', who as an infant crawls on all fours, and in old age walks leaning on a stick. I recently qualified for such a definition, being obliged to graduate to the use of a stick, after the sudden and catastrophic (in all senses) failure of both knee joints: medial meniscus and articulatory cartilage failure. I hoped that surgery, to implant twenty-first-century tungsten prostheses, might for a while reset my life's Master Clock to the middle, two-legged, phase. Small consolation that I am (I hope!) safe from the Sphinx's lethal embrace. '*Eheu fugaces, labuntur anni*', 'alas, the fleeting years slip by', was the plangent regret of the Roman poet, Horace.

Four centuries on from the time of Herodotus, and writing roughly contemporaneously with Horace, the sophisticated lawyer, politician, orator and writer, Cicero wrote, in impeccable Latin, a model for all young classical aspirants today, his dialogue on old age, *De Senectute.* He deals with the burdens of advancing years, how best to bear them, their compensations and consolations, often with surprisingly modern insights. A century or so later, the historian, Tacitus notes with economical prose the '*curvata senio membra, fluxa senio mens*', 'the bow-legged stance, the failing intellect, of our senior years'.

Palliative removal of my medial menisci, one in each knee, bought and brought me a temporary remission, measured merely in months, and one last hiking holiday with two walking poles, transiently restoring me to the four-limbed stance of the riddling Sphinx. However, the transition merely accelerated wear of the cartilaginous articulatory surfaces of the two long bones, tibia and femur, constituting the bulk of the knee joints. Waiting for right-knee surgery, as I could no longer walk unaided more than a few hundred metres, in a vain attempt to preserve some semblance of muscle mass and general fitness, I bought an exercise bike, after finding that repeated climbing and descending the stairs to a daily therapeutic total of 50 times, might be making matters worse. But so, unfortunately, also did the exercise bike. Even daily swimming 1 km in an indoors heated pool brought on pain; so much for supposed low-impact activity. However, what I did find beneficial, and without exacerbation of symptoms, was repeatedly ascending the carpeted stairs on all fours (that Sphinx again?), and descending them while hanging on manually to a system of overhead ropes jury-rigged from the balustrade bars. And every morning I would perform pull-ups from the horizontal branch of an appropriately configured tree in the garden. Eventually, I had a total knee replacement, and was instructed to prepare myself for the same to the other knee, the knee which some years previously had been causing me pain sufficient for meniscus removal as a temporary measure. However, it was then that the exercise bike proved its worth; an hour daily, pedalling on maximum resistance, not only speeded an otherwise unpleasant rehab process for the replaced knee, but also proved surprisingly beneficial even for the one awaiting the next replacement.

Why do we age? Post-reproductively, we are then all past our optimal use-by dates, and surplus to perpetuation of our species and to newly appearing generations, so there is no selective Darwinian advantage to our continuing survival. (One can, however, argue that older family members still contribute, if indirectly, to the genetic fortunes of the young by providing surrogate care and education.) And without senescence and death, the world would be knee-deep (that word again!) in redundant geriatrics. In an open world or universe, we could all remain ever young and fertile, and populate to infinity, a potential only in principle achievable by asexually reproducing single-celled organisms like the amoeba, or by cancer cells, which theoretically can all go on dividing for ever. And it may be that within our cells there lies, in part, an intracellular answer to the mysterious mechanisms of ageing. Throughout life, our cells divide and replace, as appropriate, and there may be a genetically fixed number of such divisions and replacements, a number partly governed by the little caps, or telomeres, lying at the tips of the chromosomes, and which themselves shorten with each cell division.

The telomeres seem to act like the caps at the ends of bootlaces. Modify the action of the associated enzyme, telomerase, and we may solve the problem of the vanishing telomeres and the riddling tragedy of ageing – possibly at increased risk of contracting that true immortal, cancer. Interestingly, serious exercise may slow telomere shortening; if the exact mechanism can be determined, it may open a new therapeutic window into slowing ageing. Additionally, and possibly separately, there may be present a blood fraction in the circulation of the ageing; young and old mice, with mutually crossed circulations (parabiosis), or appropriate plasma infusions, seem to reset their rates and stages of ageing, the old becoming young again in body and spirit, and the young older, at least in terms of muscle mass, bodily appearance, activity and cognition. *The Picture of Dorian Gray*? Transfusions of umbilical blood also may rejuvenate mouse brains in areas important for cognitive and memory processes. As the blood in ageing recipients contains high levels of deleterious inflammatory components derived from senescent cells, young blood may of course merely serve to dilute the old, contaminated, blood. And similarly, faecal transplants in fish, thereby altering their intestinal flora, may also provide promising new leads; the indoles, which are alkaloids, seem to be involved. In my own particular case, I may have been born just a little too early to benefit from the recent dramatic advances in stem-cell research. Appropriately injected with reprogrammed pluripotent stem cells, harvested from my own body, my knee joints might have regrown the abraded cartilage worn down by an active lifestyle. So much less messy and time-consuming than surgery. Indeed, rather than having one's body frozen at death, to be thawed for resurrection when medicine is more advanced, maybe we should merely have had frozen some of our placental blood at birth, for rejuvenating stem cells.

Another intriguing lead may come from an old observation, going back maybe 30 years (almost half a lifetime ago!) by Hayflick, who observed that whatever a mammal's weight, and however long their lifespan, they can expect to expire after roughly the same number of heartbeats, roughly 1.5 billion. Is this something to do with metabolic rate? It is the case that the bigger the body, the slower the metabolism, and if you plot metabolic rate against body mass, everything from a mouse to an elephant, excluding humans alone, falls on a straight line; and if you plot brain volume as a logarithmic function of body mass, you again get a straight line; lies, damned lies and statistics? However, there is evidence that a specific gene (DAF-2) is linked to both lifespan and metabolic rate – in the worm *Caenorhabditis elegans*! The genetic predisposition of an individual at birth, accumulated DNA damage during life, epigenetic changes and increasing immune dysregulation may all contribute to our ultimate demise. The brains of people around 90 years of age tend to have about 10 per cent less mass (Neurons? Glia? Myelin? Fluid generally?), and to have around 20 per cent less in those 100 years old, compared to those at 20 years of age – the age at which a slow decline seems to commence. However, loss of myelin, the insulating sheath around the long axonic, connecting nerve fibres, and the terminal, connecting synapses themselves, may be particularly important. Regions hardest hit are the hippocampus (memory formation, spatial aspects) and the prefrontal cortex, which manages the cognitive and executive functions – the body's veritable soul, should the latter actually exist in material form.

Guinness World Records, that endlessly fascinating compendium of all that is marvellous, unusual, enormous or tiny, as long as it is not too unseemly, correctly notes that the oldest man in the world, still alive, is 112 years of age, born in 1903 as a boy with a life expectancy, then, of only 45 or so years. Nowadays, in the developed world, it is close to 80, although only about 2 in 10,000 folk can expect to hit 100. Japanese females seem to have the longest life expectancy, although the longest well-attested female lifespan was that of the French lady, Jeanne Calment, at 122. As to whether or not it is worth it, longevity is invariably negatively correlated with quality of life, with the number of chronic medical conditions, such as heart disease, stroke, arthritis, cancer … increasing the older you get. Indeed, most folk after 60 develop at least one such malady, and by 80 maybe only one in 10 is free of any, most having two or more.

Some of the diseases accompanying an increase burden of years are Parkinson's disease, Alzheimer's disease, frontal lobar dementia and amyotrophic lateral sclerosis, and if everyone could hit 100 years of age, most folk would probably develop dementia. Are there any preventative or prophylactic measures possible? Diet (quantity – less being better, and quality – low calorie balanced diet) are promising starters, plus exercise (physical and mental), and an active social and sexual life, with managed cardiovascular function (blood pressure, etc.).

Nevertheless, any intervention, stem cells, reprogrammed heart pacemaker, drugs or otherwise, can only postpone the inevitable. Born of a mother who developed Alzheimer's in her dotage, and of a father with Parkinson's disease, two neurodegenerative disorders which in part share similar abnormal variants of the alpha-synuclein protein, a yet darker future may lurk around my own life's corner, one likely involving the onset of either or both disorders. That corner could, however, still be some distance away, as both parents hit 90, as did the two grandmothers. One grandfather, however, dropped dead on a bike ride with my then teen-aged father, to the latter's life-long shock and horror; about my other grandfather, my mother ever refused to talk. 'Oh, we don't talk about him, dear', was all she would ever say. Drink? Syphilis? Crime? Extramarital affairs? All of the above? A nice little family skeleton to rattle at the grandchildren.

Apart from the increasing fragility of bones and skin, making the consequences of adventitious cuts and falls increasingly ominous, there is the question of cognitive decline. So-called benign forgetting can manifest in inability to recall recent events (I certainly have little idea what I had for dinner two or three days ago, unless it made me unexpectedly unwell), or to remember to keep future appointments, or as increasing instances of the tip-of-the-tongue phenomenon: What's the name of that part of the old Yugoslavia where one can have great walking holidays (Slovenia)? What's the name of that small community in NW Victoria where they have long held annual footraces, with the contestants appropriately (one hopes) handicapped? The correct name 'Stawell' may pop out of hiding some time later, as long as you do not concentrate too hard in trying to remember – and a day or two later you again cannot recall that elusive name. If, however, you remember, or are cued by the word 'gift', the name will re-emerge, and all along you probably could have said how many syllables the elusive word possessed, or maybe its initial or final letter. All this suggests not so much loss from a memory store, or even loss of appropriate access routes; rather it seems as if, after a lifetime, there may be just too many interfering memories, all competing for access. In my own experience, the same items often reappear repeatedly as tip-of-the-tongue casualties.

Slowed response times have long been touted as a marker of the advancing years; however, even more important than reaction time slowing may be inconsistent or highly variable response times, implicating a possible role for attentional wandering, or even increasing neural 'noise' in processing mechanisms.

No less sinister is a gradual but inexorable decline in what's called executive function, our ability to attend to significant aspects of a situation or problem, to the exclusion of all other competing influences, and to store partial or staged solutions in working memory. Deficits here lie on a spectrum from what is often regarded as benign, age-related difficulties in handling new material, to frank dementia, with no obvious distinguishing border line or boundary.

On the market there are many games touted to exercise the mind, on the use-it or lose-it principle, and stave off the inevitable. However, recent studies suggest that most, at best, simply improve performance upon the actual tasks as practised themselves, with little or no generalisation to other tasks or to real-life situations. A possible recently identified exception may be the often violent video games beloved of the young, which involve rapid aiming at moving or disappearing enemy targets, among a welter of competing irrelevancies. Maybe these games could be developed and modified to exclude the overtly aggressive aspects.

And then there is the curious case of the drug metformin, prescribed now for half a century for type 2 diabetes, and operating via insulin control. It apparently may also possess the power to extend one's likely lifespan, although how, why, by how much and when it might first be commenced for the latter purpose, remain to be determined. Diabetes is of course much more common in older folk, but the effectiveness of metformin seems independent of the presence/absence of diabetes itself. Another drug, rapamycin, also may make mice (and men?) stay healthier, longer, although with some nasty side effects; no free lunch. One hypothesis is that such drugs may operate by clearing out senescent cells, letting the rest function better without them.

Alois Alzheimer's disease may or may not 'just' be an extension of 'normal healthy ageing' – accelerated ageing, in fact – or ageing itself maybe should be seen as a pathology in its own right, rather than just as an inevitable extension of life's natural trajectory. Alzheimer's characteristically develops over 15–20 years before cognitive problems can be diagnosed, although a few decades ago, in the 'Nuns' study', a group of ageing nuns were located having all lived in a similar, sheltered, low-stress environments; at the same time their essays, written as young teenagers, were similarly located. Complexity of syntactic and grammatical constructions, and of content, seemed to predict who was likely to go on to develop Alzheimer's in late adulthood. The mediating variable may be spare cognitive capacity – the more you have, the later you are likely to develop the condition, likelihood maybe doubling every five years after maybe 60.

Alzheimer's, the commonest form of dementia, is a progressive, degenerative disorder which attacks the brain's neurons, resulting in loss of memory functions, thought and language skills. It particularly affects cholinergic pathways, and the hippocampus. My dementing mother, in her late eighties in Wales, repeatedly asked whether it was hilly where we lived in Australia, and seemed not to notice if each time I varied the answer. She was also convinced that someone had stolen her radio, and my dead father's pyjamas from the hospital where he had died, and her confabulation was so convincing that I found myself going to various places to check up. Her mild paranoia was not altered by contrary evidence, and she was convinced that all the neighbours in her street had sold up and left the area, even though they were visible doing gardening jobs; she then would say they must have had to return to fix the garden. She was also always misplacing things. Gradually, in a care home, she lost all functions. Women seem more vulnerable to the disorder than men, partly since they tend anyway to live longer, but also, paradoxically perhaps, because after the menopause they stop producing a probably-protective female hormone, which in men continues to be available as a breakdown product of male sex hormones.

A cascade of inflammatory processes seems to be operating, which can result in neuronal hyperactivity and even epilepsy, all the likely consequence of a combination of genetic, lifestyle and environmental factors. The most important gene and indeed the earliest to be identified is the *e*4 allelic variant of the gene APOE (APOE4), which encodes apolipoprotein E (APOE). Its presence quadruples one's risk of developing the disorder, via the accumulation of amyloid-beta aggregates and plaques between cells, which were first recognised as diagnostic in 1906 by Alois Alzheimer, along with a protein, tau, that tangles within the cells (which some now say may be more important than amyloid); the *e*2 isoform promotes amyloid clearance and is protective, although unfortunately experiments in clearing amyloid have so far proved therapeutically unsuccessful. Both pathological processes lead to apoptosis and cell death. It is ironic that few people attended Alzheimer's lecture when he announced his ground-breaking findings, while the immediately following one, on compulsive masturbation, was packed to capacity. In any case, the net result of this sorry cascade of pathology is massive disturbance of neuronal circuitry, with cognitive decline paralleling progressive neuronal degradation.

At a physical level, in parallel with my declining ambulatory functions, I have become aware of a greatly increased fear and incidence of potential falls, and a slowness and unsteadiness on recovering from incipient stumbles or instability. It may be that the long axons or nerve fibres running from ankle and knee joints, and sending proprioceptive information up to the cerebellum, are becoming increasingly compromised. Proprioceptive information informs us how, for example, accurately to touch with an index finger various distal parts of the body, such as an ear, shoulder or the nose, unseen or with the eyes closed. It contributes to moment-to-moment movement and position mapping of the various parts of the body with respect to each other and to the core body and immediate environment. That map is managed jointly by the posterior parietal cortex and the interconnected cerebellum, all regions upon which it has been my privilege to work during a long professional and research life. The same explanation may account for our increasing tendency to knock hands and feet against other objects, or to knock over other adjacent items on a table when, for example, reaching for or replacing a wine bottle.

A physiotherapist friend made me a wobble board some 20 or so years ago, to help strengthen a weak ankle, which I was prone to 'roll over' or twist. It worked, but even though for years now I have balanced successfully on one leg upon the board, beneath the centre of which is affixed a hemisphere, my balance and fear of falling when, for example, attempting to negotiate a loose boulder field on a hike in the mountains, continue to worsen.

And what about that ever-interesting topic, sex? Age, like alcohol, may reduce the capacity but not necessarily the desire. The other day I saw advertised upon the side of a van 'Viagra Fences'. I suppose the aim is to imply that their fences stay up longer … Maybe we shall shortly see preparations designed to assist poor urinary flow (which I take), loss in older women of vaginal lubrication during sex, or simple domestic plumbing blockages advertised or labelled as Niagra.

We all fear old age, yet dread the alternative, an early demise, even more. That would be fine, if there should turn out to be consolations and compensations, as old Cicero himself noted two millennia ago. It all comes down to quality of life, along with a realisation that while executive functions may decline (an aspect of intelligence once known as 'fluid'), its counterpart, 'crystallised' intelligence, or a lifetime of experience and organised knowledge, may even increase, as long as there is not at the same time too rapid a concomitant decline in memory functions.

A good death is a sudden one, like that of Grandpa Bradshaw; a slow, inexorable decline is something to be feared. All of which brings me again to the question of euthanasia. I have the means, and the will, to end my days suddenly, painlessly and peacefully should the burden of living become too much to bear, and as long as my mental capacities are not too impaired to manage a gentle slide into a good night; I need not rage against the dying of the light. Yet I shall fiercely defend my right, and that of other like-minded folk, to end my days thus, despite the efforts and rantings of religious fanatics and similar bigots and control freaks, who think other people's lives are their business. For them I have only a bitter contempt, and a consoling knowledge that some time in the future at least some of them may live, or rather die, to regret their stand. As with gay marriage and homosexuality generally, euthanasia is a victimless crime, and only a crime by virtue of misguided parliamentary acts. In the meantime, dear readers, if you have not already done so, make sure to draw up, with close friends or relatives, Financial and Medical Powers of Attorney, together with an Advance Care Directive, so that your nearest and dearest can manage your affairs as you would wish when your time comes and you are incapacitated, and so arrange matters as to attempt to avert unnecessary, painful or demeaning procedures to prolong your life. Sadly, some hospitals, more commonly perhaps of a religious foundation, are said to claim that they take no notice of any Advance Care Directive, as they proudly believe that life must be prolonged as long as possible at whatever cost, whether in terms of money or human dignity. If it were merely a matter of money, I personally would by far prefer that, say, $300,000 worth of health budget towards cardiac surgery to keep me going a little longer should instead go to a young person with the prospect of a full or reasonable life ahead.

And to that, I am sure old Cicero would again have heartily concurred.

I had been writing notes for parts of this chapter at 35,000 feet, as we crossed the Amu Darya, the fabled Oxus of antiquity on the borders of northern Afghanistan. I was asked to close my window blind so that we could instead watch a video as bland, trivial and uninteresting as the food. Around me, young boys played computer games, or watched the video; older women, almost a different species in terms of skills and interests, sat quietly for amazingly long periods in apparently blank mental states. Prostatic pressures swelled the queue of their menfolk at the toilets. Having visited failing friends in the UK, I wondered how people only a little older than me must cope with the complexities of airport and embarkation; there are so many things to be aware of, and to bear simultaneously in mind. Is society better for such apparent increases in efficiency? Would my friend, now severely demented and in a home, have been so disadvantaged in an earlier, simpler era in the bosom of his family? Would he even have been seen as other than merely old, or odd? Would his paranoid delusions have had the opportunity to manifest in a simpler, less complicated and more socially coherent society? We have all lost out in an endless search for ever more efficient, economic and technical solutions for often artificial problems. Progress as an end in itself, rather than for the potential betterment of humanity as a whole.

Dementia has become almost synonymous with growing old, while the latter is a luxury (if that is the right term) which may have been absent in earlier hunter-gatherer societies; we all know what the Eskimo and Aborigines are said to have done in the way of abandoning ageing relatives unable to keep up with the group. However, Plato, Lucretius and Shakespeare all note the effect of the passing years on the intellect. Nor need one necessarily live to a very advanced age to experience, or fear, dementia, as Jonathan Swift in writing *Gulliver's Travels* knew all too well over 250 years ago:

> When they [come] to fourscore years … they have no Remembrance of anything but what they learned and observ'd in their Youth and middle Age, and even that is very imperfect … In talking they forget the common Appellation of things, and the names of Persons, even of those who are their nearest Friends and Relations. For the same reason they can never amuse themselves with Reading, because their Memory will not serve to carry them from the beginning of a Sentence to the end … neither are they able … to hold any Conversation (farther than a few general words).

Swift himself suffered progressive memory loss in his later years, protracted bouts of walking, a progressive loss of speech, and the inability to recognise acquaintances: all clear signs of Alzheimer's.

A variant of nonvascular dementia, closely related to Alzheimer's, is frontotemporal dementia, with its fairly early age of typical onset, between 45 and 60. It is characterised more by language deficits and personality changes, rather than by the more frankly memory and executive function problems of Alzheimer's.

Certain early-onset forms of Alzheimer's disease run in families, and it is of course now possible to gene test for the apolipoprotein *e4* allele which, if present, conveys a very high risk. Would we want to know? Should we know? Should others such as insurance companies have access to such knowledge? In any case, there is an exponentially increasing risk of developing dementia after the age of 60. Indeed, the disease virtually disconnects the frontal lobes, where conscious, volitional, attentional information processing occurs, from the temporal lobes where many of our factual memories are stored. The patient may still have the memories but be unable consciously to access them. That they are still there may be seen by a patient's tendency automatically to correct someone's faulty grammar while quite unable to carry on an otherwise meaningful conversation. Well over 100 years ago, the French psychiatrist, Édouard Claparède, hid tacks in his palm when shaking hands with his mildly demented patients. The next week none would greet him thus, although they could not say why, instead offering confabulatory excuses in which they clearly believed. When I was in England, I was trying unsuccessfully to remember to whom I had sent one of two postcards, while at the same time saying, without thinking, that that person (whom I then named) would be on holiday; I knew at one level while forgetting at another. We all confabulate, too, when trying automatically to make sense of ambiguous situations; thus on viewing a video of a minor traffic accident, we will describe the same scene quite differently in terms of vehicle speed and roadside furniture, depending upon whether we are asked how fast the car was going 'when it slammed into the lamppost', or 'when it bumped into the pavement'.

Patients with certain prefrontal lesions, and some Alzheimer's patients, exhibit utilisation behaviour, automatic manipulation, out of context, of objects or tools, perhaps taking the examiner's pen and writing with it. We have all, however, done something similar when, for example, we set out to change our socks and end up unthinkingly removing the rest of our garments and maybe even donning pyjamas if the latter are to hand and we are preoccupied.

At a dinner, when we were setting up a neuroscience research group, it was interesting to note that nearly everyone, in their fifties or older, was independently taking, each day, fish oil and vitamin E supplements. The latter has pronounced anti-oxidant properties, and, as tocopherol, is being studied as a possible way of slowing down Parkinson's disease. Both disorders ultimately involve oxidative stress in their neuropathology. However, maybe we should rely instead on a balanced diet and let nature take its course. Indeed, artificial supplements may be less bioavailable to the body for uptake than when taken in the context of whatever else is present in the naturally occurring substance.

When I was a child, our diet included home-grown rhubarb cooked in an aluminium pressure cooker. The oxalic acid removed all aluminium oxide, leaving the pan brilliantly clean, while we presumably ingested the result. For some time, aluminium cooking vessels have been discouraged in the light of the presence of aluminium in the neural lesions of Alzheimer's disease. At least recent evidence has tended to exonerate that metal in the aetiology of the disorder, although just as with Parkinson's disease, another metal, iron, seems to play a role in the associated inflammatory processes.

'Use it or lose it' is an adage in many contexts, and the mentally very active do seem buffered to some extent against the disorder, halving the risk, according to some estimates; although with a doubling of the incidence every five years, mental activity may only buy you that extra period. While again we do not know the direction of cause and effect, and you may only be mentally active because you start off with that amount of spare neural processing capacity to provide a reserve late in life, five years of quality life is not to be sneezed at.

So what is the quality of life if demented? My mother's distress was mostly apparent in novel situations, when there was no context to provide meaning and continuity. Without an immediate past (old memories are the last to go in dementia), she could have been quite happy in what was left to her, an immediate present. And in a sense we too are only consciously aware of the immediate present, unless we make a deliberate effort, or something untoward happens. So visits to a dementing grandma can still be rewarding to both parties, even though ten minutes later it is as if it never happened for her. And, unfortunately, with the dynamics of the disease, and greater female longevity, it is likely to be grandma you visit in the home. Tragedy really strikes when paranoid suspicion or delusions develop. Hallucinations are a different matter; they are accepted by the sufferer as non-veridical and may accompany failing sight as with macular degeneration. This is the Charles Bonnet syndrome, named after the Swiss naturalist who described the visions seen by his grandfather, whose sight was failing. My 92-year-old mother-in-law said she saw fire engines in the ward, but she knew they were not real.

The ills of age are not inevitable; my English school-friend's 94-year-old mother still made television appearances, writes political tracts and has recently attempted fiction. In the case of the then world's oldest person, Jeanne Calment in France, her CT scan, taken shortly before she died, revealed a somewhat shrunken brain, but she remained cognitively fairly unimpaired to an age twice that at which many may first experience symptoms; you can often do a lot with a little, especially if, like her, you have many long-living relatives.

If I become demented, I would, as I said, choose euthanasia, were it available, while I could still make the choice, as I believe quality of life is infinitely more important than life itself. I do not believe the argument that it would open the door for would-be beneficiaries seeking a rapid inheritance. But if the health budget is limited, would it have been better to have invested that sum in health care for the young? Who can play God and make such a decision? Diagnoses and prognoses can be wrong, just like verdicts leading to the death penalty. Death is always final.

What, you may well ask, has my research group contributed to this gloomy picture of ageing, decline and possible dementia? Just as with the *degenerative* and essentially *movement* disorders (Parkinson's and Huntington's diseases), we sought to determine some of the *cognitive* components and contributions to movement control throughout the life span, and just as with autism and many of the other developmental disorders of the frontostriatal system where *motor* aspects have been rather neglected, we addressed their possible extent; so too in *degenerative* ageing and Alzheimer's, we looked to determine the comparatively neglected *motor* aspects. We were particularly interested in fine, sequential or staged movement control – times to initiate early stages of targeting movements, times to reach peak velocity (where basal ganglia mechanisms are likely crucial), and times in deceleration in the final stages of target acquisition, where cerebellar contributions are likely to take over. We used touch-screen technology, determining, among many other parameters, velocity, acceleration/deceleration, and rates of change of acceleration/deceleration. It was not always a particularly pretty picture. But life never is.

Was that, I wonder, what lay behind Grandma's oft-repeated mantra, 'You wait till you're my age, *you'll* see!', spoken with a rising note of shrill triumph. Her other regular contributory observation was 'Old age is just creeping on.'

How long will it creep?, I wonder.

38

WHERE TO NOW?

Some forward-looking afterthoughts

Where to now? I'll personally settle for a good quality of life – freedom from dementia and an ability still to 'go bush' when the mood takes me, should I hit the Big Nine in just over another decade. By then the family genes will probably dominate, and the accumulated 'slings and arrows of outrageous fortune' – MY fortune – will by then have hit home, leaving their indelible, irreversible, stigmata. But by then, what wonderful new technical advances, 'boys' toys', may there be? I would hope to have seen ambulant imaging become a reality, mapping activity in real time as we go about our routine, or very unusual, daily lives in an 'ecologically valid' fashion. Maybe structural and functional MRI (including connectivity analyses at both levels) may sync with electrophysiological measures, capturing both very fast and more gradual processes, with the option to include, simultaneously, transcranial magnetic and/or direct-current stimulation. Such procedures would take diagnosis, assessment, management and understanding to entirely new levels. By then, it may also be possible to radio-link to individuals, even at great distances from each other, so that the donor's electrophysiological activity patterns may, via appropriate decoding and re-encoding, be fed to a recipient's brain, so that the two may share a crude simulacrum of each other's experiences and thought – 'seeing through each other's eyes', as discussed earlier. Telepathy a reality?

Paraplegics can even now regain some control of their own paralysed limbs by somewhat similar, heroic, procedures involving thought, laboriously learning to code the necessary command signals; it may not be such a great step further forward to control not just automata in this way, but even, *horrendum dictu*, someone else's limbs or thoughts.

Hippocampal implants of chips may help compensate for memory loss in ageing (yes, please!!), and maybe even extend our normal memory span – or even bypass the need for tedious grammar and vocabulary lessons altogether – enabling us immediately and faultlessly to speak in foreign tongues. The chips would need regular software updates as new words and syntactic forms evolve and continually enter the tongue encoded!

Ageing itself may too be delayed, slowed or even halted or reversed, although the limits of a limitless longevity may be something we should be careful in wishing for!

Virtual reality may become so seductive (tourism, travel, sport, sex ...) that some may choose to give up real-time life, immersed in a (to me) nightmarish extension of today's Tablet Culture, living life through one's screen, today so obsessing the young.

If, despite all such props and palliatives, one's body finally gives out, a 'body transplant' already technically feasible in principle, may be the option of last resort. But when does a body transplant not simply equate to a head transplant? After all, the two operations are identical!

And if the current advances being made by a certain European consortium to construct a complete Electronic Brain, to simulate all known aspects of human memory, cognition, and motor functions, and if the theoretical and practical issues surrounding emotions and feelings are conquered, will humans anyway thereby simply become redundant, in a universe of squabbling automata, waging endless wars upon each other, in an ever more complex and devious fashion?

No, I think at 90, I'll die happy, with all my many flaws and failings, happy to have missed a fascinatingly horrible and horribly fascinating dystopia!

Bye-bye now!

FURTHER READING

Chapter 1 The evolution of all things

Dawkins, R. & Wong, Y. (2004). *The Ancestor's Tale: A Pilgrimage to the Dawn of Life*. London: Weidenfeld & Nicolson.

Parker, S. & Roberts, A. M. (Eds). (2015). *Evolution: The Whole Story*. London: Thames & Hudson.

Stringer, C. (2012). *The Origin of Our Species*. London: Allen Lane.

Stringer, C. (2016). The origin and evolution of Homo sapiens. *Philosophical Transactions of the Royal Society of London B Biological Sciences, 371*(1698). doi:10.1098/rstb.2015.0237.

Chapter 2 Tools: tacit and tactual symbols of civilisation

Bradshaw, J. L. & Rogers, L. J. (1993). *The Evolution of Lateral Asymmetries, Language, Tool Use and Intellect*. San Diego: Academic Press.

Bradshaw, J. L. & Rogers, L. J. (1996). Primate tool use and the evolutionary development of manual asymmetry. In D. Elliott & E. A. Roy (Eds), *Manual Asymmetries in Motor Performance* (pp. 33–53). Clifton, NJ: CRC Press.

Chapter 3 Art, graffiti, juvenilia or Kilroy?

Bradshaw, J. L. (2003a). The roots of art and the European Upper Palaeolithic. *Rock Art Research, 20*(1), 9–10.

Bradshaw, J. L. (2003b). An unentrancing idea: Psychedelics and the Upper Palaeolithic. *Cambridge Archaeological Journal, 13*(2), 216–218.

Bradshaw, J. L. (2008). Ancient brushstrokes. *Rock Art Research, 25*(1), 43–44.

Clottes, J. (2008). *Cave Art*. New York: Phaidon Press.

Walsh, G. L. (1988). *Australia's Greatest Rock Art*. Bathurst, NSW: E. J. Brill/Robert Brown & Associates.

Chapter 4 Language: what tales the tongue may tell

Bradshaw, J. L. & Rogers, L. J. (1993). *The Evolution of Lateral Asymmetries, Language, Tool Use and Intellect*. San Diego: Academic Press.

Corballis, M. C. (2002). *From Hand to Mouth: The Origins of Language*. Princeton, NJ: Princeton University Press.

Lehmann, W. & Zgusta, L. (1979). Schleicher's tale after a century. In B. Brogyanyi, (Ed.), *Festschrift for Oswald Szemerenyi* (pp. 455–466). Amsterdam: John Benjamins.

Chapter 5 The child is father to the man

Sacks, O. (2015). *On the Move: A Life*. New York: Alfred A. Knopf.

Chapter 13 Eyes, a window to your thoughts

Piquado, T., Isaacowitz, D. & Wingfield, A. (2010). Pupillometry as a measure of cognitive effort in younger and older adults. *Psychophysiology, 47*(3), 560–569. doi:10.1111/j.1469-8986.2009.00947.x.

Chapter 16 Commissural connectivity

Gazzaniga, M. S. (1989). Organization of the human brain. *Science, 245*(4921), 947–952.

Gazzaniga, M. S. (2000). Cerebral specialization and interhemispheric communication: Does the corpus callosum enable the human condition? *Brain, 123*(7), 1293–1326. doi:10.1093/brain/123.7.1293.

Gazzaniga, M. S., Bogen, J. E. & Sperry, R. W. (1962). Some functional effects of sectioning the cerebral commissures in man. *Proceedings of the National Academy of Sciences of the United States of America, 48*(10), 1765–1769. doi:10.1073/pnas.48.10.1765.

Chapter 17 Harry McGurk, read my lips: ventriloquism

Nicholls, M. E. R., Searle, D. & Bradshaw, J. L. (2004). Read my lips: Asymmetries in the visual expression and perception of speech revealed through the McGurk effect. *Psychological Science, 15*(2), 138–141.

Chapter 18 Mirror, mirror on the wall: symmetrical stimuli and bimanual responses

Addamo, P. K., Farrow, M., Bradshaw, J. L., Moss, S. A. & Georgiou-Karistianis, N. (2013). Characterizing the developmental profile of effort-induced overflow across a timed trial. *American Journal of Psychology, 126*(2), 227–234.

Bradshaw, J. L. (1989). *Hemispheric Specialization and Psychological Function*. Chichester: Wiley.

Bradshaw, J. L. (1990). Methods in studying human laterality. In A. A. Boulton, G. B. Baker & M. Hiscock (Eds), *Neuromethods* (vol. 17, pp. 225–280). Clifton, NJ: Humana Press.

Bradshaw, J. L. & Nettleton, N. C. (1983). *Human Cerebral Asymmetry*. Englewood Cliffs, NJ: Prentice Hall.

Bradshaw, J. L., Nettleton, N. C., Pierson, J. M., Wilson, L. & Nathan, G. (1987). Coordinates of extracorporeal space. In M. Jeannerod (Ed.), *Neurophysiological and Neuropsychological Aspects of Spatial Neglect* (pp. 41–67). Amsterdam: North Holland.

Corballis, M. C. (1983). *Human Laterality*. New York: Academic Press.

Chapter 19 Consciousness, will and time

Bradshaw, J. L. (2007). Consciousness, will and the brain. *Australasian Science, 28*(1), 20–22.

Brooks, J. (2017). How we sense time. *Australasian Science, 38*(3), 25–27.

Crick, F. (1994). *The Astonishing Hypothesis: The Scientific Search for the Soul*. New York: Scribner.

Dennett, D. C. (1992). *Consciousness Explained*. London: Allen Lane.

Chapter 21 I didn't think I had noticed it: unconscious processing

Mattingley, J. B. & Bradshaw, J. L. (1994). How many neglects? Some considerations based on anatomy and information processing. In P. W. Halligan & J. C. Marshall (Eds), *Spatial Neglect: Position Papers in Theory and Practice* (pp. 169–172). Hove: Lawrence Erlbaum.

Mattingley, J. B., Bradshaw, J. L. & Phillips, J. G. (1992). Reappraising unilateral neglect. *Australian Journal of Psychology, 44*, 163–169.

Van den Bussche, E., Van den Noortgate, W. & Reynvoet, B. (2009). Mechanisms of masked priming. *Psychological Bulletin, 135*(3), 452–477.

Chapter 22 When recognition fails: agnosia

Grüsser, O. J. & Landis, T. (1990). *Visual Agnosias and Other Disturbances of Visual Perception and Cognition*. London: Macmillan.

Riddoch, M. J. & Humphreys, G. W. (2003). Visual agnosia. *Neurologic Clinics of North America, 21*, 501–520.

Rivolta, D., Puce, A. & Williams, M. A. (Eds). (2016). *Facing the Other: Novel Theories and Methods in Face Perception Research*. South Australia: Frontiers Media.

Weiskrantz, L. (1997). *Consciousness Lost and Found: A Neuropsychological Exploration*. Oxford: Oxford University Press.

Chapter 23 Phantom legs and neglected arms

Bisiach, E., Rusconi, M. L. & Vallar, G. (1991). Remission of somatoparaphrenic delusion through vestibular stimulation. *Neuropsychologia, 29*(10), 1029–1031.

Giummarra, M. J., Gibson, S. J., Georgiou-Karistianis, N. & Bradshaw, J. L. (2007). Central mechanisms in phantom limb perception: The past, present and future. *Brain Research Reviews, 54*, 219–232.

Mattingley, J. B. & Bradshaw, J. L. (1991). Spatial maps. *Nature, 352*, 673–674.

Mattingley, J. B. & Bradshaw, J. L. (1994). How many neglects? Some considerations based on anatomy and information processing. In P. W. Halligan & J. C. Marshall (Eds), *Spatial Neglect: Position Papers in Theory and Practice* (pp. 169–172). Hove: Lawrence Erlbaum.

Mattingley, J. B., Bradshaw, J. L. & Phillips, J. G. (1992). Reappraising unilateral neglect. *Australian Journal of Psychology, 44*, 163–169.

Ramachandran, V. S. & Blakeslee, S. (1998). *Phantoms in the Brain: Probing the Mysteries of the Human Mind*. New York: William Morrow.

Chapter 24 Is your Tuesday green? Synaesthesia

Cytowic, R. E. (2002). *Synesthesia: A Union of the Senses* (2nd ed.). Cambridge, MA: MIT Press.

Rich, A. N., Bradshaw, J. L. & Mattingley, J. B. (2005). A large-scale systematic study of synaesthesia: Is fact stranger than fiction? *Cognition: International Journal of Cognitive Science, 98*(1), 53–84.

Rich, A. N. & Mattingley, J. B. (2002). Anomalous perception in synaesthesia: A cognitive neuroscience perspective. *Nature Reviews Neuroscience, 3*(1), 43–52. doi:10.1038/nrn702.

Chapter 25 Bodily integrity and identity: is it really me?

Fitzgibbon, B. M., Enticott, P. G., Rich, A. N., Georgiou-Karistianis, N., Bradshaw, J. L. & Giumarra, M. J. (2012). Mirror sensory synaesthesia: Exploring 'shared' sensory experiences as synaesthesia. *Neuroscience and Biobehavioral Reviews, 36*(1), 645–657.

Fitzgibbon, B. M., Giumarra, M. J., Georgiou-Karistianis, N., Enticott, P. G. & Bradshaw, J. L. (2010). Shared pain: From empathy to synaesthesia. *Neuroscience and Biobehavioral Reviews, 34*, 500–512.

Geiger, J. (2009). *The Third Man Factor: The Secret to Survival in Extreme Environments*. Melbourne: Text Publishing.

Giumarra, M. J., Bradshaw, J. L., Nicholls, M. E. R., Hilti, L. M. & Brugger, P. (2011). Body identity integrity disorder: Deranged body processing, right fronto-parietal dysfunction, and phenomenological experience of body incongruity. *Neuropsychology Review, 21*, 320–333.

Giumarra, M. J., Gibson, S. J., Georgiou-Karistianis, N. & Bradshaw, J. L. (2008). Mechanisms underlying embodiment, disembodiment and loss of embodiment. *Neuroscience and Biobehavioral Reviews, 32*, 143–160.

Young, E. (2017). Game of ghosts. *New Scientist* (3150), 36–39.

Chapter 26 Empathy for pain and mirror neurons

Enticott, P. G., Kennedy, H., Rinehart, N. J., Bradshaw, J. L., Tonge, B., Daskalakis, Z. J. & Fitzgerald, P. (2013). Interpersonal motor resonance in autism spectrum disorder: Evidence against a global 'mirror system' deficit. *Frontiers in Human Neuroscience*, 7(Article 218), 1–8. doi:10.3389/fnhum.2013.00218.

Fitzgibbon, B. M., Enticott, P. G., Giumarra, M. J., Thomson, R. H., Georgiou-Karistianis, N. & Bradshaw, J. L. (2012). Atypical electrophysiological activity during pain observation in amputees who experience synaesthetic pain. *Social Cognitive and Affective Neuroscience*, 7, 357–368.

Fitzgibbon, B. M., Enticott, P. G., Rich, A. N., Georgiou-Karistianis, N., Bradshaw, J. L. & Giumarra, M. J. (2012). Mirror sensory synaesthesia: Exploring 'shared' sensory experiences as synaesthesia. *Neuroscience and Biobehavioral Reviews, 36*(1), 645–657.

Giumarra, M. J. & Bradshaw, J. L. (2009). Synaesthesia for pain: Feeling pain with another. In J. A. Pineda (Ed.), *The Role of Mirroring Processes in Social Cognition* (pp. 287–307). Tokowa, NJ: Humana Press.

Rizzolatti, G., Sinigaglia, C. & Anderson, F. (2008). *Mirrors in the Brain: How Our Minds Share Actions, Emotions, and Experience*. Oxford: Oxford University Press.

Chapter 28 Huntington's disease, the Lady of the Lake and the hunt for the gene

Dayalu, P. & Albin, R. L. (2015). Huntington disease, pathogenesis and treatment. *Neurologic Clinics, 33*(1), 101–114.

Durr, A., Gargiulo, M. & Feingold, J. (2012). The presymptomatic phase of Huntington disease. *Revue Neurologique, 168*(11), 806–808.

Georgiou, N., Bradshaw, J. L., Phillips, J. G., Bradshaw, J. A. & Chiu, E. (1995). The Simon effect and attention deficits in Gilles de la Tourette syndrome and Huntington's disease. *Brain, 118*, 1305–1318.

Georgiou, N., Phillips, J. G., Bradshaw, J. L., Cunnington, R. & Chiu, E. (1997). Impairments of movement kinematics in patients with Huntington's disease: A comparison with and without a concurrent task. *Movement Disorders, 12*(3), 386–396.

Huntington, G. (1872). On chorea. *Medical and Surgical Reporter of Philadelphia*, 26(15), 317–332.

Nguyen, L., Bradshaw, J. L., Stout, J. C., Croft, R. & Georgiou-Karistianis, N. (2010). Electrophysiological measures as biomarkers in Huntington's disease: Review and future directions. *Brain Research Reviews, 64*, 177–194.

Phillips, J. G., Bradshaw, J. L., Chiu, E. & Bradshaw, J. A. (1994). Characteristics of handwriting in patients with Huntington's disease. *Movement Disorders, 9*, 521–530.

Walker, F. O. (2007). Huntington's disease. *Lancet, 369*(9557), 218–228.

Chapter 29 Parkinson's disease: when go turns to slow

Cunnington, R., Iansek, R., Bradshaw, J. L. & Phillips, J. G. (1995). Movement-related potentials in Parkinson's disease: Presence and predictability of temporal and spatial cues. *Brain, 118*, 935–950.

Cunnington, R., Iansek, R., Johnson, K. A. & Bradshaw, J. L. (1997). Movement-related potentials in Parkinson's disease: Motor imagery and movement preparation. *Brain, 120*, 1339–1353.

Georgiou, N., Iansek, R., Bradshaw, J. L., Phillips, J. G., Mattingley, J. B. & Bradshaw, J. A. (1993). An evaluation of the role of internal cues in the pathogenesis of Parkinsonian hypokinesia. *Brain, 116*, 1575–1587.

Kalia, L. V. & Lang, A. E. (2015). Parkinson's disease. *Lancet, 386*(9996), 896–912.

Parkinson, J. (1817). *Essay on the Shaking Palsy* (pp. 1–3). London.

Sveinbjornsdottir, S. (2016). The clinical symptoms of Parkinson's disease. *Journal of Neurochemistry, 139*, 318–324.

Chapter 30 Musicians' dystonia: a brain out of tune

Lim, V., Bradshaw, J. L., Nicholls, M. E. R. & Altenmüller, E. (2004). Abnormal sensorimotor processing of pianists with focal dystonia. In S. Fahn, M. Hallett & M. DeLong (Eds), *Dystonia 4* (pp. 267–273). Philadelphia, PA: Lippincott, Williams and Wilkins.

Chapter 31 Clothes-pegs, sex, hobbies, addiction and gambling

Feil, J., Sheppard, D., Fitzgerald, P. B., Yuecel, M., Lubman, D. I. & Bradshaw, J. L. (2010). Addiction, compulsive drug seeking and the role of frontostriatal mechanisms in regulating inhibitory control. *Neuroscience and Biobehavioral Reviews, 35*, 248–275.

Lorains, F. K., Stout, J. C., Enticott, P. G. & Bradshaw, J. L. (2017). Gambling disorder. In N. J. Rinehart, J. L. Bradshaw & P. G. Enticott (Eds), *Developmental Disorders of the Brain* (2nd ed., pp. 231–250). London: Routledge.

Chapter 33 A god of the gaps and dental distress

Dawkins, R. (2006). *The God Delusion.* London: Bantam.

Nelson, K. (2011). *The God Impulse: Is Religion Hardwired into the Brain?* London: Simon & Schuster.

Chapter 34 The little brain

Corben, L. A., Georgiou-Karistianis, N., Bradshaw, J. L., Evans-Galea, M. V., Churchyard, A. J. & Delatycki, M. B. (2012). Friedreich ataxia: Characterising the neuropathological and neurobehavioural phenotype in Friedreich ataxia: A systematic review. In A. J. Hannan (Ed.), *Tandem Repeat Polymorphisms: Genetic Plasticity, Neural Diversity and Disease* (pp. 169–184). New York: Springer.

Hocking, D. R., Bradshaw, J. L. & Rinehart, N. J. (2008). Fronto-parietal and cerebellar contributions to motor dysfunction in Williams syndrome: A review and future directions. *Neuroscience and Biobehavioral Reviews, 32*, 497–507.

Hocking, D. R., Rinehart, N. J., McGinley, J. L., Galna, B., Moss, S. A. & Bradshaw, J. L. (2011). Gait adaptation during obstacle crossing reveals impairments in the visual control of locomotion in Williams syndrome. *Neuroscience, 197*, 320–329.

Hodos, W. (2009). Evolution of cerebellum. In M. D. Binder, N. Hirokawa & U. Windhorst (Eds), *Encyclopedia of Neuroscience* (pp. 1240–1243). Berlin: Springer.

Kraan, C. M., Hocking, D. R., Bradshaw, J. L., Fielding, J., Cohen, J., Georgiou-Karistianis, N. & Cornish, K. M. (2013). Neurobehavioral evidence for the involvement of the FMR1 gene in female carriers of fragile X syndrome. *Neuroscience and Biobehavioral Reviews, 37*, 522–547.

Chapter 36 STROKE: the hour that struck

Henseler, I., Regenbrecht, F. & Obrig, H. (2014). Lesion correlates of patholinguistic profiles in chronic aphasia: Comparisons of syndrome-, modality-, and symptom-level assessment. *Brain, 137*(3), 918–930.

Manasco, M. H. (2013). *Introduction to Neurogenic Communication Disorders.* Burlington, VT: Jones and Bartlett.

Mattingley, J. B., Bradshaw, J. L. & Phillips, J. G. (1992). Impairments of movement initiation and execution in unilateral neglect: Directional hypokinesia and bradykinesia. *Brain, 115*, 1849–1874.

Chapter 37 I'm as old as I feel

Ballard, C., Gauthier, S., Corbett, A., Brayne, C., Aarsland, D. & Jones, E. (2011). Alzheimer's disease. *Lancet, 377*(9770), 1019–1031. doi:10.1016/S0140-6736(10)61349-9.

Bellgrove, M. A., Phillips, J. G., Bradshaw, J. L., Hall, K. A., Presnell, I. & Hecht, H. (1997). Response programming in dementia of the Alzheimer type: A kinematic analysis. *Neuropsychologia, 35*, 229–240.

Bowen, R. L. & Atwood, C. S. (2004). Living and dying for sex. *Gerontology, 50*(5), 265–290.

Querfurth, H. W. & LaFerla, F. M. (2010). Alzheimer's disease. *The New England Journal of Medicine, 362*(4), 329–344.

Rose, M. R. (1991). *Evolutionary Biology of Aging*. New York: Oxford University Press.

INDEX